Information Processing Systems:

AN INTRODUCTION TO MODERN, COMPUTER-BASED INFORMATION SYSTEMS

Information Processing Systems:

AN INTRODUCTION TO MODERN, COMPUTER-BASED INFORMATION SYSTEMS

WILLIAM S. DAVIS   Miami University

ADDISON-WESLEY PUBLISHING COMPANY   Reading, Massachusetts
Menlo Park, California
London • Amsterdam • Don Mills, Ontario • Sydney

ISBN 0-201-00999-4
BCDEFGHIJK-BP-79

TO BILL, TERRY, AND CARLA

Preface

The computer is today a dominant force in our society. Its use continues to grow year by year. These machines keep getting faster, more reliable, less expensive, smaller, and easier to use—the newer pocket calculators provide a perfect illustration of these trends. The promise of better performance at lower cost leads to an inescapable expectation of even more growth in the future; computers *will be* an integral part of our daily lives. A basic understanding of these machines and their effect on us is essential to the modern educated man or woman.

Most existing introductory-level textbooks present computer concepts from a late-1960s perspective. Most of the material remains valid—computers still work pretty much as they did back in the 1950s. But the emphasis is shifting. In the late 1960s, efficient use of a very expensive piece of office equipment, the computer, was the key to data processing economics, putting a premium on "good," tight programming, and making such topics as computer arithmetic and the internal functioning of the machine very important. Today, efficient use of the entire information processing *system* has become the objective.

This book presents basic information processing and computer concepts in a readable and, hopefully, entertaining manner, integrating newer techniques and modern technologies by progressing smoothly from the traditional "basics" to the idea of a total information processing system. Along the way, such topics as data base management, structured programming, operating systems, virtual memory, top-down system design, minicomputers, microcomputers, intelligent terminals, distributed data processing, teleprocessing, and telecommunications will be introduced in context (rather than simply added on). A discussion of elementary "breakeven" economics is presented to give the student an appreciation for *why* computers are used. In later chapters, this same concept is applied to a number of modern techniques for using a computer, helping the student to gain an understanding of the importance of economic "trade-offs" in selecting among various alternatives. In short, the objective of this book is to present the computer from the perspective of the late 1970s and the 1980s.

For the past several years, I have been teaching computer concepts to college students. Many, many introductory texts have crossed my desk. Most seem to follow a pattern, presenting much the same material in much the same order. This book is different. Perhaps a few paragraphs on the very unusual approach taken in preparing this book will help to spotlight these differences.

The process began, as is so often the case, with the author's sense of discontent with available introductory-level information processing texts. I developed a proposal and submitted it to Addison-Wesley. They liked it, and we began working in earnest.

Normally, as most authors can probably tell you, the process of developing a text follows a standard path, from manuscript, to galleys, to pages. But this book is different. After I had written the first five chapters and prepared a detailed outline, Addison-Wesley's Editor of Computer Sciences, Mr. Bill Gruener, and I set out on a tour of a number of colleges, universities, and community colleges to solicit, firsthand, the comments and suggestions of professional educators teaching in computer-related fields. There is always a danger that a textbook will present material from a very parochial, "my school" point of view. We wanted very much to avoid this problem. The feedback provided by this tour has proven to be invaluable.

Two of my primary objectives in writing this book were readability and pedagogical soundness. A typical student knowing nothing about computers or information processing should be able to read this book and learn from it. Claiming readability and effectiveness is one thing; actually doing something to achieve these objectives is something else. Thus, a second rather unique approach was introduced into the textbook development process. I enlisted the aid of Dr. Allison McCormack, an Assistant Professor of English at Miami University, an expert in constructing and criticizing written English and a computer novice. Her help in converting my sometimes too technical material into a more readable form is deeply appreciated. In addition to this rather mundane service, Dr. McCormack also helped to test the effectiveness of the text as a teaching tool. Her task was to develop a series of questions from each chapter for eventual use in a study guide. A person who can develop good questions about a subject knows that subject. Allison and I are quite proud of the study guide written to accompany this text. She obviously learned.

Finally, the manuscript was finished. Another objective was technical accuracy; thus the finished product was submitted to an in-depth technical review by a number of experts. I would like to express my sincere appreciation to three of my reviewers: Mr. William Herlihy, Mr. George Miller, and Mr. George Williams, for their especially solid reviews. Needless to say, their suggestions led to numerous refinements and improvements.

This book is different. The material is tightly structured, building step by step from basic to advanced concepts. Emphasis is placed on the technology of the late 1970s. The very title, *Information Processing Systems*, emphasizes the product of computers—information—rather than the machines themselves.

The book has been divided into five parts. Part I covers the broad range of modern computer applications and shows the student **why** computers are used. Building on this basic overview, Part II covers basic computer concepts, introducing most of the key hardware and software ideas covered in a traditional "introduction to the computer" course. Part III represents a departure from most traditional texts, covering data management concepts in some depth. Data and information are, after all, the whole point of using computers.

Many of the concepts presented in the first three parts are really old ideas. Computers still work in much the same way as they did back in 1952. By the time we reach Part IV, however, we are ready to begin discussing the most modern, most up-to-date techniques and technologies. Finally, in Part V, we come back to the very broad perspective of Part I, reexamining the spectrum of computer applications and considering a number of computer-related problems in light of what we have learned. The final chapter discusses trends and opportunities in the computer field.

A few final personal notes before we begin. Several years ago, I entered the computer field as a programmer. Since that time, I've programmed professionally in several languages (assembler, PL/1, COBOL, and RPG), worked as an operator (informally, during those "graveyard shift" debugging sessions) on both large computers and minicomputers, worked as a professional systems analyst, and served as a consultant for a number of firms. Since starting my teaching career, I've worked at a small private school (Lafayette College in Easton, Pennsylvania), a large, public, residential campus (Miami University in Oxford, Ohio), and a community college (Miami's branch campus in Hamilton, Ohio). All these experiences have contributed to the writing of this book. I sincerely hope you find it interesting, useful, and informative.

Hamilton, Ohio
December 1977

W.S.D.

Abridged Contents

Contents

FILE PROCESSING   *PART* **III**

INFORMATION SYSTEMS   *PART* *IV*

The
Computer
Impact

The Computer Impact

A FEW DAYS IN THE LIFE OF BOB SMITH

Bob Smith is a typical guy. He's married, has two children, and lives in a small house in a suburban development outside a large city. He has a pretty good job—not the most exciting work in the world, but he likes it and the pay is not bad.

It's Friday afternoon—payday. Along with thousands of his co-workers Bob eagerly awaits his weekly wages, neither knowing nor caring that his work record for the prior week was analyzed, his earnings calculated, and his check printed by a computer.

At 4:15 P.M. the end-of-shift buzzer sounds, and the nightly race to the parking lot begins. On the way out, Bob must stop to punch his time card. He inserts a card containing his name and employee number into the proper slot of a small blue machine, waits a fraction of a second, retrieves the card, places it in a rack, and rushes to his car. By punching his time card, Bob really sent the following message to a computer: "Bob Smith left at exactly 4:16 today." This little piece of data will be used in preparing the following week's pay.

Bob is the third member of his four-person car pool to reach the parking lot. Only two months ago, he didn't even know two of his three fellow riders. In response to a tight energy situation, the company's computer was programmed to suggest possible car pools by matching home addresses and work schedules.

The trip through the city is paced by computer-controlled traffic signals. A short stretch of turnpike costs twenty-five cents; the card Bob receives on entering and returns on leaving the toll road will eventually be processed by the state's computer.

Friday means a stop at the bank. As Bob waits in line, he can't help but notice the strangely shaped black numbers at the bottom of his paycheck and on the deposit slip from his checking account. The numbers are printed with a special magnetic ink and allow the bank's computer to read the documents.

Finally, it's Bob's turn. He inserts his plastic bank card into the slot in the 24-hour automated teller and types in his personal code number; in response, the heavy metal cover rises, exposing a set of push buttons. He pushes the one marked "Checking Account Deposit," and drops his paycheck through a slot; he then pushes two other buttons indicating his desire to withdraw fifty dollars in cash, and the machine dispenses the money. This 24-hour teller is a small special-purpose computer. As he leaves the bank, Bob enjoys a momentary thought about the pleasant conversations he used to have with the tellers. But the lines are shorter today and, after all, you can't fight progress.

Bob's credit card covers the cost of a full tank of gas. He leaves behind a copy of the sales slip which will eventually be read by the oil company's computer as it compiles future bills. The next stop is home, where Bob is enthusiastically greeted by his wife, Nancy, whom he met through a computer dating service.

Awaiting him is a stack of bills delivered with the aid of computer-read zip codes. Bills for electricity, gas, the mortgage, insurance, department store purchases, a magazine subscription, and the family doctor are neatly piled on his desk, every bill prepared and addressed by a computer. Bob writes a check (a message to the bank's computer) to cover each bill, and stuffs both the check and the bill into the proper preaddressed return envelope. "Next month," he thinks, "I'm going to sign up for the new bill-paying service being offered by the bank and let them simply transfer money from my account to cover some of the bills; why should I take the time to write all these checks?" The new service is part of the bank's Electronic Funds Transfer system to be implemented, as you may have guessed, through the bank's computer.

Friday is grocery night for the Smiths. As they move through the aisles, their selections are aided by computer-generated unit price information. At the checkout counter, a clerk simply moves packages over a small electronic reader, making sure that the preprinted product code is in the proper position. The product code identifies the brand and size of the package; once read, this information is sent along to the store's computer, where the current price of the item is found and added to the bill. After all the Smiths' purchases have been scanned, the clerk pushes a button and a detailed list is printed. Bob presents his bank card; the clerk inserts it into a card reader similar to that used on the 24-hour bank teller and, in a fraction of a second, funds have been transferred from Bob's checking account to the supermarket.

For the past few weeks, Nancy has been on a health-food campaign, serving her family a series of well-planned, balanced, nutritious, tasty, and reasonably priced meals. The menus were printed in the local newspaper. They had been planned by a computer.

The Smiths' favorite television program won't be on tonight; it was canceled because its rating, calculated by a computer, was too low. Fortunately, a baseball game is being televised. The antics of some cartoon characters on the million-dollar, computer-controlled scoreboard are of particular interest to the children.

The ball game is interrupted several times to report on the progress of our latest space flight. Such space probes would, of course, be impossible without the aid of computers.

A major topic of discussion on the late news is a charge made by a group of politicians that computers may have influenced the results of a recent statewide election. It seems that several hours before the polls closed, a computer predicted the outcome based on an analysis of sample "key" precincts. Perhaps a number of potential voters, having heard or read about this prediction, decided to stay home, feeling that their vote wouldn't mean anything anyway.

A special feature on the sports report is a discussion of how the computer is used to rate college football players who are eligible for the professional draft. The final news item is a reading of a computer-generated weather report indicating that there is a "thirty-percent chance of precipitation" for Saturday.

For the past few years, Bob has been attending evening and weekend classes at a local university in hopes of eventually earning a degree. Saturday morning is registration time for the next semester so, after breakfast and a quick scan of the morning newspaper (the type was set by computer, by the way), he heads for the city again. The registration process consists of filling out a number of computer-readable forms, because class registration and billing are computerized at this university.

Later that afternoon, Bob's golf game shows marked improvement as he shoots a very strong eighty-five. Perhaps a new set of computer-designed golf clubs had something to do with it. Some of the luster is lost, however, when Nancy cards an eighty-two using his old, cut-down set.

On the way home from the golf course, Bob and Nancy decide to stop and do some shopping at their favorite department store. Selecting a number of items from stock, they approach a checkout clerk, presenting Nancy's credit card in payment. As a normal part of processing the credit sale, the clerk inserts the card into a small machine; within a second or two, a green light winks on, indicating that the credit sale is approved. Actually, the little machine sent Nancy's credit card number to a central computer, which checked a list of stolen credit cards and made sure that Nancy had consistently paid her bills before granting its approval.

Saturday's supper, again planned by computer, is eaten a bit earlier than usual; Bob and Nancy plan an evening at the racetrack. There, their attention is centered on a large electronic tote board, where the rapidly changing odds on each race are flashed. The track's computer recalculates these odds every ninety seconds, basing its computations on the actual amount of money wagered on each horse. Right after the fifth race, it begins to rain (the weather bureau's computer had estimated a thirty-percent chance).

On the way home, Bob is stopped by a state police officer for exceeding the speed limit. The officer radios the numbers of Bob's driver's license and automobile registration back to headquarters, where a quick check of the police department's computer files shows that the car has not been listed as stolen and that Bob's record shows no recent traffic convictions. This information is radioed back to the officer who simply warns Bob not to exceed the speed limit again.

As the officer leaves and Bob and Nancy resume their trip home, we too will leave this brief narrative of a day or two in the lives of a typical American couple living in the last quarter of the twentieth century.

THE COMPUTER IMPACT

Not too many years ago, Bob and Nancy Smith might have been characters from science fiction. As recently as the late 1950s, the computer was almost unknown outside a few large universities and research centers. Yet today, a few short years later, the impact of the computer on the everyday life of a typical citizen of the United States is staggering, rivaling that of television and the automobile.

The computer is with us literally from birth until death. In the hospital, the fact of a new birth is reported to a number of hospital and government computers. Several tests are performed, some with the assistance of a computer, to ascertain and ensure the health of the newborn. Nurses are reminded of the proper medication and diet for both baby and mother by the hospital's computer. Upon their departure, the proud parents are presented with a bill prepared by computer. At life's opposite pole, the fact and cause of an individual's death are reported to a number of hospital, government, and scientific computers, perhaps providing an important clue in the fight against cancer or heart disease.

Education takes up a significant part of our early years. Information processing machines—another, perhaps more accurate name for computers—are becoming an increasingly important factor in our educational system. Most large universities, many smaller colleges, and quite a few high schools use the computer to schedule classes, print grade reports, and maintain scholastic records. A number of examinations (the Scholastic Aptitude Test, College Entrance Examination, and many IQ tests, to name a few) are graded by computer. In some schools, a few courses are actually taught by computers.

After our formal education is completed, we enter the work force, and what could be more important to us than our paycheck? Most are prepared by computer. In addition to preparing pay checks, business people handle billing, maintain accounting and tax records, make credit decisions, and keep track of merchandise by computer. Manufacturers often assign the computer the job of scheduling and controlling production and, in some cases, have a computer guide a specific machine through the process of cutting or shaping a piece of metal or plastic without human intervention.

In the financial arena, the stock market has been computerized to a high degree, and almost every banking transaction (checks, deposits, savings account deposits and withdrawals, bond purchases) involves the bank's computer.

The police and other law enforcement agencies use the computer to keep track of stolen automobiles, analyze evidence, and identify fingerprints. Several law officers' lives have been saved when a request for information on a car they had just stopped was answered with a computer-generated report, returned in a few seconds, indicating that the occupants of the car in question had previously been reported as armed and dangerous. In some communities, the computer, using statistical techniques, identifies high-crime areas, in effect predicting the most likely locations for a crime. Lawyers also use the computer to help research court cases.

The government is probably the biggest user of computers in this country. Income tax returns are checked and tax records maintained by computer. Social security, the highway trust fund, welfare, medicare, student loans, government payrolls, automobile registrations—the list of government operations that depend on the computer, at least for record keeping, is practically endless. Even our national defense system, from the early-warning system to the delivery of a missile, could not operate without the computer.

Not even sports are immune. Several National Football League teams have banded together to take advantage of computerized scouting reports and draft choice ratings. Some teams even use the computer to analyze an opponent's past games and predict the most likely play in certain situations. Television coverage of the recent Olympic Games highlighted some extremely accurate computer-controlled timing devices. The computer is actually becoming an active participant in a number of newer "sports," with computer chess and other, similar games gaining in popularity.

The entire space program and much current scientific research in such fields as atomic physics, cellular biology, and astronomy would not be possible without the computer. Engineers design bridges, chemists identfy compounds, and geographers draw maps with the aid of these modern marvels.

The computer, directly or indirectly, affects almost every phase of our modern way of life; except for a few hermits, it is difficult to find an individual who has never heard the word "computer" or handled (but not bent, folded, spindled, or mutilated, of course!) a data processing card. Yet, to the average person, the computer is shrouded in myth and mystery. Why? Where do our ideas about computers originate?

THE COMPUTER IN SCIENCE FICTION

In his classic novel *1984*, George Orwell described a future totalitarian society. To many people, the combination of the computer and modern bugging devices seems to provide the technology to make Orwell's nightmare come true; we may not have this society yet, but it is technologically feasible.

Many moviegoers remember HAL, the electronic villain of *2001, A Space Odyssey*; HAL, a computer, attempted to take control of a spaceship in order to hide his (its) own error. In yet another film, *COLOSSUS, the Forbin Project*, a massive computer in the United States teams up with its counterpart in a foreign country and takes over the world.

Other authors echo this theme. The computer has become the Frankenstein's monster of our modern folklore. Examples abound, including such tales as Ira Levin's *This Perfect Day*, Michael Crichton's *The Terminal Man*, and Harlan Ellison's short story "I Have No Mouth and I Must Scream."

In *Fail-Safe* by Eugene Burdick and Harvey Wheeler, the failure of a computer circuit is responsible for a nuclear disaster. Robots, mechanical men with computers for brains, are popular "bad" guys. A few authors (Isaac Asimov in *I, Robot* and Robert A. Heinlein in *The Moon is a Harsh Mistress*, to name two) have attempted to show computers and nonhuman intelligence in a more positive light. Artoo-Deetoo and See Threepio are considered by many to be the real heroes of *Star Wars*. But the reader of science fiction usually sees the computer as a sinister, evil, almost living thing. Is this what computers are really like? No! Hopefully, after reading this book, you'll agree.

THE COMPUTER IN THE NEWS

Every so often, a newspaper article describes how a computer wrote a paycheck for one million dollars, or issued a bill for $0.00 with a fifty-cent service charge for nonpayment, or refused to issue a magazine subscription to a sailor on the USS Enterprise because there were too many other subscribers with the same mailing address, or made some other, equally ridiculous mistake. We all enjoy a good laugh, comment on the stupidity of the machine, and remind ourselves that humans are still needed and still superior to machines. Is this portrayal of the computer as an incredible bungler accurate? Again, no! But a correctly written check, or a valid bill, or a properly handled magazine subscription does not make the news.

Occasionally, in the science supplement of a Sunday newspaper, the computer is credited with aiding a physicist in finding a new subatomic particle, or with helping an astronomer find a new quasar. Such stories are of great interest—to another physicist or astronomer.

The space program provides an excellent perspective on how the popular press covers the computer. Without the computer, there would be no space program. Only once, however, during the Apollo series, did the computer receive any substantial news coverage. It failed, and the moon landing was completed manually. The picture presented by the news media is highly inaccurate.

TECHNICAL ARTICLES BY COMPUTER PROFESSIONALS

Doctors, lawyers, engineers, and most other professional groups have their own technical journals, and computer professionals are no exception. Such periodicals are not meant for the casual reader; computer experts contribute to technical, computer-oriented magazines as a means of communicating with other computer professionals in a highly technical, seemingly "foreign" language which, so far as the average person is concerned, simply adds to the mystique of the computer.

FUTURE SHOCK

Television is relatively new, but it was preceded by radio, the movies, and the theater. Very few of us, to be sure, really understand the details of broadcasting, but we can accept television.

Automobiles have been around for a hundred years or so. Before the automobile, we had horse-drawn carriages. We all feel reasonably comfortable with a car. We understand them, at least well enough to know how to drive them. Very few of us are capable of taking a car apart and putting it back together, but we have all come to accept the automobile.

Computers are different. They are expensive; even the rich family down the street doesn't own a computer. Most of us have never even seen one. Not only do we not know how they work, we don't even know what they do! People who actually work with computers seem to be somehow different or strange, speaking a language only they and their peers can understand. Computers perform bookkeeping functions such as payroll preparation and inventory maintenance—nonphysical jobs that we've always associated with thinking. Do computers actually think? Computers don't move. We can't see what they're doing. And that scares us.

The computer, like an automobile or a television set, is just a machine. It's expensive and complex, but it's just a machine. So why do we fear them? We don't hesitate to turn on a strange television set. We don't hesitate to drive a borrowed or rented car. But we wouldn't think of entering a computer room and turning on the computer.

Perhaps one reason why we feel less than comfortable with computers is the apparent suddenness with which they have exploded into common use. A few years ago, no one we knew had even heard of the computer; now, they're everywhere. Where did these machines come from?

A BRIEF HISTORY OF THE COMPUTER

The Beginnings

As soon as humans moved from a barter economy to a monetary economy, the need for numbers, computation, and the keeping of records became apparent. As early as 3000 B.C., numbers were in use in some parts of the world. The first real computational aid, the abacus, was developed in China as early as 2600 B.C. (by some accounts), and moved to Greece and Egypt by about 1000 B.C. This simple counting device is still in common use in many parts of the world. Arabic numbers and the concept of zero were also developed during this very early period of human history.

For centuries, little happened that was to prove of any real consequence in the development of the modern computer. The first true mechanical aid to computation was an adding machine invented by Blaise Pascal in 1642. The machine worked, but was a financial failure due to the inability of mid-seventeenth century industry to manufacture gears and linkages with the precision necessary to ensure accuracy. In 1694, Gottfried Wilhelm Liebniz took the idea of a mechanical calculator one step further, inventing a machine capable of multiplication. Like Pascal's adding machine, it was a failure due to a lack of engineering and industrial technology.

The next two centuries saw significant advances in the fields of electronics and manufacturing. A brief look at the discoveries made in electricity in the early 1800s illustrates a very important phenomenon—the fact that scientific discovery tends to feed on itself. In 1786, Galvani became the first man to identify electric current; it seems hard to believe that prior to 1786, we didn't even know that electric current existed! In 1800, the first wet battery was developed. By 1834, using the current generated by such batteries, electromagnetism, electrical generation, the rotary generator, and the electric motor had all been invented. From nothing to electric motors in a few decades! Why this sudden explosion of activity? As is so common in science and technology, one new idea makes other experimentation possible, which in turn gives rise to another new idea, which in turn gives rise to more, and on and on until, in a surprisingly brief period of time, knowledge has advanced tremendously.

One very important development of the early 1800s occurred in France where, in 1806, a man named Joseph Jacquard invented the Jacquard loom, an automatic weaving machine controlled by punched cards. Jacquard was not attempting to invent a computer or a mechanical aid to computation, but his idea of using punched cards to hold information would be borrowed by a number of true computer pioneers, as we'll see later.

The most interesting computer pioneer of the nineteenth century was Charles Babbage. His ambition was to build an "analytical engine" capable of performing automatically many complex mathematical operations. By 1843, he had drawn up detailed plans for a machine incorporating almost every major component and function of a modern computer! Why wasn't it built? Simply because the manufacturing technology of the day was not equal to the task. Technology had advanced tremendously since the days of Pascal and Liebniz, but not far enough. The work of Charles Babbage was largely forgotten, not to be rediscovered until *after* his ideas had been implemented by other men almost a century later.

The Middle Years: 1880 Until World War II

The United States Constitution requires that a census be conducted every ten years. The census of 1880 took seven and one-half years to complete. Growth trends made it quite obvious that the 1890 census would take even longer to tabulate—eleven years was considered a reasonable guess. This meant that the Census Bureau would have been counting the 1890 results as the 1900 numbers began rolling in! And the future promised only falling further and further behind with little or no hope of ever getting even.

The problem was tackled by a consultant to the Census Bureau named Herman Hollerith. His inspiration was Jacquard, the French inventor who, some years before, had automated a weaving machine by punching control information into cards. If a pattern of holes in a card could represent weaving instructions, why couldn't similar holes stand for numbers? As the data for the 1890 census began to come in, Hollerith had it punched into cards.

To read and tabulate this data, he borrowed ideas from the rapidly developing field of electricity. Cards do not conduct electricity, since paper is a very good insulator. If a card is placed on a metal surface and a series of metal pins is brought into contact with the card, the paper material effectively separates the pins from the metal surface, cutting off the flow of electricity. Except, of course, where there is a hole. Here, the pin goes through the hole and contacts the metal, allowing a current to flow. Hollerith's device simply counted the number of times that current actually flowed through a given wire as the cards were fed one at a time by hand. Each wire corresponded to one possible hole position on the card; each hole position represented one value of one census statistic; thus, the counts gave the results of the census. The 1890 census was completed within two years.

Why was Hollerith successful when such men as Pascal, Liebniz, and Babbage had failed? Were his ideas any better? Not really, but by 1890, electronics and manufacturing technology had advanced to the point where Hollerith's ideas could be implemented.

By the late 1920s, card-tabulating equipment had become quite common throughout the United States. In 1935, IBM was successful in obtaining the largest (to that day) card-tabulating equipment contract when the social security system came into being. Significant improvements had, of course, been made, but the equipment was based essentially on Hollerith's original idea.

In 1939, Howard Aiken of Harvard University began working on a machine to solve polynomials; by 1944, with the help and financial support of IBM, the MARK I, the very first electromechanical computer, was unveiled. The modern age of the computer had begun.

The Development of Computers: 1945 through 1950

War tends to accelerate invention. One important war-related project took place at the University of Pennsylvania, where a team under the leadership of John W. Mauchly and J. Presper Eckert, Jr., set out to make a computer to aid in the construction of ballistics tables. The result—ready in 1945, two months *after* the surrender of Japan—was christened the ENIAC (Electronic Numerical Integrator and Calculator). The ENIAC was the first electronic computer.

After the ENIAC was completed, Mauchly and Eckert continued their work, developing an improved model, the EDVAC, in 1946. An important addition was the stored program concept suggested by John vonNeumann, a member of the team working on this project and an outstanding mathematician in his own right.

The First Generation: The 1950s

Mauchly and Eckert left the university, founded a corporation to manufacture computers, and, in 1951, sold a computer named UNIVAC I to the Census Bureau (the machine was retired in 1963, and now rests in the Smithsonian Institute). The age of the computer was well under way.

The 1950s marked the computer's first generation. The precise dates of this generation are difficult to pinpoint exactly—the beginning is set somewhere between 1950 and 1954, and the end generally falls somewhere around 1958 or 1959. What really distinguishes the first generation from subsequent generations is technology. The key electronic component of a first-generation computer was the electronic tube. By today's standards, these machines were quite slow, being capable of executing approximately 1000 instructions per second. They were also rather small, holding perhaps 10,000 to 20,000 characters of data in their main memories. The electronic technology, speed, and size of a machine identify it as first generation; the dates are of secondary importance.

By 1956, IBM had taken a marketing lead that it has yet to relinquish, selling the IBM 650 and 700 lines of machines. Other key competitors included Monroe, NCR, Burroughs, RCA, Underwood, and, of course, UNIVAC. (Notice that we've stopped talking about individual inventors and have begun to discuss corporations instead. A modern computer is composed of complex electronic and mechanical parts, well beyond the capabilities of any single individual.)

The Second Generation: 1960 through 1965

The field of electronics was not idle during the 1950s. Perhaps the most important discovery was the transistor, a device which won the 1956 Nobel Prize for three American scientists. By 1957, Burroughs had developed a fully transistorized computer for the Air Force. The higher speed and greater reliability of transistors marked the end of the electronic tube-based first-generation computers, and ushered in the second generation.

By 1960, first-generation computers were virtually obsolete. Transistors are smaller, faster, and more reliable than electronic tubes. As a result, a second-generation computer using transistors rather than electronic tubes was physically smaller, much faster (1,000,000 as opposed to 1000 instructions per second), and much more reliable than its first-generation counterpart. Such computers as the Honeywell 800, Burroughs B5500, IBM 1400, IBM 7090, Control Data Corporation 1604, and UNIVAC 1107 had become big sellers, with the improved reliability derived from solid-state electronics making such machines attractive to the business market.

Beyond the field of electronics, the second generation saw a tremendous improvement in techniques for using computers, with such concepts as operating systems, time-sharing, and user-oriented languages coming into common use. Right now, these terms probably don't mean much to you, but by the time you finish the book, they will.

You may have noticed that we haven't even *mentioned* any individuals in our brief discussion of the computer's second generation. The size, complexity, and cost of these machines made them corporate rather than individual devices.

The big news of the second generation was a phenomenal growth in computer use. As recently as 1950, the number of computers available in the world could be counted on a single individual's fingers; by 1965, the value of installed computers had risen to an estimated three to four *billion* dollars.

The Third Generation: 1965 to the Present

The field of electronics was not dormant during the period of the second generation—major advances were made in the areas of printed and integrated circuits. As a result of these advances (Fig. 1.1), electronic devices became even more compact, faster, more reliable, and less expensive. IBM's System/360 and (currently) System/370 computers, the dominant machines of the period, use these modern integrated circuits, as do the most current products of Control Data Corporation, Burroughs, Sperry Rand (UNIVAC), Honeywell, NCR, and others. By the mid-1970s, the value of installed computers had risen above 24 billion dollars.

An important third-generation trend lies in the rapid development of minicomputers and microprocessors, small (as the names imply) and relatively inexpensive machines which are often dedicated to a specific task or application. Many firms are currently active in this field, with Digital Equipment Corporation being one of the leaders.

Major advances in applications and techniques include multiprogramming, multiprocessing, microcoding, and virtual memory—terms that may not mean much to you now, but will be recognizable soon. Many observers today believe that we are actually in a fourth generation.

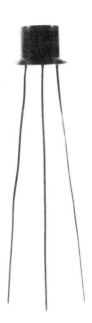

Fig. 1.1
A first-generation tube, a second-generation transistor, and a third-generation integrated circuit. Note the difference in size.

CURRENT TRENDS AND FUTURE PROJECTIONS

Look back at the time scale we've been using in describing the history of data processing. In the beginning, we were talking about centuries; in the middle period, techniques were developed over decades; since 1950, everything has happened in a matter of years. The first generation began around 1950; by 1960, first-generation computers had become obsolete, supplanted by the transistorized machines of the second generation; by 1965, integrated circuits spawned a third generation, which, in turn, was pushed aside by improved equipment in the early 1970s. The growth has been almost exponential (Fig. 1.2). At the same time, computers have gotten better and better. In Fig. 1.3, we see a number of trends projected on a single graph. Over the past several years, the speed and reliability of electrical devices such as the computer have risen tremendously, while the size and, more important, the cost of these devices have tended to drop just as dramatically. Consider the modern pocket calculator, which illustrates all these trends.

Why is the product improving while the cost is dropping? Very few products follow this pattern. But the computer is unique. It actually participates in its own improvement! Let's explain that last statement. A computer is the culmination of centuries of progress in many different areas of science and technology—electronics, chemistry, manufacturing, engineering, and others. The computer is a very complex piece of equipment; designing and building

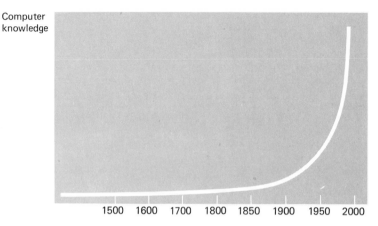

Computer knowledge

1500   1600   1700   1800   1850   1900   1950   2000

Fig. 1.2
The growth
of the computer.

one is a very complex task. Early computers proved very valuable in performing the computations necessary to plan and analyze new technology, thus accelerating further development. This led to better computers. Better computers meant that the scientist and engineer could do an even better job of designing and planning even better circuits which, in turn, led to even better computers. The same trend can be seen in manufacturing, where the ability of a computer to control production or test a product for quality has led to more efficient production which, in turn, through lower cost and better quality, has made the computer more readily available which, again in turn, has led to greater use of the computer in manufacturing. It's a spiral, with one improvement making the next improvement possible. This interrelationship among science, technology, and the computer is what has made the explosive development we're now experiencing possible.

Fig. 1.3
Current trends.

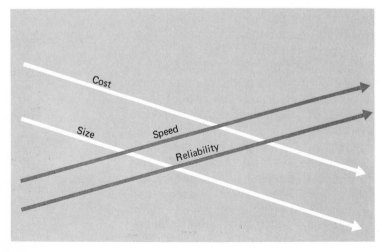

Cost

Size

Speed

Reliability

Time ⟶

And what of the future? Look for a continuation of the trend toward physically smaller but more and more powerful computers. Already, computers small enough to fit in a briefcase but more powerful than UNIVAC I are being offered for sale. The trend toward lower cost will also continue. Look for a proliferation of small computers (as opposed to calculators) in the not too far distant future, with very powerful devices falling into the price range of an automobile. A knowledge of the computer is in fact essential to the modern educated man or woman.

FUTURE SHOCK—AGAIN

One of the most interesting and perhaps most significant books of the early 1970s was Alvin Toffler's *Future Shock*. In this thought-provoking study, Mr. Toffler puts forth the idea that our society suffers from "future shock," which is caused by a too rapid rate of change. Everything seems to be changing today: the pace of life itself, life-styles, family relationships, science, jobs, everything. We find it confusing, and maybe even a bit terrifying. If any single machine can be said to represent change, it's the computer. A mere few decades ago, there weren't any; now they're everywhere. And their use is growing with new applications appearing almost daily.

Perhaps the most terrifying intrusion of the computer into our daily lives is in the area of employment. We've all heard of people being replaced by computers. Actually, *machines* have been replacing people for almost as long as we have been using tools, but *computers* replace clerks, bank tellers, and supermarket cashiers—people who are doing *nonphysical* work. That kind of change scares us. Is it any wonder that we misunderstand and almost fear these machines? Is it any wonder that a new set of myths has grown up around the computer?

Like any machine, the computer can be used for good or evil purpose. So long as most people think of the computer as an awe-inspiring "supermachine" best left to the relative handful of "experts" who are capable of really understanding it, the potential for evil is enormous. To properly control, we must first understand. Few of us can take an automobile apart and put it back together, but most of us know enough about the automobile to at least sense when something goes wrong. Likewise, few of us will ever build our own computer, but we should at least understand how these machines work and what they can (and cannot) do. The basic principles of the computer are actually quite simple.

The objective of this book is to present basic computer concepts in an easy-to-read, easy-to-follow way, concentrating on the underlying ideas rather than the technical terms. Once the concepts have been covered, we'll begin to cover typical applications of the computer, emphasizing those computer capabilities that make it a valuable tool in a given application. When we're finished, you should have a pretty good idea of how computers work and what they can and cannot do. Hopefully, real understanding will replace the myths which have come to be associated with the computer.

KEY WORDS	SUMMARY

computer

first generation *(B)*

information processing machine

integrated circuit

microcomputer

minicomputer

second generation *1960 1965*

third generation

1965 to present

The computer has become a dominant force in our society, reaching into many areas of our daily lives. Its growth, sluggish for centuries, has been nothing short of phenomenal in recent years. Yet to most of us, the computer is shrouded in myth and mystery. A primary objective of this book is to "de-mythologize" these machines.

EXERCISES

1. See if you can find any evidence of the computer in your daily life. Keep track of the number of times that you come across a punched card, a check, or a piece of mail addressed by a computer (if the name is printed in all capital letters, it's pretty safe to assume that it has been addressed by a computer), or are required to fill out an application form or an order form.

2. Look through this evening's newspaper and see how many articles and features you can find which involve the computer in some way. Check such items as stock market prices or baseball records, which are frequently computer-prepared. Check the "help-wanted" section for such positions as computer operator, programmer, systems analyst, analyst, keypunch operator, or any position beginning with the words "data processing."

3. Read one of the books or short stories mentioned in the section on the computer in science fiction and make a note of your reaction. Reexamine your reaction after you have finished this course.

4. In our discussion of the development of computers, we tried to show how many different fields of science and technology have contributed. Choose another field, such as construction, television, or the automobile, and analyze its development in much the same way.

OTHER REFERENCES

Three very interesting books on the subject of computer history are

1. Harmon, Margaret (1975). *Stretching Man's Mind: A History of Data Processing.* New York: Mason/Charter.
2. Rodgers, William (1974). *Think: A Biography of the Watsons and IBM.* New York: New American Library.
3. Rosenberg, Jerry (1969). *The Computer Prophets.* New York: Macmillan.

Why Computers Are Used

Chapter 1 illustrated just how widespread is the use of computers in our modern industrialized society. Our objective in this chapter is to explain *why* they are used. We will begin by showing the importance of information in our complex society, indicating that a computer is an information processing machine. One example of a typical information processing application, that of payroll, will be used to illustrate the economics of information processing—computers will be used if they can do a job at a lower cost than human beings. A computer's two main "skills," speed and accuracy, will also be discussed.

INFORMATION

When we think of modern American business and industry, we tend to think of the corporate giants—firms such as General Motors, Ford, Chrysler, IBM, and General Electric. These companies, however, were not always big; many began as single-owner proprietorships. One person invented a new product or a new service, or thought of a better way of performing some task, and decided to go into business. In the beginning, these firms tended to be literally "one-man bands," with the owner designing, manufacturing, selling, servicing, and planning a product, and performing the necessary record-keeping functions in his or her spare time.

Eventually, if the product or service was a good one, the demand became too great for one individual to handle, and a partner or some hired help entered the scene. Soon a few salespeople, an accountant or two, and a handful of workers to help build the product were added. The proprietor, however, still exercised complete control over the business.

In a modern, large, multinational corporation, such personal control becomes impossible. How can the president of General Motors *possibly* be familiar with the details of the manufacturing, design, and marketing of all GM cars? Because of its size, the modern corporation has become very tightly organized, with lines of command and control that rival those of the military. The president sits at the top of this typical organizational pyramid (Fig. 2.1), with a vice-president in charge of each of the major functions. The vice-presidents, in turn, have a number of middle-level managers reporting to them. Eventually, we reach the level of the "front-line" manager who is responsible for the people who actually perform the manual tasks. The sheer size and complexity of a modern corporation makes such organization essential.

The big problem faced by management is one of coordinating these groups. What happens, for example, if the sales department suddenly recognizes a decline in the demand for lime-green refrigerators, but manufacturing continues to build lime-green refrigerators? Without tight management control, this situation can happen (as it did with the hula hoop and oversized automobiles). Back in the days of the single proprietorship, the fact that one individual was personally responsible for all phases of the operation made such an event unlikely, but no one individual can exert such total control today. How can the president and the other officers of a large corporation control such complex operations?

Through **information.** What exactly is meant by the term information?

Perhaps the best way to illustrate the concept of information is through an example. Let's assume that the vice-president in charge of sales is to approach the president with a request that the company begin offering lime-

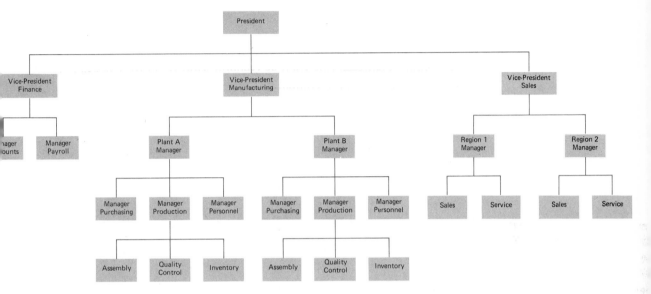

Fig. 2.1
A typical corporate organization chart.

green refrigerators for sale. It's probably reasonable for the president to assume that the vice-president has looked into the sales potential very carefully, and firmly believes that "if lime-green refrigerators were available, our salespeople could sell them." To the president, the knowledge that "lime-green refrigerators will sell" becomes a single fact; i.e., a single piece of **data.**

Is this enough? Can the president, on the basis of this single piece of data, commit the company to the building and distribution of lime-green refrigerators? Probably not. Can they be built? The president might ask manufacturing or engineering for an opinion. Let's assume that the answer is "yes, they can be built." The president now knows that the sales force can sell them *and* that the company can build them. Is this enough? Again, probably not. Can they be built at a reasonable price? Once more, the president might ask engineering for an opinion. Engineering, we'll assume, estimates that "we can build them for $1.00 more per unit than the standard white unit." Now the president knows that the company can sell them and build them, and that it will cost $1.00 more per unit to build a lime-green refrigerator. Now, perhaps, the president can make a decision.

Examine this process carefully, because it illustrates an important concept. The president began with a number of individual pieces of *data*, each of which, by itself, was not enough to support a decision. It was only when the president had combined a number of different pieces of data, that he or she had enough to support a decision. By combining data in a meaningful way, the president has created *information* (Fig. 2.2). Information has meaning. Data are merely individual facts which must be combined or "processed" in some way in order to give them meaning.

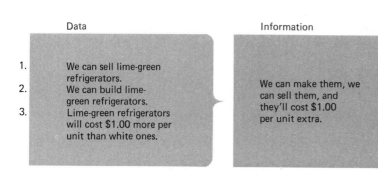

Fig. 2.2
Data is combined to form information.

Let's assume that on the basis of the information available on the sales and manufacturing potential for lime-green refrigerators, the president decides to offer this product for sale. Data has been combined to form information, this information has supported a decision, and the resulting decision has led to action: start producing the refrigerators. What if some of the data had been incorrect? What if there really were no demand for lime-green refrigerators? What if a sudden increase in the cost of lime-green paint pushed the extra cost up to $25.00 per unit? The organization must have a mechanism for correcting wrong decisions.

This mechanism is usually implemented through such tools as budgets, quotas, and targets. Each salesperson might be assigned a quota of 250 lime-green refrigerators, to cite one example. If salesperson A reports only 200 sales, we have a fact. If salesperson B reports 300 sales, the average of 250 units each seems to indicate that sales are right "on target"—we now have information. If, however, salesperson B also reports 200 lime-green refrigerators sold, the average of only 200 units, when compared to the quota or target of 250 per salesperson, seems to indicate that sales are not going as well as expected—information of another sort. Management can now make another decision, to cut production or stock the product in hopes that sales will pick up, resulting in another action.

Thus we can see that the information flow through an organization is cyclic in nature (Fig. 2.3). Data is combined to form information. Information supports decision making. A decision (hopefully) leads to action. The

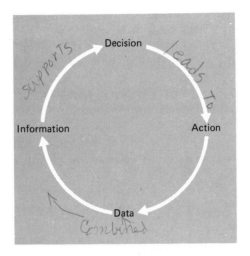

Fig. 2.3
The information feedback cycle.

results of an action can be measured; these measurements produce additional data which can be combined to form additional information which, in turn, can be used to support the decisions that "fine tune" the process.

A modern large organization consists of a number of separate functional groups whose activities must be coordinated. Information is the key to this coordination. Each of the functional groups produces information which is used to communicate with the other groups. Using a business concern as an example, let's begin with the engineering department, where a product is designed, generating a set of engineering drawings. Other engineers design the equipment needed to build and inspect the product. Still another group of engineers is responsible for planning the production process. The result is a set of detailed instructions for manufacturing the product—information.

How large should the plant be? To answer this question, the marketing department gathers a different type of information, conducting a series of market surveys in an attempt to estimate the market and sales potential of the product.

Once the plant is in operation, the need for information continues. The sales department reports each sale by filling out a special form—an order. The sum of all unfilled orders makes up the "backlog." If the backlog indicates that large numbers of the product have been ordered but not yet made, then increase production. Information provided by the sales department thus has a direct impact on the production process. Should the company continue making lime-green refrigerators? If the backlog for lime-green models is small, no; if the backlog is large, yes.

It's one thing to say that manufacturing needs the information provided by sales or that sales needs the information provided by manufacturing. It's quite another thing to actually provide that information. How, for example, can sales data be made available to other functions in the organization? The sales department writes an order form for each order. Is it reasonable to expect manufacturing to work with thousands and thousands of individual orders? Of course not. Manufacturing personnel are not interested in the details of the individual orders; what they need is summarized information—in

Fig. 2.4
The computer as an information warehouse.

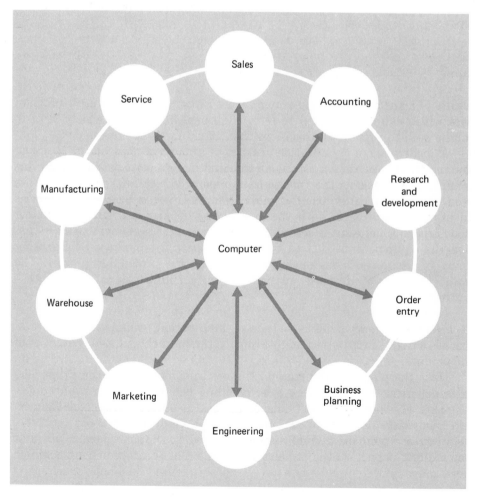

other words, how many units of product A must be produced in a given month? Someone or some group must "process" the sales data, combining and summarizing the data on individual orders to produce information which is useful to manufacturing. To achieve this objective, many firms have an order entry department or a similar group. The function of such a department is purely clerical; they process the paperwork. Similar groups exist throughout the organization, translating the data produced by one group into the information needed by another.

As a company continues to grow, even this arrangement becomes unwieldy. A greater volume of sales produces a greater volume of paperwork; eventually, even the best manual paperwork system is overwhelmed. Enter the computer. A computer is very good at addition, subtraction, multiplication, division, sorting, counting, accumulating—in short, all those functions that are normally handled by clerical people. If the computer is placed in a (logically) central position (Fig. 2.4), each of the major functions in the organization can communicate its own detailed data into the computer. The computer can then summarize the data, feeding it back to the individual functions as required. Thus, the computer acts as a sort of information warehouse, accepting data from various locations, processing it, storing it, and releasing it on request. The computer thus allows a major portion of paperwork handling to be automated.

Does this mean that all the clerical jobs in the country are about to be taken over by the computer? Most definitely not! The fact that a task *can* be automated does not necessarily mean that it *will* be automated. Computers are expensive, and big companies do not purchase expensive equipment simply to replace people. Equipment is purchased only if it saves money. Perhaps the best way to visualize this process is through an example. Let's take a look at a very common data processing activity, payroll preparation, as it is performed in three different firms.

PAYROLL PROCESSING

Everyone who works expects to be paid, and we all have a pretty good idea of how our pay is calculated. First, we know our hourly pay rate. Second, we know how many hours we've worked. Multiplying these two numbers gives us our gross pay, but, as we all know, this is not our take-home pay. The government takes a portion to cover income taxes, the amount varying with the income level. Another portion goes to the Social Security Administration to help pay the costs of our social security system. Other payroll deductions might cover union dues, credit-union loan repayments, savings, bond purchases, state taxes, local taxes, and a myriad of other things. Subtracting all these deductions from our gross pay yields our actual take-home, or net, pay.

This is a pure data processing or information processing activity, with the hours worked provided by the employee on a time sheet or a time card, the data on pay rates kept in the employee's folder or by the boss and the data defining proper amounts for deductions provided by the government, the union, the employee, and others. Someone must put all this data together, or process it, in order to prepare a valid paycheck. Let's see how three different firms might handle this information processing problem.

Payroll Processing in a Small Business

For quite a few years, Tony has operated a service station at the corner of Fifth and Main. He has a good reputation for high-quality work and claims numerous regular customers. Tony employs seven people: two mechanics and five part-time attendants. Let's watch him as he prepares his weekly payroll.

On Monday morning, Tony posts a work schedule for the week in the station. Throughout the week, changes are simply noted on the schedule—Tom's Wednesday morning history test might prompt him to switch nights with Judy. Early Saturday evening, after closing the station for the weekend, Tony removes the schedule and takes it home. This record of the number of hours worked by each employee is essential data; we can call it Tony's basic *input* document.

Saturday evening is payroll time. Tony always starts with Lou, his number-one mechanic and second in command. The schedule shows that Lou worked from 8.00 A.M. until 5:00 P.M. (nine hours) Monday through Friday and from 9:00 A.M. until 1:00 P.M. on Saturday. Although it isn't actually on the schedule, Tony knows that Lou took an hour for lunch on each nine-hour day. Working on a sheet of scratch paper, Tony quickly computes Lou's total hours for the week: 44. Lou is paid $4.75 per hour. A simple multiplication (44 × $4.75) gives Lou's gross pay for the week; it's $209.00.

Next, Tony computes the income-tax deduction. The government publishes a set of income-tax withholding rates every year; this set of tables is circulated in a booklet called "Circular E." In this booklet are the tables Tony must use in preparing payroll. (A copy of the appropriate tables has been reproduced in Fig. 2.5.) Lou has a wife and one child living at home; thus, Tony must subtract $43.20 ($14.40 times 3 dependents) from Lou's gross pay before entering the table—this subtraction leaves $165.80 of taxable wages. Tony now enters the tax table. Since Lou's taxable wage lies between $96 and $173, the amount of tax to be withheld is $8.16 plus 20% of all earnings over $96. Tony computes the "excess" portion of earnings ($165.80 minus $96.00 equals $69.80), finds 20% of this amount (20% of $69.80 is $13.96), adds this amount to the base tax ($8.16 plus $13.96 equals $22.12), and ends up with the amount of federal income tax that must be withheld from Lou's pay.

WEEKLY PAYROLL PERIOD

(a) Single person—including head of household				(b) Married person			
If the amount of wages is:		The amount of income tax to be withheld shall be:		If the amount of wages is:		The amount of income tax to be withheld shall be:	
Not over $25 0				Not over $48 0			
Over—	but not over—		of excess over—	Over—	but not over—		of excess over—
$25	−$67 . . . . . 16%		−$25	$48	−$96 . . . . . 17%		−$48
$67	−$115 . . . . $6.72 plus 20%		−$67	$96	−$173 . . . . $8.16 plus 20%		−$96
$115	−$183 . . . . $16.32 plus 23%		−$115	$173	−$264 . . . . $23.56 plus 17%		−$173
$183	−$240 . . . . $31.96 plus 21%		−$183	$264	−$346 . . . . $39.03 plus 25%		−$264
$240	−$279 . . . . $43.93 plus 26%		−$240	$346	−$433 . . . . $59.53 plus 28%		−$346
$279	−$346 . . . . $54.07 plus 30%		−$279	$433	−$500 . . . . $83.89 plus 32%		−$433
$346	. . . . $74.17 plus 36%		−$346	$500	. . . . $105.33 plus 36%		−$500

Fig. 2.5
A federal income tax table: Weekly payroll period. Multiply the number of dependents claimed by the employee by $14.40. Subtract the resulting amount from gross pay. The result is the employee's taxable wage. (*Source: Circular E, Employer's Tax Guide,* Department of the Treasury, Internal Revenue Service Publication 15. Revised April 1976, pp. 17–18.)

Next, the social security tax must be computed. The current social-security tax rate is 5.85% of gross pay. Since Lou's gross pay is $209.00, the deduction for social security is $12.23 (5.85% of $209.00).

Other deductions, such as state tax, local tax, and so on, would be computed in much the same way; let's simply assume that there are no more deductions and move along to the computation of take-home pay.

Net, or take-home, pay is found by subtracting all deductions from gross pay. In Lou's case, Tony subtracts the $22.12 for income tax and the $12.23 for social security tax from Lou's gross pay of $209.00, leaving a net pay of $174.65. A check for this amount is made out to Lou.

Tony is now ready to tackle Ralph's pay. First, the total number of hours that he worked is determined—the source is the work schedule. Hours worked is then multiplied by the hourly pay rate, giving gross pay (with only seven employees, Tony knows everyone's pay rate). The gross pay figure allows income tax to be computed through the tax tables. The social security deduction is 5.85% of gross pay. Net pay is found by subtracting these two deductions from gross pay, and a check is written.

He now moves on to the part-time workers, repeating what should, by now, have become an obvious pattern:

1. Find total hours worked from the schedule.

2. Multiply hours worked by the employee's hourly pay rate to get gross pay.

3. Find income tax from the tax table.

4. Multiply gross pay by 0.0585 to get the social security tax.

5. Subtract income tax and social security tax from gross pay to find net pay.

6. Write a paycheck.

Note that the exact same sequence of computational steps is repeated for each employee.

Every computation is checked and double-checked for accuracy, but mistakes still happen occasionally. The arithmetic is not difficult; multiplication and subtraction, even with decimal numbers and percentages, are elementary-school skills. But Tony hates this job; it's just too repetitive, too boring, and too exacting.

Tony spends roughly an hour a week on his payroll. Why not do the work on a computer? A computer, even a small one, cannot be rented for much less than $1000 per month. Even though he loathes this part of his job, Tony is not willing to spend $1000 per month just to save an hour a week of his time. The service station is just too small for a computer.

Payroll Processing in a Larger Firm

The *Evening News* employs approximately 700 people, some as reporters and others as proofreaders or typesetters. Still other individuals are involved in running the presses, selling ads, or delivering the newspapers. Although the company would certainly not be considered huge (or even big), no single individual would be capable of personally exercising total control over all these functions, making subdivision necessary.

Payday is once a week, on Friday. Since the company is a bit larger than Tony's service station, some of the informality disappears from the payroll process. Rather than simply relying on handwritten attendance records, employees record their comings and goings by punching a time clock. Since it is not reasonable to expect any one individual to keep everyone's pay rate in mind, personnel records are maintained. But the computations performed and tables used by the *News* are identical to those used by Tony; if they tried to do the job any differently, the *News* would be in violation of federal law. An individual's pay is still computed by the following six steps:

1. Find total hours worked (from the time card).

2. Multiply hours worked by the employee's hourly pay rate (from personnel records) to get gross pay.

3. Find income tax from the tax tables.

4. Multiply gross pay by 0.0585 to get the social security tax.

5. Subtract income tax and social security tax from gross pay to find net pay. (With a larger firm such as the *Evening News*, other deductions are likely, but we'll ignore them.)

6. Write a paycheck.

This procedure must be repeated once for each employee. Tony went through it seven times, needing about an hour to complete the work. The *News* must repeat the cycle seven hundred times; one hundred hours would seem a reasonable estimate of the time required to complete the job. If we assume that the company is on a standard forty-hour work week, that amounts to the services of 2½ people. Adding various employee benefits to the basic pay of these employees means that it would probably cost the *News* at least $1000 per month for each employee; given 2½ people, that's a total of $2500 just to produce the payroll. A computer can be rented for around $1000 per month. It looks like a good deal.

But it's a bit more complex than that. In order to use a computer, even a small one, an operator is needed. A computer operator is a highly skilled individual who expects to be paid more than the average employee. Let's assume a total labor cost of $1500 per month, including benefits. The operator and the computer will cost the *News* $2500 per month; they can save the *News* $2500 per month. Should the *News* shift payroll computations to the computer? The answer is not clear; perhaps other applications of the machine will produce other savings and "tip the balance" in the computer's favor.

Payroll Processing in a Large Corporation

Tinhorn Steel is one of the largest corporations in the country; the local plant alone employs nearly seven thousand people. Laws regarding income tax and social security tax do not change as a firm grows larger; thus Tinhorn faces the same tax-withholding requirements as Tony's service station and the *Evening News*, and an individual employee's pay is computed by the same procedure used in the two smaller firms. Yet Tinhorn Steel uses a computer.

Tony repeated this set of calculations seven times a week, spending about an hour on the job. The *News* repeated the same computations 700 times, needing about 100 hours, or the services of 2½ people, to do the job. Tinhorn Steel, with 7000 employees in the local plant, must repeat the cycle 7000 times, spending about 1000 hours per week on payroll! Again, if we assume a forty-hour work week, that amounts to 25 full-time employees doing nothing but multiplying hours worked by hourly pay rate and so on. At $1000 per employee, that's $25,000 per month just to *produce* the paychecks for the other 6975 employees.

As we stated earlier, a computer can be rented for roughly $1000 per month. With the services of an operator, a programmer, and a data processing manager included, the total cost of computerized payroll won't exceed $6000 or $7000 per month. That's considerably less than $25,000. Tinhorn uses a computer because the computer is cheaper. It's that simple. Whenever

1. A task can be completely defined by a series of repetitious, computational or logical steps,

2. The task must be repeated many times,

the computer may provide a solution. Both characteristics—well-defined steps repeated many times—are present in the vast majority of commercial computer applications.

THE BREAKEVEN POINT

Why should the number of repetitions make such a big difference? If a computer rents for $1500 per month, the rental cost remains the same whether the machine is used to compute one, two, seven hundred, or several thousand pay checks. The computer is a **fixed-cost item.** Human labor, on the other hand, is a **variable-cost item.** If the cost of producing one paycheck by hand is one dollar, the cost of producing two is two dollars, five hundred cost $500, and ten thousand, at $1 each, $10,000.

Take a look at Fig. 2.6. Along the horizontal or x-axis, we have the number of repetitions; along the vertical or y-axis, we have the total cost. The horizontal line marked "computer cost" shows that the cost of doing a job such as payroll does not change as the number of repetitions changes; it costs the same to compute one paycheck as it does to compute 10,000. (This is not entirely true; more checks means more paper and more ink and more paper handling, but the variable part of the computer cost is very small.) The slanted line marked "manual cost," starting at zero and going up and to the right, shows how the cost of processing checks by hand increases with each check. Eventually, as the number of repetitions increases, the "manual" line crosses the "computer" line. To the left of this point, the cost of doing the job by hand is less than the cost of using the computer; to the right of this point, the cost of using the computer is less than the cost of doing the job by hand. This point is called the **breakeven point.** The breakeven point defines a critical number of repetitions. If a company has fewer employees and, hence, fewer paychecks than this crucial number, the job will probably be done by hand. If employment exceeds this number, the computer will probably be used.

Actually, this idea is not so unusual if you think about it. Why, for example, do we use a shovel to dig a few postholes but switch to a steamshovel

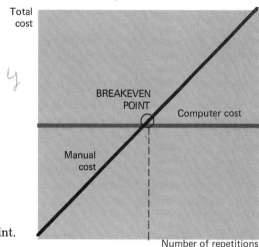

Fig. 2.6
The breakeven point.

to dig a basement for a new house? Given enough people and enough shovels, a basement could be dug by hand, but with such a large task, the use of the machine saves money (and time). Why does a teacher grade classroom examinations by hand while lengthy exams such as the Scholastic Aptitude Test (SAT) are graded by machine? Again, it's a question of cost. Why do we type letters but print newspapers and books? Try to picture two million copies of the latest paperback bestseller being produced by monks with quill pens; even at the ridiculously low wage of one dollar per hour, the cost of a book produced in this manner would be beyond all but the most wealthy.

The breakeven concept is an important one. Manual labor is a variable cost; machine labor is a fixed cost. As the number of repetitions or copies increases, the cost of manual labor creeps closer and closer to the breakeven point; when the breakeven point is crossed, the machine will be used. This is the underlying motivation behind *all* forms of "automation"; if the machine is cheaper to use than human labor, the machine will be used. There is nothing sinister about it. Automation is not designed to put people out of work; automation is intended to save money.

SIMILAR COMPUTER APPLICATIONS

Let's assume that we're selling cars and specializing in a single model. The cars on our lot make up our inventory. Each time we sell a car, we subtract one from inventory; each time a new shipment arrives from our supplier, we add the incoming cars to our inventory. The current number of cars in inventory is an important statistic; we use this number to determine whether or not to order additional cars. The computations are very easy—simple addition and subtraction.

At a more realistic automobile dealership with dozens of different models, the problem is a bit more complex, but manual records are still adequate. What happens, however, in a big department store, or a supermarket, or an industrial warehouse, where thousands of different products must be controlled and tracked? Paper-and-pencil inventory systems do not have a chance in such complex environments. The calculations are no more difficult; it's just that there are so many more of them to perform. Computers are frequently used to keep track of inventory.

Billing is another good example of a common computer application. A small company might write its bills by hand, but how can a large bank-credit-card system possibly process millions of individual purchases each month by hand? Instead, individual sales and credit slips are read into the computer and sorted and grouped by account number, and the resulting bills are compiled and printed by computer.

Banks face similar problems. To update checking account balances, all checks must be subtracted from the old balance and all deposits must be added. Again, it's simple addition and subtraction. If only a few dozen accounts are involved, this job presents no problem. But what if the bank has 100,000 or more accounts? Would you enjoy doing nothing but adding deposits and subtracting checks for eight hours a day, day in and day out? Adding interest to savings accounts is a similar problem. The computations are easy—all you do is find an account's minimum balance for the period and multiply by a constant interest rate. But, ten thousand times?

A small library can easily track its circulation by handwritten documents or 3×5 card files. But what about the big metropolitan library or the large university library? A small school can easily compute every student's grade point average manually, but if Ohio State or Stanford University were to try this approach, first-term averages *might* be ready by the end of the second term.

A surprising percentage of modern computer applications are really nothing more than this—very simple computations repeated many, many times. These applications represent nothing more nor less than the automation of tedious clerical functions.

THINGS HUMANS CANNOT DO

One of the most exciting stories of the late 1960s and the early 1970s was the conquest of space. Without the use of computers, however, the moon landings would have been impossible. This fact was underscored when, on one Apollo mission, an accident forced cancellation of the flight and raised the specter of three humans marooned in space. No human being could possibly have computed the necessary changes in flight plans rapidly enough to have saved the lives of the astronauts; only a computer could have done the job.

Consider the number of variables involved in trying to hit the moon with a rocket. The earth is spinning on its own axis and moving through space. Wind is a factor, and wind velocities can vary significantly as a rocket moves through the earth's atmosphere. The moon is a moving target. Even the gravitational attraction of the sun and the other planets must be taken into account. The problem is one of complexity and speed—people just can't manipulate all these variables rapidly enough.

Air-traffic control around a major airport is a similar problem. Each airplane can be viewed as a point in space defined by its ground location (e.g., eight miles out at five degrees east of due north), an altitude, a speed, and a direction of travel. A few planes present no real problem, but what happens when fifteen or twenty planes are circling and waiting for landing instructions, and another dozen are on the ground waiting to take off? Although human decisions are still essential in air-traffic control, the computer provides crucial assistance by tracking all air traffic and alerting the air-traffic controller of potentially dangerous situations before it's too late.

Our national air defense system provides another example of how computers can be used to perform tasks that are beyond normal human capability. Let's say that an unidentified aircraft is spotted over northern Canada. Is it a regularly scheduled flight? A check of all airline schedules might answer this question. Is it possible that a regularly scheduled flight might be off course due to weather conditions? Factoring worldwide weather reports into airline flight schedules might answer this question. Is it a private flight with an itinerary filed with the Civil Aeronautics Board? Before a human being could finish all of these checks, a real enemy threat would be exploding over Chicago. Computer assistance is essential.

Let's slow down for a moment and evaluate what we've been reading. Although none of the above situations can be handled entirely by people, human beings *can* solve the equations necessary to support a space flight or control air traffic or track an unidentified aircraft. People developed these equations and procedures; the computer is doing nothing that people have not already done. It's just that people can't perform these tasks quickly enough. The computer's skill is one of speed, not intelligence.

A COMPUTER'S SPEED

A computer is an electronic device. One of its capabilities is addition. A computer adds by simply allowing electrical current to pass through a series of circuits, in something like the time it takes a light bulb to begin to glow once the switch has been turned on. Instantaneous? Not quite, but the time is certainly well below human comprehension.

One second is an extremely long period of time to a computer. Even on a small, "slow" computer, the execution of an instruction takes less than one **millisecond,** which is (1/1000) one thousandth of a second. That's 1000 instructions per second. Even a millisecond is a long period of time to a large, modern, more expensive computer; many machines are capable of executing an instruction in one **microsecond**—one millionth (1/1,000,000) of a second —or less. New models are beginning to push into the **nanosecond** range (see Fig. 2.7). A nanosecond is one thousandth of one millionth, or one billionth, of a second (1/1,000,000,000); in one nanosecond, light travels one foot! [The next step is the **picosecond,** one millionth of one millionth of a second (1/1,000,000,000,000)!]

These speeds are inconceivable to the human mind. Let's use an analogy in order to put computer speeds into perspective. To travel from New York City to Los Angeles is a trip of roughly 3000 miles. How long would it take a human being to walk it? Assuming we can find someone who would like to try, a good steady walking pace would be about three miles per hour, meaning that some 1000 hours would be consumed in actually walking. Since people must take time to eat and sleep, let's assume that our walker averages

In the computer, the basic operations can be done within the order of a

NANOSECOND

One thousandth of a millionth of a second.

Within the half second it takes this spilled coffee to reach the floor, a fairly large computer could—

(given the information in magnetic form)

Debit 2000 checks to 300 different bank accounts,

and *examine the electrocardiograms of 100 patients and alert a physician to possible trouble,*

and *score 150,000 answers on 3000 examinations and evaluate the effectiveness of the questions,*

and *figure the payroll for a company with a thousand employees.*

and a few other chores.

Photo courtesy of IBM.

Fig. 2.7
The speed of modern computers is pushing into the nanosecond range.

ten hours a day of actual forward motion. A total of 100 days or 2400 hours would be needed to make the entire trip.

Jet airplanes have made the trip in three hours. Comparing the jet plane to the man, we find that

$$2400/3 = 800,$$

meaning that a jet plane is 800 times as fast as a human being.

Remember the estimate of some 1000 hours (or 60,000 minutes) needed to complete a 7000-employee payroll if the job were to be done manually? A computer, even a small, millisecond computer, can easily handle the same payroll in about ten minutes. Using the same kind of ratio as above,

$$60,000/10 = 6000,$$

we find that a computer is *6000* times as fast as human beings. The jet would have to make the trip from New York to Los Angeles in *twenty-four minutes* in order to enjoy the same speed advantage over a walking human that a computer enjoys over a computing human.

Actually, the computer's speed advantage is even greater than the above analogy indicates. The slowest part of almost any computer system is the card reader. The estimate of ten minutes for a 7000-employee payroll was based on a 700-card-per-minute card reader setting the pace, and not on actual computer speeds. If we were to concentrate on the computer itself, the jet plane would have to make a 3000-mile trip in but a fraction of a minute in order to enjoy a similar speed advantage. *Computers are fast!*

A COMPUTER'S ACCURACY

A wall switch can be used to turn on a light bulb. When the switch is moved to the "on" position, electricity flows through a wire and the bulb lights. Move the switch to the "off" position, and the light goes out. A repeat of this little experiment will cause electricity to flow through the *same* wire and light the *same* bulb, and our experience tells us that no matter how often the experiment is repeated, we can expect the same result. Eventually, of course, the bulb burns out or the switch begins to wear and the experiment "fails," but, for the most part, the electrical circuit designed to control the light bulb is very "accurate."

The computer performs arithmetic and other functions through the use of electricity. Passing the same type of electrical current through the same wires will produce the same result time and time again. Thus, a computer is "accurate." Of course, the electronic circuits of a computer are much more complex than the electronic ciruits which control a light bulb, but once the circuit has been designed, built, and fully tested, it is every bit as predictable.

The computer almost never makes a mistake. Electrical failures do, of course, occur on occasion, but due to the advanced electronics used in modern computers, such failures are quite rare.

Imagine again a 7000-employee payroll being prepared manually. Imagine yourself working eight hours a day, five days a week, fifty weeks a year, doing nothing but multiplying hours worked by hourly pay rate to get gross pay. Do you think that you might possibly make an occasional mistake? Unlike a human being, a computer does not suffer from boredom or fatigue. A computer has no emotions. *Computers are accurate.*

WHY ARE COMPUTERS USED?

As we have seen, computers are very fast and very accurate. Unfortunately, they are also very expensive. On some highly repetitious jobs, its speed and accuracy allows a computer to do the work at a lower cost than human beings; because of the high cost of the computer, however, this only occurs when the job must be repeated many times. In other cases, the computer is used to do jobs which just could not be done by unaided human beings—such jobs as air-traffic or space-flight control. On these jobs, people can do the needed calculations; they just can't do them fast enough.

In other words, computers are used for economic reasons. They allow us to handle certain functions at a lower cost than would otherwise be possible, and they allow us to perform tasks that we could not do otherwise.

At the beginning of this chapter, we discussed the importance of information to a modern organization. Since then, we've been concentrating on specific examples of information processing—the payroll application, the inventory application, the billing application, and others, but we really haven't described the interrelationships between these individual data processing applications and the various functions of the organization. The accounting department, for example, is very interested in the information produced by the payroll programs. Sales is certainly concerned with inventory data, as is accounting. Information contributed by all these individual applications contributes to the organization's *data base.* If we assume that this text is your first introduction to the computer and the field of information processing, the term data base is a bit too advanced to fully define in this chapter; thus, we will build the background necessary to understand this concept over the next several chapters. In Part II of the text, we'll concentrate on how the computer actually works. This material will provide the background needed to understand the concepts of files and file processing, which will be presented in Part III. Finally, in Part IV, we'll introduce some basic system concepts, showing how the computer can be treated as the information warehouse we described in the first few pages of this chapter. The final section of the text, Part V, will concentrate on present trends and possible future directions for the computer or information processing field, ending with a discussion of the social impact of the computer.

SUMMARY

We began by pointing out the importance of information in a modern complex organization; information is crucial to planning and control. The computer was described as an information processing machine and as an information warehouse. Next, a typical application—payroll—was traced through a series of three firms of different sizes, the major objective being an illustration of the breakeven concept: If a repetitious task is performed enough times, the computer becomes cheaper than a manual operation. Other examples of the "many repetitions of a simple job" application were presented. The computer was then shown to be capable of performing tasks which, without the computer, would be impossible. The major advantages of a computer—its tremendous speed and accuracy—were also discussed.

KEY WORDS

automation

breakeven point

computer

data base

feedback

fixed cost

information

information processing

input

microsecond

millisecond

nanosecond

organization

variable cost

EXERCISES

1. Find out how the manager of a local service station or grocery store handles payroll.

2. Which of the following tasks might be suitable for the computer? Why?
   a) Grading a multiple-choice test
   b) Grading a piece of creative writing
   c) Conducting a drill session in basic mathematics
   d) Teaching the basic rules of grammar
   e) Teaching art
   f) Addressing a few envelopes
   g) Addressing several thousand copies of a magazine

3. One major topic covered in this chapter was the breakeven point. Explain what it means in your own words. See if you can think of a number of examples in which this concept comes into play.

4. One example of computer use cited in the first chapter was the continual recomputation of betting odds at a racetrack. Why can't people do this job?

Basic Computer Concepts

How a Computer Works

3

OVERVIEW

This chapter begins with an analogy showing a group of human beings performing the basic functions of a computer. Following the analogy, these functions will be related to the components of a real computer. This material serves as an overview of Part II, providing a framework against which to study the material in Chapters 4–9.

HOW A COMPUTER WORKS: AN ANALOGY

To gain some appreciation for how computers work and what a programmer does, let's imagine a group of people who function in much the same way as a computer does. A manager and his two secretaries share a suite of three offices (see Fig. 3.1). The manager sits at a desk in the middle room; except for the two secretaries, he has absolutely no contact with the outside world.

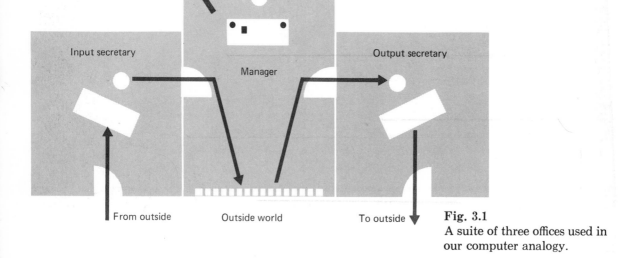

Input secretary

Output secretary

Manager

From outside   Outside world   To outside

Fig. 3.1
A suite of three offices used in our computer analogy.

This is a very efficient operation. One of the manager's aides is responsible for handling all information coming *into* the office; he's the input secretary, and his job is to allow the outside world to communicate *to* the man in the middle room. The other secretary, the output secretary, provides a communication link *from* the manager to the outside world.

Imagine the extreme isolation of this man. He sees and hears nothing unless that information comes from the input secretary. As the work is completed and results are sent outside, he must *assume* that the output secretary delivers them properly.

The middle room bears closer examination. Hanging on the front wall are 250 numbered chalkboards (Fig. 3.2). These chalkboards will be used to hold the data being processed by the manager.

Next to the boss's desk is a small, portable chalkboard, the work space (Fig. 3.3). It's divided into three parts: "A," "B," and "ANSWER." This work space will be used in computations.

On the desk itself (Fig. 3.4) are two buttons: one to call the input secretary, and one to call the output secretary. In the center of the desk is a deck

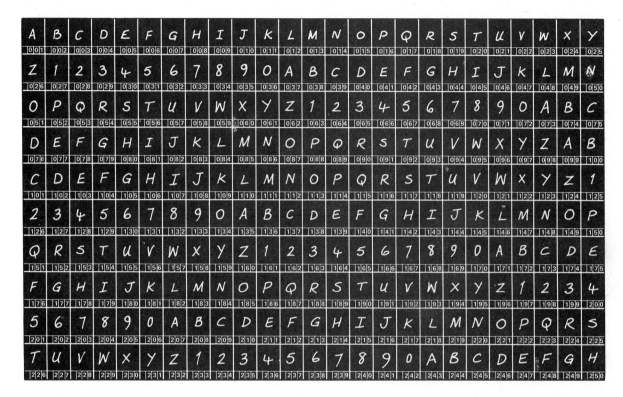

Fig. 3.2
The front wall is covered with 250 numbered chalkboards.

A	
B	
Answer	

Fig. 3.3
The work space.

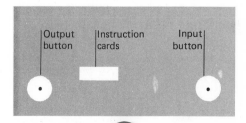

Fig. 3.4
The desk.

of instruction cards, which we discuss in more detail later.

In addition to the "single source in/single source out" mode of operation, the manager has a number of other, very serious limitations. He's pretty good at basic arithmetic and can copy accurately, but he can't handle more than two numbers at a time, and his only possible response to a direct question is a simple yes or no.

He's rather lazy too, with absolutely no personal initiative. Our hero does only (and exactly) what he is told to do—nothing more and nothing less. That's the purpose of the cards in the middle of the desk; they're his instructions. Another individual, a programmer, must put together a series of instruction cards telling the boss how to prepare a payroll; a complete copy of this program is shown in Appendix A.

GETTING STARTED: INPUT

The first instruction card reads

   1. PUSH INPUT BUTTON.

Following his instructions to the letter, the manager pushes the input button and settles back to wait. A buzzer sounds on the input secretary's desk; the secretary grabs the first input record, enters the middle room, and begins copying the information onto the numbered chalkboards.

This office uses a standard form which is exactly 80 characters long (Fig. 3.5); any information that is to be communicated to the manager *must* be submitted on this standard document. Also, as the input secretary enters the

Fig. 3.5
The first input record.

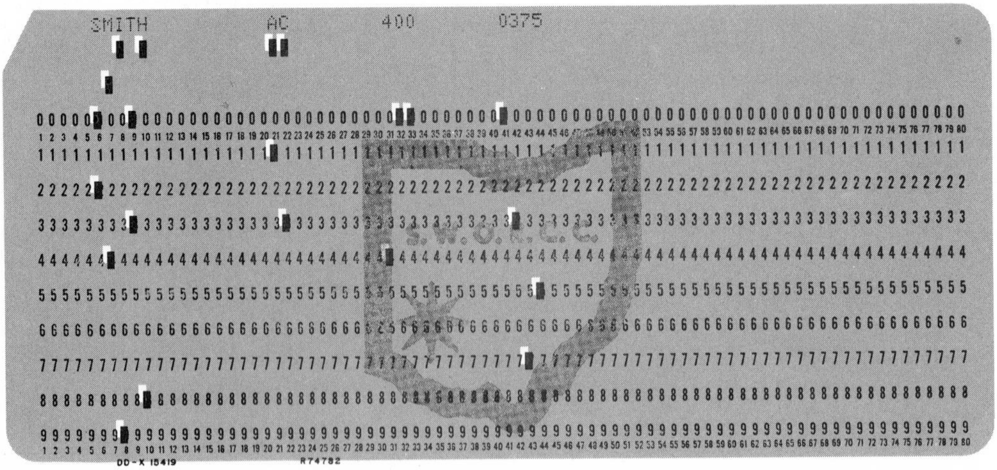

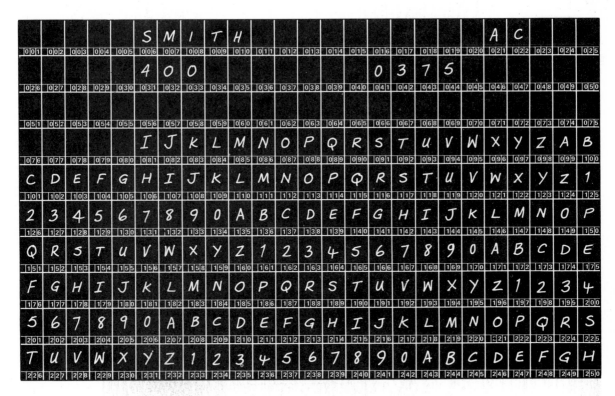

Fig. 3.6
The memory chalkboards after the first input record has been added.

room and begins to copy information onto the numbered slates, the secretary will *always* start with slate number one.

The first record (Fig. 3.5) is for a man named A. C. Smith, who worked 40.0 hours and is paid 3.75 per hour. The secretary, armed with eraser and chalk, copies this information onto the first 80 numbered slates, one character to each slate (Fig. 3.6). Columns 1 through 5 (in Fig. 3.5) are blank, so chalkboards 1 through 5 are erased and left blank. The name "SMITH" is found in positions 6 through 10; thus, it is copied onto slates 6 through 10. When he has finished, the input secretary has reproduced—letter for letter, number for number, blank for blank, and position for position—an exact duplicate of the input record on the numbered chalkboards.

PROCESSING THE DATA

Computing Gross Pay

Having completed his work, the input secretary exits, closing the door behind him. The input operation finished, a buzzer sounds, interrupting the manager's brief nap. He turns over the first instruction card, revealing the second instruction:

2. COPY THE THREE SLATES STARTING WITH SLATE 31 ONTO WORK SPACE A.

He does as he is told, and turns to the next card:

3. COPY THE FOUR SLATES STARTING WITH SLATE 41 ONTO WORK SPACE B.

and the next:

4. MULTIPLY.

As he completes this series of operations, the work space looks like Fig. 3.7. The three instructions told him to copy the number of hours worked from slates 31, 32, and 33 (the same positions that this field occupied on the input record) onto work space A, to copy the hourly pay from slates 41, 42, 43, and 44 onto work space B, and to multiply these two numbers together, giving gross pay.

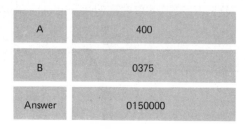

Fig. 3.7
The work space after the computation of gross pay.

Note how mechanical the operation is. Our human computer is not in the least concerned with the meaning of his work; he simply takes one number from "here," and another number from "there," and multiplies them. He could just as well be doing a junior high school math lesson or a computation in subatomic physics—they're all the same to him.

Note also the extreme detail of these instructions. It's not enough simply to tell our hero to multiply two numbers together; he must be told exactly where to find the numbers. If, by mistake, the third instruction said to copy the four slates starting with slate 40 instead of 41, he would have dutifully copied a blank followed by the digits 037 onto his work space B, and computed gross pay at 37 cents an hour. (You may have spotted a complete absence of decimal points. Decimal-point alignment, as we'll see later, is handled by the programmer.)

In the next instruction:

5. COPY THE ANSWER ONTO THE SEVEN SLATES STARTING WITH SLATE 81.

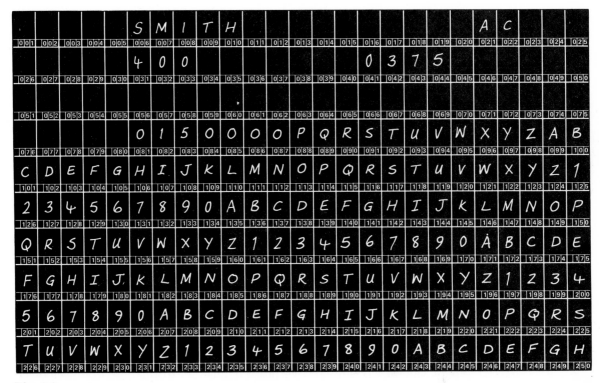

Fig. 3.8
The memory chalkboards after the computation of gross pay.

the programmer tells the manager in the middle room to save the result of his computation; unless he is told otherwise, he will simply destroy this result when he performs the next computation. Following step 5, the memory chalkboards look like Fig. 3.8.

Computing Social Security Tax

The computation of social security tax is similar to the computation of gross pay. First, gross pay is copied from the chalkboards (where step 5 stored it) onto the work space:

6. COPY THE SIX SLATES STARTING WITH SLATE 81 ONTO WORK SPACE A.

To get social security tax, we must calculate 5.85 percent (the current tax rate) of the employee's gross pay, hence:

7. COPY "585" ONTO WORK SPACE B.
8. MULTIPLY.

and

9. COPY THE ANSWER ONTO THE NINE SLATES STARTING WITH SLATE 88.

The result, social security tax correct to six decimal places, now exists on the memory blackboards (the actual step-by-step contents of these blackboards can be seen by referring to Appendix A).

Computing Income Tax

Income tax is computed by selecting a tax rate from a set of tables—the more you earn, the higher the rate. Rather than use the complex tables described in Chapter 2, we'll invent a very simple set of rates for our example: If gross pay is less than $100.00, five percent of gross pay is deducted; otherwise, ten percent is deducted. Instruction 10:

10. COPY THE SIX SLATES STARTING WITH SLATE 81 ONTO WORK SPACE A.

gets our human computer started. Now we (the programmers) are ready to tell him how to select the proper tax rate. We start with a question:

11. IS THE NUMBER ON WORK SPACE A LESS THAN 010000?

which tells him to compare gross pay with $100.00 (remember, decimal points aren't carried). There are two possible answers to this question: yes or no. Based on the answer, we'll tell the manager how to select the correct rate.

Suppose the answer is "yes." If gross pay *is* less than $100.00, then the proper tax rate is five percent. The relevant instructions are shown in Fig. 3.9; by following these instructions, the boss, given a "yes" answer to the question posed in step 11, would skip to card 15, where he would be instructed to copy "05" (for five percent) onto work space B and then multiply.

Suppose the answer is "no." Following the question of step 11, the manager would *not* skip to card 15; he would go instead to card 13 where he would be instructed to copy "10" (for ten percent) onto work space B and then to skip to card 16 where the desired multiplication would be performed. Finally, in either case, the answer would be copied to the chalkboards.

Our human machine has answered a simple yes/no question and, based on the answer, has been able to change the sequence of instructions. A more complex tax structure would require more questions, but the logic is essentially the same. This is an extremely valuable skill.

Computing Net Pay

Net pay is simply gross pay minus all deductions. Since our hero is restricted to the processing of two numbers at a time, the computation involves two distinct steps: subtract social security tax from gross pay and then subtract

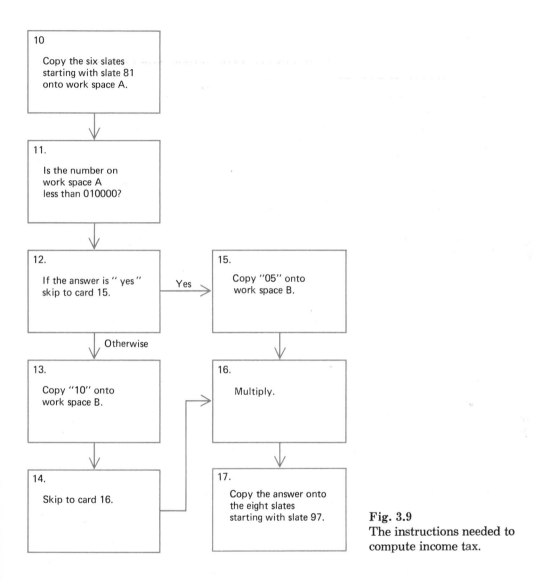

Fig. 3.9
The instructions needed to
compute income tax.

income tax from this partial answer. The instructions needed to perform these functions are shown in Fig. 3.10.

FINISHING UP: OUTPUT

On input, the input secretary produced an exact copy of a single record on the memory boards. Output works in just the opposite manner—the manager prepares an exact copy of a single line of output on the slates, and then

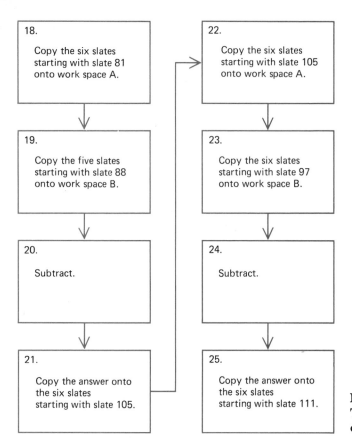

18.

Copy the six slates starting with slate 81 onto work space A.

19.

Copy the five slates starting with slate 88 onto work space B.

20.

Subtract.

21.

Copy the answer onto the six slates starting with slate 105.

22.

Copy the six slates starting with slate 105 onto work space A.

23.

Copy the six slates starting with slate 97 onto work space B.

24.

Subtract.

25.

Copy the answer onto the six slates starting with slate 111.

Fig. 3.10
The instructions needed to compute net pay.

calls the second secretary who transcribes it, position for position, to a standard form. (For those who are interested in the exact details, see instructions 26 through 34 in Appendix A.)

Before we move on, take a look at instruction 32 (in the Appendix):

32. COPY "." ONTO SLATE 225.

That's how the decimal point gets into the final answer; the programmer tells the computer to put it there.

STARTING OVER

The last three instructions are especially interesting:

35. HAVE ALL EMPLOYEES BEEN PROCESSED?
36. IF "YES" THEN QUIT.
37. GO TO CARD #1.

Because of these three cards, the program will be executed over and over again until all payroll records have been processed. Without this capability, how could our human processor handle a 7000-employee payroll? He would need a complete set of instructions for each employee—that's 7000 × 34, or 218,000, cards! This is another indication of the importance of the ability to respond to a yes/no question and to change the sequence of instructions based on the answer.

OUR ANALOGY: A SUMMARY

The man in the middle room did just about everything that a computer can do. Computers can request single records of *input* data, with the input device making a character-by-character copy in the computer's memory or storage. In much the same way that our human data processor copied information from the numbered chalkboards onto his workboard, the computer can copy information from one memory location to another. The computer can add, subtract, multiply, and divide, but (normally) with only two numbers at a time. The machine can compare two numbers or two letters and answer such questions as "Is the first positive?" "Is it negative?" "Is it zero?" "Is the first bigger than the second?" "Is it smaller?" "Are they equal?" In each case, the only possible answers are "yes" or "no"; a **branch instruction** can be executed based on the answer. On output, information is simply transferred from the computer's memory or storage to some output device which assumes responsibility for printing or otherwise "outputting" it.

That's about it. No one would ever think of hiring a person who works like the guy we've been describing, unless, of course, he or she knew that the worker is capable of handling 1000 sets of computations per minute without making a mistake.

REAL COMPUTERS

The point of this analogy has been to simulate a real computer. Let's examine the key components of such a machine. Every computer consists of three basic parts: an input device, the computer itself, and an output device (Fig. 3.11). The input and output secretaries in our example represent, as you've

Fig. 3.11
The basic parts of any computer system.

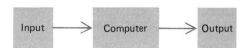

probably guessed, the input and output devices, respectively; the manager represents the computer. Within the computer are a number of key components: the **central processing unit,** where computations and other logical functions are performed (the manager himself), **storage** or **memory** (the numbered chalkboards), and **registers** (the work space). These components are shown in Fig. 3.12.

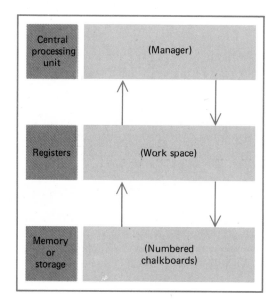

Fig. 3.12
The component parts of a computer.

Throughout the remainder of this section, we'll be looking at each of these major components in more detail. Chapter 4 is devoted to basic input and output concepts. Chapter 5 concentrates on the computer's memory or storage, while Chapter 6 discusses the central processing unit, registers, and other logical **hardware.** We'll consider **software** in Chapters 7 and 8; software (or programs) was simulated by the deck of instruction cards in the above analogy. Chapter 9 will attempt to pull all these ideas together by presenting a complete computer-based system in a manner similar to the one used in this chapter, but in considerably more technical terms. As you read the material in these next several chapters, the analogy you've just completed should serve as a useful point of reference, tying all the concepts together in a single framework.

Know

SUMMARY

This chapter introduced the basic functions of a computer through an analogy, showing humans performing the computer's various tasks. Two secretaries simulated input and output. An individual known as the manager played the part of the central processing unit. Numbered chalkboards simulated the computer's memory, while a workboard took the place of registers. A deck of instruction cards was used to show the basic idea of a program.

EXERCISES

1. Take paper, a pencil, and a pocket calculator, and lay out a system for computing payroll using as input the records described in this chapter. Explain how you would simulate each of the key computer components: input, output, the central processing unit, memory, registers, and the program.

2. Visit a real computer center. Try to identify each of the major computer components.

KEY WORDS

branch

central
processing unit

computer

input

input device

instruction

memory

output

output device

processing

program

programmer

record

register

software

storage

Input and Output

In Chapter 3, we used an analogy to introduce the primary functions of a computer. As you may recall, the two secretaries represented input and output. In this chapter, we'll be discussing equipment which actually supports input and output: card readers, printers, card punches, MICR and OCR hardware, terminals, and other types of equipment. In addition, we'll introduce the concepts of buffering and control units.

THE PUNCHED CARD

The most widely known of all computer input or output documents is the **punched card**; it's hard to imagine anyone in our present society who has never seen one. This familiarity makes the card an excellent choice for introducing basic input and output concepts.

Let's begin by analyzing the card itself. A punched card (Fig. 4.1) is divided into eighty **columns**, each of which is subdivided into twelve **rows**. The columns are numbered from 1 through 80 (predictably); you can find the column numbers between the 0's and the 1's in Fig. 4.1. The rows run down the card: 12, 11, and 0 through 9. Originally, the card was intended to be used for numerical data only (Hollerith's census application); thus, early cards had only ten punch positions per column, 0 through 9. These are known as the **numeric positions**. Later, when the need for alphabetic data arose, the **zone** positions, rows 12 and 11, were added.

Fig. 4.1
A punched card.

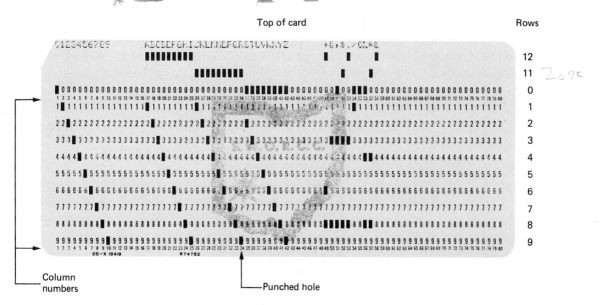

Top of card

Rows

12

11

0

1

2

3

4

5

6

7

8

9

Column numbers

Punched hole

Each column of a card holds one **character**—a letter, a digit, or a special symbol such as a punctuation mark. The position of holes punched in the column determines the character. In Fig. 4.1, column 1 contains only a single hole in the 0 row; thus the column contains the digit zero. Column 2 contains a single punched hole in the 1 row; hence, it contains the digit one. Letters are represented by two punches, a zone and a numeric, in the same column; column 17, for example, contains punches in rows 12 and 1, which, taken together (Fig. 4.1), designate the letter A. The various special symbols are similarly represented by combinations of hole patterns; the punched card code is summarized in Fig. 4.2.

Character	Punched Card Code	Hole Pattern
0	0	001000000000
1	1	000100000000
2	2	000010000000
3	3	000001000000
4	4	000000100000
5	5	000000010000
6	6	000000001000
7	7	000000000100
8	8	000000000010
9	9	000000000001
A	12,1	100100000000
B	12,2	100010000000
C	12,3	100001000000
D	12,4	100000100000
E	12,5	100000010000
F	12,6	100000001000
G	12,7	100000000100
H	12,8	100000000010
I	12,9	100000000001
J	11,1	010100000000
K	11,2	010010000000
L	11,3	010001000000
M	11,4	010000100000
N	11,5	010000010000
O	11,6	010000001000
P	11,7	010000000100
Q	11,8	010000000010
R	11,9	010000000001
S	0,2	001010000000
T	0,3	001001000000
U	0,4	001000100000
V	0,5	001000010000
W	0,6	001000001000
X	0,7	001000000100
Y	0,8	001000000010
Z	0,9	001000000001
¢	12,2,8	100010000010
.	12,3,8	100001000010
(	12,5,8	100000010010
+	12,6,8	100000001010
&	12	100000000000
!	11,2,8	010010000010
$	11,3,8	010001000010
*	11,4,8	010000100010
)	11,5,8	010000010010
;	11,6,8	010000001010
—	11	010000000000
/	0,1	001100000000
,	0,3,8	001001000010
%	0,4,8	001000100010
?	0,7,8	001000000110
:	2,8	000010000010
#	3,8	000001000010
@	4,8	000000100010
'	5,8	000000010010
=	6,8	000000001010
"	7,8	000000000110
blank	no punch	000000000000

Fig. 4.2
The punched card code.

Notice how consistent the code is. The numbers 0 through 9 are represented as punches 0 through 9, respectively. The letters A through I are all assigned a zone punch of 12, and, within this zone, are simply numbered from 1 to 9. The letters J through R all have a zone punch of 11, and are numbered in normal succession within this zone; the letters S through Z have a zone punch of 0 (yes, zero is sometimes a zone) and are numbered 2 through 9, respectively. Compare this code to the complexity of the Morse code. Which one would you prefer to memorize? This code makes sense!

Take special note of the third column of Fig. 4.2, marked "hole pattern." The computer is an electronic device. It's relatively easy to design an electronic device to recognize things as being either "on" or "off." This type of yes/no or on/off logic is easy to implement on a punched card, because in any given possible punch position, there either is or is not a hole. What the rightmost column of Fig. 4.2 illustrates is the presence (1) or absence (0) of a hole in each of the twelve rows within a given column of a card; this pattern of "hole or no hole" is what really represents the individual character.

Reading the Data

Paper (a punched card is made from a particular type of paper) is a good electrical insulator; in other words, paper will *not* conduct an electrical current. This simple fact provides the basis for a technique for reading these documents. Let's say that we were simply to lay a card on a metal surface and touch each of the 960 possible punch positions (80 columns times 12 rows per column equals 960 different possible punch positions) one at a time with an electronic probe (see Fig. 4.3). If there were no hole in a given punch position, the card would serve to separate the probe from the metal surface, thus preventing the flow of electricity. If, however, there were a hole, the probe would drop through the hole and contact the surface, thus allowing a current to flow through the wire. The presence or absence of electrical cur-

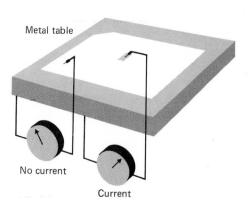

Metal table

No current

Current

Fig. 4.3
An experiment to illustrate how a punched card is read.

rent in the wire has exactly the same meaning as the presence or absence of a hole in the card; we have succeeded in converting a pattern of holes into a pattern of electricity, thus "reading" the data.

Of course, the technique of reading one punch position at a time with a manual probe is much too inefficient for practical use. A more realistic approach would be to design a brushlike device containing 960 different probes, one for each possible punch position, and to read all positions at the same time. We must also be concerned with feeding the cards into the read mechanism; manual feeding might have been acceptable in Hollerith's day, but it isn't now. One of the most common feed-and-read mechanisms in use today consists of a metal cylinder and a set of metal "fingers" (Fig. 4.4).

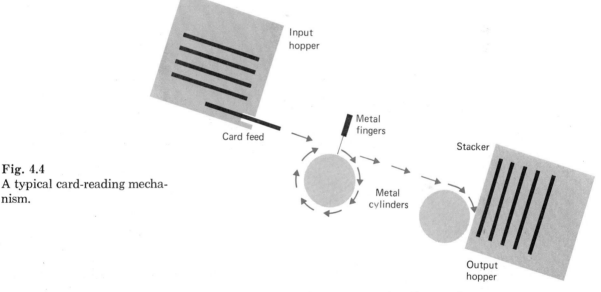

Input hopper

Card feed

Metal fingers

Stacker

Metal cylinders

Fig. 4.4
A typical card-reading mechanism.

Output hopper

Using this device cards are moved from the input hopper one at a time and wrapped around the metal cylinder. The metal fingers, one for each of the twelve rows (or one for each of the 80 columns on some machines), are allowed to simply drag over the card; if there is a hole, the finger drops through and contacts the cylinder, thus allowing a current to flow. Since the cylinder rotates at a fixed speed, the time to go from column 1 to column 2 to column 3 and so on is constant, allowing the machine to distinguish between individual columns. Card readers of this type are capable of reading as many as 600 cards per minute.

Another important property of a card is its opacity; in other words, light won't go through it. Except, of course, where a hole has been punched. This property is the basis for another general type of card reader, one based on a photoelectric circuit. A photoelectric cell emits electricity when struck by

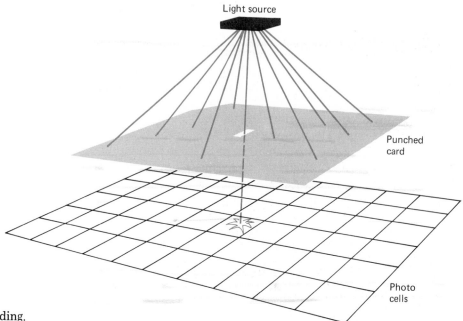

Fig. 4.5
Photoelectric card reading.

light. Imagine a bank of 960 of these cells (Fig. 4.5), one for each possible punch position. If a card were placed on top of this bank of cells and a light were shined on the card, the card would block the light, preventing it from hitting the photoelectric cells; hence no current would flow. Except, again, where a hole had been punched in the card. At these spots, light would stream through to the photoelectric cells, causing an electrical current to be generated. Once again, some wires would have a current and others would not; the card, having been converted to an electrical pattern, is read.

The photoelectric process involves less physical contact than do the mechanical contact approaches to card reading; thus, card readers utilizing the photo-cell approach are capable of a bit more speed—1000 cards per minute is not an uncommon rate. An example of a typical card reader is shown in Fig. 4.6.

Preparation

So far we've been discussing how to read a pattern of holes in a punched card. But how are the holes made in the card in the first place?

The most common mechanism for punching data into cards is the keypunch (Fig. 4.7). A keypunch, as the name implies, is a keyboard device, looking much like a typewriter. Instead of using paper, however, the key-

Fig. 4.6
A typical card reader—this
one is a card reader/punch.

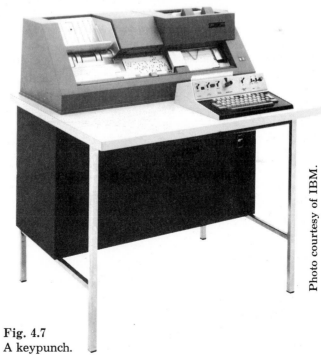

Fig. 4.7
A keypunch.

punch is equipped with a card-feed mechanism which moves one card at a time into the punching position; as a key is depressed, the hole pattern associated with that key is punched into the card. Most keypunches have a printer that prints the content of each column at the top of the card, thus facilitating visual checking.

The most common type of keypunch punches a single column of data as the key is depressed. Other keypunches, called **buffered keypunches**, allow the operator to type an entire card of data, visually check that data, depress a button, and then (and only then) actually punch the data into the card. The big advantage of a buffered keypunch is in data accuracy; if an error is made when initially entering the data, the operator has the ability to spot and correct the error before actually punching the card.

Closely associated with keypunching is the process of verification. A **verifier** looks very much like a keypunch. Once data has been keypunched, it is moved to the verifier where a different operator re-keys it; the verifier marks any cards on which the two operators disagree, allowing these cards to be isolated and corrected.

A common computer output device is a card punch. Perhaps the best way to understand how a card punch is used is through an example—let's use payroll again. Each employee in a plant requires a weekly time card containing, among other things, the individual's name, social security or employee number, department number, and actual time worked. Except for the actual time worked, all of this information is known at the beginning of the week,

Fig. 4.8
A port-o-punch card.

Photo courtesy of IBM.

before the card is prepared. Rather than repeat the slow, expensive, manual keypunching operation on this known data every week, a deck of partially prepunched cards (containing name, social security number, and department number) can be prepared by the computer through a card punch at a rate of 300 to 500 cards per minute with almost perfect accuracy, leaving only the actual hours worked to be filled in by the keypunch operators. Punched-card output can be used in a number of similar applications.

Another technique for preparing punched cards is the **port-o-punch** system shown in Fig. 4.8. In this system punch positions are prescored and the holes are later created by manually pushing out the hole with a stylus. This type of card is often used in vote tabulation. A ballot is inserted into a small plastic case, and the voter uses a stylus to punch the card in positions that correspond to his or her choices for the various offices; these individually prepared cards can then be read into a computer for tabulation. Other types of portable, one-card-at-a-time devices are also available.

The 96-Column Card

Although the 80-column card is considered an industry standard, there are other types of cards. One of the most important alternatives is the 96-column card used in small computers (Fig. 4.9). On this card, data is punched in three sections—columns 1 through 32 are on the top, columns 33 through 64 are in the middle, and columns 65 through 96 are on the bottom. Rather than

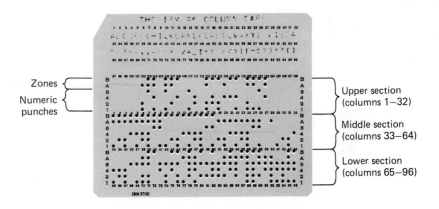

Fig. 4.9
The 96-column card.
(*Note:* The alphabet
begins in column 33.)

the usual twelve rows per column, the 96-column card has only six—from bottom to top, they are 1, 2, 4, 8, A, and B, respectively. The first four are numeric punches; the last two are zone punches. The number 1 is just a 1 punch; the number 2 is a 2 punch; the digit 3 is a 1 *and* a 2 punch; the digit 7 is 1, 2, and 4 punches in the same column (just add the punches together). Letters of the alphabet consist of a zone punch plus a combination of numeric punches. Actually, the coding scheme is quite similar to the standard 80-column code.

The 96-column card is smaller and it contains more data. Why hasn't it totally replaced the 80-column card? Basically because so many companies have such a large investment in programs and equipment that are based on the 80-column card.

CHARACTERS, FIELDS, RECORDS, AND FILES

In our discussion of the punched card, we concentrated on how individual *characters* can be punched and read. Actually, we are interested in more than the individual characters. In Chapter 3, we described an input record, transparently a punched card, on which columns 6 through 20 were said to contain the individual's name, columns 21 and 22 his or her initials, 31 through 33 the hours worked, and 41 through 44 this same person's pay rate. Each of these groupings of characters has a meaning of its own. Such character groupings are called **fields**. A field is simply a group of characters having a logical meaning.

The individual who simulated a computer in Chapter 3's analogy needed *all* the data on a single card in order to compute one person's pay. *The collection of data fields needed to support one cycle of a program is called a* **record**. When using punched cards, one card typically contains one record; this is why punched card equipment is sometimes called **unit record** equipment. A program normally reads one record of data, processes this record, and produces a record of output; the program then moves on to the next record, repeating the cycle.

In any firm that uses the computer to produce its payroll, there will almost certainly be a large number of employees, each of whom has a time card. Each time card is one record, providing the data needed to compute that individual's pay. The collection of all the time cards is called the time-card file. *A* **file** *is a collection of all the records of a given type.* A program processes a file by reading the records in that file one at a time until the entire file has been processed.

We should note at this point that many computer applications call for the input and output of multiple files in a single program; we'll discuss such applications in later chapters.

PRINTERS

Typewriters

The simplest computer output device is basically an electric typewriter. A mechanical typewriter (Fig. 4.10a) works through a series of levers. When a key is depressed, a lever causes a type hammer to move forward and smash into a ribbon and the paper, leaving behind the impression of a character. On an electric typewriter (Fig. 4.10b), the connecting levers are replaced by an electrical switch; as the key is depressed, the switch is closed, causing a type hammer to smash into a ribbon and the paper. Since the typewriter is just a machine, it doesn't care where the electrical impulse comes from; thus, by sending the proper electrical signals to the typewriter, a computer can close the proper switches and cause a message to be printed. This is essentially how the computer prepares printed output.

An electric typewriter, modified, of course, for use with a computer, can also be used as an input device; each typed character can be converted to an electrical pattern and sent to the computer.

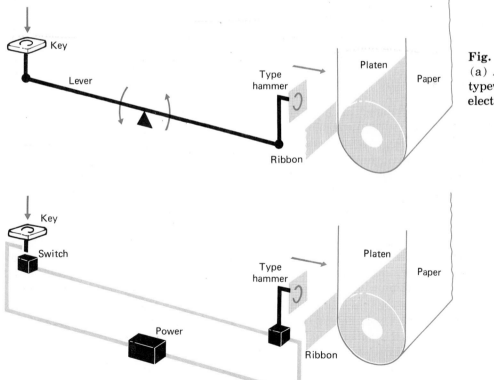

Fig. 4.10
(a) A mechanical typewriter. (b) An electric typewriter.

There are several different types of **printers** in common use. **Impact printers** which use a type hammer, ribbon, and paper, are probably the most common; they are relatively inexpensive and are capable of printing at speeds in the neighborhood of 20 to 30 characters per second.

Matrix printers are beginning to grow in popularity. On a matrix printer, the letters and numbers on the type slugs are replaced by a matrix of wires; by controlling which wires are allowed to strike the ribbon and the paper, a dot pattern forming the desired letter or number is left behind. (It's quite similar to the electronic scoreboard, on which a pattern of lights in a square matrix can be made to display the score or a message.)

Non-impact printers are also available. As the name implies, a non-impact printer forms letters without actually striking the paper. Many approaches to non-impact printing are commercially available; most rely on specially treated paper. One technique called radiation printing selectively burns the paper, leaving characters (or diagrams) behind. Another approach utilizes a jet of ink which "spits" a pattern of dots to form characters. Heat-sensitive paper is used in a number of thermal techniques, where the equivalent of type is heated as the paper passes by, leaving behind an impression of a character. Non-impact printing is (or can be) a bit faster than impact printing, and it's certainly far less noisy. The disadvantages of non-impact printing are two: the specially treated paper is expensive, and it's next to impossible to make more than one copy at a time.

Line Printers

Computer reports can be extremely lengthy. To insist that such reports be printed at 20 or 30 characters per second is unreasonable—assume a 132-character line, 50-lines per page, and a 200-page report, and compute the print time at 25 characters per second. At that rate, it would take over 14 hours to produce! To support the printing of large reports, **line printers** (Fig. 4.11) are used. A typewriter prints one character at a time; a line printer prints one line at a time.

It's not quite correct to say that a line printer prints a full line at a time. One common approach to line printing (probably the easiest to visualize) consists of a rotating cylinder holding on its surface a complete set of the numbers, letters, and symbols (the character set) available to this printer (Fig. 4.12); there is one set of characters for each possible print position. In front of the cylinder is a set of type hammers—again, one for each print position. The cylinder is constantly rotating and as the desired character moves over the paper, the hammer is fired and the character is printed. It's possible that one, a dozen, or even one hundred characters might actually be printed at the same time. The real speed advantage of a line printer, however, results from the fact that it is not necessary to move a type element or

Fig. 4.11
A line printer.

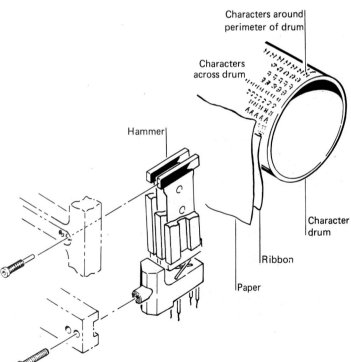

Fig. 4.12
A print mechanism for a line
printer. (Illustration courtesy
of Dataproducts Corporation,
Woodland Hills, California.)

a carriage in order to space the characters. Other common approaches put the character set on a series of moving rods or on a moving chain; the result is the same, with the character being printed as it moves into the proper position. Try to picture a typewriter with one type-ball for each and every print position, and you'll have a good mental image of how a line printer works.

Line-printer speeds range (in popular models) from a few hundred lines per minute into the 1000 to 1500 line-per-minute range. Non-impact line printers are also available, enjoying the same advantages and disadvantages as their typewriter counterparts.

CHARACTERS, FIELDS, RECORDS, AND FILES REVISITED

A printed report (Fig. 4.13) can, if properly prepared, be very easy to read. The column headers at the top of each page clearly identify the meaning of each field, and the individual fields are evenly spaced across the page to give an attractive appearance. How is this result achieved? How can the printer be made to space and to print column headers?

The answer to both questions is the same: The computer, under control of a program, tells it to. The programmer first lays out a column header and codes the instructions necessary to instruct the computer to set up this header in memory. Once the header is set up, it is sent to the printer. A similar method is used for spacing: The programmer determines the proper number of blanks, instructs the computer to set up a line of output containing these blanks, and the resulting line is sent to the printer.

Let's put it another way. The printer prints individual *characters* without regard for their logical relationship; the grouping of characters into fields is a logical function which is performed within the computer (and, of course, within the mind of the person reading the report). The same principle holds true on a card reader which simply sends one independent character at a time into the computer; the task of grouping these characters into fields is a logical function belonging to the computer itself.

OTHER UNIT RECORD MEDIA

The computer is not limited to card reader input and printer output; other media, many designed to handle a particular type of application, exist. One of the better known alternatives is **MICR**, which stands for Magnetic Ink Character Recognition. The oddly shaped black numbers on the bottom of every bank check are printed in a special machine-readable magnetic ink.

INVENTORY MASTER LIST

PART NUMBER	DESCRIPTION	STOCK ON HAND	REORDER POINT	REORDER QUANTITY	REORDER PENDING
0001	EMERY PAPER, SHEET	1530	78	1500	
0002	COMPACTOR	278	10	300	
0007	BALL POINT PEN	1888	51	2000	
0013	ADDING MACHINE RIBBON	78	21	100	
0017	FLAG POLE	85	43	100	
0020	PAINT BRUSH	563	28	550	
0025	V-BELT	1643	85	2000	
0032	BEVERAGE COOLER	697	20	700	
0037	3/4 ELBOW	258	95	325	
0040	COPIER	772	39	825	
0043	ACETATE SOLVENT - PINT	271	22	300	
0052	ALCOHOL, QUART BOTTLE	492	32	500	
0058	THUMB TACKS - BOX	616	87	615	
0063	EXPOSURE METER	292	61	340	
0071	METAL FOIL - ROLL	414	36	500	
0074	RANGE HOOD	195	34	250	
0080	AWNING	338	20	400	
0085	GARDEN TRACTOR	151	33	175	
0091	SEARCHLIGHT	840	79	800	
0095	AIR FILTER	836	45	1000	
0099	TRIPOD	595	55	600	
0107	HEAT LAMP	619	32	700	
0108	BOOK REST	949	70	1000	
0109	AIR BRUSH	42	65	200	X
0115	HOT WATER HEATER	78	11	100	
0124	DOCK COVER	922	133	850	
0127	VINAL - YARDS	554	93	900	
0128	SEWER TAPPER	919	70	1000	
0136	NYLON SILK SCREEN	84	25	250	
0143	HINGE	233	110	200	
0148	ADHESIVE TAPE, ROLL	1157	704	700	
0153	CHICKEN WIRE - FEET	616	98	600	
0159	PRESSURE COOKER	830	79	800	
0166	BARBED WIRE, FEE	774	96	2000	

Fig. 4.13
An example of a printed report.

INVENTORY MASTER LIST

PART NUMBER	DESCRIPTION	STOCK ON HAND	REORDER POINT	REORDER QUANTITY	REORDER PENDING
0170	OPTICAL FILTER	647	45	1400	
0172	RIVETS – POUNDS	825	29	1000	
0178	AIR COMPRESSOR	22	85	500	X
0184	HEATING PAD	60	83	1300	X
0189	KITCHEN EXHAUST FAN	169	62	400	
0194	TWO-WAY RADIO	277	20	350	
0202	ACETYLENE TOURCH	2	10	75	X
0207	BOOKSTAND	1911	71	2000	
0208	AIR GUAGE – HOSE TYPE	1359	77	2000	
0212	FM RADIO	410	61	500	
0230	AM RADIO	34	45	750	X
0231	FAN COIL ENCLOSURE	478	53	500	
0234	FLOWER POT	1379	403	1000	
0239	ALUMINUM PIPE, FEET	1884	297	1600	
0243	AEROSOL CONTAINER	1732	376	2000	
0247	ELECTRIC SAW	840	310	600	
0248	TABLE PAD	207	120	400	
0252	DYNAMITE	832	53	1000	
0255	BASEBALL	889	71	1000	
0262	OIL FILTER	648	99	750	
0264	HOE	177	98	250	
0271	ACOUSTICAL TILE, BOX	1499	94	1500	
0276	UNIT HEATER	934	75	1000	
0280	SHOVEL	933	79	1000	
0283	GOGGLES	100	81	325	
0287	ROPE – FEET	651	35	700	
0294	ICE MAKER	201	66	250	
0295	AIR DRYER	736	37	700	
0304	CAMERA CASE	325	59	300	
0309	PAINT ROLLER	706	72	700	
0311	AUTOMOBILE CLOCK	232	92	400	
0318	RAKE	24	19	250	
0323	BARREL – WOODEN	96	67	100	
0324	POLISHING CLOTH	903	60	1000	
0329	METAL BOX	31	7	240	
0333	FIRE HOSE – FEET	269	56	300	
0337	ALARM	616	397	1250	
0344	PROJECTION SCREEN	614	194	500	

The first of these three fields identifies the bank; the second field (Fig. 4.14) identifies the individual account number; and the third field, added after the check has been cashed, shows the amount of the check. Once these three fields have been read, the bank has all the information it needs to update an individual's checking account. A MICR reader, similar in appearance to a card reader, converts the magnetic intensity of a MICR character into an electrical pulse (or pulses), thus reading it.

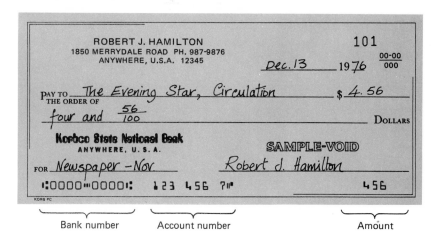

Fig. 4.14
MICR fields on a chart.

Another common technique for entering data into a computer is called Optical Character Recognition, or **OCR.** Under OCR, typed and even carefully handwritten characters are read directly by a machine. One method of reading OCR characters breaks a possible print position into a matrix of dots and measures the reflectance of each dot—white paper reflects considerably more light than a black mark on that white paper does. The pattern of high and low reflectance defines the character.

A simplified version of OCR is known as **mark sense.** Most students have been exposed to mark sense—those test sheets on which you are expected to blacken the space between the two parallel lines corresponding to the correct answer provide a perfect example. Like OCR, mark sense relies on the reflectivity of light from white or lightly colored paper; unlike OCR, the meaning of a mark sense character is derived from the position of a mark rather than from the shape of a character.

Perhaps the major competition for the punched card today is provided by a number of **key-to-tape** and **key-to-disk** systems (Fig. 4.15). Essentially, these devices work much like a keypunch, with an operator entering one character at a time via a keyboard. The data, rather than going directly onto a card, is displayed on a small cathode-ray tube (like a television set). Once an entire record has been entered, the operator visually checks the data for ac-

Fig. 4.15
Operators preparing computer input data on a
key-to-tape system.

curacy before depressing a button which causes the data to be recorded (so far, it's pretty much like a buffered keypunch). Rather than punching a card, however, the key-to-tape or key-to-disk devices record the data on magnetic tape or magnetic disk. The use of tape and/or disk allows data to be read into the computer at rates much higher than are possible with punched cards.

Another common input and (occasionally) output medium is **punched paper tape** (Fig. 4.16). In a manner analogous to punched cards, characters can be represented on paper tape as a pattern of punched holes. The most popular format divides the tape into eight channels that run parallel with the tape. Each character consists of a pattern of holes and no holes cutting across the tape.

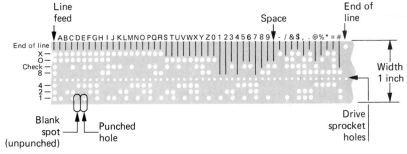

Fig. 4.16
An 8-channel
punched
paper tape.

On a punched card, a record is either 80 or 96 columns or characters long. The limiting factor is the length of the card. On a printer, the size of a record is limited to the length of a print line. What is the limit of a paper tape record? How long is the tape? Although it's usually classified with card readers and printers (because of its speed), paper tape is *not* a unit record medium. A paper tape record can be almost any length.

TERMINALS

In our discussion of typewriters earlier in this chapter, we mentioned the possibility of using such devices to input data to a computer. When a typewriter device is used in this way, it is called a **terminal** (Fig. 4.17). Often, terminals are used for both input and output.

In Chapter 2, we discussed the speed of computers, using such terms as microsecond and nanosecond to describe computer capabilities. Compare your own typing speed to a machine capable of adding over one million numbers in one second. Unless you are very unusual, the comparison favors the computer.

It is unrealistic to expect an expensive computer to wait while we type our one or two characters per second. Instead, as we type, our characters are

Fig. 4.17
A terminal.

Photo courtesy of Teletype Corporation.

stored in a **buffer,** which is part of the terminal (Fig. 4.18). As we complete the line, our final act is to hit the RETURN key, moving the carriage back to the left margin. At this signal, the complete line (or record) of data can be transferred into the computer at something closer to computer speeds.

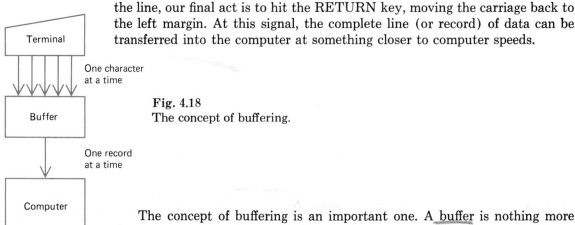

One character
at a time

One record
at a time

Fig. 4.18
The concept of buffering.

The concept of buffering is an important one. A buffer is nothing more than temporary memory or storage. Its function is to allow the speed of input or output devices to more closely match the speed of the computer. Although the need is not as obvious, buffering takes place on card readers and printers, too; a rate of 600 cards per minute may seem very fast, but, to a computer, it's really quite slow. Rather than force the computer to wait for the card reader to read each column one at a time, the contents of the individual columns are placed in a buffer, with the actual transfer of data taking place after the complete record has been read. On a line printer, a complete record is moved from the computer to a buffer, and the individual characters are fed to the printer one at a time. If you think about it, it's possible to print position 100 before printing position 10 on a line printer; without buffering, would this be possible?

Typewriters are not the only variety of terminal in common use. **Cathode-ray-tube** terminals, essentially television sets with a keyboard and the ability to display characters (Fig. 4.19), are becoming increasingly popular. Often called *CRT*s or *tubes*, these terminals allow for the rapid display of a limited amount of information.

One growing application of CRTs is in data entry; essentially, a CRT terminal can be used to replace a keypunch. When keypunching, the keypunch operator transfers data from a **source document,** such as a time sheet or an engineering drawing, to a punched card; eventually, the card is read into a computer. Using a CRT, the terminal operator can enter the data through the keyboard and *directly* into the computer. To simplify the task of the terminal operator, a pattern identifying the data that must be entered can be displayed on the screen; note, in Fig. 4.19, the words NAME, STREET, CITY, STATE, and ZIP. Using this approach, all the operator need do is fill in the blanks.

The use of a CRT rather than a keypunch for preparing computer input data tends to produce more accurate data. Why? Basically, for two reasons.

Fig. 4.19
A cathode-ray-tube (CRT)
terminal.

Photo courtesy of Control Data Corporation.

First, since a CRT terminal is normally attached to a computer, the computer can be used to check on the accuracy of the data, making such comments as "There is no such customer number," or "Four hours is a bit low for a typical work week; are you sure the decimal point is in the right place?" Little things such as misplaced decimal points and inverted digits (1324 rather than 1234) are very common human errors; the computer is very good at catching such errors.

The second reason for the improved accuracy of CRT-based data entry has to do with the ability to capture data closer to its source. For example, imagine that you are a salesperson and that you have just written an order. The chances are that your order will go directly to an order-entry clerk or a secretary who types the order and checks it for accuracy. Next, the typed order is sent to keypunch, where it is copied to a punched card and, eventually, submitted to the computer. What exactly is done in the keypunch operation? The data is copied from one document to another. Period! It's just copied. And copying is a source of error. (Try typing the material on this page, and then have someone count your errors.)

Why not allow the order-entry clerk or secretary who typed the order in the first place to enter the data directly into the computer? Using a CRT terminal, this person could produce computer input data with roughly the same effort needed to type the document in the first place. Thus the keypunch step could be completely bypassed, eliminating both a cost and a significant source of error. In some firms, the salesperson is responsible for entering order information via a CRT, thus eliminating the need for an order-entry specialist.

Besides eliminating copy errors, placing data entry responsibility close to the source of the data has another important impact on data accuracy. What would happen, for example, if a timekeeper dropped a decimal point and submitted a total of 400 (rather than 40.0) hours worked for an individual employee during a given week? The keypunch operator would probably punch 400, but a professional timekeeper entering the data through a CRT would immediately recognize the absurdity of a 400-hour work week and correct the data on the spot. The individual whose actions produce the data should know what the data should be, an advantage that a professional keypunch operator would almost certainly not enjoy.

In addition to being accurate, CRT data entry tends to be a bit faster than keypunching, simply because the data is entered directly into the computer and does not have to go through another device (a card reader) before becoming available to the computer. Combining the quicker data accessibility with improved accuracy makes CRT data entry quite attractive; more and more organizations are using this approach.

Management is also beginning to make heavy use of CRT terminals. Information is essential to good management, and the computer is a virtual treasure trove of information. In many modern offices, the manager has at his or her disposal an on-line CRT connected directly to the computer. By asking simple questions such as "What's the current stock on hand for part number 228654?" the manager can selectively query the computer's data base. This approach is rapidly developing into a very important management tool; it's the key to a management information system, a topic we'll be discussing in more detail later.

We've considered some of the advantages of CRTs, but there are also disadvantages. Several years ago, the argument was that CRT terminals were more expensive than typewriter terminals. This is no longer true; advances in electronics have brought the cost of a CRT terminal into a very competitive range.

Another common argument holds that whenever CRT terminals are used, special equipment and special programs must be available to support them. (We'll consider this equipment and software in more detail in a later chapter.) But these special support modules must be present for any terminal, not just a CRT.

Actually, the biggest argument against the use of CRTs is the fact that they produce only an image on a screen rather than a hard copy on paper. The user of a CRT is glued to the terminal, while the user of a typewriter terminal can tear off information and carry it to "where the action is." A "hard copy" terminal leaves a complete audit trace of all the day's activities;

it is very difficult to accurately trace what has happened on a CRT. What's better, a CRT or a hard copy terminal? It depends on the application.

Buffering is essential on a CRT terminal. The image on a cathode-ray tube screen is not permanent and must be constantly refreshed by retransmitting the image. One alternative would be to have the computer simply retransmit the data several times a second, but a computer has better things to do with its time. A more reasonable approach is to send the data to a buffer, allowing electronic circuits within the terminal to refresh the image from the buffer as required.

Special-purpose Terminals

Other terminals are designed to perform special functions. Consider, for example, **data entry terminals** such as the one shown in Fig. 4.20. These terminals typically consist of a card reader, a badge reader, and a simple keyboard. A worker might, upon entering a manufacturing plant in the morning, insert his or her badge into the terminal, thus reporting the time of arrival to the computer. Upon completing a unit of work, this same individual might insert this badge (for personal identification) and a card identifying the

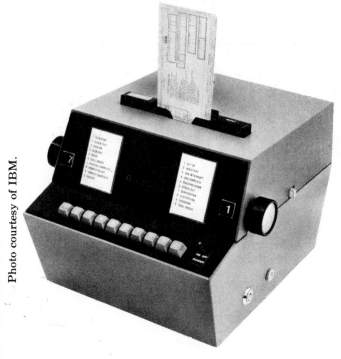

Fig. 4.20
A simple data-entry terminal.

Photo courtesy of IBM.

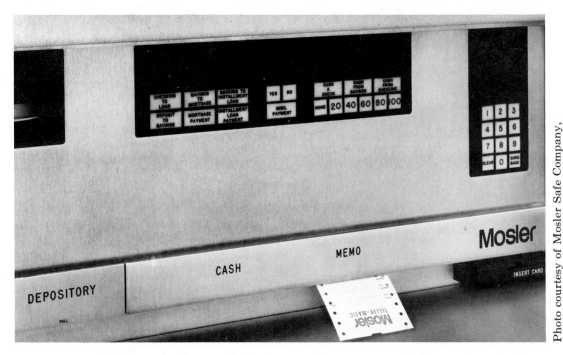

Photo courtesy of Mosler Safe Company, an American Standard Company.

Fig. 4.21
An automatic teller.

work just completed into the machine, using the keyboard to report such variable data as quantity. This approach, often called **source data automation**, eliminates the need for keypunching the data at a later time.

The idea of capturing data at the source is also quite prevalent in retailing, with cash registers either being directly connected to a computer or producing machine-readable register tapes. Even more common are the little terminals that allow a salesclerk to enter an account number and the amount of a purchase into a credit verification system. You've probably seen these at the local department store.

In some supermarkets, a scanning device, a special type of terminal, can read the bar codes printed on most packages, allowing the store's computer to locate the current price and update the store's inventory. Even banks, with various automatic-teller devices (Fig. 4.21), are using special-function terminals.

CONTROL UNITS

Throughout this chapter, we've been discussing the need for buffering. In many cases, the physical buffer is not located in the input or output device itself, but resides in an intermediate device called a **control unit** (Fig. 4.22).

Fig. 4.22
The relative position
of a control unit.

The control unit sits between the **I/O** (for input/output) **device** and the computer acting, with its buffering capability, as an intermediary.

Control units perform another, less obvious function as well. Consider the many different I/O devices we've discussed in this chapter. The 80-column card uses a code derived from the twelve possible punch positions in each column. The 96-column card uses a six-hole code. Paper tape uses a code based on eight different hole positions. A printer expects an electrical impulse which can be converted to a switch position, so that the proper hammer can be fired. A MICR device reads magnetic intensity. An OCR or mark sense device reads the degree of reflected light. Imagine the complexity of a computer capable of dealing with all of these different forms of electronic codes!

In order to save expense and to simplify the design of the computer, the task of converting all these codes is housed in a control unit. The control unit for the card reader (Fig. 4.23) accepts punched card code and converts it to a standard computer code (for the computer being used). The printer's control unit (Fig. 4.23) accepts this standard computer code and converts it electronically into the pulses that fire the proper print hammers. Similarly, with each input or output device, the intermediate control unit always works with the standard computer code on the computer's side and whatever code is called for on the device side. Thus, no matter what the electronic characteristics of the device might be, the computer always "sees" the same code (we'll introduce some common codes in the next chapter). This control unit function is called **standard interface.**

Fig. 4.23
The standard interface function.

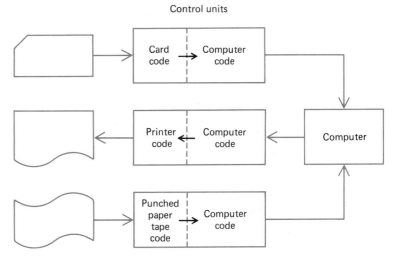

SUMMARY

In this chapter, we've introduced a number of basic input and output devices including card readers, printers, card punches, MICR, OCR, mark sense, and terminals. Key concepts included the use of codes to stand for characters, buffering, and the standard interface function of control units.

EXERCISES

1. Keypunch your name and address into a data processing card.
2. What is a field?
3. What is a record?
4. What is a file?
5. Explain buffering.
6. What are the functions of a control unit? What does standard interface mean?
7. Explain how a line printer differs from a character printer.
8. What advantages do key-to-disk and key-to-tape systems enjoy over standard punched cards?
9. Data on cards and other unit record media is stored as a series of independent, coded characters. Why is this desirable?
10. Explain how a card reader works.
11. A major topic in this chapter is the use of CRT terminals for data entry. What are the advantages of this approach over keypunching?

KEY WORDS

buffer	character	keypunch	OCR	source document
buffered keypunch	control unit	key-to-disk	paper tape	standard interface
card column	data entry	key-to-tape	port-o-punch	terminal
card punch	data entry terminal	line printer	printer	unit record
card reader		mark sense	punched card	verification
card row	field	matrix printer	record	verifier
cathode-ray tube terminal	file	MICR	source data automation	
	impact printer	nonimpact printer		

Memory or Storage

OVERVIEW

In this chapter, we will be discussing main memory devices, the computer component that was simulated by numbered chalkboards in Chapter 3. We begin with a brief introduction to binary numbers, the key to understanding how memory works. Once this basic foundation has been laid, various codes and data formats will be introduced. Memory addressing will also be covered.

COMPUTER MEMORY

In Chapter 3, we used an analogy of numbered chalkboards to illustrate how data is stored within a computer. In this chapter, we will analyze a number of real memory devices. The word *memory* is a somewhat unfortunate choice in that it implies a human capability; *storage* is a better word, but memory is so commonly used that it has become accepted.

How does computer memory work? How does it differ from human memory? Let's continue using the analogy of the chalkboard. Information—instructions for a test, the time and location of a meeting, answers to a homework assignment—can be written on a chalkboard. So long as this information remains on the board, it can be read or copied by anyone who enters the room; the chalkboard allows for perfect recall of the original information. Board space is, however, limited; eventually, the portion of the board containing the information will be erased and reused. Once this happens, the data is lost forever. It can, of course, be rewritten, but the original piece of data is gone.

Computer memory is analogous to an electronic chalkboard. Once information enters a computer's memory, it stays there exactly as entered; the computer has the ability to recall totally this data. Computer memory is, however, limited in size. Eventually, all memory is filled, and a portion must be erased and reused; when this happens, the computer is left with absolutely no recall of the information initially recorded in this location. The computer has both perfect recall and perfect "forgetfulness."

Obviously, there's no little person with a piece of chalk running around inside a real computer. How can a memory device be implemented electronically?

A computer is an electronic device. People are not, at least not in the common sense. We easily manipulate ten different digits, twenty-six different letters (both upper case and lower case), and any number of punctuation marks and other symbols. Such diversity is not convenient for an electronic device. Thus, before learning exactly how a computer stores information, it's necessary to spend a little time studying what the computer actually stores—its equivalent of our numbers, letters, and special symbols. Thus we begin a brief introduction to the **binary number system.**

THE BINARY NUMBER SYSTEM

Modern digital computers are disgned to work with *binary* data; thus a basic appreciation of the binary number system is essential if you are to gain a real understanding of how a computer works. It is *not* essential that you become extremely proficient in handling binary numbers. You do *not* have to begin thinking in binary, and personal difficulties in converting from decimal to binary and back again will *not* doom you to certain failure in any computer-related course. Even the professional programmer finds proficiency in handling pure binary numbers to be, at best, of marginal importance. Should you decide to major in a computer-related field, you will eventually encounter a real need for working with binary data. At this point, however, what is really important is that you realize that it's not only possible to store and manipulate binary data, but that this approach makes a great deal of sense on a computer. The purpose of this section is to give you an appreciation for the value of using binary and to create in your mind a willingness to accept the use of binary data on a computer as being reasonable, quite possible, and very sensible.

Since the decimal numbering system is more familiar to most of us, let's start our discussion of binary numbers by taking a close look at a few decimal numbers. Consider the two numbers 3 and 30. Both contain a common digit, a three, but we all know that we are looking at two different numbers. What's the difference between the three in the number 3 and the three in the number 30? The answer is its position: The first three is in the units position, and the second three is in the tens position. Closer analysis reveals that the number thirty (30) is really another way of saying "three tens and no ones."

To put it another way, *any* decimal number consists of a series of digits— 0, 1, 2, 3, 4, 5, 6, 7, 8, 9—written in precise, relative positions. The number twenty-three is written as 23, while a different combination of the same two digits, 32, represents a completely different number.

Take a look at the number 3580; what is really represented by this combination of digits is

```
3580
   │││└──── units ─────────→   0 times      1 =      0
   ││└───── tens ──────────→  +8 times     10 =     80
   │└────── hundreds ──────→  +5 times    100 =    500
   └─────── thousands ─────→  +3 times   1000 =   3000
                                                 ──────
                                                   3580
```

In other words, to find the value of *any* number, multiply each digit by its positional (or place) value, and add these products. This is known as the **digit-times-place-value rule.**

Take a closer look at the sequence of place values. In the example shown above, we started with 1, then went to 10, then 100, then 1000. What would you expect the next higher place value to be? It would, of course, be 10,000. Just add one more zero. What does this really mean? We started with 1. To move up to the tens position, we multiplied this starting value by 10 (our **base** —this is a base-ten numbering system). The hundreds position, stated another way, is 10×10. The thousands position is $10 \times 10 \times 10$. Next comes the ten-thousands position: $10 \times 10 \times 10 \times 10$. Do you perceive a pattern? Each time we move up one position, we multiply by one more ten.

Eventually, we reach a point where it becomes a bit tedious to write down all those tens. You probably know that 10×10 can be written as 10^2 and that $10 \times 10 \times 10$ can be written as 10^3; the exponent or "power" of ten indicates the number of times that the number is to be multiplied by itself. This saves writing a lot of zeros when a number becomes very large. Numbers expressed in this way are written in **scientific notation.**

100,000	10,000	1000	100	10	1
	$10 \times 10 \times 10 \times 10$	$10 \times 10 \times 10$	10×10	10	1
10^5	10^4	10^3	10^2	10^1	10^0

Fig. 5.1
Decimal place values.

In Fig. 5.1, we have written a series of place or positional values along a horizontal line, showing these same values, in scientific notation, below the line. Starting at the right, we find that the number 1 can be written as 10^0; in fact, by mathematical definition, *any* number (except zero) raised to the zero power is equal to 1. Given this starting point, the place values for the decimal numbering system can be written as 10, the base, raised to a series of sequential integer powers—0, 1, 2, 3, 4, 5, 6, 7, ...

Let's summarize a few of the key ideas brought out in our discussion of decimal numbers. First is the idea of place or positional value represented by the base ten (10) raised to a series of sequential integer powers. The use of the digit zero (0) to represent "no value" in a given position is the second key concept. Third, a total of ten digits—0, 1, 2, 3, 4, 5, 6, 7, 8, 9—are needed to write decimal numbers. Finally, only values less than the base (in this case, ten) can be written in a single position; numbers exceeding ten must be written in at least two positions.

There is nothing to restrict the application of these rules to a base-ten numbering system. If the positional values are represented as powers of two instead of ten, we have the framework of the base-two or binary numbering system (Fig. 5.2). As in the decimal numbering system, the digit zero (0) is needed to represent "no value" in a given position. In addition to zero, the binary numbering system needs only one other digit, a one (1), in order to form numbers. Why only these two digits? Only values less than the base can be represented in a single position. Since the base of the binary system is two (2), only numbers less than two can be so represented—0 and 1.

32	16	8	4	2	1
$2 \times 2 \times 2 \times 2 \times 2$	$2 \times 2 \times 2 \times 2$	$2 \times 2 \times 2$	2×2	2	1
2^5	2^4	2^3	2^2	2^1	2^0

Fig. 5.2
Binary place values.

Once again, as in the decimal numbering system, the digit-times-place-value rule still works; it's just that the place values are different, representing powers of *two* rather than powers of ten. Consider, for example, the binary number 1101. Using the digit-times-place-value rule and remembering that we have a binary number, we can perform the following analysis:

$$
\begin{array}{l}
1101 \\
\quad 2^0 \text{ or units} \longrightarrow 1 \text{ times } 1 = 1 \\
\quad 2^1 \text{ or twos} \longrightarrow +0 \text{ times } 2 = 0 \\
\quad 2^2 \text{ or fours} \longrightarrow +1 \text{ times } 4 = 4 \\
\quad 2^3 \text{ or eights} \longrightarrow +1 \text{ times } 8 = 8 \\
\hline
\qquad\qquad\qquad\qquad\qquad\qquad\quad 13
\end{array}
$$

giving us the decimal equivalent of the binary number 1101.

Any whole number can be written in binary. How do we tell the difference between a binary 11 (which is equal to three in decimal) and a decimal eleven? Normally, the binary number is enclosed within a set of parentheses, and a subscript is used to indicate the base—for example, $(1101)_2$. This is merely a convenient way of differentiating between numbers with different bases.

We use the base-ten system because we are used to it; since our childhood, the numbers 1, 2, 3, 4, 5, 6, 7, 8, 9, and 10 have been drilled into us. There is, however, nothing inherently "better" about base-ten numbers; in fact, if humans were to have six fingers on each hand, we might well be using a base-twelve number system in our everyday activities. Since we all know base-ten, base-ten is convenient for us. That's why we use it.

For a computer, an electronic device, binary numbers are much more convenient to use than are base-ten numbers. Since data representation requires only the two digits, 0 and 1, the computer, using binary numbers, can work with the simple on/off logic of electrical circuits. Binary is truly an electronic numbering system.

Other number systems, notably **octal** or base-8 (Fig. 5.3) and **hexadecimal** or base-16 (Fig. 5.4), are also used with computers The octal system uses powers of eight to represent positional values, using the digits 0, 1, 2, 3,

32,768	4096	512	64	8	1
$8 \times 8 \times 8 \times 8 \times 8$	$8 \times 8 \times 8 \times 8$	$8 \times 8 \times 8$	8×8	8	1
8^5	8^4	8^3	8^2	8^1	8^0

Fig. 5.3
Octal or base-8 place values.

65,536	4096	256	16	1
$16 \times 16 \times 16 \times 16$	$16 \times 16 \times 16$	16×16	16	1
16^4	16^3	16^2	16^1	16^0

Fig. 5.4
Hexadecimal or base-16 place values.

4, 5, 6, and 7 within this framework. The hexadecimal system uses powers of sixteen and the digits 0, 1, 2, 3, 4, 5, 6, 7, 8, 9, A, B, C, D, E, and F. Note that, in a base-16 number system, the individual digits range from 0 through 15.

Let's clear up a possible point of confusion right now. There are *no* computers that actually work in octal or in hexadecimal; they all work in binary. The value of the base-8 and base-16 number systems lies in the ease of conversion to or from binary, a circumstance which allows numbers written in these systems to be used as a shorthand for displaying the actual binary contents of a computer's memory. Each octal digit is equivalent to *exactly* three binary digits (Fig. 5.5); each hexadecimal digit is equivalent to *exactly* four binary digits (Fig. 5.6).

When a program goes wrong, the programmer often finds it necessary to look at a "dump" of the contents of the computer's memory in order to figure out what happened. If the data were in pure binary form, this dump would consist of page after page of an almost blinding pattern of 0's and 1's (see Fig. 5.7—try staring at the binary data in this figure for a while, and then stare at a white wall). If, however, the octal number system is used to represent this data in a shorthand form, three binary digits can be reduced to a single octal digit; should the programmer actually need the individual bits, conversion is very straightforward. Using the hexadecimal system, four binary digits can be represented by each "hex" digit with no loss of data.

With the everincreasing cost of paper, saving the programmer's eyesight is not the only benefit to be gained from using the octal and hexadecimal systems to represent binary data in a shorthand form. A twelve-page binary

Octal	Binary	Octal	Binary
0	000	4	100
1	001	5	101
2	010	6	110
3	011	7	111

Fig. 5.5
Octal-to-binary conversion table.

Hexadecimal	Binary	Hexadecimal	Binary
0	0000	8	1000
1	0001	9	1001
2	0010	A	1010
3	0011	B	1011
4	0100	C	1100
5	0101	D	1101
6	0110	E	1110
7	0111	F	1111

Fig. 5.6
Hexadecimal-to-binary conversion table.

dump would need only four pages if converted to octal and only three pages if converted to hexadecimal. (See Fig. 5.7.)

The shorthand—whether octal or hexadecimal—used on a particular machine depends on the internal circuitry of the computer. Some computers group data into six-bit chunks, meaning that octal will almost certainly be used. Others group data into eight-bit chunks, hence the use of hexadecimal. But these two number systems have nothing to do with how the computer actually works; they are just used for convenience.

Throughout the remainder of this text, we'll be talking about the manipulation of binary data by the computer. When we refer to binary data, we are simply talking about a string of 0's and 1's. Occasionally, we'll concentrate our attention on one or two of these binary digits, using the term **bit**, which is an acronym for *binary dig*it. The bit is the basic building block of the computer.

Fig. 5.7
Octal and hexadecimal as binary shorthand. Note how much more readable and compact octal and hexadecimal representations are.

```
                    Binary
110010101011  000101001000  101100001111
011001100001  100000100011  011101010100
000100000010  011111110000  000010000101
100100100100  100001011111  100000011001

        Octal                  Hexadecimal

6253 0510 5417            CAB 148 B0F
3141 4043 3524            661 823 754
0402 3760 0205            102 7F0 085
4444 4137 4031            924 85F 819
```

CODES

We have seen that numbers can be represented in binary form. Patterns of 0's and 1's can, however, be used to represent more than numerical data. In Morse code, for example, letters are represented by a pattern of dots and dashes; for instance, (. . . − − − . . .) is the international distress signal SOS. If we were to substitute a 1 for each dot and a 0 for each dash, we would have a binary code capable of communicating letters as well as digits. Braille is another example of a code which, at its core, is binary; there either *is* or *is not* a raised dot.

A game that you probably played as a child involves the coding of secret messages. A very common code in such games simply converts each letter to a number, with 1 meaning A, 2 meaning B, and so on. Using such a code,

8–5–12–16

can be interpreted to mean "H–E–L–P." Why are the dashes used? Is 851216 really "HELP," or is it "HEABAF"? The dashes are used to separate letters and allow the reader to make sense of the code.

Suppose we were to take a different approach and decide that each and every letter will be represented by exactly two digits—A is 01, B is 02, J is 10, K is 11, and so on. Now our message can be written as

08051216

without any dashes. Since each and every letter is represented by exactly two digits, all we need do is break the message into two-digit groups. We have a **fixed-length code.**

Suppose we were to do the same thing with the binary number system. Starting with only the numbers 0 through 9, we might write the binary equivalent of each digit and use the resulting four-bit number as a *code* (Fig. 5.8). Using this code, the number 12 could be *represented* as 00010010. Note that we are *not* talking about the binary number system right now; we are talking about a code. If we were to take the string of digits $(00010010)_2$ and treat it as a binary *number*, we would have

1 times 2^1,   plus 1 times 2^4,   or 18,

Decimal	Code	Decimal	Code
0	0000	5	0101
1	0001	6	0110
2	0010	7	0111
3	0011	8	1000
4	0100	9	1001

Fig. 5.8
A binary code for decimal digits.

A	11 0001	S	01 0010
B	11 0010	T	01 0011
C	11 0011	U	01 0100
D	11 0100	V	01 0101
E	11 0101	W	01 0110
F	11 0110	X	01 0111
G	11 0111	Y	01 1000
H	11 1000	Z	01 1001
I	11 1001		
		0	00 1010
J	10 0001	1	00 0001
K	10 0010	2	00 0010
L	10 0011	3	00 0011
M	10 0100	4	00 0100
N	10 0101	5	00 0101
O	10 0110	6	00 0110
P	10 0111	7	00 0111
Q	10 1000	8	00 1000
R	10 1001	9	00 1001

Fig. 5.9
The six-bit BCD code. Other unlisted codes
are used for special symbols.

which is *not* 12. Coded numbers and real numbers are not the same, simply
because the code ignores positional value.

Many computer applications require *alphabetic* as well as *numeric* data;
thus, something more than this simple numeric code is needed. One solution
to this problem is the six-bit **BCD code** (Binary Coded Decimal) shown in
Fig. 5.9. Using this code, individual characters are represented by a series of
six bits: two zone bits and four numeric bits. The letters A through I are all
assigned zone bits 11. Since A is the first letter in this group, its numeric part
is 0001; B, being the second letter in the group, has the numeric part 0010;
C is 0011, and so on. In other words, a zone-bit configuration of 11 is attached
to a numeric part which indicates the relative position of the letter within the
group. A second group of letters, J through R, is assigned zone bits 10; once
again, the numeric bits show the relative position of each letter within the
group. The letters S through Z are formed by attaching numeric bits 0010
through 1001, respectively (that's 2 through 9) to zone bits 01 (there are
only eight letters in this group, which explains the unusual start). Numbers
all have zone bits 00 followed, essentially, by the number itself expressed in
binary. The digit zero deviates somewhat to allow for the existence of a blank
character. It's actually a fairly simple code. All things considered, it makes a
great deal more sense than the code Mr. Morse developed for the telegraph.

In Chapter 4, we talked a bit about control units. Do you remember the
standard interface function? The control unit, on input, accepts whatever
code is used by the I/O device and converts it to computer code (Fig. 5.10).
On output, the control unit accepts computer code, transforming it to whatever the output device requires in the way of a code. BCD is sometimes used
as an internal computer code. The I/O devices treat each character as a sepa-

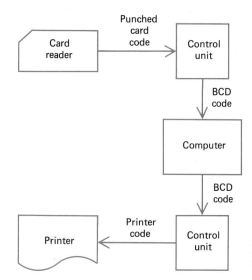

Fig. 5.10
The function of a control unit.

rate entity, passing their own codes along to a control unit where the data is converted to BCD and stored (or copied) into the computer's memory as separate and independent characters. The job of putting the individual characters together to form fields is a logical function performed by the computer under the control of a program.

One point should be restated at this time. Coded data and numeric data are not the same. The two decimal digits 12 obviously form the number twelve which, in pure binary form, is $(1100)_2$. Using the BCD code, the digit 1 is 000001, and the digit 2 is 000010; putting them together yields

$$
\begin{array}{l}
000001000010 \qquad or \\
\quad\quad\quad\ \lfloor\ \ \ \lfloor\!\!\!-\!\!\!-\ 1 \text{ times } 2^1 = \ \ 2 \\
\quad\quad\quad\ \lfloor\!\!\!-\!\!\!-\ +1 \text{ times } 2^6 = 64 \\
\quad\quad\quad\quad\quad\quad\quad\quad\quad\quad\quad\overline{66}
\end{array}
$$

which is *not* 12. A card reader passes individual digits to a computer in BCD form. If, however, the two digits in question really do mean twelve, we *must* have a mechanism for converting from *coded* form to *numeric* form. Fortunately, most computers possess special instructions to perform this conversion.

The code allows individual characters of data to be transferred between the computer and its input and output devices. The code also allows these individual characters to be stored in the computer's memory. The computer, under program control, groups these characters into logical fields and per-

| Character | EBCDIC | | ASCII-8 | |
	Binary	Hex	Binary	Hex
A	1100 0001	C1	1010 0001	A1
B	1100 0010	C2	1010 0010	A2
C	1100 0011	C3	1010 0011	A3
D	1100 0100	C4	1010 0100	A4
E	1100 0101	C5	1010 0101	A5
F	1100 0110	C6	1010 0110	A6
G	1100 0111	C7	1010 0111	A7
H	1100 1000	C8	1010 1000	A8
I	1100 1001	C9	1010 1001	A9
J	1101 0001	D1	1010 1010	AA
K	1101 0010	D2	1010 1011	AB
L	1101 0011	D3	1010 1100	AC
M	1101 0100	D4	1010 1101	AD
N	1101 0101	D5	1010 1110	AE
O	1101 0110	D6	1010 1111	AF
P	1101 0111	D7	1011 0000	B0
Q	1101 1000	D8	1011 0001	B1
R	1101 1001	D9	1011 0010	B2
S	1110 0010	E2	1011 0011	B3
T	1110 0011	E3	1011 0100	B4
U	1110 0100	E4	1011 0101	B5
V	1110 0101	E5	1011 0110	B6
W	1110 0110	E6	1011 0111	B7
X	1110 0111	E7	1011 1000	B8
Y	1110 1000	E8	1011 1001	B9
Z	1110 1001	E9	1011 1010	BA
0	1111 0000	F0	0101 0000	50
1	1111 0001	F1	0101 0001	51
2	1111 0010	F2	0101 0010	52
3	1111 0011	F3	0101 0011	53
4	1111 0100	F4	0101 0100	54
5	1111 0101	F5	0101 0101	55
6	1111 0110	F6	0101 0110	56
7	1111 0111	F7	0101 0111	57
8	1111 1000	F8	0101 1000	58
9	1111 1001	F9	0101 1001	59

Fig. 5.11
The EBCDIC and ASCII-8 codes. Once again, unlisted bit combinations are used to represent punctuation marks and other special symbols; these symbols are not shown since the pattern of the code is not as obvious. A full listing of these codes can be found in almost any reference manual.

forms any data format conversions needed to produce meaningful data. Any code will do, so long as it is known and consistently applied. Two codes enjoying great popularity on modern computers are IBM's **EBCDIC** (Extended Binary Coded Decimal Interchange Code, pronounced "ebb-see-dic") and the **ASCII-8** code of the American Standards Institute (Fig. 5.11). Both are eight-bit codes; hence, the hex shorthand. If you glance back at the punched-card codes of Chapter 4, you should recognize the hole/no-hole pattern as still another binary code.

PHYSICAL MEMORY DEVICES

As we can see from the preceding discussion, the ability to manipulate just two characters—a 0 and a 1—limited though it may seem, gives us all kinds of capabilities. We can treat a given combination of 1's and 0's as a pure binary number, giving us the ability to manipulate numbers. Alternatively, we can treat the string of bits as coded data and subdivide it into code groups, giving us the ability to handle alphabetic messages. (Incidentally, computer codes are almost universally fixed-length codes because it is easier to design electronic equipment around a fixed-length format than around a variable-length format.) Anything that can be done with numbers and letters can be done with bits.

How do we go about storing these bits? Almost any device that is capable of holding two states—a light (on/off), a wire (current flowing/no current flowing), an electronic tube (current/no current), a transistor (current/no current), a switch (open/closed)—can be used to store bits. Some devices are better than others, but all could work.

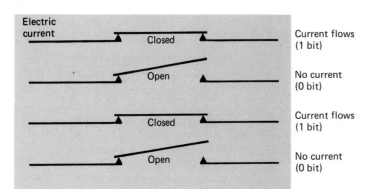

Fig. 5.12
Electromagnetic relays as storage devices.

Early computers used electromagnetic relays similar to those shown in Fig. 5.12. An open switch stored a 0-bit; a closed switch stored a 1-bit. To read the contents of memory, all the computer had to do was to pass a current across the wires. If the current flowed, the switch must have been closed, indicating a 1-bit; if no current flowed, the switch must have been open, indicating a 0-bit. However, electromagnetic relays proved to be too bulky, too slow, and too costly, and they have disappeared from the market as memory devices. The big breakthrough leading to their demise was the development of **magnetic core** memories.

Magnetic core memory takes advantage of the directional properties of a magnet and of the relationship between electricity and magnetism. It is made from tiny donut-shaped rings (cores) of magnetic material (Fig. 5.13). We've

Fig. 5.13
A close-up of magnetic core memory. Each tiny donut-shaped core is about the size
of the head of a pin.

all played with bar magnets as children, and most of us know about the north
and south poles of a magnet—magnets possess directional properties. But how
do we tell the north from the south pole on a ring magnet? Actually, what
gives a magnet its directional properties is the alignment of the electronic
forces within the material. If enough individual molecules are lined up in the
right direction, we have a magnet; that direction determines which is the
north and which is the south pole. On a ring magnet, this alignment results
in clockwise or counterclockwise magnetization (Fig. 5.14), giving us the
necessary two states. We'll arbitrarily use the clockwise state (although the
other choice would be just as good) to indicate a 1-bit and the counterclockwise state to indicate a 0-bit, and design a computer memory around this
assumption.

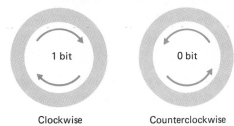

Fig. 5.14
The two states of a magnetic core.

Clockwise   Counterclockwise

Core memory is fairly fast, with "slow" core being capable of transferring close to two million characters per second, and "fast" core nearly four million characters per second. The cost of core is approximately one-half cent per bit, and until recently, that price was hard to beat. However, newer solid-state technologies have begun to produce memory devices that are cost-competitive with core, while offering substantially better performance at transfer rates of over eight million characters per second.

Most computer manufacturers are beginning to shift from core to solid-state memories on their latest computers. The primary reason for this is cost. Today, core and solid-state memories are cost-competitive, with core perhaps enjoying a slight edge. But core manufacture is a predominantly manual process, while solid-state devices are made by largely automated processes. The trend in manual labor costs is up; the cost of automated production tends to remain, at worst, constant.

Figures 5.13 and 5.15 show, respectively, core memory and a type of solid-state memory, MOSFET (for Metal Oxide Semiconductor Field Effect Transistor), which is used in the IBM 5100 portable computer, among other places. Solid-state memory is compact, highly reliable, and very fast, and its use is

Fig. 5.15
Solid-state memory chips. These MOSFET (for Metal Oxide Semiconductor Field Effect Transistor) chips each hold 24,576 bits of storage capacity; they are used in the IBM 5100 computer. Yes, that is a teaspoon of sugar.

Photo courtesy of IBM.

growing. Costs are actually dropping on these newer memory technologies. The days of core dominance are numbered.

Computer people often refer to a machine's **main memory** as core. In the past, it really was core, and the name made sense. Today, however, most new computers no longer use core, although the term continues to be used to describe the main memory. Over the years, this usage has created a new meaning for the word core: main memory. It will probably continue be used in this context, in spite of the swing to semiconductor memories.

ADDRESSING MEMORY

Individual bits might be stored on cores or on solid-state devices but, at any rate, we store bits. As we saw earlier in the chapter, bits can be grouped together to form coded characters or binary numbers. Every digital computer has the ability to group bits.

Since IBM is the largest supplier of computers in the world, the reader is more apt to have access to an IBM computer than to the product of any other manufacturer; thus, we will use the IBM System/370 series of computers as an example of how bits are grouped and **addressed**.

The basic unit of memory on an IBM System/360 or System/370 computer is a set of eight bits called a **byte** (Fig. 5.16). Two codes, EBCDIC and ASCII-8, use eight bits to identify a single character. IBM uses the EBCDIC code, storing one EBCDIC ("ebb-see-dic") character in each byte.

A very simple addressing scheme is used to allow the programmer to indicate a specific byte location in a program. The bytes are numbered sequentially. The first byte in memory is byte number 0 (Fig. 5.16), the second is number 1, the third is number 2, and so on, until all bytes in a given memory

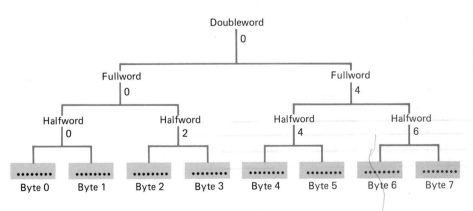

Fig. 5.16
Addressing main memory on an IBM System/370.

have been numbered (the largest possible address in an IBM System/360 or System/370 computer is 16,777,215).

Not all data in the computer is character data; at times, numeric data is needed. If the computer were limited to groupings of eight bits, the largest number that could be stored would be $(11111111)_2$ or $(FF)_{16}$, which is 255. That is not even big enough to compute take-home pay. Additional data groupings are needed. Thus, most computers have the ability to handle a **word** of data.

On an IBM machine, groups of 16 bits or two bytes are wired together to form **halfwords** (see Fig. 5.16), and groups of 32 bits or four bytes (or two halfwords) are wired together to form (as you may have guessed) **fullwords.** A halfword, assuming that the first bit is used as a sign, can hold a maximum value of $(0111111111111111)_2$, which is 32,767. A fullword of 32 bits can hold numbers in excess of two billion!

Note (Fig. 5.16) the location of halfwords and fullwords. The first two bytes combine to form the first halfword; bytes 1 and 2 do *not* form a halfword because they are not wired together to form a halfword. Similarly, bytes 0, 1, 2, and 3 form a fullword, but bytes 2, 3, 4, and 5 do not (again, because they are not wired to form a fullword). The address of each halfword is the number of the byte beginning that halfword—0, 2, 4, 6, 8, 10, and so on. Note that they are all divisible by two. The address of each full word is the number of the byte beginning that fullword—0, 4, 8, 12, 16, and so on, all of which are divisible by four.

Why is it necessary to wire certain memory locations together to form words and halfwords? One byte isn't big enough to hold a meaningful number; more space is needed. Also, the number is a single entity that must be handled as a single entity so as to maintain positional value. By wiring two bytes together to form a halfword, the designers of the IBM System/370 have given the computer the capability of manipulating 16-bit numbers. The fullword allows for the manipulation of 32 bits at a time—an even larger number. At the top of the memory hierarchy is the **doubleword,** 64 bits or two fullwords long, which allows for the manipulation of 64 bits at one time in support of certain operations.

Since character fields are of undetermined length, it makes sense to design a machine that allows these fields to be manipulated one character (byte) at a time, thus providing the flexibility needed to work with fields of unpredictable length. The programmer can instruct the computer to manipulate single bytes, groups of two bytes (halfwords), groups of four bytes (fullwords), or groups of eight bytes (doublewords), depending on the type of data being processed.

Not all manufacturers of computers use the IBM approach. On many computers, for example, the basic addressable unit of memory is the word, with words rather than bytes being consecutively numbered. Even the length of a word is subject to variation—16-bit computers and 24-bit computers are common (actually, almost any length will work). Some computers even use a variable-length word.

MEMORY CONTENTS: DATA TYPES

Coded data (EBCDIC on an IBM machine) comes into the computer from an input device and is stored in memory, with one coded character occupying one memory location or byte. (Typically, for example, an 80-character card will be copied into 80 *consecutive* memory locations.) During processing, this data may be rearranged and copied into different memory locations, but the basic rule of storing one character per byte holds. The rule is, of course, different on word-addressed machines; a 24-bit word-addressed machine might, for example, store three EBCDIC or ASCII-8 characters or four BCD characters in a single word, but the principle is the same.

Numeric data is different, requiring more than a single memory location. On an IBM machine, the first step toward conversion from coded data to numeric data is called **packing.** Consider the number 123 in EBCDIC form (hexadecimal shorthand):

F1F2F3

The zone bits are needed to allow for differentiation between letters and digits, but they cause problems in attempting to work with the *number* 123 rather than the individual *digits* 1, 2, and 3. Packing strips the zone bits away, leaving

123F

behind; F is the zone bits previously attached to the low-order digit and serves as a plus sign. Many computers can actually perform arithmetic on such *packed decimal* data.

The next step up the numeric ladder is binary data. Pure binary numbers are stored in halfwords (if small) or fullwords. Arithmetic using binary data is much more efficient than similar arithmetic performed on packed decimal data because with binary data, the computer can manipulate the entire number at one time, rather than byte by byte, which is how the computer must work with packed decimal data. Most computers contain an instruction to convert packed decimal data to binary and another instruction to reconvert binary data to packed decimal; we must eventually get our answers back into coded form if a printer is to be able to print them. These operations use the doubleword described above.

In addition to character, packed decimal, and binary data, many scientific computers are capable of handling information stored in a fourth form: **floating-point.** Scientists frequently find it necessary to work with extremely large (astronomical distances) and extremely small (subatomic) measure-

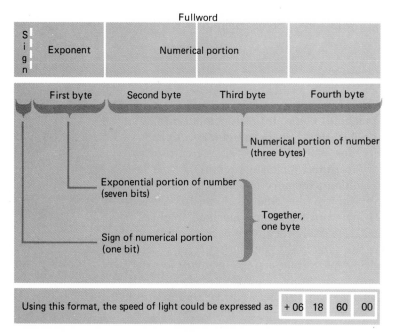

Using this format, the speed of light could be expressed as + 06 18 60 00

Fig. 5.17
Floating-point data format.

ments. Traditionally, scientific notation is used to represent such numbers; for example, the speed of light, 186,000 miles per second, is written as 0.186×10^6 in scientific notation. The whole and fractional portions hold the number; the exponent, the power of ten, locates the decimal point. A binary fullword can be made to hold a number in scientific form if it is subdivided into exponent and number portions (see Fig. 5.17).

Program instructions can also be stored in the computer's memory; they represent still another type of internal information.

DISTINGUISHING FIELD TYPES

A computer's memory can be used to store character data, packed decimal data, binary data, floating-point data, and program instructions. How can the computer possibly tell one type of data from another? It can't, at least not without the help of a programmer. The programmer is responsible for designating certain areas of memory as data areas and others as instruction areas. The programmer is also responsible for identifying the type of data stored in each memory location. The programmer must be very careful not to mix data with instructions.

Instructions are executed in the computer's central processing unit (CPU), the subject of the next chapter.

SUMMARY

In this chapter, we introduced the basic concepts of computer memory or storage devices. The chapter began with a discussion of the binary number system, the language of the computer. Key concepts included digit and positional value, the zero (0) digit, and the computer's need for only two digits—0 and 1. The octal and hexadecimal number systems were introduced as convenient shorthands for binary data.

Following the introduction to binary numbers, several binary codes were introduced, including BCD, EBCDIC, and ASCII-8. Finally, we entered a discussion of physical storage media. Until recently, core was *the* primary memory device. Lately, computer technology has been shifting to solid-state memories.

Memory is grouped and addressed within a computer. IBM groups every eight bits together to form a byte; the individual bytes are consecutively numbered from zero up to the limit of a given installation's available memory, thus providing an addressing scheme. Bytes are grouped to form halfwords, which are subsequently grouped to form fullwords; fullwords are themselves grouped into doublewords. Other manufacturers use different schemes for grouping and addressing memory; many use the word as the basic addressable unit.

Memory can be used to hold many different types of data. Character data is stored in coded form, one character per byte or several characters per word. Packed decimal data is also stored in bytes; it's an intermediate step between character data and binary data, and can be used in arithmetic on some machines. Binary data is stored in halfwords or fullwords; the computer's ability to manipulate the entire number at one time makes such data the most efficient type for arithmetic. Many computers can handle floating-point data as well. Finally, memory is used to hold instructions, a topic we'll discuss in more detail in subsequent chapters.

EXERCISES

1. Why is the binary number system so well suited to the computer?

2. What is meant by place or positional value?

3. Explain the digit-times-place-value rule.

4. Explain the difference between coded and numeric data.

5. Relate the concept of binary codes to the punched-card code presented in Chapter 4.

6. How is main memory addressed?

7. How can the computer tell the difference between coded data, numeric data, and instructions?

8. Integrated circuits and solid logic memories are beginning to replace core in many modern computers. Why?

9. Why are the octal and hexadecimal number systems used with computers?

10. Computers with an 8-bit basic addressable unit of main memory probably use EBCDIC or ASCII-8 internally. A 24-bit word-addressed machine might use BCD. Why?

KEY WORDS

address	control unit	numeric data
alphabetic data	core memory	octal
ASCII-8	decimal	packed decimal
base	digit	positional value
binary	digit-times-place-value rule	scientific notation
binary coded decimal (BCD)	EBCDIC	semiconductor memory
binary number system	floating-point data	standard interface
bit	hexadecimal	storage
byte	main memory	word
code	memory	
coded data	number system	

Computer Logic: the Central Processing Unit

OVERVIEW

Chapter 5 introduced the key ideas of memory; in Chapter 6, we'll concentrate on the other key component of the computer itself, the *central processing unit* or CPU. We'll discuss the basic operations that can be performed by the CPU and then show how these functions are implemented through the computer's instruction set.

The chapter concludes with a discussion of a hardware system, tying together the computer, its I/O devices, control units, and channels. Also included is an optional discussion of computer circuits and the integrated-circuit manufacturing process.

101

THE CENTRAL PROCESSING UNIT: BASIC FUNCTIONS

Returning to our analogy of Chapter 3, we recall that the manager was responsible for performing a number of logical functions. His first job was, as you remember, to turn over an instruction card and figure out what the programmer wanted him to do. His list of choices was limited to the following:

1. Add two numbers.

2. Subtract one number from another.

3. Multiply two numbers.

4. Divide one number into another.

5. Copy a field from one memory location (or a register) to another.

6. Compare two numbers or fields and branch (i.e., changing the sequence of instructions), depending on the result of the comparison.

7. Request input of a record.

8. Request output of a record.

Once he decoded the instruction, his next task was to execute it. The boss simulated a computer's **central processing unit**; the CPU does electronically exactly what the manager did manually.

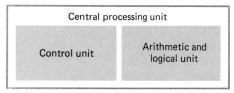

Fig. 6.1
The central processing unit.

The CPU is divided into two parts (Fig. 6.1): the **control unit** and the **arithmetic and logical unit**. The function of the control unit is to get a single instruction and to decode it. Once the control unit has figured out what is to be done, control is turned over to the arithmetic and logical unit, which does it. The first step in this cycle is called instruction time, or **I-time**. The second step, involving the arithmetic and logical unit, is called execution time, or **E-time**. Completion of both parts represents one **machine cycle** (Fig. 6.2). That's how a computer works: The control unit figures out what is to be done and turns control over to the arithmetic and logical unit, which performs the task and turns control back to the control unit, which decodes the

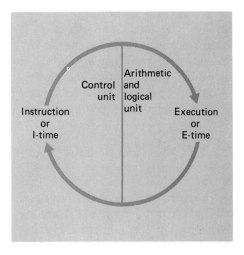

Fig. 6.2
A machine cycle.

next instruction and returns control to the arithmetic and logical unit, and on and on in a cyclic pattern.

MACHINE INSTRUCTIONS

On page 44, we listed the basic functions available to our "human computer" of Chapter 3. That's about all a real computer can do, too: add, subtract, multiply, divide, copy, handle simple yes/no logic, ask for input, and ask for output. There are different kinds of *add* instruction—halfword adds, fullword adds, packed decimal adds, floating-point adds—and a similar collection of instructions for each of the basic functions, but they still basically pertain to simple arithmetic, copying, simple logic, and I/O. In Chapter 5, we discussed a number of different types of data, both coded and numeric, indicating that a computer cannot perform arithmetic on coded data, and that numeric data cannot be properly interpreted by an I/O device. To simplify the necessary handling of both types of data, most computers have instructions to convert data from one type to another. PACK, for example, is IBM's instruction for converting EBCDIC-coded data to packed decimal form. With the addition of these data-conversion instructions, we're looking at a computer's complete repertoire.

What exactly do we mean by an **instruction**? Perhaps the best way to visualize the meaning of an instruction is to look at a familiar, close relative of the computer—the pocket calculator. Let's assume that we have a number in the calculator's memory and wish to add another value to it. Depending on the type of calculator we are using, either we enter the number and push the ADD (or +) button, or we push the ADD (or +) button and enter the number; the result in both cases is the same, a very rapid computation of the correct sum. The typing or keying of the number is an input operation. Pressing the ADD (or +) button causes the two numbers in question to be allowed to pass through the addition circuitry. The display of the answer is an output operation. In effect, each function button on the calculator represents one instruction in the calculator's instruction set.

THE STORED-PROGRAM CONCEPT

On the calculator, each action (each instruction) involves two distinct steps on the part of the person using the machine. First is a "decision" phase ("What should I do next?") analogous to the function of the control unit of the central processing unit. Second is an "action" phase (push the proper button) analogous to the function of the arithmetic and logical unit.

A computer does *not* work by pushing buttons. The approach described in the preceding paragraph is fine for computing your own grade point average or your own take-home pay, but picture the problems involved in pushing the right buttons in the right sequence 20,000 times to compute everyone's grade point average or everyone's take-home pay. Impossible!

Imagine a mechanical device capable of pushing the right buttons in the right sequence. To help visualize this device, think of a player piano with a paper or rubber roll controlling the striking of the keys. Given such a device, the problem of multiple repetitions would disappear. To do a given computation 20,000 times, we would merely turn the machine on and let it run 20,000 times. The right buttoms would be depressed in the right sequence with mechanical precision.

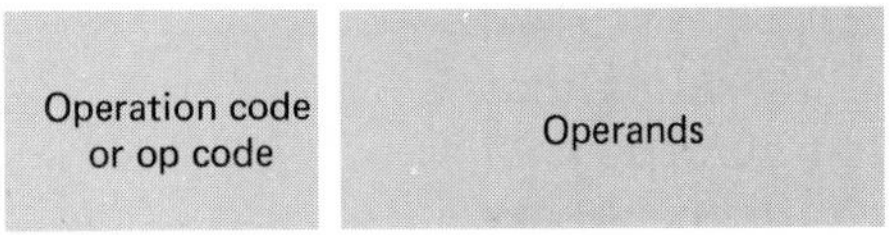

Operation code or op code	Operands

Fig. 6.3
An instruction.

The computer works in much the same way. Rather than using buttons, a computer uses *instructions*. The format of an instruction (Fig. 6.3) is pretty simple, consisting of an operation or **op code** telling the machine *what* to do (add, subtract, multiply, divide, compare, copy) and a series of **operands** providing the machine with such information as

1. Where in memory data can be found,

2. Where in memory an answer is to be placed,

3. The length of an element of data.

A **program** is simply a series of these instructions stored in main memory. The control unit of the CPU goes into memory, *fetches* one of these instructions, and decodes it. The op code of the instruction tells the machine what to do (this is equivalent to telling it which button to push) and the operands tell the machine what elements of data to do it to. After decoding the instruction, the control unit passes control to the arithmetic and logical unit, which executes the instruction. Then it's back to the control unit, which fetches the next instruction and repeats the cycle.

What makes this approach particularly effective is the fact that the program is stored in the computer's main memory in electronic form. Once an instruction is in the computer, it is nothing more than a string of binary digits. This means that no mechanical motion is involved in executing an instruction. Why is the lack of mechanical motion important? Mechanical motion is very slow when compared with the very rapid speed of electricity moving through a wire; also mechanical components tend to wear out.

Thus we have a **stored program**, so called simply because it is stored in main memory. The program controls the CPU by guiding it through the right instructions in the right sequence. One program might guide the CPU through the computation and printing of payroll checks. Another might cause the machine to compute an arithmetic average, while still another program might read a magnetic tape and print a list of address labels. Since the program exists only as a pattern of binary 1's and 0's in main memory, it is easy to change. By reading a new program (from cards, tape, or a direct access device) into main memory, a computer that had been processing payroll is transformed into an inventory machine or an accounting machine. By simply changing the program, the same set of hardware can be used for any number of different applications; this *general-purpose* nature of the computer is one of its more powerful features.

The ability to work under control of a stored program is what distinguishes a computer from a calculator. (Some of our newer calculators are actually programmable, making the dividing line a bit fuzzy.) We'll cover programming in more detail in Chapters 7 and 8.

THE COMPUTER'S INSTRUCTION SET

A computer adds by allowing two binary numbers to pass through a set of electrical circuits. It multiplies by allowing two binary numbers to pass through another set of electronic circuits. It copies by using still another set of circuits. In fact, each instruction valid on a given computer has its own set of circuitry. The collection of all these electronic components is known as the computer's **instruction set.**

On early computers, these instructions were handwired. They were very expensive, and modifications were made only after careful study. On a modern

Fig. 6.4
The modular design of a modern computer. This photograph of a Honeywell Level 6 minicomputer shows a CPU, main memory, and control for a number of peripheral devices and communication lines implemented on a series of circuit boards.

computer, the circuits are equally complex, but modern production methods have reduced the cost and improved reliability tremendously.

On a modern computer, a set of instruction circuits might be placed on individual circuit cards or boards. These electronic components are then slipped into a cabinet (Fig. 6.4) to form the computer. This approach makes the selection of an instruction set a bit more flexible. A business data processing installation might, for example, decide *not* to purchase the floating-point instruction set, having no need for it; the mainframe supplier can easily comply with the customer's wishes by simply pulling or not installing the card containing the floating-point instruction set.

A growing trend in the computer industry is the use of **microprogramming.** On a microprogrammable computer, the owners can design and code their own made-to-order instruction set. A good example of this can be found on the function keys of some of the more expensive pocket calculators. Many such calculators contain a key for finding square roots. By simply entering a number and depressing the SQUARE ROOT key, the desired result can be directly computed; in effect, the calculator has a square-root instruction. By using microprogramming, a similar square root instruction could be added to the instruction set of a regular computer. Most computers, as we've mentioned above, are restricted to requests for I/O, copy and compare operations, and simple arithmetic. Although it is possible to estimate a square root with a great deal of accuracy by using only addition, subtraction, multiplication, and division, a special square-root instruction would be a lot faster and at least as accurate. In the days of handwired computers, this would have been economically impractical. Today, with microcoding, such complex instructions make sense, particularly on a scientific computer.

When we think of the term *hardware,* we think of something solid, such as a cabinet or a group of wires. Programs are *software;* they exist as patterns of binary 1's and 0's in main memory, or on tape or disk, or as a pattern of holes in a punched card. (In effect, the only reason we need the card is to hold the holes together; the program is the part that isn't there.) The instruction set is somewhere between these two extremes. It's not software because it exists in the form of a physical card or a collection of physical circuits. But the fact that it can be easily modified makes it somewhat less permanent than the word hardware implies. The term **firmware** has thus evolved to describe such computer components.

REGISTERS

How does data or an instruction get from main memory to the CPU? On many computers, the answer is "through the registers." A **register** acts as a path or conduit, connecting the two major components of the computer.

Once again, it seems that the best way to explain the functions of a register is by referring to the familiar pocket calculator. We've already seen that the electronic circuits of a calculator are analogous to a CPU. Since most calculators have very limited memory, let's say that our main memory is a sheet of scratch paper. If we wish to add two numbers, it is first necessary to transfer them from the scratch pad (our main memory for this analogy) into the calculator; we do this by keying in the numbers to be added, digit by digit. In effect, we have transferred the data from main memory into a register.

Most computers are designed in a similar manner. Data is first stored in main memory. If two numbers are to be added, one (or both) must first be copied into a register before the ADD instruction can be executed.

Following execution of an ADD on a calculator, the answer is usually displayed (the display is nothing more than a visual copy of what is in the register) so that the operator can copy it to the scratch paper (main memory). Following the execution of an ADD instruction on a computer, the answer is usually dropped into a register, allowing a subsequent instruction to copy it into main memory.

Registers exist in many different forms. On some computers, they are part of main memory; on others, the registers are part of the CPU; and on still others, they lie in between. Some machines use general-purpose registers, which are available for both addressing and arithmetic. On other computers, the addressing and arithmetic functions are separated. In some cases, the programmer may have access to two special registers called the ACCUMULA-TOR and the COUNTER, the functions of which should be apparent if you've ever tried to compute a simple average. Many machines have special registers for handling floating-point arithmetic.

The size of a register and the number of registers on a machine varies from manufacturer to manufacturer. Most often, the word size used on a given computer matches the register size; common word sizes include 16, 24, and 32 bits.

Although the size, number, and type of registers can vary, their function remains constant; they are used to transfer information between the CPU and main memory.

A COMPUTER: THE WHOLE PACKAGE

We have finally reached the point where we can put all the components of a computer together. At the top of Fig. 6.5, we see the central processing unit, better known as the CPU, where all the logical and control functions of the computer are carried out. The CPU is subdivided into two parts: the control

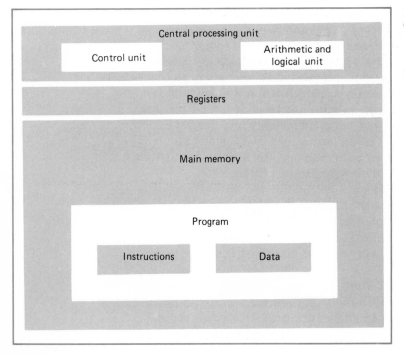

Fig. 6.5
The entire computer.

unit and the arithmetic and logical unit. The control unit is responsible for figuring out exactly what the computer is to do next; the arithmetic and logical unit is responsible for doing it.

At the bottom of the figure is the computer's main memory, consisting of a series of magnetic or electronic devices, each capable of existing in either of two states (0 or 1). These individual bits are grouped together to form bytes, characters, words (depending on the computer manufacturer), or, in general, memory locations. On almost all computers, these memory locations are addressed by assigning them consecutive numbers beginning with 0; we can find the address of a given memory location by simply counting how many memory locations it is away from the first one.

Between the CPU and main memory are a number of registers, which serve as pathways or conduits connecting these two components. Registers on a given computer might be located in memory or in the CPU; Fig. 6.5 illustrates their *logical* position.

According to many sources, the term central processing unit should be applied to the entire computer; in other words, everything shown in Fig. 6.5. If this definition were applied, the CPU would actually include main memory and the registers. However, the standard definition clearly limits the term central processing unit to "the interpretation and execution of instructions," which is the meaning assigned to the term in this text. Although the broader definition of the CPU is technically not correct, you'll still find many people using it.

Another term used to describe a computer is **mainframe**. To many, a computer's mainframe is simply the CPU. Others include the registers and main memory in the definition. Still others argue that the mainframe consists of every component which is actually included in the same physical "box" as the CPU; this latter definition seems to be the one that is currently popular. Thus, we speak of a computer's mainframe, which houses a CPU, main memory, registers, and perhaps other electronic components as well.

MEMORY CONTENTS

Memory can hold program instructions and data; both, of course, are stored in binary form. How can the computer tell the difference between instructions and data? It can't. It is the responsibility of the programmer to keep them separate.

THE MEMORY, OR MACHINE, CYCLE

As we've already discussed, the computer executes instructions by following a very simple cyclic procedure. The first part of this cycle, called I-time or instruction time, consists of the control unit of the CPU fetching from memory and decoding one instruction. During execution time, or E-time, the arithmetic and logical unit of the CPU performs the desired operation on the elements of data specified in the instruction. The cycle then repeats, with the control unit fetching and decoding the next program instruction and the arithmetic and logical unit actually doing what has been requested.

Now that we've covered many of the key concepts of memory, registers, and the CPU, we can take a closer look at this cycle, using a specific example. A brief program segment designed to add two numbers is shown in Fig. 6.6. (We won't show the instructions or data in their actual binary form, but will leave that exercise for a later chapter.) As its first act, the control unit fetches and decodes the first of these four instructions, which reads:

LOAD THE FULLWORD STARTING AT MEMORY LOCATION 1000 INTO REGISTER 3.

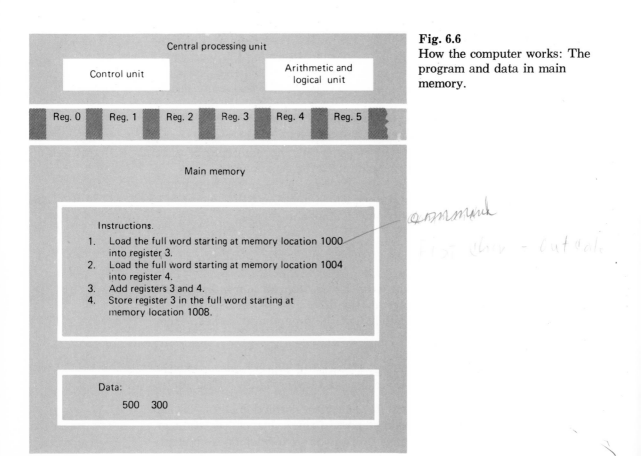

Fig. 6.6
How the computer works: The program and data in main memory.

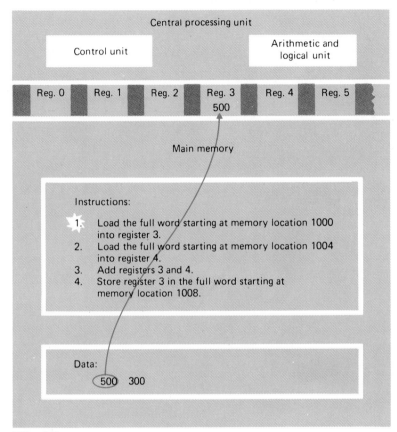

Central processing unit

Control unit

Arithmetic and
logical unit

Reg. 0   Reg. 1   Reg. 2   Reg. 3   Reg. 4   Reg. 5
                              500

Main memory

Instructions:

1. Load the full word starting at memory location 1000
   into register 3.
2. Load the full word starting at memory location 1004
   into register 4.
3. Add registers 3 and 4.
4. Store register 3 in the full word starting at
   memory location 1008.

Data:
    500   300

Fig. 6.7
The first element of data is loaded into register 3.

Having decoded the instruction, the control unit turns control over to the
arithmetic and logical unit, which loads the fullword starting at memory location 1000 into register 3 (Fig. 6.7). Now it's the control unit's turn again;
the next instruction:

LOAD THE FULLWORD STARTING AT MEMORY LOCATION
1004 INTO REGISTER 4.

is fetched and decoded and, in the second phase of this memory cycle, the
arithmetic and logical unit performs the expected task (Fig. 6.8). Back to the
control unit and the next instruction:

ADD REGISTERS 3 AND 4.

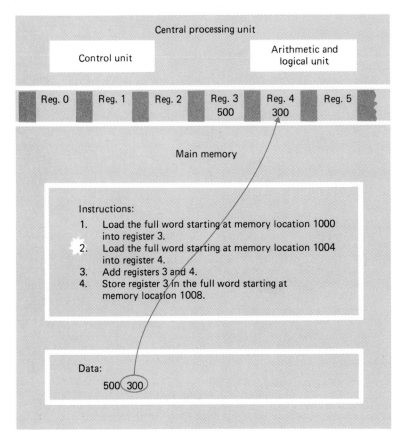

Fig. 6.8
The second element of data is
loaded into register 4.

again with predictable results. Note that the answer is placed in register 3,
the first register specified in the instruction (Fig. 6.9). The control unit now
goes after the next instruction, fetching and decoding:

STORE REGISTER 3 IN THE FULLWORD STARTING AT
MEMORY LOCATION 1008.

The arithmetic and logical unit does as it has been told, and the result is
shown in Fig. 6.10. Do you remember, from our discussion in Chapter 3 how
our "human computer" copied data from the chalkboards (memory) to his
workboard (registers), did all computations on the workboard (registers),
and copied the answer back to the chalkboards (memory)? You've just seen
how these same functions are carried out on a real computer.

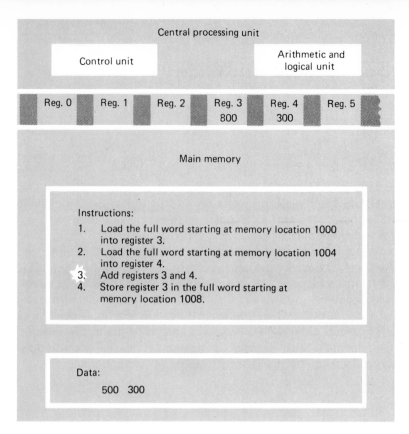

Fig. 6.9
The two registers are added, with the sum being placed in register 3.

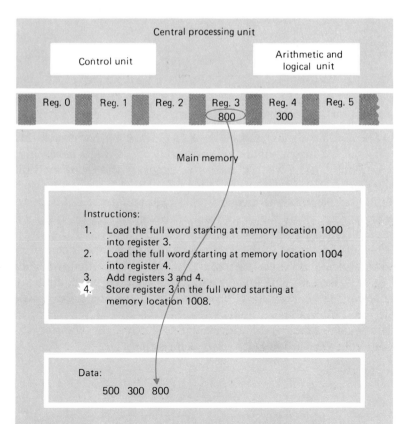

Fig. 6.10
The answer is stored back in memory.

TYING IN INPUT/OUTPUT

In the preceding discussion, we mentioned the presence of *data* in the computer's memory; how did it get there? From an input device. The whole point of using a computer is to read a record of input data, process this data within the computer, and then write a record of output, repeating the cycle again and again. The computer *system* is not complete without input and output devices. How are these devices attached to the computer?

The control unit, as you may remember, is responsible for converting the code used by the I/O device (the card reader's 12-bit code, for example) into the computer's internal code, a function known as standard interface. Another hardware component, a *channel*, is frequently placed between the control unit and the computer (Fig. 6.11); we'll explain the functions of a channel in the next several paragraphs. One point should be made, however, before we begin: The "control unit" associated with an I/O device is quite different from the control unit of the CPU, which decodes instructions.

Fig. 6.11
Input and output devices are attached to the computer through control units and channels.

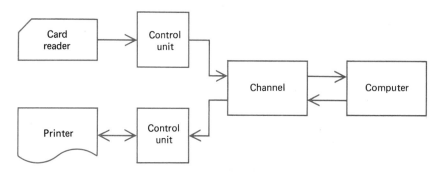

There are a number of logical functions that must be performed during an I/O operation. Let's use a simple example, that of reading a card, to illustrate. What is really meant when a computer requests the input or transfer of "one card's worth" of information from a card reader? If we assume a standard 80-column card is used, it means that 80 characters of data are to be moved, one at a time, from the card reader through a control unit, where they are converted into EBCDIC (or similar coded) form, and then into 80 consecutive memory locations in the computer's main memory. There are two very important logical functions that must be performed in support of the transfer of data. The first function is counting. How is the equipment to "know" that exactly 80 characters of data have been transferred if it doesn't count them? Counting is a logical function.

The other logical function is addressing. Following the transfer of the 40th character from the card to, let's say, memory location 1023, where does

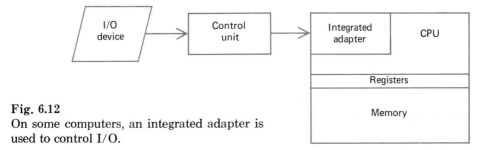

Fig. 6.12
On some computers, an integrated adapter is used to control I/O.

the 41st character go? Memory location 1024, obviously. How do we get from 1023 to 1024? Simple—we add 1. Addition is also a logical function.

Within a computer, logical functions are performed by the CPU. Thus on early computers, the CPU was responsible for physically controlling an I/O operation by keeping track of the number of characters transferred and the address of the "next" character in main memory. Many modern computers, particularly minicomputers and other small or midsized machines, still use the CPU in this way, attaching control units to a device called an **integrated adapter** (Fig. 6.12), which is physically located in the same "box" as the CPU. These integrated adapters function by "stealing" machine cycles from the CPU to support the character-counting and addressing operations.

There is nothing wrong with cycle stealing; it is a reasonable and fairly inexpensive way of controlling I/O. When the central processing unit is concentrating its energies on counting characters and updating addresses, however, it isn't performing useful work on an application program. On a smaller machine, this does not represent a great deal of waste, but as computers become bigger and faster and as more and more input and output devices are attached to the mainframe, controlling each and every I/O operation becomes a burden. The solution to the problem is the **channel**, which is essentially a minicomputer placed between one or more control units and the computer. The channel's functions are to count characters and update main memory addresses, thus taking over responsibility for controlling an I/O operation and freeing the central processing unit to perform other tasks.

Most computers support two different types of channels. The first, called a **multiplexer** (Fig. 6.13), is designed to attach low-speed I/O devices such as card readers and printers. Compare the speed of a card reader—a rate of perhaps 1000 characters per second—with the speed of a computer, which is capable of manipulating millions of characters per second. Obviously a computer can easily keep up with a number of card readers. The multiplexer allows dozens of low-speed I/O devices to be handled concurrently by overlapping, or *multiplexing*, their operation, getting one character from a card reader, sending one character to a card punch, sending one character to a

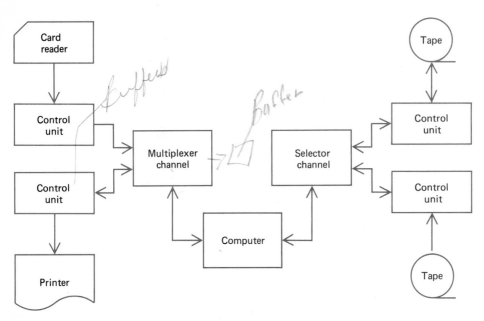

Fig. 6.13
Multiplexer channels are used to connect slower I/O devices; selector channels are used for high-speed I/O.

printer, and then coming back to the card reader to wait for the next character to be read at the relatively low rate of 1000 characters per second.

Multiplexing implies buffering. Think about it for a minute: How can a device such as a multiplexer channel possibly handle a number of devices concurrently without some means of "taking up the slack" when the inevitable conflict occurs? In our discussion of buffering (Chapter 4), we mentioned the need for a buffer to overcome the rather obvious disparity between the speed of a human typist and that of a computer, indicating that the buffer is frequently found in the control unit. Buffering at the control unit level is important to the proper functioning of a channel. What happens, for example, if a multiplexer channel is working on so many concurrent operations that it doesn't get back to a given card reader before the "next" column is read? With the use of buffering, the card reader simply drops the character into the control unit's buffer and proceeds to the next column; when the channel does get back to the card reader, it will find the data in the buffer.

In order to avoid possible conflicts in transferring data into main memory, many channels contain buffers. The steps involved in a typical I/O operation, to cite one example, begin with data moving from a card through a card reader and into a control unit's buffer, from the control unit into the multiplexer channel's buffer, and, eventually, into main memory.

High-speed input and output devices, such as magnetic tape, disk, and drum (to be covered in detail in a subsequent chapter), are normally attached to the computer through a different type of channel called a **selector** (Fig. 6.13). Unlike the multiplexer channel, a selector channel is designed to handle the transmission of data between main memory and a single I/O device at a time. Since these devices are relatively fast, the advantages of overlapping or multiplexing I/O operations are not as great. In effect, a selector channel serves as a high-speed data path connecting a single I/O device to the computer, with data being transferred in what is known as the *burst mode*. After completing an operation, the channel can then be used to connect the computer to another high-speed I/O device. A selector channel, like its multiplexer counterpart, counts characters and updates addresses, freeing the central processing unit from this responsibility.

Although the so-called high-speed devices (such as tape, drum, and disk) are very fast when compared with card readers and printers, they are still quite slow in relation to the computer's internal-processing speeds. On some extremely fast computers, special selector channels actually overlap a number of high-speed I/O operations; these channels are called **block multiplexers.**

COMPUTER SYSTEMS

We have now covered all of the major components of a **computer system** (see Fig. 6.14). Let's put the pieces together. The system begins with the computer itself, which is subdivided into three major parts: the central processing unit (CPU), registers, and memory. Within memory, we find both program instructions and data; since programs and data are stored as nothing more than a pattern of 1's and 0's on a two-state device such as core (or its equivalent), they are easily changed, allowing the machine to process a number of records and then to switch quickly to another program that can process several "different" records.

The central processing unit is subdivided into two parts: the control unit and the arithmetic and logical unit. The control unit is responsible for getting (fetching) an instruction from memory and decoding it—in other words, for figuring out what the program is to do. Control is then transferred to the arithmetic and logical unit, which executes the specified instruction. Next, it's back to the control unit, where the process is repeated. The registers serve as paths or conduits connecting main memory and the CPU.

Outside the computer, we find low-speed I/O devices such as card readers and printers attached to the computer first through a control unit (Fig. 6.14), which buffers the data and converts the code of the input or output device to the code expected by the computer (standard interface), and then through a multiplexer channel, which again buffers the data and performs the

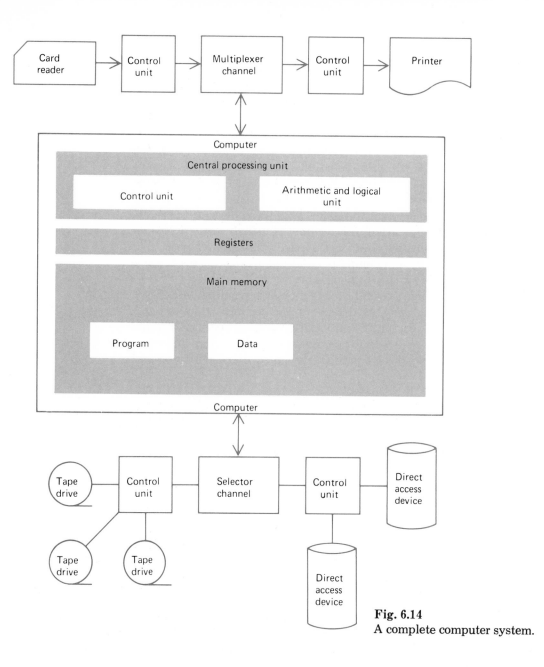

Fig. 6.14
A complete computer system.

logical functions of counting characters and keeping track of main-memory addresses. A multiplexer channel can multiplex or overlap a number of I/O operations.

High-speed I/O devices such as tape, disk, and drum are attached (Fig. 6.14) first through a control unit and then through a selector channel. A selector channel performs the same counting and addressing functions that a multiplexer does, but it doesn't overlap I/O operations, transmitting data between main memory and one device at a time in burst mode.

All these components together compose a typical computer system. The term *system* is important, since it implies a collection of different components, all of which must work together to achieve an objective. Without input data, the computer, which is a data processing machine, would have no data to process. Without control units and channels, the input of data would be impossible. Once in the computer, data is processed through the combined efforts of memory, registers, and the control unit and arithmetic and logical unit of the central processing unit. Of course, without output, there's no point in processing data. Computers work for the benefit of people, not computers; thus, if people cannot read and analyze the computer's results, those results are meaningless. All parts of the system must work in concert; the failure of any one part means the failure of the system.

We've covered the hardware components of this system in some detail. Software will be covered in Chapters 7 and 8, and additional details on data are left for Part 3.

ELECTRONICS

First-generation computers used electronic tubes as their primary component. During the second generation, transistors began to supplant tubes. Today, solid-state and integrated circuits are the rule. As we progress from generation to generation, computers become faster, more reliable, smaller (Fig. 6.15), and, on a cost-per-computation basis, less expensive. The reason for these improvements is technology, as we move from the use of tubes to transistors to solid-state logic, the electronic components become faster, more

Fig. 6.15
A comment on the trend in computer size. (Reprinted with permission of *Datamation.*® Copyright 1975 by Technical Publishing Company, Greenwich, Connecticut.)

'We've lost the main processing unit'

reliable, smaller, and less expensive. Today, we have nanosecond computers that almost never fail, that can fit inside a typical briefcase, and that can be purchased for under $10,000! It won't be long before personal computers are available for considerably less than the cost of a new car!

BOOLEAN LOGIC*

The functions of a central processing unit are performed electronically. This implies a collection of electronic circuits. What do they look like? Let's talk in logical terms first; a bit later in the chapter, we'll describe the physical appearance of the circuits.

In the mid-1800s, George Boole developed a new type of logic which today bears his name: Boolean algebra. Boolean algebra allows complex mathematical and logical problems to be solved by manipulating two conditions: true or false. The computer is a two-state device (using 0 or 1), making Boolean logic ideal for use on a computer. Most modern digital computers are based on **Boolean logic.**

At its core, Boolean logic requires only three basic logic blocks: AND, OR, and NOT. The functions of each of these logic blocks are summarized in Fig. 6.16. These simple gates can be combined to perform a number of more complex functions. (A diagram of a circuit designed to add two bits is shown in Fig. 6.17.) All of the functions performed by a computer are implemented through a combination of these three basic building blocks.

This is not to imply that making a computer is simple. A single function might involve thousands of logic blocks, and their interrelationship is so critical that a seemingly insignificant error such as using an extra inch of wire can throw electrical timings so far off as to make the circuit unusable. But design complexities do not change the fact that a computer is *basically* constructed from these three building blocks.

Microcoding, or microprogramming, essentially involves writing instructions for the actual AND, OR, and NOT logic needed to implement a larger function (such as finding a square root). The microcode is then converted into an electrical circuit.

INTEGRATED CIRCUITS

We have been talking about integrated circuits for some time now, beginning with the discussion of noncore main memory in Chapter 5. What exactly do these circuits look like? How are they made? To gain even a basic understanding of integrated circuits, it is first necessary to understand how a transistor works.

Matter is composed of atoms. An atom consists of a nucleus of positively charged and electronically neutral particles surrounded by negatively charged elec-

---

* Over the next several pages, we will be describing the physical characteristics of the circuits that are used to build computers. Presentation of this material was intentionally postponed until now, since many instructors will consider it to be optional.

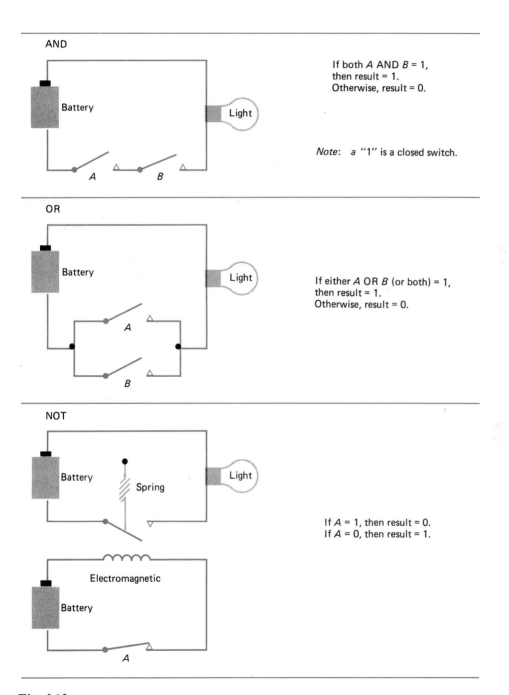

AND

If both *A* AND *B* = 1,
then result = 1.
Otherwise, result = 0.

Note: a "1" is a closed switch.

OR

If either *A* OR *B* (or both) = 1,
then result = 1.
Otherwise, result = 0.

NOT

If *A* = 1, then result = 0.
If *A* = 0, then result = 1.

Fig. 6.16
The three basic Boolean logic blocks.

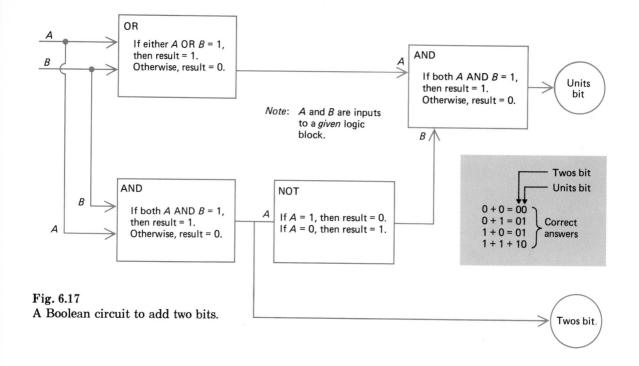

Fig. 6.17
A Boolean circuit to add two bits.

trons (Fig. 6.18); the model looks like a solar system; the nucleus represents the sun, and the electrons represent the planets.

A chemical compound is a combination of atoms. In some compounds, the combination of atoms of different types results in one or more *extra* electrons (Fig. 6.18);

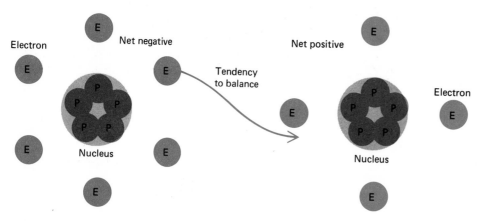

Fig. 6.18
Basic chemistry: Materials with an excess of electrons are negatively charged, while materials with a scarcity of electrons are positively charged.

in other compounds, the opposite is true, with a *scarcity* of electrons present. There is a strong tendency for extra electrons to migrate to a compound with a scarcity of electrons; all we need do to encourage this is to provide a path, such as a wire.

Transistors take advantage of this basic electrical fact. Starting with a neutral material (like silicon), a spot with a positive electrical charge is created (see Fig. 6.19). Flanking this spot are two negatively charged areas. An electrical current can flow from the outer negative areas into the middle positive area, but no current can flow in the opposite direction. The designer of electrical circuits can do wonders with these "one-way-only" components. (Incidentally, we could have created a transistor with a negative center flanked by two positive areas; in such a device, current could flow from the middle only.)

The transistor is one key component in an integrated logic circuit. These circuits are "grown," using a combination of chemical and photographic techniques. The starting point is a slice of silicon material (Fig. 6.20a). An oxide is allowed to form on the surface of this material (Fig. 6.20b). Next, a photographic mask is laid on top of the surface and, through a series of light exposures, selected portions of the silicon dioxide surface are weakened. Acid is used to wash the surface; this acid bath removes all the silicon dioxide from the weakened areas, leaving behind a hole or window through the oxide coating to the raw silicon below (Fig. 6.20c). The material is now placed in a special oven and bombarded with (in this example) negatively

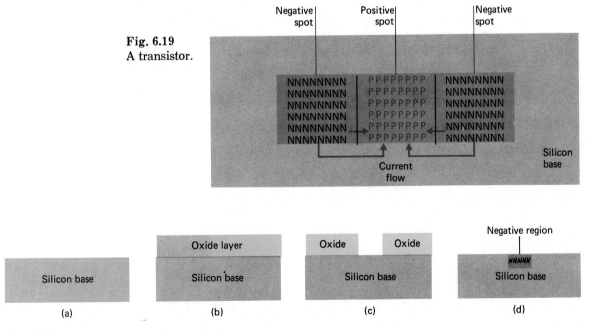

Fig. 6.19
A transistor.

Fig. 6.20
The first steps in "growing" a transistor: (a) the starting point—silicon; (b) the oxide layer grows; (c) after photographic etching; and (d) a negative area remains after bombardment.

charged materials. A final bath removes all the oxide. The result (Fig. 6.20d) is a slice of electronically neutral silicon with an isolated negatively charged area.

After completing these steps, the process is repeated with a different mask; the second series of steps is illustrated in Fig. 6.21. As a result of these two steps, we now have a transistor on a slice of silicon. Other steps might cut other windows to be followed by a bombardment with metal ions, thus creating an electrical path roughly equivalent to a printed wire. Using this approach, complete logical circuits can be created.

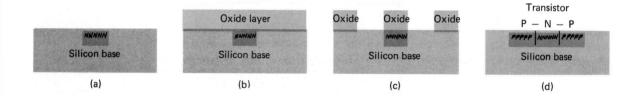

(a)   (b)   (c)   (d)

Fig. 6.21
The second steps in "growing" a transistor: (a) the starting point; (b) the oxide layer grows; (c) after photographic etching; and (d) positive areas remain after bombardment.

Nothing in this brief discussion says that the process is limited to producing one transistor or one circuit on a single slice of silicon. In fact, the photographic masks are normally reproduced time and time again, yielding thousands of circuits on a single slice.

The big factors in determining the cost of these circuits are density and yield. The cost of producing a single slice is actually almost constant: It doesn't matter whether we put 10 or 10,000 circuits on the slice. We still must use the same number of masks and the same number of process steps.

Let's assume a cost of $100 per slice as an example. If we made only a single transistor, we would have a $100 transistor, which is quite expensive. However, if we were able to squeeze 1000 transistors onto the slice, we would have 1000 ten-cent transistors. Yield has a similar impact. Let's say that our process is running at a 50-percent yield, meaning that of the 1000 transistors on the slice only 500 are good; at a cost of $100 for all of them, the final cost is 20 cents per transistor. But as the yield gets better, the cost per transistor drops. Both of these factors have an impact on the electronics industry today; circuits are being made at greater and greater densities and the manufacturing yield of the process keeps getting higher. The net result is declining cost—a perfect example of this trend is the decreasing cost of pocket calculators.

Fig. 6.22
An integrated circuit chip. This one, shown resting on a penny, is the heart of a five-function digital watch.

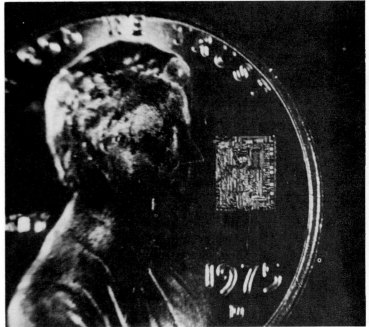

Photo courtesy of Texas Instruments Corporation.

In order to simplify the handling of these integrated circuits, they must be packaged. The first step in this process is to cut a slice into individual circuits (Fig. 6.22), which are called *chips*. Next, these circuit chips are bonded to small carriers, resulting in a component such as the microprocessor shown in Fig. 6.23. These individual components can be soldered or otherwise connected to a card (Fig. 6.24) or a board. The cards and boards can be easily assembled to build a computer (Fig. 6.25) or, for that matter, almost any electronic device.

Perhaps the best way to visualize the trends in electronic development is to look at two different machines that existed nearly 25 years apart. Back in the early days of computer development (around 1952), the best-known computer was the UNIVAC I. It was quite large, weighing about four tons and consuming 575 square feet, the better part of a good-sized room. Its memory could hold approximately 12,000 of today's characters. It could execute almost 4000 instructions in one second, and it cost about $2,000,000. Today, a briefcase-sized machine with over 32,000 characters of main memory capable of performing in excess of one million instructions per second can be purchased for around $15,000 or less. That's progress!

Where will it all end? The ultimate is probably a complete CPU plus associated main memory on a single slice of silicon that is perhaps from 2½ to 3 inches in diameter. It's theoretically possible!

Fig. 6.23
A chip mounted on a carrier.

Photo courtesy of Texas Instruments Corporation.

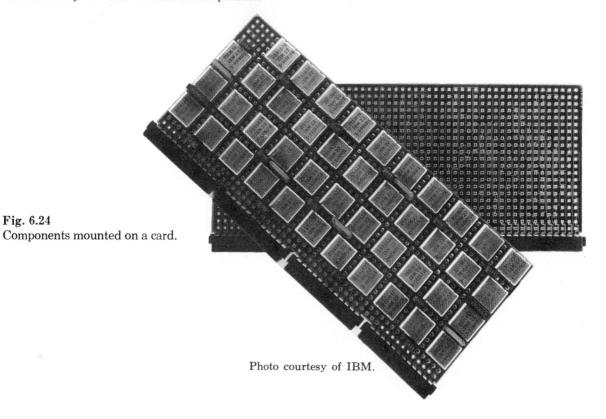

Fig. 6.24
Components mounted on a card.

Photo courtesy of IBM.

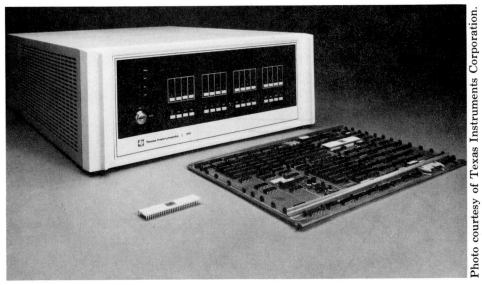

Photo courtesy of Texas Instruments Corporation.

Fig. 6.25
An example of modular computer design. Chips are attached to carriers, which in turn are put together to build a computer.

SUMMARY

The main focus of this chapter was the computer's central processing unit, or CPU. We began with a discussion of the functions performed by the two main components of the CPU, the control unit and the arithmetic and logical unit. I-time (or instruction time) and E-time (or execution time), the two components of a machine cycle, were defined and illustrated, along with the idea of a stored program.

Registers and channels, both multiplexer and selector, were introduced and placed in context. We then moved into a discussion of the computer system, showing how I/O devices, control units, channels, main memory, registers, the central processing unit, and data fit together.

Finally, in a section that many instructors may have considered to be optional, we spent some time discussing the physical nature of the CPU, touching on the three basic logical building blocks of a modern computer (the AND, OR, and NOT functions of Boolean algebra) and describing how integrated circuits are manufactured.

EXERCISES

1. Explain what is meant by a computer's machine cycle.

2. What are the functions performed by the control unit of the central processing unit?

3. What is the difference between the control unit of the CPU and the control unit that is found between the computer and an I/O device?

4. What is meant by a stored program?

5. Explain how the idea of a stored program allows a computer to be a general-purpose machine.

6. What functions are performed by a channel?

7. Explain the difference between multiplexer and selector channels.

8. What is meant by a computer's instruction set?

9. OPTIONAL   The cost of modern integrated circuits continues to decline. Can you give any reasons?

10. OPTIONAL   Follow the circuitry of the two-bit adder (Fig. 6.17) and see how it actually performs the following additions

    a) $0 + 0 = 00$ b) $0 + 1 = 01$
    c) $1 + 0 = 01$ d) $1 + 1 = 10$

KEY WORDS

arithmetic and logical unit

buffer

burst mode

central processing unit (CPU)

channel

computer system

control unit

control unit portion of CPU

data

execution time (E-time)

firmware

general-purpose computer

hardware

hardware system

I/O device

instruction

instruction set

instruction time (I-time)

integrated
adapter

integrated circuit

machine cycle

main memory

mainframe

microprogram-
ming

multiplexer
channel

operand

operation (op)
code

record

register

selector channel

software

stored program

OPTIONAL
KEY WORDS:

AND

Boolean logic

chip

NOT

OR

Software: Problem Definition and Planning

7

OVERVIEW

To this point, we've covered the major hardware components of a computer system in some detail. Software (the actual programs) is different. It's not a physical thing (like hardware) that can be seen or felt; to a certain extent, it's much like a thought. Because of the uniqueness of this topic, we'll devote the next two chapters to a discussion of software. In Chapter 7, we will concentrate on the logic of a program, emphasizing what it does rather than how it is implemented. The problems of defining and planning the program will be discussed. Key ideas will include flowcharts, decision tables, structured programming, modular programming, and top-down program design. The implementation and maintenance of a program on a computer will be presented in Chapter 8.

The intent of this chapter is to clearly illustrate that programs must be carefully planned by human beings before being implemented on a computer. Planning is a thought process, and not a mechanical or electronic process. Don't lose sight of this basic idea.

131

SOFTWARE: BASIC CONCEPTS

In the analogy used in chapter 3, the computer "program" was simulated by a deck of 3×5 file cards; our human computer, as you may recall, determined what to do next by turning over the cards one at a time. In Chapters 5 and 6, we have mentioned that program instructions are really stored in main memory and that the central processing unit is responsible for "fetching" one instruction at a time and executing it. In the next two chapters, we'll be looking at software in more detail.

Software is another term for programs. Hardware is physical, while software is *not*. Within the computer, a program is nothing more than a pattern of 1's and 0's in memory, existing only so long as the power remains on. You can't see software, nor can you feel, smell, taste, or hear it.

The transient nature of software allows a computer system to be very flexible. At any given moment, the computer might be running a payroll program, with the collection of hardware components, working under control of a program, producing paychecks from time cards. A few minutes later, following completion of the payroll job, a new program might be placed in the computer, allowing the same collection of hardware components to compute and print end-of-term grade reports for 20,000 students. Another program change might allow a mathematician to use the same hardware to analyze a large amount of data. Still another program change might convert the same physical machine into an inventory processor. The flexibility of software allows a computer to become a true general-purpose machine.

What is a program? In Chapter 6, we discussed the computer's instruction set. Most computers are restricted to various forms of the following basic functions:

1. Addition,

2. Subtraction,

3. Multiplication,

4. Division,

5. Copying,

6. Simple yes/no logic,

7. Requesting input,

8. Requesting output, and

9. Converting data from one type to another.

A *program* is nothing more than a series of these instructions. That statement does oversimplify the concept a bit, since the instructions must be the right instructions in the right sequence, but that is *basically* all a program is.

In Chapter 6, as you may recall, we discussed the idea of a stored program. We began by pointing out that in order to solve a problem on a pocket calculator, it is necessary to attack the problem step by step. We then imagined a machine capable of pushing the proper buttons in the correct sequence, in effect putting the calculator under automatic control.

This is essentially what a program does for a computer. The program consists of a series of instructions that tell the computer, step by step, exactly what it is to do. Each instruction tells the computer to perform one of its basic functions—addition, subtraction, multiplication, or any of the other skills listed above. The sequence of instructions determines the order in which these instructions will be performed. A correctly written program will cause the computer to convert input data to accurate output information.

THE PROGRAMMING PROCESS

Programs do not simply "spring into being." Where do they come from? Programs are written by *programmers.* Some human being must tell a computer, step by step, exactly what must be done before a computer can do anything. How does a programmer go about writing a program?

Programming is not quite a science; there is a touch of art involved. Thus it is not surprising to find that different programmers go about the task of writing a program in different ways. There are, however, a number of clearly identifiable steps that are almost always involved in the programming process and that provide a convenient framework for studying this process. In very general terms, these steps are to

1. Define the problem,
2. Plan a solution,
3. Implement that solution, and
4. Maintain the program or programs.

In this chapter, we'll concentrate on the first two steps, leaving the discussion of implementation and maintenance for Chapter 8.

PROBLEM DEFINITION

The first of these steps, problem definition, asks a key question: "What is it we want to do?" It would seem as though this is an obvious starting point, but problem definition tends to be the most frequently bypassed step in the entire process. Almost every computer installation in the country produces at least one report that no one wants and no one uses, a situation that we can probably attribute to the fact that the programmer never thought to ask, "What exactly do you want me to do?"

Thus it is essential that we know what we are going to do *before* we start to do it. Common sense? Sure. But all too often common sense is ignored.

In this chapter and in Chapter 8, we'll be following through on the payroll application introduced in Chapter 3, actually converting the "program" of that analogy to a real computer program. Our problem definition is to develop and write a program to compute net pay and print paychecks for a number of individuals.

One final comment before we move on to planning. Who is responsible for defining the problem? In some organizations, it's the programmer who, hopefully, arrives at a definition by talking with those who will eventually use the information produced by the program. In other organizations, this responsibility belongs to the systems analyst, another professional whose job we will examine in detail in Part IV of the text. Part of the analyst's job is to clearly define (and in some cases, plan) the work to be done by the programmer.

PLANNING

Planning is a more detailed step. By this stage, the fact that a program will be created has been established, and what is needed is a detailed set of specifications to guide the programmer as he or she begins programming. It is still a good idea to know exactly where you are going before you start, thus the planning step is often subdivided into a number of separate steps, starting with a very general view of the solution to the problem and gradually adding more and more detail.

Often the programmer will begin the planning process by carefully analyzing the problem, perhaps with the help of a systems analyst. We have already determined what must be done during the problem-definition stage; the question now is to define, in very general terms, the steps which must be taken to achieve that objective. For our payroll program, we might define the following key steps:

1. Compute gross pay.

2. Compute income tax.

3. Compute social security tax.

4. Compute any other deductions.

5. Subtract all deductions from gross pay to get net pay.

6. Print or type a paycheck.

Notice how general this first planning stage is. We haven't attempted to define *how* any of these basic steps will actually be implemented; we concentrate instead on *what* must be done.

Now we begin to add detail. How do we compute gross pay? Usually the computation is simply one of multiplying the number of hours worked by the hourly pay rate. But what about overtime? Often, the number of hours worked over 40 in a given week are paid at 1½ times the normal pay rate, but some organizations use slightly different rates. What about weekend and holiday hours? Do we calculate a double-time pay rate for those hours? It is essential that all the rules for computing gross pay be clearly defined *before* the programmer begins coding.

How are we to compute income tax? Once again, before the programmer begins to write the instructions to compute income tax, the rules must be clearly defined. In this case, the Internal Revenue Service publishes a booklet, Circular E, which very clearly defines the various income tax rates for different levels of income and different pay periods. Figure 7.1 shows a weekly tax table taken from this document.

Social security tax appears to be a much simpler computation; it is calculated as 5.85 percent of gross pay. But there is a limit. Once total gross pay for the year passes a cutoff figure, social security tax is no longer withheld. This must be taken into account before writing the program.

Other deductions follow a similar pattern. How exactly is state income tax computed? What about local income tax? Are union dues to be withheld? Under what circumstances? What about "bond of the month" plans or credit union payments? All these questions must be answered before the program can be completed. A program is much more than just a series of instructions.

Fig. 7.1
A federal income tax withholding table. Multiply the number of dependents claimed by $14.40. Subtract the result from gross pay to get taxable wages. (*Source: Circular E, Employer's Tax Guide,* Department of the Treasury, Internal Revenue Service Publication 15, revised November 1976, pp. 17–18.)

WEEKLY PAYROLL PERIOD

(a) Single person—including head of household			(b) Married person		
If the amount of wages is:	The amount of income tax to be withheld shall be:		If the amount of wages is:	The amount of income tax to be withheld shall be:	
Not over $25 0			Not over $48 0		
Over—	but not over—	of excess over—	Over—	but not over—	of excess over—
$25	−$67 . . . . . 16%	−$25	$48	−$96 . . . . . 17%	−$48
$67	−$115 . . . . $6.72 plus 20%	−$67	$96	−$173 . . . . $8.16 plus 20%	−$96
$115	−$183 . . . . $16.32 plus 23%	−$115	$173	−$264 . . . . $23.56 plus 17%	−$173
$183	−$240 . . . . $31.96 plus 21%	−$183	$264	−$346 . . . . $39.03 plus 25%	−$264
$240	−$279 . . . . $43.93 plus 26%	−$240	$346	−$433 . . . . $59.53 plus 28%	−$346
$279	−$346 . . . . $54.07 plus 30%	−$279	$433	−$500 . . . . $83.89 plus 32%	−$433
$346	. . . . $74.17 plus 36%	−$346	$500	. . . . $105.33 plus 36%	−$500

This is not to imply that *everything* must be completely defined before the first instruction can be written. More frequently, planning and implementation overlap a bit, with the program being written in stages. We will discuss this in more detail later.

Let's return to the program we're actually going to be implementing—a simplified version of the payroll problem. Gross pay is simply the number of hours worked multiplied by an hourly pay rate; for our purposes, we will ignore overtime. Social security is a straight 5.85 percent of gross pay. The income tax rate structure we'll use is a simple one:

Gross less than	Tax is
$100.00	5% of gross
Infinity	10% of gross

For this example, we will ignore all other deductions. After going through the detailed planning of this program, we will, however, spend some time discussing how we might approach a more complex problem.

DETAILED PLANNING

We began the planning process by defining, in very general terms, the steps involved in computing payroll. We then proceeded to define in detail the rules for implementing each of these steps. We are now about to begin the process of restating these rules in terms of the basic functions of a computer. Thus, we enter the final planning stage—detailed planning.

If you look back at the steps required to compute payroll, you'll see that they could be applied to *any* technique for computing payroll: using either simple paper and pencil, a desk calculator, or a computer. Also, our general analysis concentrated on the computation of only a single individual's net pay. Now that we've defined the detailed rules for each of those general steps, we're ready to begin defining how we might implement payroll *on a computer*. We're moving from very general planning to very detailed planning, step by step.

Incidentally, you may be wondering why "detailed planning" has been given its own topic heading. Isn't detailed planning a part of planning? Yes it is, but it's very important that you understand the value of step-by-step planning, because many realistic computer problems are much too complex to allow even the best programmer to simply jump in and begin working with the details. By giving detailed planning its own heading, we are emphasizing the importance of this step-by-by approach.

Programmers use a number of different tools to aid in this detailed planning step. Two of the more commonly used tools are flowcharting and decision tables.

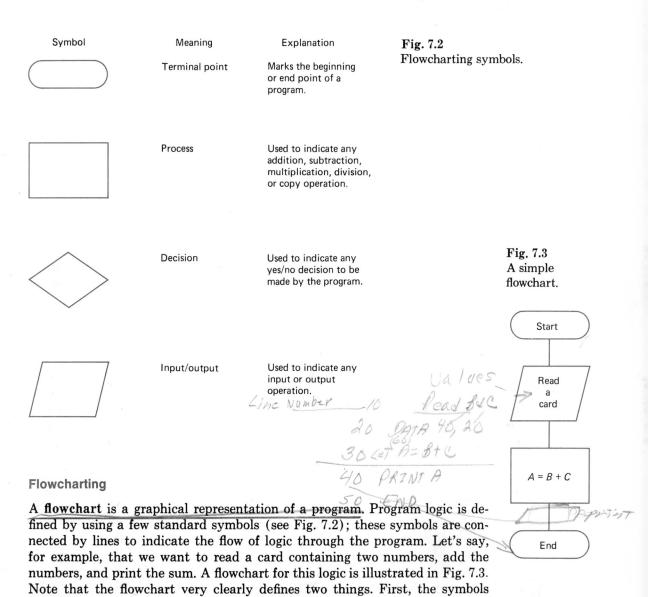

Symbol	Meaning	Explanation
(terminal point symbol)	Terminal point	Marks the beginning or end point of a program.
(process symbol)	Process	Used to indicate any addition, subtraction, multiplication, division, or copy operation.
(decision symbol)	Decision	Used to indicate any yes/no decision to be made by the program.
(input/output symbol)	Input/output	Used to indicate any input or output operation.

Fig. 7.2
Flowcharting symbols.

Fig. 7.3
A simple
flowchart.

Handwritten notes:

Values

Line Number ___ 10 ___ Read B & C

20 DATA 40, 20

30 Let A = B + C

40 PRINT A

50 END

Flowcharting

A **flowchart** is a graphical representation of a program. Program logic is defined by using a few standard symbols (see Fig. 7.2); these symbols are connected by lines to indicate the flow of logic through the program. Let's say, for example, that we want to read a card containing two numbers, add the numbers, and print the sum. A flowchart for this logic is illustrated in Fig. 7.3. Note that the flowchart very clearly defines two things. First, the symbols identify the individual logical steps in the program. Second, following the lines connecting the symbols clearly defines the sequence of these steps. In other words, in addition to telling what must be done, a flowchart also defines the order in which these steps must be performed.

There are a few simple, generally accepted rules governing the flowlines. The normal direction of flow is from top to bottom or from left to right; arrowheads are used if the direction of flow is anything else. Flowlines can cross, but it is not a recommended practice. In general, the idea is to keep things as simple and as straightforward as possible.

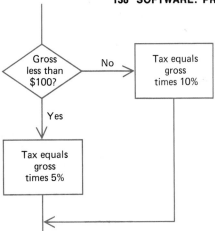

Fig. 7.4
A decision point in a flowchart.

Let's consider an example of simple decision logic. Since we're going to be computing income tax, our income tax rate structure (if gross pay is less than $100, then the tax is 5 percent of gross; otherwise, the tax is 10 percent of gross) can support an excellent example (Fig. 7.4). Note that within the diamond-shaped symbol we asked a question: "Is gross pay (computed in a prior step) less than $100?" How many different possible answers are there to this question? Only two: yes or no. If the answer is yes, income tax is computed at a 5-percent rate by simply following the flowline marked "yes." If the answer is no, we move (in this example) to the right along the flowline marked "no," compute the tax at a 10-percent rate, and rejoin the mainline of the program. Arrows have been added for clarity.

You are probably wondering if there is any significance to the fact that we moved down the flowchart for "yes" and to the right for "no." Although there are local standards within a given organization, there is no nationally accepted standard practice. All that is really important is that the programmer be consistent. A flowchart, you must remember, is merely an aid to planning.

Now we're about ready to begin a flowchart of our payroll program. The finished product is shown in Fig. 7.5. Let's go through it step by step; the steps have been numbered to aid in this process. Follow the flowchart carefully as we move through the program, and be sure that you understand exactly what happens in each and every step. The steps are as follows:

1. This is the start of the program.

2. Read a card containing an employee's name, the number of hours worked, and the hourly pay rate. Remember that the computer is an information processing machine. Its basic pattern is to read a record of data, process that data, and write a record of information.

3. Here, we have reached a decision point: Is this the last card? There are two possible answers: yes or no. A computer "knows" that a job is done

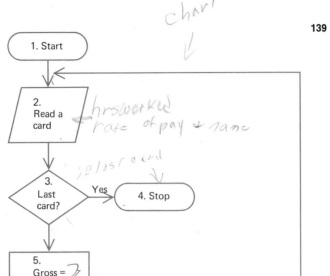

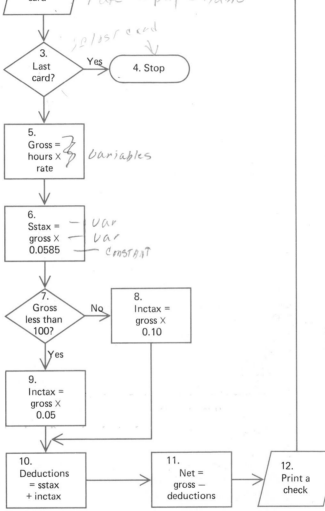

Fig. 7.5
A flowchart of our payroll program.

(handwritten annotations on the figure:)
hrsworked
rate of pay & name
if last card ↓
Variables
Var — Var — Constant

only when the programmer tells it so. In this program, a special card containing no actual data will be placed at the end of the deck. When the computer reads this card, it "knows" that the job is completed.

4. This is the end of the program, reached only when the last card has been read.

5. Gross pay is computed by multiplying the number of hours worked by the hourly pay rate. Why must this *follow* the reading of an input card?

6. Social security tax is computed by multiplying gross pay by 5.85 percent (which is, in decimal terms, 0.0585). Why must this step follow the computation of gross pay?

7. This decision is the first step in the computation of income tax; instructions 7, 8, and 9 have already been described in some detail (see Fig. 7.4).

8. If gross pay is *not* less than $100, then income tax is 10 percent (0.10) of gross pay.

9. If gross pay *is* less than $100, then income tax is 5 percent of gross pay. Why must the computation of income tax follow the computation of gross pay? Would it be possible to compute income tax before computing social security tax? Sure you could. Do you have to know the social security tax in order to compute income tax?

10. In order to get total deductions, we add income tax and social security tax.

11. Net pay is computed by subtracting total deductions from gross pay. Why couldn't we compute net pay before this point in the program?

12. Finally, we print a check.

Note the flowline that follows step 12. It goes back to the top of the program —specifically, back to step 2. Why do you suppose this is done? The answer is simple: Having read one record of data, processed this data, and written one record of output information, we are ready to repeat the process on another record of data. This is called a **loop**. The ability to loop—to go back and repeat a number of instructions—means that the programmer need only solve the problem once and simply repeat those steps for subsequent data. (Before we move on, it is important that you completely understand the flow of logic shown in the flowchart of Fig. 7.5. If you weren't sure of the answers to all of the questions asked in the step-by-step description of the flowchart, go through it again.)

Having developed a flowchart of our program, we have just about completed the planning phase. The flowchart of Fig. 7.5 very clearly shows, step by step, exactly what the computer must do in order to compute payroll. Coding the program now becomes a task of simply translating this logic into the proper computer language, a problem that we will discuss in Chapter 8.

Programmers and Flowcharting

Not all programmers use flowcharts in planning their programs. Flowcharting is simply a tool that allows us to visualize the logic of a program. Flowcharting is extremely valuable to the beginning programmer, but once an individual has gained considerable experience as a programmer, it becomes just as easy (if not easier) to visualize logic in a programming language. Programming languages, as we'll see in Chapter 8, are languages having specific punctuation and grammer rules and possessing a certain style of their own. Much as the true expert in a foreign language learns to *think* in that language, the expert programmer learns to think in COBOL, or FORTRAN, or assembler language; and once an individual has reached this point, a flowchart becomes almost an impediment rather than an aid to thought. Thus it is not surprising to find that most skilled programmers do not actually use flowcharts for planning purposes.

Does this mean that the study of flowcharting is a waste of time? Certainly not! Designing flowcharts is an excellent way to train your mind to think in the kind of logical pattern required by a computer.

There is another use for flowcharts that even the best programmers have come to accept as essential. A flowchart is a great *documentation* tool. After a program has been written (possibly even years later), it is often necessary to go back and make corrections and changes. Given a flowchart, the programmer finds it much easier to figure out exactly what the program does.

Decision Tables

A programmer will sometimes use a **decision table** as a supplement to a flowchart, particularly when a related set of conditions makes the logical flow of a program very complex. As an example, let us assume that the basketball coach has asked us to look through the student records and produce a list of all full-time male students who are at least 6 feet 5 inches in height and who weigh at least 180 pounds. We might want to write a program that will check the records for us, asking the following questions:

1. Is the student male?

2. Is the student taking at least 12 credit hours?

3. Is the student at least 77 inches tall?

4. Does the student weigh at least 180 pounds?

If the answer to all four questions is yes, we want to print the student's name and address; if we receive a single "no," however, we will simply move on to the next student.

With four logical tests, we have a fairly complex program segment. However, by using a decision table, we can express these four tests and their necessary conditions in an easy-to-follow, standard way.

A rough outline of a decision table is shown in Fig. 7.6. The table is divided into four segments: a condition stub at the upper left, a condition entry at the upper right, an action stub at the lower left, and an action entry at the lower right. Within this framework, we'll list our questions (the condi-

Condition stub	Condition entry
Action stub	Action entry

Fig. 7.6
The framework of a decision table.

tions) in the condition-stub section (Fig. 7.7). Below the questions, we'll list our possible actions in the action-stub section. Note that each of our questions is restricted to a yes or no response.

Now we can begin to fill out the decision table. The first question (Fig. 7.7) has two possible answers: yes or no. These answers are listed in the condition-entry section of the table: "Y" for yes and "N" for no. If the answer to the first question happened to be yes, would we have enough information to make a decision? No; we would still have three more questions to go through. But if the answer to the first question happened to be no, we would know enough to take a specific action, ignore this student, and move on. To indicate this fact, we put an "X" in the action-entry section of the decision table directly under this "N" response (see Fig. 7.7). Continuing on a question-by-question basis, we will eventually produce the table shown in Fig. 7.7. Reading the table carefully, you will notice that the first action (list the student's name and address) is called for only when all four conditions are true. You will also notice that a single response of no to any of the four conditions is enough to support the alternate decision (skip to the next student). The decision table has allowed us to express a fairly complex series of yes/no conditions and their associated actions in a standard, easy-to-follow format.

The only part of our payroll program that might call for a decision table is the computation of income tax, although it is doubtful that a programmer would consider anything as relatively simple as a tax table to be worth the effort. A more realistic application of this tool is in the computation of state or local income taxes, where the amount collected depends on a number of

Is the student male?	Y	N		
Is the student taking at least 12 credit hours?	Y		N	
Is the student at least 77 inches tall?	Y			N
Does the student weigh at least 180 pounds?	Y			N
List the student's name and address.	X			
Skip to the next student.		X	X	X X

Fig. 7.7
A decision table for the basketball problem.

complex conditions such as place of residence, place of employment, tax rate collected by the government of the place of residence, and so on.

Not all programmers use standard flowcharts and decision tables. Many have devised their own personal techniques. However, if flowcharts and decision tables are to be used for documentation purposes rather than as a planning tool, standardization is essential.

Defining Data Format

The first real step in the flowchart of the payroll program (see Fig. 7.5) was to read a card. In the description of the flowchart, the fact that this card contained an employee's name, the number of hours worked, and hourly pay rate was mentioned. That's about all we, as human beings, would need to figure out the meaning of the fields on the card. However, a computer needs a bit more.

A card reader "reads" the data punched on a card one column at a time, transferring the data into the computer one character at a time. Within the computer, these individual characters must be put together to form fields. It is the responsibility of the programmer to tell the computer exactly how to do this.

Before the programmer can possibly tell the computer exactly what to do, the programmer must know. Thus another step in the planning process involves laying out, column by column, the contents of the data cards; an example of the card layout for our payroll program is shown in Fig. 7.8. Every data card must be keypunched in exactly the same way in order for the program to work. The employee's name, for example, must *always* start in column

Fig. 7.8
Input card format for the payroll program.

Card columns	Field length	Content
1 – 5	5	Blanks — unused
6 – 20	15	Last name
21 – 22	2	Initials
23 – 30	8	Blank — unused
31 – 33	3	Hours worked to nearest tenth
34 – 40	7	Blank — unused
41 – 44	4	Hourly pay rate
45 – 80	36	Blank — unused

6 and must *always* consume exactly 15 columns; hence the name "ROSE" would be followed by eleven blanks, while, on another card, the name "COTTERMAN" would be followed by six blanks.

A similar argument can be stated for output. What exactly does a paycheck look like? Consider your own personal checks for a moment. Does it make any difference where you write the name of the person or organization to be paid? Does it make any difference where you write the amount of the check? The answer, of course, is yes. For a human being, a simple instruction such as "enter the amount of the check on the line found on the right-hand side of the check about one-third of the way down from the top" would be more than adequate. Using a computer, however, we must be a bit more precise. An example of how a single line of output might be carefully defined for eventual computer use is shown in Fig. 7.9.

Carefully defining the format of each record input to or output from a program is an important part of the planning process.

Positions	Field length	Content
1 – 10	10	Blank
11 – 12	2	Initials
13	1	Blank
14 – 28	15	Last name
29 – 38	10	Blank
39 – 46	8	Net pay
Balance of line		Blank

Fig. 7.9
Output line (check) format for the payroll program.

PROGRAM PLANNING: A SUMMARY

The main objective of program planning is to carefully define a solution to a problem down to the point where it can be implemented on a computer. Ideally, the solution should be so well defined following planning that programming (the subject of Chapter 8) becomes little more than the translation of this solution into "computerese." Planning is a step-by-step process, beginning with a very general view of the problem and gradually introducing detail until a computer solution is clearly defined.

STRUCTURED PROGRAMMING

To avoid confusion, the sample payroll program used in this chapter has been kept simple. Realistically, however, the computation of payroll is much more complex. Federal income tax tables use many more than the two different rates that we used. Many states have an income tax patterned after the federal system. City taxes are also common. Social security tax is computed at a standard rate, but only up to a maximum figure. Add other possible deductions too numerous to mention, and you get an idea of the complexity of the problem.

Each of these deductions taken by itself is not very complex; a good programmer can easily handle them. They become difficult to deal with only when they are combined. In many computer installations, rather than attempt to write a single, huge program, a series of separate modules or subprograms tied together by a control module, the **mainline,** is written. This approach is one of the underlying principles of modular programming, or **structured programming.**

A flowchart depicting a program designed along modular lines is shown in Fig. 7.10. Note that the mainline contains very few actual computations. Instead, the mainline *links* to computational modules; control passes to the module for a computation and then returns to the mainline. By reading only the mainline, you get a pretty good idea of what the program is doing; it's just that all the details have been moved out to the subroutines. In effect, the mainline of a modular, structured program greatly resembles the generalized list of "things to be done" that represented the first step in the planning of our program.

There are a number of distinct advantages to this approach. Obviously, by restricting logic modules to a single function, the program becomes a series of very simple steps rather than a massive "kludge." This makes the program easier to write, easier to correct, and easier to test. How can this be so? Consider that if we were to write a payroll program without modularization, every instruction would have to be in place before testing could begin. If, however, a modular approach were taken, we might start with only the mainline, using very simple "dummy" modules for each of our deductions—income tax at a common ten percent and state tax at a constant one percent, for example. As we completed each module, it could be added to the total package; since modules are introduced one at a time, we would know that if anything goes wrong, the fault must lie with the new module. Thus a program can be tested and corrected a piece at a time, and that's a lot easier than trying to do the job all at once.

Another important advantage to using modular programming is simplified program maintenance. For example, if tax rates were to change, it would be

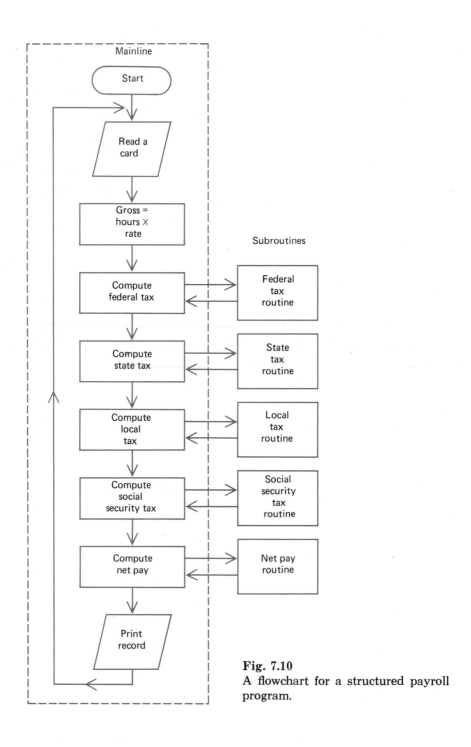

Fig. 7.10
A flowchart for a structured payroll program.

necessary to change the program to accommodate the new rate structure. How often does this happen? Taking state, local, and federal taxes into account, a change in tax rates can probably be expected at least once a year. If a program were written as a series of separate modules, a change in federal income tax rates could be handled by changing only the income tax subroutine, leaving the remainder of the program alone.

There is one more advantage to modular programming. Most real-life computer applications are big and rather complex. Such programs cannot be written by a single individual within a reasonable period of time; hence, teams of programmers are assigned. The modules represent an obvious basis for dividing the work.

Modular, structured programming is being adopted by more and more firms as the advantages of this approach become more widely known. We'll return to this topic in Chapter 8.

THE TOP-DOWN APPROACH

Another idea often attributed to the proponents of structured programming is the *top-down approach* to program planning and design. Essentially, working from the top down means that we begin with a general view of the solution to a problem, gradually introducing details layer by layer. This is the procedure we followed in this chapter. We began with a very general problem definition. Moving on to the planning stage, we first constructed a simple list of the steps needed to solve the problem. Next, each of these steps was defined. Finally, the definitions were converted to a form suitable for beginning the actual writing of a program.

IMPLEMENTATION AND MAINTENANCE

Having covered problem definition and planning, we are now ready to move on to the next two stages in the programming process: implementation and maintenance. *Implementation* is the task of converting the solution to a problem into a form suitable for a computer's use; in other words, by implementation we mean actually writing a program. Implementation involves *coding* (the actual writing of the program), *testing* to make sure the program is correct, *debugging* (the removal of errors), and *documentation*. Program *maintenance* involves a number of activities that take place after the program is completed; this includes making any necessary changes and removing any errors not detected in the testing phase. We will describe these steps in Chapter 8.

KEY WORDS	SUMMARY

KEY WORDS

data format

decision table

documentation

flowchart

general-purpose
computer

instruction

link

loop

mainline

maintenance

modular
programming

problem definition

program

program
implementation

program planning

programmer

software

stored program

structured
programming

subroutine

systems analyst

top-down
approach

SUMMARY

This chapter began with a basic definition of software and then moved into a discussion of the programming process. The four major steps in this process are (1) problem definition, (2) planning, (3) implementation, and (4) maintenance.

Problem definition, as the term implies, involves determining exactly what must be done. It is essential that the programmer know the purpose and intent of a program before beginning to write that program.

The planning stage represents an attempt to fully define a specific solution to the point of implementation on a computer. Starting with a general view of the essential steps in the program, details are added layer by layer until a detailed plan, often in the form of a flowchart and/or several decision tables, is produced. This step-by-step approach is known as top-down program design.

Two planning tools, flowcharts and decision tables, were described in some detail, and a flowchart of the payroll application first discussed in the analogy of Chapter 3 was prepared. We then considered a more realistic example of payroll processing, using this example as a basis for discussing the value of structured, modular programming.

EXERCISES

1. What is software? How does it differ from hardware?

2. What is a program?

3. What is meant by problem definition? Why is it important that this step be completed first?

4. What is the objective of the planning phase of the program development process?

5. What is a flowchart? Develop a flowchart showing all the steps involved in starting an automobile.

6. Why don't all professional programmers use flowcharting as a planning tool? Does the fact that many professional programmers skip flowcharting mean that flowcharting is useless? Why or why not?

7. What is a decision table?

8. Why is it necessary to fully define the format of each and every record to be input to or output by a program?

9. Discuss some of the advantages of the structured, modular approach to large-scale programming.

10. What is meant by a top-down approach to program planning and design?

Software: Programming

Continuing with the discussion of the programming process that we began in Chapter 7, this chapter covers the implementation and maintenance steps. Program implementation refers to the task of actually writing and testing a program. Beginning with an individual instruction, we'll build from a number of basic concepts, through groups of instructions, to the idea of assembler and compiler languages. We will then introduce the concept of program logic by showing how the simple payroll program that we planned in Chapter 7 can be implemented in each of several languages, using this example as a mechanism for describing some of the key characteristics of these languages. The chapter ends with a comparison of the several languages and a discussion of the costs of programming.

THE PROGRAMMING PROCESS

The four basic steps in the programming process are definition, planning, implementation, and maintenance. We have already covered the first two in some detail; we must now turn our attention to program implementation and maintenance.

By program implementation, we mean the task of actually converting a problem solution, existing perhaps in the form of a flowchart, into a computer *program.* This task involves a number of clearly identifiable steps. The first of these is **coding;** in other words, actually writing the instructions. It's a rare programmer who can write error-free code; thus a second step in this process is program **debug,** which simply means removing the errors (or *bugs*) from the program. The final step is program **testing.** In this step, the program is used to process realistic, representative data, and the results are compared with expected results. These three steps overlap a great deal, with errors frequently being detected during testing and removed (debugged) by recoding portions of the program.

Maintenance begins after the program is finished. As an example, return once again to our payroll program. Income tax rates change from year to year, and the new rates must be incorporated into the program; such program changes are part of maintenance. Another common maintenance problem involves the removal of bugs that, for some reason or another, had not been removed during the implementation stage. It's almost impossible to test a program for every possible contingency; even the best of plans will always miss one or two extreme or unusual conditions.

Since maintenance begins after the program has been written, it involves some special problems. The original programmer may well have forgotten the program, hence needing a refresher, or he or she may have left the organization, meaning that someone else must find and fix the bug or make the modification. If a program is to be successfully maintained, it is essential that a very clear and complete description of the logic of the program be available.

A detailed description of a program is normally prepared as part of the implementation stage in a step known as **documentation.** Program documentation consists of program listings, flowcharts, decision tables, narrative descriptions, data formats, and any other information that might help a future maintainer to understand the program. Many organizations have standard formats for program documentation. Frequently the original programmer is required to prepare an acceptable documentation package before a program is officially declared finished. Without good program documentation, maintenance becomes very difficult, if not impossible. Ideally, the programmer should be preparing documentation throughout the implementation stage, integrating this essential task into his or her daily activity.

Programming is the task of actually writing a program; it involves all four steps. A *program* is a series of instructions that tells a computer what to do.

What do these instructions look like, and how do they fit together to form a program?

AN INSTRUCTION

In Chapter 6 we explained how the central processing unit gets an *instruction* from main memory and figures out what is to be done, turning control over to its arithmetic and logical unit for the actual execution of the instruction. Obviously, if a computer is to work in this way, each instruction must contain the information needed to tell the CPU what to do.

A typical instruction (Fig. 8.1) contains two major fields: an **operation code** (or op code) and a series of **operands.** The op code tells the machine *what* to do: add, subtract, multiply, divide, copy, compare, ... The operands tell the computer "what to do it *to*." For example, if we, as programmers, wanted to instruct the computer to add the contents of registers 2 and 3, the parts of our instruction might be the following:

Op code	ADD REGISTERS
Operands	
First	2
Second	3

The op code tells what is to be done (ADD REGISTERS), while the operands tell what memory locations or registers are to participate in the operation (registers 2 and 3 in this example).

Let's look at another situation. What if our application calls for us to copy an employee's name from the image of an input card (in main memory) to the image of an output line that we are in the process of building in main memory? What is it that we want to do? Copy, or MOVE, data from one memory location to another. Let's assume that the individual's name starts

Fig. 8.1
The parts of a typical computer instruction.

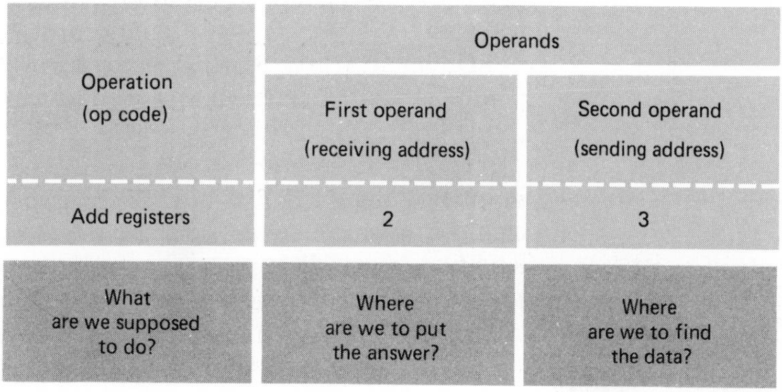

Operation (op code)	Operands	
	First operand (receiving address)	Second operand (sending address)
Add registers	2	3
What are we supposed to do?	Where are we to put the answer?	Where are we to find the data?

at memory location 1000, and we want to make a copy of this field at memory location 2000. Our instruction might contain the following:

Op code	MOVE
Operands	
First	2000
Second	1000

Why is the target address given first? The designers of the computer used in this example decided that data would move from the second operand location to the first operand location. This decision is an arbitrary one, but if you want to use this computer, that's the way it is. Once you understand the rules, the instruction very clearly says that the data found at memory location 1000 is to be moved to memory location 2000. There is no ambiguity. What do we mean by memory location? Remember (see the discussion in Chapter 5) that every character, or byte, or word (depending on the computer) in main memory is assigned a number indicating its relative position away from the first memory location. This relative position is called an *address*. By memory location, we mean address.

A SINGLE LOGICAL OPERATION: ADDING TWO NUMBERS

Now let's see how a series of instructions can be used to perform a simple logical function such as the addition of two numbers.

Before getting into the actual instructions, it might be wise to review briefly a few hardware concepts. Data, once in the computer, is stored in main memory. Data is processed in the central processing unit. In order to add two numbers, it is first necessary to copy (or LOAD) them into registers, the conduits connecting memory and the CPU. Following addition, we will probably want to copy (or STORE) the answer from a register (where the CPU places it) into memory. Thus, a task as simple as the addition of two numbers really involves four distinct instructions (Fig. 8.2): LOAD/LOAD/ADD/STORE. Instructions, like data, are stored in main memory, which is capable of storing only patterns of 1's and 0's; thus an instruction at the machine level *must* exist in binary form.

On an IBM System/360 or System/370 computer, the op code for loading a number from memory into a register is

01011000

in binary; thus, the first of these four instructions (Fig. 8.3) begins with this eight-bit operation code. The second eight bits are subdivided into two parts: The first four indicate the register that is to receive the data (register 3) and the second four bits hold an index register, a field that we are not using in this instruction. The final 16 bits hold the address of the sending field in main

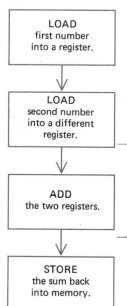

Fig. 8.2
Adding two numbers on a computer.

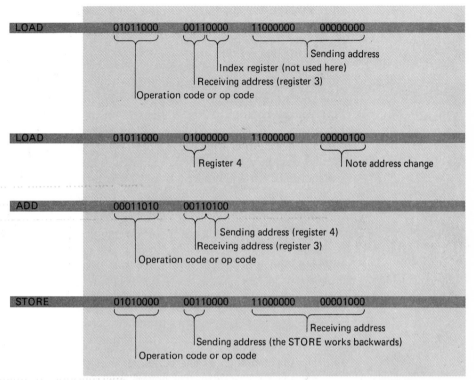

LOAD 01011000 00110000 11000000 00000000
Sending address
Index register (not used here)
Receiving address (register 3)
Operation code or op code

LOAD 01011000 01000000 11000000 00000100
Register 4
Note address change

ADD 00011010 00110100
Sending address (register 4)
Receiving address (register 3)
Operation code or op code

STORE 01010000 00110000 11000000 00001000
Receiving address
Sending address (the STORE works backwards)
Operation code or op code

The complete set of four instructions (*see if you can find the* ADD *instruction*)

0101100000110000110000000000000001011000010000001100000000000010000011010001101000101000000110000110000000000001000

Fig. 8.3
The instruction needed to add
two numbers.

memory (in other words, where, in main memory, the number that is to be loaded into register 3 can be found).

The second instruction (Fig. 8.3) is another load instruction, so its op code is identical to that of the first instruction. Note, however, that the first operand indicates register 4 rather than register 3 and that the address of the second operand field in memory is also different. This is a different instruction; it loads a different number into a different register.

Next is the add instruction, whose op code is

00011010

The first operand (four bits) indicates register 3; the second operand (the next four bits) indicates register 4; this instruction (see Fig. 8.3) adds registers 3 and 4, dropping the sum into register 3 (the receiving address register).

Finally, the answer is copied back into main memory. The op code for a store instruction is

01010000

in binary. The first operand identifies register 3 as the one that is to be stored; the second operand gives the address (main memory) where it is to be stored.

At the bottom of Fig. 8.3 is the string of bits representing these four instructions. In the early days of computing, programs were written at this level. Imagine how difficult it would be to find one incorrect bit in that string. And we're only looking at four instructions. A typical program might consist of thousands of such instructions! Fortunately, programmers don't have to get down to the "bit level" anymore because we have assembler and compiler programs to help simplify the task of writing a program.

AN ASSEMBLER PROGRAM

Coding at the binary level is difficult to put it mildly. Even in the early days of data processing, many programmers took shortcuts. One common approach was to write the program in a shorthand form, as follows:

```
LOAD    3,1000
LOAD    4,1004
ADD     3,4
STORE   3,1008
```

After coding the program at this level, the programmer could logically "desk-check" it before converting the **mnemonic codes** shown above to true binary. The conversion was straightforward; the programmer knew that when "LOAD" was coded, he or she really meant $(01011000)_2$ and that "3" really meant $(0011)_2$. Essentially, the programmer converted the program from his or her own mnemonic (meaning "sounds like") language by replacing each field with its binary equivalent, perhaps using a simple conversion table to aid in this translation process.

Why not write a program to take these mnemonic codes to binary? Logically, the conversion process is fairly simple: Just match the coded operation with an entry in a table and, when an equal code is encountered, substitute. Figure 8.4 shows a series of mnemonic operation codes which are valid on IBM's System/360 and System/370 computers, along with their associated binary op codes. Using the codes in this table, it is relatively easy to convert mnemonic operation codes to their binary equivalents. Can this be done by a program? Of course. All we're dealing with is the yes/no logic available to a computer.

Description	Mnemonic	Binary op code
Add memory to register	A	01011010
Add register to register	AR	00011010
Branch on condition	BC	01000111
Compare memory locations	CLC	11010101
Compare registers	CR	00011001
Divide register by memory	D	01011101
Divide register by register	DR	00011101
Load from memory into register	L	01011000
Move data (copy)	MVC	11010010
Multiply register by memory	M	01011100
Multiply register by register	MR	00011100
Store register in memory	ST	01010000
Subtract memory from register	S	01011011
Subtract register from register	SR	00011011

Fig. 8.4
Some typical mnemonic operation codes
(IBM System/360 and System/370).

To illustrate this idea, let's try converting a mnemonically coded instruction such as

AR   3,4

to a binary instruction. The op code is AR. Refer to Fig. 8.4, and start at the top. Is AR equal to A? Obviously not. Move along to the next op code. Is AR equal to AR? Yes! We've found the correct op code. Our table tells us to use

00011010

as the binary op code for this instruction. What about the operands? Do you remember the computer instructions designed to convert data type? Simply convert the "3" and the "4" to binary, and you have a complete instruction

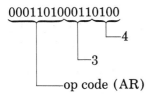

Other instructions can be converted using the same method.

The program that performs this job is called an **assembler.** An assembler program (Fig. 8.5) reads a programmer's **source code,** written in the mnemonic language, and converts it to **object code,** which is another term for machine-level binary code. A programmer writing at this level is said to be programming in an *assembler-level* language.

Note the instructions in Fig. 8.5. We load a value into register 3 by coding

L   3,A

which is much easier to understand than its binary equivalent

0101100000110000110000000000000

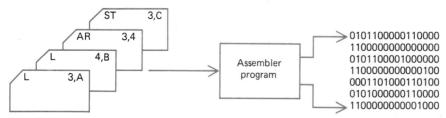

Fig. 8.5
An assembler program.

The responsibility for converting assembler-level instructions into machine-level object code belongs to the assembler program. All the programmer must do is follow the rules.

We do pay a price for this benefit. We are no longer writing programs that can be directly executed on a computer. Programming is now a two-step operation: (1) load the assembler program and convert the source code to object code, and (2) load and execute the object code.

Most computer mainframe manufacturers provide an assembler program with their machine. There are no national standards on assemblers; they vary significantly from manufacturer to manufacturer. However, these languages do share one common feature: The programmer codes one mnemonic instruction for each machine-level instruction.

COMPILERS

Why must the programmer code two loads and a store just to add two numbers? Logically, all he or she wants to do is add; the loads and store are used because that's the way the machine works. Why not assume these steps? That's the basic idea behind a **compiler** (Fig. 8.6).

A scientist or engineer who wishes to add two numbers would probably express the problem as an algebraic equation:

$$C = A + B.$$

Fig. 8.6
A FORTRAN compiler.

The computer may need the two loads and the store, but the programmer logically has no need for anything but the add instruction. Why not let a program take care of inserting these instructions, particularly when we know

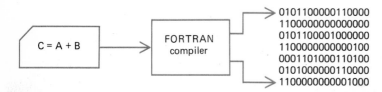

that in almost all cases, the addition of two numbers involves essentially these same four instructions?

FORTRAN, which stands for FORmula TRANslator, was developed in the mid-1950s with exactly this idea in mind. The FORTRAN programmer can express program logic by writing a series of instructions which look very much like algebraic expressions, ignoring the details of exactly how these operations will be implemented on a given computer. These source statements are fed into a FORTRAN compiler, which converts or translates the statements into acceptable machine-level object code (Fig. 8.6).

Note, by comparing Figs. 8.5 and 8.6, that the same object code is produced by both the assembler program and the FORTRAN compiler. This shouldn't surprise you. The instructions that are actually executed by the computer *must* be binary instructions. You must have valid binary instructions in the computer before it can do anything.

Why use an assembler at all when the compiler-level language is obviously so much easier? As we'll see a bit later, the assembler language programmer, who is coding at a one-to-one level (in other words, one assembler instruction yields one machine instruction), can take certain shortcuts, producing somewhat shorter and faster-running programs.

FORTRAN is not the only compiler language in use today. One of the most common languages is COBOL, the COmmon Business Oriented Language. COBOL, as the name implies, is a business language designed to handle business problems. It reads much like standard English, as you can see by looking at the instruction to add two numbers shown in Fig. 8.7. COBOL source statements must be written according to the rules of COBOL. They are submitted to a COBOL compiler, which converts or translates the source code into machine-level object code (see Fig. 8.7), much as before.

Other compilers which we'll just mention at this time include BASIC (Beginners's All-purpose Symbolic Instruction Code), APL (A Programming Language), PL/1 (Programming Language One), RPG (Report Program Generator), ALGOL (ALGOrithmic Language), GPSS (General Purpose System Simulator), and many, many more. If you were to define your own set of rules for producing valid machine-level code, you could design your own personal compiler. More often, however, assemblers and compilers are provided by the computer manufacturer.

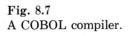

Fig. 8.7
A COBOL compiler.

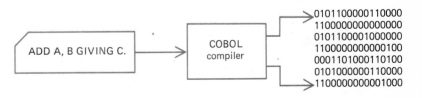

PROGRAM LOGIC

So far, we have considered an individual instruction and a group of instructions needed to support a single logical operation. Let's move ahead one more step and put these pieces together to make a complete program. The program with which we will be working is a payroll program, specifically the version first introduced in the analogy of Chapter 3 and flowcharted in Chapter 7. In this chapter, the flowchart will be converted into actual program code.

Since we will be implementing the payroll program from the plan developed in Chapter 7, the flowchart has been reproduced in this chapter for easy reference (Fig. 8.8). Rather than concentrate on any single language, the program will be written in four of the more common programming languages: BASIC, FORTRAN, COBOL, and assembler. The key characteristics of a language will be discussed first, and then the payroll program will be coded. Read carefully each version of the program, relating the steps to the flowchart shown in Fig. 8.8. The intent of this section is to give you a feel for these languages, and *not* to teach you how to write original programs.

BASIC

We will begin with one of the easier to use languages, BASIC. A BASIC program consists of a series of program *statements*, each one instructing the computer to take a specific action. BASIC statements are written in a form similar to algebraic notation. Rather than being forced to worry about memory locations and addresses, the programmer manipulates *variables* and *constants*.

The key statement supporting all processing steps (represented by a rectangle in a flowchart) is the LET statement. The statement

    10   LET A = B

indicates, for example, that a copy of what is currently stored in the memory allocated to variable B is to be copied into the space allocated to variable A.

Variables are represented by a single letter of the alphabet or by a single letter followed by a digit; valid variables include A, A0, A1, B, C, D, D0, D8, and so on. Constants are represented as simple numbers, with or without a decimal point; the constant π is, for example, 3.1416.

Perhaps the best way to illustrate the LET statement is through an example. The formula for finding the area of a circle is

    Area $= \pi \cdot \text{radius}^2$.

A BASIC LET statement to perform this computation is

    5   LET A = 3.1416 * R ** 2

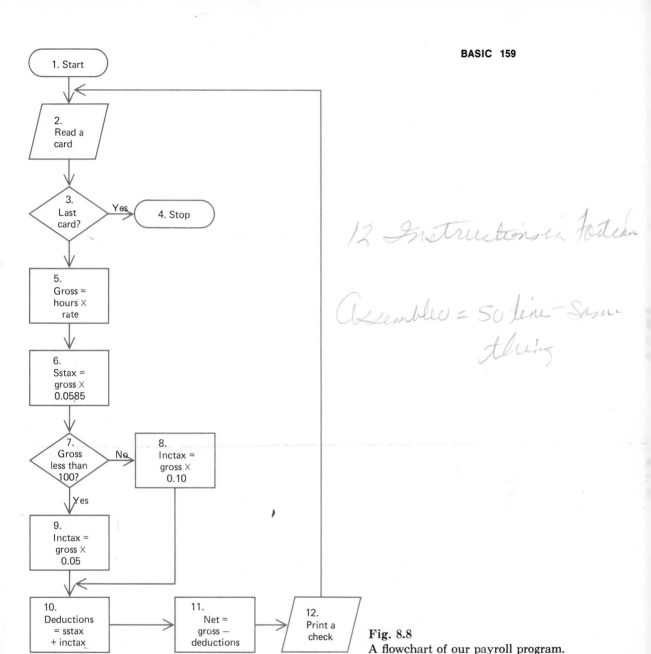

Fig. 8.8
A flowchart of our payroll program.

Note that on the left side of the equal sign only a single variable, A, is found. The LET statement really says, "Do whatever is indicated on the right side of the equal sign, and then copy the answer into the variable indicated on the left side of the equal sign."

To the right of the equal sign is an *expression* defining the arithmetic steps involved in computing, in this case, the area of a circle. The expression consists of variables, constants, and *operators*. Valid operations include addition (a + sign), subtraction (a − sign), multiplication (indicated by *, an asterisk), division (a slash, /) and exponentiation (a double asterisk, **). In some versions of BASIC, an arrow pointing upward (↑) is used to indicate exponentiation.

By combining these components, we get a valid LET statement. The statement

10   LET A = 0.5 * B * H

computes the area of a triangle using the formula

Area = $\frac{1}{2}$ · (base) · (height).

To compute gross pay, we might write

10   LET G = H * R

where H represents the number of hours worked and R represents the pay rate. This statement

10   LET G = H * R

can be interpreted as follows:

1. Multiply whatever is currently found in the variable H by whatever value is currently stored in the variable R.

2. Copy the answer into the variable G.

You will note that these two statements imply that there must be some value already stored in variables H and R *before* this statement can be executed. How do these values get there? Basically (no pun intended!), there are two ways. First, we might write a series of BASIC statements. The statements

10   LET H = 40

15   Let R = 4.25

20   Let G = H * R

would cause the computer first to copy the constant 40 into variable H and then to copy the constant 4.25 into variable R. Now, when the third instruction is executed, both variables on the right side of the equal sign have values, and the multiplication can take place. Do you remember the process of substitution in algebra? We are simply substituting an actual value for a variable before using that variable in a computation.

Rather than coding the actual value of a variable in a LET statement, we can instruct the computer to request the values through an INPUT statement. The statements

10   INPUT H,R

20   LET G = H * R

would first get values for H and R from an input device, store these values in the space allocated to the two variables, and then perform the multiplication, storing the answer in G.

The INPUT statement is coded by typing the word INPUT, followed by a list of variables separated by commas; the computer will expect a value for each and every variable in the list. The statement

5   INPUT X,Y,Z

for example, represents a request for three values from an input device.

What if the programmer wants to see the results of a computation? Output can be obtained by using a PRINT statement. The BASIC program segment

5   INPUT R

10   LET A = 3.1416 * R ** 2

15   PRINT R,A

would get a value for R from an input device, compute the area of a circle of this radius, and display the values of both the radius and the area on an output device (a printer or a terminal). The PRINT statement is coded by typing the word PRINT followed by a list of the variables to be printed, separated once again by commas.

It makes little sense to write a computer program to compute the area of a single circle; pocket calculators can do this job quite easily. What if, however, we needed to compute the areas of dozens of circles? Performing the same steps over and over again would become tedious; we might consider writing a program in this case.

Recall the concept of a *loop* introduced in Chapter 7. By coding the solution to a problem once and then telling the computer to go back and repeat those instructions, we can have the computer go through a program any number of times. If we are to take advantage of looping in BASIC, we must have a method for identifying individual instructions and a special instruction to to tell the computer to go back to the top of the program. In BASIC, individual instructions are identified by assigning a number to each statement; in fact, every instruction *must have* a valid statement number. The instruction that tells the computer to go back to the top of the program is the GO TO. The program

10	INPUT R
20	LET A = 3.1416 * R ** 2
30	PRINT R,A
40	GO TO 10

tells the computer to get a value for R from the input device, compute the area of a circle of this radius, print the radius and the area, and then go back to statement number 10 and repeat the program.

There is only one problem with this little program; how can the computer tell when we have computed the areas of all the circles in which we are interested? It can't; the computer will just keep asking for more input data. We must have a mechanism to tell the computer when we are finished. By using an IF statement, we can have the computer perform a logical test. The program

10	INPUT R
15	IF R < 0 THEN 50
20	LET A = 3.1416 * R ** 2
30	PRINT R,A
40	GO TO 10
50	END

includes an IF test after the INPUT statement. If the value for the radius provided by the programmer is less than (the < symbol) zero, the program *branches* to statement number 50, which says END. The END statement is how the programmer tells the computer to quit. If a value is less than zero, it is negative. Since a negative radius is impossible, this is a good "end-of-data" test.

The IF statement allows the programmer to compare a variable to a constant or to another variable. Possible conditions include equal to (=), less than (<), greater than (>), and any combination of two of these conditions. The general form of the instruction is

IF condition THEN statement number.

If the condition is true (if R is less than zero, in our example), then the branch to the indicated statement takes place; if the condition is not true, no branch takes place and the program continues on to the next instruction in sequence. We'll be using the IF statement for two purposes in our payroll program: first, to test for the end of data, and second, to find the proper income tax rate.

Know diffrence between different languages

Let us now take a look at the payroll program as it might be coded in BASIC (Fig. 8.9). The sample program is very heavily documented with numerous comments to help guide you through the logic. Comments in BASIC are identified by the letters REM following the statement number; the comments are *not* actually part of the program, serving merely to explain.

Fig. 8.9
Payroll in BASIC.

rem- documentations describe program

```
100 REM  * * * * * * * * * * * * * * * * * * * * * * * * * *
105 REM  * THIS PRØGRAM CØMPUTES AND PRINTS AN INDIVIDUAL'S  *
110 REM  * TAKE HØME PAY. WRITTEN BY W.S. DAVIS, 11/1/77.    *
115 REM  * * * * * * * * * * * * * * * * * * * * * * * * * *
120 REM
125 REM  * * * * * * * * * * * * * * * * * * * * * * * * * *
130 REM  * THE PRØGRAM STARTS BY GETTING ØNE INPUT RECØRD. *
135 REM  * THE RECØRD CØNTAINS THE FØLLØWING FIELDS:        *
140 REM  *    NS      EMPLØYEE NAME                          *
145 REM  *    IS      EMPLØYEE INITIALS                      *
150 REM  *    H       HØURS WØRKED TØ NEAREST 1/10           *
155 REM  *    R       HØURLY PAY RATE                        *
160 REM  * * * * * * * * * * * * * * * * * * * * * * * * * *
165          INPUT NS.IS.H,R
170 REM  * * * * * * * * * * * * * * * * * * * * * * * * * *
175 REM  * IF HØURS WØRKED IS NEGATIVE, THIS IS THE LAST RECØRD. *
180 REM  * * * * * * * * * * * * * * * * * * * * * * * * * *
185          IF H < 0 THEN 350
190 REM  * * * * * * * * * * * * * * * * * * * * * * * * * *
195 REM  * WE NØW CØMPUTE GRØSS PAY AND SØCIAL SECURITY TAX. *
200 REM  * VARIABLE G HØLDS GRØSS; VARIABLE S HØLDS TAX.     *
205 REM  * * * * * * * * * * * * * * * * * * * * * * * * * *
210          LET G = H * R
215          LET S = G * 0.0585
220 REM  * * * * * * * * * * * * * * * * * * * * * * * * * *
225 REM  * WE NØW CØMPUTE INCØME TAX. IF GRØSS PAY IS LESS   *
230 REM  * THAN $100, THE TAX RATE IS 5%; ØTHERWISE, THE     *
235 REM  * RATE IS 10%. THE VARIABLE I HØLDS INCØME TAX.     *
240 REM  * * * * * * * * * * * * * * * * * * * * * * * * * *
245          IF G < 100.00 THEN 260
250          LET I = G * 0.10
255          GØ TØ 280
260          LET I = G * 0.05
265 REM  * * * * * * * * * * * * * * * * * * * * * * * * * *
270 REM  * NEXT, WE CØMPUTE TØTAL DEDUCTIØNS, USING THE VARIABLE D.*
275 REM  * * * * * * * * * * * * * * * * * * * * * * * * * *
280          LET D = I + S
285 REM  * * * * * * * * * * * * * * * * * * * * * * * * * *
290 REM  * FINALLY, WE CØMPUTE AND PRINT NET ØR TAKE-HØME    *
295 REM  * PAY, USING THE VARIABLE N.                        *
300 REM  * * * * * * * * * * * * * * * * * * * * * * * * * *
305          LET N = G - D
310          PRINT NS;' , ;IS, 'S';N
315 REM  * * * * * * * * * * * * * * * * * * * * * * * * * *
320 REM  * GØ BACK AND READ ANØTHER CARD.*
325 REM  * * * * * * * * * * * * * * * * *
330          GØ TØ 165
335 REM  * * * * * * * * * * * *
340 REM  * TERMINATE THE PRØGRAM.*
345 REM  * * * * * * * * * * * *
350          END
```

CRT or Read Statement?

fields

Give 140, 145, 150, 155 values

Getting valuable

There are a few points in this program that have not yet been covered. Do you remember the difference between coded and numeric data within a computer? The variables and constants described in the preceding discussion were all numeric. When the programmer wishes to store alphabetic data in coded form, a variable name consisting of a letter of the alphabet followed by a dollar sign ($) is used. In the payroll program (Fig. 8.9), the programmer's name and initials are stored in variables named N$ and I$, respectively. Alphabetic constants are represented by a string of characters between a set of apostrophes; in statement 310, for example, the ',' and '$' tell the computer to actually print a comma and a dollar sign.

Note also the statement numbers: They run from 100 to 350 in increments of five. The programmer may use any numbering scheme desired, so long as the program statements are in sequential order. Leaving gaps is advantageous in that additional statements can be easily inserted into the program if necessary; statement number 112, for example, would be inserted between statements 110 and 115.

Read the program in Fig. 8.9 carefully, comparing it with the flowchart shown in Fig. 8.8. If you follow it step by step, you should have little trouble understanding the logic.

FORTRAN

The first of the compiler languages, FORTRAN was designed to support mathematical and scientific applications. Thus, it is not surprising to find that FORTRAN statements, like BASIC statements, resemble algebraic expressions.

Like BASIC, FORTRAN allows the programmer to write statements by using a combination of variables, constants, and operators. The operators are the same: + for addition, − for subtraction, * for multiplication, / for division, and ** for exponentiation. The variables and constants are, however, a bit different.

The most obvious difference between FORTRAN and BASIC variables lies in the number of characters that the programmer may use in a variable name. A FORTRAN variable consists of from one to six letters or digits, the first of which must be a letter. Valid FORTRAN variable names include X, X1, RADIUS, AREA, and TAX. Given these longer names, the FORTRAN programmer can more clearly indicate the actual operations to be performed; for example,

$$AREA = 3.1416 * RADIUS ** 2$$

Note that the added clarity is for the benefit of the programmer (documentation); it doesn't matter to the computer.

In BASIC, a number is a number. In FORTRAN, there are two different kinds of numbers: *integers* and *real numbers*. An integer, as the name implies, is a whole number without fractional part. A real number has a fractional part. Do you recall the difference between pure binary numbers and floating-point numbers (see Chapter 5)? Integers are pure binary numbers; a FORTRAN real number is stored in floating-point form. The computer is a bit more efficient when using pure binary, but the mathematician or scientist has frequent need for very large and very small values; hence the floating point.

The first letter in the variable name determines the type of variable. Names beginning with I, J, K, L, M, or N identify integer variables; names beginning with any other letter are real. Constants are written as numbers, much as they are in BASIC. A real constant contains a decimal point, and any constant written without a decimal point is assumed to be an integer. In the FORTRAN statement for the area of a circle shown above, the constant 3.1416 is real, while the constant 2 is an integer.

Except for the number of characters in a variable name and the two different types of numeric data, a FORTRAN *assignment statement* looks like a BASIC LET statement without the LET. The area of a triangle might, for example, be computed by:

AREA = 0.5 * BASE * HEIGHT

Gross pay might be found by coding:

GROSS = HOURS * RATE

As in BASIC, every variable appearing in an assignment statement must have been assigned an actual value before the statement is executed. Thus we could code:

HOURS = 40.0

RATE = 4.25

GROSS = HOURS * RATE

and use the combination of these three statements to compute gross pay for an individual who worked 40 hours and who earns $4.25 per hour.

Once again, the data can be input from an input device rather than initialized through an assignment statement. In FORTRAN, the basic input statement is the READ statement. The general form of a READ statement is:

READ (n,m) list

where "n" is the number of an input device, "m" is the number of a FORMAT statement, and "list" is a list of the variables to be read. The statement

READ (5,15) X,Y,Z

gets values for variables X, Y, and Z from device number 5.

The READ statement requires further explanation. First let's consider the device number. In BASIC, the programmer is usually working through a terminal; thus it is reasonable to assume that INPUT means, "Get some data from the terminal." FORTRAN is a bit more general, being designed for use with terminals, punched cards, or any other input or output medium. Rather than have a series of different statements for each of the different possible input or output devices, FORTRAN uses the device number to designate a specific piece of I/O equipment. The actual numbers used can vary with the computer installation, but "1" or "5" are commonly used to designate a card reader, and "2" or "6" are typical printer device numbers.

The second number enclosed within the parentheses of the READ statement identifies the associated FORMAT statement. What is a FORMAT statement? It is a column-by-column description of the input or output record. For example, let's say that during the planning stage we determined that an input card to a program designed to compute the area of a triangle would contain the following data fields:

Columns	Contents
1–5	base, correct to two decimal places
6	blank
7–11	height, correct to two decimal places

A FORMAT statement to describe this card is:

FORMAT (F5.2,X,F5.2)

Within the parentheses, the card format is described column by column. The first field, F5.2, indicates that the first variable is real (the F), is five digits long (the 5), and that two digits are to be assumed to the right of the decimal point (the 2). The next field, X, indicates that one column on the card is to be skipped before encountering the next value, which is another five-digit real number with two digits to the right of the decimal point.

The function of the FORMAT statement is to describe, column by column or position by position, the format of an input or output record. An F-type format item, as we've seen, is used to designate a real variable. An X-type format is used to indicate blank or unused spaces. Integer values are designated by an I-type format item; for example,

FORMAT (I6)

indicates a six-digit integer value.

By combining a READ statement and a FORMAT statement, we have a very flexible set of I/O instructions. The instructions

READ (5,10) HOURS, RATE

10   FORMAT (F3.1,F4.2)

will result in values for both hours and rate being read from device number 5 (the card reader); instruction number 10 describes the precise format of the input card.

Output also uses a combination of statements—the WRITE and FORMAT statements. The WRITE statement looks very much like a READ statement:

WRITE (n,m) list

The "n," "m," and "list" have the same meaning as before.

Note the use of statement numbers in FORTRAN. A statement number need be assigned only when the programmer wishes to refer to a statement. Since FORMAT statements are always referenced by a READ or a WRITE, a FORMAT statement always has a number. The only other time that a statement number is needed is when the programmer wishes to branch to a given point in a program.

FORTRAN also has an IF statement; its general form is:

IF (condition) expression

An example of the FORTRAN IF is shown in the following program:

```
1       READ (5,11) RADIUS

11      FORMAT (F5.2)
        IF (RADIUS .LT.0) GO TO 99
        AREA = 3.1416 * RADIUS ** 2
        WRITE (6,12) RADIUS, AREA

12      FORMAT (X,F6.2,3X,F9.4)
        GO TO 1

99      STOP
        END
```

The IF statement tests the condition enclosed within the parentheses. If the condition is true (if RADIUS is less than zero, in our example), then the expression following the parentheses is executed; in this case, the computer would branch to statement number 99, and stop. If the condition is not true, the computer continues on to the next statement in sequence.

One of FORTRAN's main advantages is the tremendous collection of scientific and mathematical subroutines that are available in support of this language. FORTRAN has been around for quite some time, and many common scientific problems have already been solved. Rather than "re-invent the wheel," the FORTRAN programmer can simply attach several subprograms to his or her own program, linking to these routines through a CALL statement.

```
C
C     * * * * * * * * * * * * * * * * * *
C     * THIS PROGRAM COMPUTES AND PRINTS   *
C     * AN INDIVIDUAL'S TAKE-HOME PAY.     *
C     *    WRITTEN BY: W.S. DAVIS          *
C     *                NOVEMBER 1, 1977.   *
C     * * * * * * * * * * * * * * * * * *
C
      DIMENSION NAME(4)
      REAL NET,INCOME
C
C     * * * * * * * * * * * * * * * * * * * * * * * *
C     * THE PROGRAM STARTS BY READING THE NAME, INITIALS,  *
C     * HOURS WORKED, AND PAY RATE. THE FORMAT STATEMENT,  *
C     * NUMBER 10, DESCRIBES THE FIRST TWO AS ALPHABETIC   *
C     * FIELDS. HOURS WORKED IS A DECIMAL NUMBER WITH ONE  *
C     * POSITION TO THE RIGHT OF THE DECIMAL POINT. THE    *
C     * PAY RATE IS A FOUR DIGIT NUMBER WITH TWO           *
C     * POSITIONS TO THE RIGHT OF THE DECIMAL POINT.       *
C     * * * * * * * * * * * * * * * * * * * * * * * *
C
    1 READ (5,10,END=99) NAME,INIT,HOURS,RATE
   10 FORMAT (4X,4A4,A2,8X,F3.1,7X,F4.2)
C
C     * * * * * * * * * * * * * * * * * * * *
C     * COMPUTE GROSS PAY AND SOCIAL SECURITY TAX.*
C     * * * * * * * * * * * * * * * * * * * *
C
      GROSS = HOURS * RATE
      SSTAX = GROSS * 0.0585
C
C     * * * * * * * * * * * * * * * * * * *
C     * FIND TAX RATE AND COMPUTE INCOME TAX. *
C     * * * * * * * * * * * * * * * * * * *
C
      IF (GROSS .GE. 100.00) GO TO 25
         INCOME = GROSS * 0.05
         GO TO 30
   25    INCOME = GROSS * 0.10
C
C     * * * * * * * * * * * * * * * * * * *
C     * COMPUTE TOTAL DEDUCTIONS AND NET PAY. *
C     * * * * * * * * * * * * * * * * * * *
C
   30 DEDUCT = INCOME + SSTAX
      NET = GROSS - DEDUCT
C
C     * * * * * * * * * * * * * * * * * * * * *
C     * PRINT A PAY CHECK AND GO BACK TO THE TOP. *
C     * * * * * * * * * * * * * * * * * * * * *
C
      WRITE (6,50) INIT,NAME,NET
   50 FORMAT (10X,A2,4A4,10X,'$',F7.2)

      GO TO 1
   99 STOP
      END
```

Fig. 8.10
Payroll in FORTRAN.

The FORTRAN version of our payroll program is shown in Fig. 8.10. Comments are identified by the letter "C" in the first position of the line. Like the BASIC REM statements, these comments are not actually part of the program; they serve instead as an aid to documentation.

FORTRAN is designed for mathematical operations; thus the language is not very good at handling non-numeric data. The DIMENSION statement near the top of the program (Fig. 8.10) sets aside four fullwords (16 bytes in total) to hold the employee's name. The name is read in statement number 1 under control of an A-type format item. The REAL statement identifies the variables NET and INCOME as being real variables; had we not so indicated, the FORTRAN compiler would have assumed that these variables were integer (they begin with one of the letters between I and N), and simply ignored the decimal point. Both net pay and income tax have fractional parts.

The READ statement (number 1) contains an extra field:

1   READ (5,10,END = 99) NAME,INIT,HOURS,RATE

It is standard procedure in many computer centers to place a special end-of-data marker at the end of a deck of data cards; this marker might take the form of a special card with a number of unusual characters (/*, or /&, or //, or EOD) punched in the first several columns. By coding END=99, the programmer is telling the system that when this special card is encountered, the computer is to branch to instruction number 99.

Once again, read the program (Fig. 8.10) carefully, comparing it step by step to the flowchart shown in Fig. 8.8.

COBOL *most widely used*

The COmmon Business Oriented Language (COBOL) was designed, as the name implies, with business data processing in mind. Business computer applications usually involve the processing of files; payroll, inventory, accounts receivable, and accounts payable are typical examples. Such applications tend to be long-lived; in other words, once a payroll program is written, it will probably be used for years. Therefore, the maintainability of these programs is of great concern. This places a premium on documentation, and COBOL is designed to be almost self-documenting.

Every COBOL program is divided into four divisions. The first of these, the IDENTIFICATION DIVISION, contains such information as the name of the program, the name of the programmer, and remarks concerning the function of the program. The primary purpose of the IDENTIFICATION DIVISION is documentation.

The second division of a COBOL program is called the ENVIRONMENT DIVISION. Here, the environment in which the program is designed to run is clearly spelled out, including such information as the make and model of the computer for which the program was written and a list of all the I/O devices used by the program. In addition to providing important documentation, the ENVIRONMENT DIVISION houses the code needed to logically link the program to its I/O devices.

Following the ENVIRONMENT DIVISION is the DATA DIVISION, where the format of each input and output record is defined. Consider, for example, the input card to the "area of a triangle" program described on p. 166. In COBOL's DATA DIVISION, the format of this record might be defined as follows:

```
01   INPUT-CARD.
     02  BASE        PICTURE IS 999V99.
     02  FILLER      PICTURE IS X.
     02  HEIGHT      PICTURE IS 999V99.
     02  FILLER      PICTURE IS X(69).
```

These PICTURE clauses have been used to describe, column by column, the entire 80 columns of the card. The variable called BASE is a five-digit number with two digits to the right of the decimal point; the 9 identifies a numeric character, and V designates the implied location of the decimal point. The second item of data, called FILLER, has as its PICTURE a single X, which designates a non-numeric field. Next comes the HEIGHT, another numeric field. The final field, holding the unused remainder of the card, is also called FILLER. FILLER is a special name that can be used to identify any and all data fields not actually referenced by a program.

In the DATA DIVISION's FILE SECTION is listed the format of each input and output record. In the WORKING-STORAGE SECTION, work space to hold intermediate results, column headers, and other work areas can be defined.

All variables must be defined in the DATA DIVISION. A COBOL variable name can consist of from 1 to 31 characters; letters, digits, and the dash (—) character are valid. Why such large names? COBOL, remember, was designed with the idea of self-documentation in mind. Since the programmer has 31 characters to work with, names like SOCIAL-SECURITY-NUMBER can be used. This very clearly indicates the content of a field, and therefore aids documentation.

The final division of a COBOL program is the PROCEDURE DIVISION. It is here that the actual logic of the program is coded. The designers of COBOL wanted to create a language that is easy to read; thus a COBOL statement is much like an English-language sentence, complete with a verb and a period at the end. COBOL arithmetic is performed by statements such as the following:

```
ADD A,B GIVING C.
```

```
MULTIPLY HOURS-WORKED BY PAY-RATE
         GIVING GROSS-PAY.
```

In BASIC and FORTRAN, input and output statements are designed to read values of individual variables; in COBOL, we read and write entire records. The statement

```
READ CARD-FILE, AT END GO TO END-OF-JOB.
```

reads a single record of the card file; both the file and the record must be defined in the DATA DIVISION. The AT END clause attached to the READ statement is a test for the special end-of-data card. When this card is encountered, the program will branch to location END-OF-JOB.

Output is controlled through the WRITE statement, as in:

WRITE PAY-CHECK AFTER ADVANCING 2 LINES.

PAY-CHECK is the name of a record defined in the DATA DIVISION. The AFTER ADVANCING clause controls printers spacing; in this case, the printer is to skip two lines and then print.

The IF statement in COBOL is a bit different. Its general form is as follows:

IF condition expression1 OTHERWISE expression2.

This is known as IF ... THEN ... ELSE ... logic. First, the condition is tested. If the condition is true, then the first expression is executed. If the condition is false, then the second expression is executed.

IF ... THEN ... ELSE ... logic is extremely useful. Consider, for example, the following statement:

IF GROSS-PAY IS LESS THAN 100.00
MULTIPLY GROSS-PAY BY 0.05
GIVING INCOME-TAX.

OTHERWISE MULTIPLY GROSS-PAY BY 0.10
GIVING INCOME-TAX.

What if the condition is true (GROSS-PAY is less than 100.00)? Then IN-COME-TAX will be computed at a five-percent rate. What if the condition is not true? INCOME-TAX will be computed at a ten-percent rate. An easy way to remember how IF ... THEN ... ELSE logic works is to remember the following sentence:

IF condition-is-true THEN do-this;
OTHERWISE do-this-instead.

Business computer applications are typically large, involving many different programmers. Under such conditions, structured modular programming makes a great deal of sense. Typically, the necessary linkage between the program's mainline and its subroutines is achieved by using the PERFORM statement. In its most basic form, the PERFORM statement causes the computer to branch to a subroutine and then to come back to the mainline following execution of the subroutine statements. The instruction

PERFORM INCOME-TAX-ROUTINE.

might well imply that the programmer has instructed the computer to link to an income tax computation routine, compute the tax, and return.

Fig. 8.11
Payroll in COBOL.

```
IDENTIFICATION DIVISION.
  PROGRAM-ID. SALARY.
  AUTHOR. DAVIS.
  REMARKS. THIS PROGRAM COMPUTES AND PRINTS AN INDIVIDUAL'S
           TAKE-HOME PAY.


ENVIRONMENT DIVISION.
  CONFIGURATION SECTION.
    SOURCE-COMPUTER. IBM-370-168.
    OBJECT-COMPUTER. IBM-370-168.
  INPUT-OUTPUT SECTION.
  FILE-CONTROL.
    SELECT CARD-FILE ASSIGN TO UT-S-SYSIN.
    SELECT PRINT-FILE ASSIGN TO UT-S-SYSOUT.




DATA DIVISION.
  FILE SECTION.
  FD CARD-FILE, LABEL RECORD IS OMITTED,
                BLOCK CONTAINS 0 RECORDS,
                DATA RECORD IS TIME-CARD.
  01 TIME-CARD.
     02 FILLER         PICTURE X(5).
     02 EMPLOYEE-NAME  PICTURE X(15).
     02 INITIALS       PICTURE X(2).
     02 FILLER         PICTURE X(8).
     02 HOURS-WORKED   PICTURE 99V9.
*    HOURS WORKED ARE TO THE NEAREST 1/10 HOUR.
     02 FILLER         PICTURE X(7).
     02 PAY-RATE       PICTURE 99V99.
     02 FILLER         PICTURE X(36).


  FD PRINT-FILE, LABEL RECORD IS OMITTED,
                 BLOCK CONTAINS 10 RECORDS,
                 DATA RECORD IS PAY-CHECK.
  01 PAY-CHECK.
     02 FILLER         PICTURE X(10).
     02 INITIALS       PICTURE X(2).
     02 FILLER         PICTURE X(1).
     02 EMPLOYEE-NAME  PICTURE X(15).
     02 FILLER         PICTURE X(10).
     02 NET-PAY        PICTURE $$999.99.
     02 FILLER         PICTURE X(36).


  WORKING-STORAGE SECTION.
     77 SOCIAL-SECURITY-TAX PICTURE 9999V99.
     77 INCOME-TAX          PICTURE 9999V99.
     77 DEDUCTIONS          PICTURE 9999V99.
     77 GROSS-PAY           PICTURE 9999V99.
```

A COBOL version of our payroll program is shown in Fig. 8.11. There are a few points not mentioned in the above discussion. Look first at the DATA DIVISION. The line beginning "FD   CARD-FILE" contains a reference to a LABEL RECORD, and the next line holds a BLOCK CONTAINS clause. The first of these clauses identifies the type of label used on this file; the second identifies the blocking factor. A detailed explanation of the meaning of these two clauses is beyond the scope of this book; don't get hung up on them, as they are not really crucial to an understanding of the program.

Moving along to the PROCEDURE DIVISION, the first and next-to-last instructions are, respectively, two OPEN statements and two CLOSE statements. The purpose of these statements is, at the beginning of the program, to make sure that the I/O devices required are ready to be used and,

```
      PROCEDURE DIVISION.
           OPEN INPUT CARD-FILE.
           OPEN OUTPUT PRINT-FILE.


       PAY-COMPUTATIONS.
           READ CARD-FILE, AT END GO TO END-OF-JOB.
           MULTIPLY HOURS-WORKED BY PAY-RATE GIVING GROSS-PAY.


   *     *** * * * * * * * * * * * * * * * * * * * * * ***
   *     *** THE CURRENT SOCIAL SECURITY TAX RATE IS 5.85%.***
   *     *** * * * * * * * * * * * * * * * * * * * * * ***
           MULTIPLY GROSS-PAY BY 0.0585 GIVING SOCIAL-SECURITY-TAX.


   *     *** * * * * * * * * * * * * * * * * * * * * * * ***
   *     *** FOR THIS EXAMPLE, WE'LL USE A VERY SIMPLE INCOME TAX **
   *     *** RATE SCHEDULE: IF GROSS PAY IS LESS THAN $100.00,    ***
   *     *** THE TAX RATE IS 5%; OTHERWISE, THE RATE IS 10%.      ***
   *     *** * * * * * * * * * * * * * * * * * * * * * * ***
           IF GROSS-PAY IS LESS THAN 100.00
                   MULTIPLY GROSS-PAY BY 0.05 GIVING INCOME-TAX;
               OTHERWISE MULTIPLY GROSS-PAY BY 0.10 GIVING INCOME-TAX.


           ADD INCOME-TAX , SOCIAL-SECURITY-TAX GIVING DEDUCTIONS.
           MOVE SPACES TO PAY-CHECK.
           SUBTRACT DEDUCTIONS FROM GROSS-PAY GIVING NET-PAY.
           MOVE CORRESPONDING TIME-CARD TO PAY-CHECK.
           WRITE PAY-CHECK AFTER ADVANCING 2 LINES.
           GO TO PAY-COMPUTATIONS.


       END-OF-JOB.
           CLOSE CARD-FILE.
           CLOSE PRINT-FILE.
           STOP RUN.
```

at the end of the program, to return the devices to the system so they can be used by another program.

Finally, we must consider the target of a GO TO statement. In BASIC and FORTRAN, statements are assigned numbers, and a branch instruction simply refers to the number of the target statement. In COBOL, a *paragraph name* is assigned to each branch point; examples in the program shown in Fig. 8.11 are PAY-COMPUTATIONS and END-OF-JOB.

Read the program in Fig. 8.11 carefully, comparing the PROCEDURE DIVISION step by step with the flowchart shown in Fig. 8.8.

ASSEMBLER LANGUAGE

Unlike the compiler languages that we have discussed, there is no standard, nationally accepted assembler language. Every mainframe manufacturer provides an assembler-level language uniquely suited to a specific computer model. Any assembler language would do for the following discussion; we have chosen IBM System/360–System/370 assembler simply because it is the most commonly used assembler language.

The assembler language programmer codes one mnemonic instruction for each machine-level instruction that the computer is to execute. The programmer is also responsible for laying out the actual memory locations that will hold input and output records and intermediate results.

An assembler language version of the payroll program is shown in Fig. 8.12. Comments in assembler language are indicated by the presence of an asterisk (*) in the first column of the source statement; as was the case with the other languages, comments have been heavily used to promote readability.

The program begins with a number of strange-looking instructions which, according to the comments, handle standard register conventions. Essentially, these instructions take care of locating the program in memory, providing a "base" or starting point for addressing. In COBOL, these functions were a hidden part of the IDENTIFICATION DIVISION.

At the bottom of Fig. 8.12(a) are two *data control blocks*. These blocks handle communications with the I/O devices. In COBOL, the SELECT and ASSIGN statements in the ENVIRONMENT DIVISION (see Fig. 8.11) took care of this job. In both FORTRAN and BASIC, this responsibility was assumed by the compiler, which merely added the proper code to the object module.

Part (b) of Fig. 8.12 contains the instructions which lay out memory locations to hold the input card, output record, and work areas; find the equivalents in the COBOL program (Fig. 8.11).

The actual logic of the program is shown in part (c) of the figure. Using the comments as a guide, read the program, relating the logic back to the flow-

```
*       * * * * * * * * * * * * * * * *
*       * THIS PROGRAM COMPUTES AND PRINTS    *
*       * AN INDIVIDUAL'S TAKE-HOME PAY.      *
*       *    WRITTEN BY: W.S. DAVIS           *
*       *             NOVEMBER 1, 1977        *
*       * * * * * * * * * * * * * * * *
*
```

```
BEGIN    STM    14,12,12(13)
*        * * * * * * * * * * * * * * *
*        * STANDARD REGISTER CONVENTIONS.*
*        * THE BASE REGISTER IS 12.        *
*        * * * * * * * * * * * * * * * *
         BALR   12,0
         USING  *,12
         ST     13,SAVEAREA+4
         LA     13,SAVEAREA
         B      GO
```

```
SAVEAREA DC     18F'0'
```

```
*        * * * * * * * * * * * * * * * *
*        * DATA CONTROL BLOCK FOR CARD INPUT.*
*        * * * * * * * * * * * * * * * *
*
CARDIN   DCB    DDNAME=SYSIN,DSORG=PS,MACRF=GM,EODAD=QUIT
```

```
*        * * * * * * * * * * * * * * * * *
*        * DATA CONTROL BLOCK FOR PRINTER OUTPUT.*
*        * * * * * * * * * * * * * * * *
*
PRINTER  DCB    DDNAME=SYSOUT,DSORG=PS,MACRF=PM
```

Fig. 8.12(a)
Payroll in assembler language.

```
*          * * * * * * * * * *
*          * INPUT CARD FORMAT.*
*          * * * * * * * * * *
*
TIMECARD DS      0CL80
         DS      CL5
NAME     DS      CL15         EMPLOYEE NAME
INITIALS DS      CL2          EMPLOYEE INITIALS
         DS      CL8
HOURS    DS      CL3          HOURS WORKED
         DS      CL7
RATF     DS      CL4          HOURLY PAY RATE
         DS      CL36


*
*          * * * * * * * * * * *
*          * FORMAT FOR PAY CHECKS.*
*          * * * * * * * * * * *
*
CHECK    DS      0CL132
         DC      CL10' '
INIT     DS      CL2          EMPLOYEE INITIALS
         DC      C' '
EMPLOYEE DS      CL15         EMPLOYEE NAME
         DC      CL10' '
NETPAY   DS      CL9          NET PAY OR TAKE HOME PAY
         DC      CL85' '


*
*          * * * * * * * * * * * * * * * * * *
*          * WORK SPACE FOR INTERMEDIATE RESULTS.*
*          * * * * * * * * * * * * * * * * * *
*
WORK     DS      D            WORK AREA
GROSS    DS      CL8          STORAGE AREA FOR GROSS PAY
INCOME   DS      CL8          STORAGE AREA FOR INCOME TAX
SSTAX    DS      CL8          STORAGE FOR SOCIAL SECURITY TAX
EDIT     DC      X'5B202120202042020'   EDIT FIELD FOR NET PAY
```

Fig. 8.12(b)
Payroll in assembler language.

```
GO        OPEN   (CARDIN,INPUT)
          OPEN   (PRINTER,OUTPUT)


START     GET    CARDIN,TIMECARD
*


*         * * * * * * * * * *
*         * COMPUTE GROSS PAY.*
*         * * * * * * * * * *
*
          PACK   WORK,HOURS
          CVB    4,WORK      GET HOURS INTO REGISTER 4 IN BINARY FORM
          PACK   WORK,RATE
          CVB    5,WORK      GET RATE INTO REGISTER 5 IN BINARY FORM.
          MR     4,4         MULTIPLY HOURS BY RATE TO GET GROSS.
          D      4,=F'10'    ALIGN TO TWO DECIMAL PLACES.
*                            REGISTER 5 NOW CONTAINS GROSS PAY.
          CVD    5,WORK
          UNPK   GROSS,WORK    STORE GROSS PAY IN MEMORY.
          OI     GROSS+7,X'F0'


*
*         * * * * * * * * * * * * * * *
*         * COMPUTE SOCIAL SECURITY TAX.*
*         * * * * * * * * * * * * * * *
*
          LR     7,5         COPY GROSS INTO REGISTER 7.
          M      6,=F'585'   COMPUTE TAX TO SIX PLACES.
          D      6,=F'10000' ALIGN TO TWO PLACES.
          CVD    7,WORK
          UNPK   SSTAX,WORK  STORE SS TAX IN MEMORY.
          OI     SSTAX+7,X'F0'
```

Fig. 8.12(c)
Payroll in assembler language.

```
*
*          * * * * * * * * * * * * * * * * * * * *
*          * DETERMINE RATE AND COMPUTE INCOME TAX.*
*          * * * * * * * * * * * * * * * * * * * *
*
           C      5,=F'10000'    COMPARE GROSS TO $100.00.
           BNL    TEN                      IF NOT LOW, SKIP TO LABEL 'TEN'
           L      8,=F'5'        IF LOW, RATE IS 5%.
           B      COMPUTE
TEN        L      8,=F'10'       IF GROSS IS GREATER THAN OR
*                                EQUAL TO $100, RATE IS 10%.
COMPUTE    LR     9,5            COPY GROSS INTO REGISTER 9.
           MR     8,8            INCOME TAX TO FOUR PLACES.
           D      8,=F'100'      ALIGN TO TWO PLACES.
           CVD    9,WORK
           UNPK   INCOME,WORK    STORE INCOME TAX IN MEMORY.
           OI     INCOME+7,X'F0'


*
*          * * * * * * * * * * * * * * *
*          * COMPUTE TOTAL DEDUCTIONS. *
*          * * * * * * * * * * * * * * *
*
           AR     7,9            ADD INCOME TAX AND SS TAX.


*
*          * * * * * * * * * *
*          * COMPUTE NET PAY.*
*          * * * * * * * * * *
*
           SR     5,7            SUBTRACT DEDUCTIONS FROM GROSS PAY.
```

Fig. 8.12(d)
Payroll in assembler language.

```
*
*           * * * * * * * * * * * * * * * *
*           * MOVE NAME INTO OUTPUT LINE. *
*           * * * * * * * * * * * * * * * *
*
            MVC    EMPLOYEE,NAME
            MVC    INIT,INITIALS
*
*           * * * * * * * * * * * * * * * * * * *
*           * EDIT NET PAY FOR PRINTING.         *
*           * INCLUDE DECIMAL POINT AND DOLLAR SIGN.*
*           * * * * * * * * * * * * * * * * * * *
*
            MVC    NETPAY,EDIT
            CVD    5,WORK
            ED     NETPAY,WORK+4   GET NET PAY INTO OUTPUT LINE.
            MVI    NETPAY,X'40'    BLANK OUT FIRST DOLLAR SIGN.


*
*           * * * * * * * * * * * * * * * * * * * * * *
*           * PRINT A PAY CHECK AND GO BACK FOR MORE DATA.*
*           * * * * * * * * * * * * * * * * * * * * * *
*
            PUT    PRINTER,CHECK
            B      START
```

Fig. 8.12(e)
Payroll in assembler language.

```
*           * * * * * * * * * * * * * * * * * * * * *
*           * FOLLOWING END OF DATA, TERMINATE PROGRAM. *
*           * * * * * * * * * * * * * * * * * * * * *
*
QUIT        CLOSE  CARDIN
            CLOSE  PRINTER
            L      13,SAVEAREA+4       STANDARD REGISTER CONVENTIONS.
            LM     14,12,12(13)
            BR     14
            END
                   =F'10'
                   =F'585'
                   =F'10000'
                   =F'5'
                   =F'100'
```

Fig. 8.12(f)
Payroll in assembler language.

chart shown in Fig. 8.8. A few things will look a bit different from the other programs. The PACK instruction, for example, converts the EBCDIC (coded) data coming from the input card into packed-decimal (numeric) form. The CVB (Convert to Binary) instruction converts the packed-decimal number into pure binary form and places it in a register. These functions are, of course, performed in every program, but are transparent to the compiler programmer.

Further along in Fig. 8.12(c) is a divide instruction. Without going into unnecessary details, we note that the division operation is needed to ensure decimal point alignment. You'll find similar instructions throughout the program each time that a decimal point alignment is needed.

The "tax table" in part (d) of the figure looks a bit unusual in that we seem to be comparing gross pay to "10000." Recall that the computer cannot handle a decimal point. How would you write $100.00 without the decimal point?

Near the bottom of Fig. 8.12(d) are two instructions which illustrate the advantages of assembler language. Because the registers in which we computed gross pay, social security tax, and income tax have been carefully selected, the computation of total deductions and net pay can be done by simply adding the registers containing the two deductions and then subtracting this total from the register containing gross pay. In any compiler-level language, such foresight would have been impossible; intermediate results would have been stored in main memory and reloaded into registers before computations could be performed.

Figure 8.12(e) shows how an output line is set up in memory and subsequently sent to the printer before the program branches back to find another card and repeat the cycle. The ED (edit) instruction places an actual decimal point and a dollar sign in the result. Near the bottom of part (e) are the instructions which terminate the program after the last card has been encountered.

Once again, read the program carefully, relating the logic to the flowchart shown in Fig. 8.8; the program comments will serve as a guide. Note that, in an assembler-level program, the instructions which actually convert data from coded to numeric form and the instructions which actually move data between memory and registers must be coded. These instructions were present in the object-level or machine-level code produced by the various compilers, but they did not have to be coded by the programmer. This is one way in which a compiler simplifies the programmer's task.

THE COMPILATION PROCESS

At numerous points in this chapter, we have mentioned the use of a compiler. Let's now pull all these ideas together and make sure that you understand the entire process.

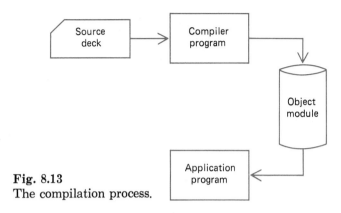

Fig. 8.13
The compilation process.

A programmer codes a program in a *source language*, such as assembler, COBOL, FORTRAN, or BASIC. No computer is capable of executing these source statements directly. Before program execution is possible, the source program must be translated into machine-level code, in other words, binary instructions. A program at the machine level is called an **object module.** A flowchart of this translation process is shown in Fig. 8.13.

A compiler is a program designed to translate source statements, written according to a specific set of rules, into object code. It is important to remember that different compilers are different: A COBOL compiler *cannot* produce valid object code from a FORTRAN source deck. There are COBOL compilers, FORTRAN compilers, BASIC compilers, assemblers, and many other compilers, one for each different source language. Source statements must be written according to the rules imposed by the compiler being used; otherwise, valid machine-level statements will *not* be produced.

The compilation process (Fig. 8.13) is a two-step process. First the proper compiler (or assembler) program must be loaded into memory. The compiler reads the source statements and translates them into object-module form; usually, the object module is written to a high-speed storage medium such as magnetic tape or disk, although punched-card output (an *object deck*) is sometimes used. Later, this object module is itself loaded into the computer's main memory, and the *application program* begins to execute.

Incidentally, not all object modules can be directly loaded and executed. Programmers often make use of subprograms and other prewritten modules that must be added to the object code by another special program called a linkage editor. We'll discuss this program in more detail in Chapter 10.

THE PROGRAMMING PROCESS: A SUMMARY

A program is a set of instructions written to guide a computer through some process. Programs do not simply "spring into being"; they must be planned and written by people. The process of creating a program involves at least four distinct steps: problem definition, planning, implementation, and mainte-nance.

Problem definition is the process of determining exactly what must be done. It is very important that the programmer know exactly what must be done before attempting to implement a solution. A perfect program designed to solve the wrong problem is useless.

The planning stage involves moving from this definition to the point at which a specific solution can be implemented on a computer. Ideally, planning should be done in steps, with a general overview of a solution gradually being developed into a specific, detailed plan. Useful planning aids include flowcharts and decision tables.

During implementation, the solution to a problem is converted into an actual computer program. The implementation stage involves four clearly recognizable steps: coding, debugging, testing, and documentation. Often these four steps overlap.

The final stage in the program development process is maintenance, which begins after the program is finished. Program maintenance involves such tasks as making necessary program changes and removing any bugs not detected during the implementation stage.

THE COST OF A PROGRAM

Every program, to a greater or lesser degree, involves all the steps listed above. A cost can be associated with each step. Problem definition and planning take time, and the time of a professional programmer or systems analyst costs money. Coding and program maintenance also consume the time of the programmer. In addition to labor costs, these last two steps also involve computer expenses, since programs must be debugged and tested on the machine. The total cost of developing and implementing a program is the sum of all these costs.

Program implementation and maintenance are active tasks. The programmer sitting at his or her desk writing code is obviously doing something. The programmer debugging at the computer console is obviously busy. Problem definition and planning, on the other hand, are passive in nature, involving considerable thought. Is the programmer who is sitting at a desk and thinking really accomplishing something, or merely "goofing off"?

Many people equate physical activity with progress; thus it is not surprising to find programmers (and managers) who want to skip the definition and planning stages and "begin doing something." This is a mistake. If, during problem planning, an error in the problem definition is encountered, all that is lost is a few hours of labor time. But what if this same error were not detected until a major portion of the program had been coded? Then not only planning time, but also programmer coding time and computer expenses are lost. The further into the programming process we get, the more costly it becomes. The earlier an error can be detected, the less time and money is wasted in solving the wrong problem. Good, careful planning helps to ensure that errors will be detected early in the process.

Another, perhaps even greater, danger inherent in immediately beginning active program implementation without adequate planning is the natural reluctance of people to admit failure, scrap a program, and start over. The chances are that once a program is written it will not be discarded. The result is a program which processes information that no one wants or needs. Such programs represent a complete waste of human and computer resources. The cause is usually poor planning.

Documentation is another thankless task. It's part of the program implementation stage, but the documentation really isn't needed until the maintenance step. Programmers tend to want to take shortcuts on documentation, preferring to move on to another program. To the original programmer concerned with implementing a program, documentation may seem like a waste of time, but without proper documentation, maintenance is very difficult, if not impossible. All too often, the poorly documented program will not be maintained at all, but simply rewritten. The cost of starting over is much higher than the cost of documentation.

LANGUAGE SELECTION

What's the best language? At the risk of sounding like a politician during an election year, we would have to say that it depends. COBOL is a file-processing language designed to be most efficient on such typical business applications as updating ledgers, producing accounting reports, handling payroll, and keeping track of inventory. BASIC and FORTRAN, on the other hand, were designed with scientific and mathematical problems in mind.

The typical COBOL application is *I/O bound*, involving the reading of an input record, the execution of a few simple computations, and the writing of a record of output during each program cycle. Mathematical applications are more apt to be *compute bound*, performing many computations on a relatively small amount of data. COBOL stores data within the computer in coded form, ready for I/O, converting to numeric form only when an arithmetic instruction is encountered. FORTRAN converts data to numeric form as soon as it enters the computer; thus all data is in a form suitable for computation. Given these facts, it's not surprising to find that COBOL is very good at handling I/O-bound business programs but is quite inefficient when working with mathematical computations. FORTRAN, on the other hand, is excellent on computer-bound programs, but leaves something to be desired when it comes to handling I/O.

The assembler language programmer can control the type of data on a variable-by-variable basis, converting from coded to numeric form (or vice versa) only when absolutely necessary. The direct, one-assembler-instruction-for-one-machine-instruction mode of this language allows for other efficiencies as well. A good assembler language programmer can write a program that is smaller (in terms of memory size) and that executes more quickly than a similar program written in any compiler-level language. But an assembler-level program takes longer to code, is tougher to document and to debug, and is more difficult to maintain than a compiler language program.

So, what is the best language? Again, it depends on the application. For an I/O-bound business program, COBOL may well be the choice. The scientist wishing to analyze some data will probably select FORTRAN, BASIC, or a similar computation language. Some programs are designed to remain in main memory at all times; others (a production-control data-collection program, for example) may be used thousands of times per day. The "on-the-computer" execution costs of such a program may well outweigh the additional coding, debugging, documentation, and maintenance costs of assembler language, making assembler the best choice. Language selection is a function of the particular application. A language should be selected with the idea of keeping *total* program cost (including execution costs) to a minimum.

In spite of assembler's greater "on-the-computer" efficiency, the trend today is very strongly toward the use of compiler languages. There are several reasons for this. Using a compiler means lower programming costs but higher execution costs. Using assembler means higher programming costs but lower execution costs. As the cost of computer hardware drops, the cost of executing a program also drops. Programming is a labor-intensive activity, and the cost of human labor has risen dramatically over the past several years. Since the total cost of a program is the sum of program development and program execution costs, by reducing program development costs, the use of a compiler language tends to reduce total program costs, hence the trend toward compiler languages.

One final comment about assembler. An assembler language is unique to a given model of computer. Compiler languages are not; with relatively minor modifications, a FORTRAN or COBOL program can be made to run on almost any computer. By using assembler, the programmer is virtually committing his or her organization to a single supplier.

SUMMARY

In this chapter, we covered the last two steps in the program development process: implementation and maintenance. The chapter began at the bottom, with a single instruction. The parts of a typical instruction, operation or op codes and operands, were discussed.

Next, we moved up to a series of instructions designed to perform a single logical function—adding two numbers. The instructions were first shown at a binary, machine level and subsequently, in assembler, FORTRAN, and COBOL; in this way, the basic idea of compilation was introduced.

Moving up one level, we showed the logic of a typical application, payroll, and proceeded to write this program in BASIC, FORTRAN, COBOL, and assembler language. The idea of compilation, with source statements being converted to an object module, was then covered.

The chapter ended with a review of the steps involved in the programming process: definition, planning, implementation, and maintenance. The cost of each of these factors was pointed out, and the total cost of a program defined. Language selection was then discussed from the viewpoint of trying to minimize total program cost.

In Chapter 9, we will show how a simple program is actually executed on a computer.

EXERCISES

1. Why is it necessary to have instructions to convert data from coded form to numeric form and back again?

2. Explain the two major parts of a typical instruction: the op code and the operands.

3. Why must machine-level programs be in binary form?

4. What advantages are derived from using the mnemonic codes of an assembler language rather than coding at the machine level?

5. What is a compiler?

6. What is a source program or source module?

7. What is an object module?

8. It has been said that once a problem has been fully defined, the task of programming it becomes one of simply translating the solution into a computer programming language. Do you agree? Why or why not?

9. Relate the several steps involved in the programming process to the total cost of a program.

10. Each programming language has its strengths and weaknesses. Compare an assembler and a compiler language, using the steps in the programming process as a guide. Explain why COBOL is better than FORTRAN on programs with a great deal of I/O.

KEY WORDS

application program	IF ... THEN ... ELSE ... logic
assembler language	instruction
BASIC	machine-level program
bug	maintenance
COBOL	mnemonic code
coded data	numeric data
coding	object code
comments	object module
compiler	program
constant	program testing
debug	source code
documentation	statement
execution	variable
FORTRAN	

The Computer System

In Chapter 3, the basic functions of a computer were introduced through an analogy. Since that time we have discussed in some detail input and output, memory, the central processing unit, channels, control units, and programs. In this chapter, we will actually load a program into main memory and follow the operation of the entire computer system as the program is executed step by step.

THE HARDWARE SYSTEM

The hardware system on which we'll be running this example is shown in Fig. 9.1. The computer contains the usual components: a CPU, registers, and main memory. A single multiplexer channel serves to connect the input and output devices to the computer. Our input device is a card reader; as you can see (Fig. 9.1), there is a control unit between the input device and the channel. The output device is a printer; again, a control unit serves as an interface.

Fig. 9.1
The hardware system used in our example.

Poised at the input side of the card reader, we find a number of cards, each containing one record of data (Fig. 9.1). Associated with the printer is the paper that will eventually be used to display the results of our example.

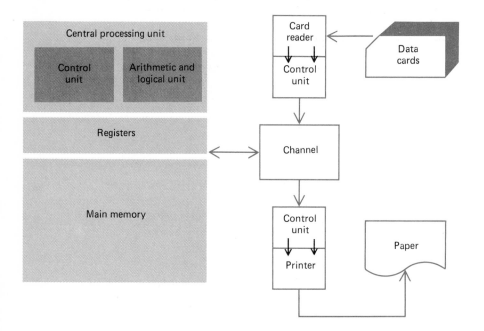

THE PROGRAM

The hardware system shown in Fig. 9.1 is nothing more than a collection of very expensive office furniture without a program to provide control. For this example, we'll be using a program that is designed to compute an average.

Let's discuss this problem a bit before we try to code it. If you were asked to compute an average—let's say, the average grade on an exam taken by all the members of your class—how would you go about solving this problem?

You might

1. Write all the numbers in a column.

2. Add the column of figures.

3. Count the number of figures in the column.

4. Divide the sum by the count giving the average.

Now we'll make the job a bit easier by giving you a few machines to aid in making these computations—specifically, a pocket calculator and a mechanical counter. Given this equipment, you might view the problem in a different way. First of all, a pocket calculator doesn't add a column of figures in the same way that you would. When using such a device, you enter the first number, add the second to it, add the third to the sum of the first two, and so on. A calculator adds two numbers at a time. This process is sometimes called accumulation.

The availability of a mechanical counter might change your view of the counting process too. Why go back after adding or accumulating the numbers and count them? Why not simply add 1 to the counter as each number is added to the accumulator? Your method of computing an average with electronic and mechanical aids might include the following steps:

1. Set the accumulator to 0.

2. Set the counter to 0.

3. Add a number to the accumulator.

4. Add 1 to the counter.

5. If there are any more numbers to be added, return to step 3; otherwise, continue on to step 6.

6. Divide the accumulator by the counter to get the average.

What we have here is a program. It's a series of logical steps which, if followed to the letter, will always result in the computation of an arithmetic average. Although the form of the program is not quite suitable for the computer, it is, logically speaking, a program.

As we begin to analyze this program from a computer's point of view, we must keep in mind the fact that a computer is not a human being. We are capable of exercising independent judgment; a computer is not. The most obvious point of difference, at least in this problem, lies in how people and computers discover that there is no more data to be processed. Consider the fifth step in the set of directions listed above: "If there are any more numbers to be added, return to step 3; otherwise, continue on to step 6." How do we determine that there are no more numbers? "Simple," says the human, "there aren't any more numbers!" We'd be insulted if someone were to imply that such a simple exercise in logic was beyond us.

This kind of logic *is* beyond the computer. A computer is, as you may remember, restricted to simple yes/no logic. What if a line in our column of figures were to be left blank? What if the numbers were continued on a second or third page? What if a few extra numbers were written along the margins? These situations would pose no problem for us, but such variables involve more than simple yes/no logic.

A computer gets its data from some input device—in our example, a card reader. We cannot allow the computer to assume that if there is no more data in the card reader, there is no more data to be processed. What if the operator hasn't yet loaded some of the cards? What if the card reader breaks down? What if another program is in the card reader immediately following ours? A human being would be capable of dealing with these problems, but a computer needs a very complex program to deal with every possible contingency.

All this discussion amounts to a very lengthy way of stating something very simple: A computer must be provided with an unambiguous mechanism for determining when there is no more data to be processed. With card input, this objective is usually achieved by using a special "last card." The letters "EOD" might be punched in the first three columns of this last card; the first two columns might contain the characters "/*" or "/&"; or the card might start with "$EOJ". Any combination of unique characters will do equally well. Given this end-of-data marker, the process of identifying the end of data becomes a simple yes/no decision, as follows:

1. Read a card.

2. Are the first two columns equal to /*?

3. If yes, it is the last card.

4. If no, it is not the last card.

With these ideas in mind, look at the flowchart shown in Fig. 9.2. We start by setting the accumulator and the counter to zero, just as we did before. Next, following the arrows, we read a card. Next comes the test for the last card; this test must follow the read instruction because we don't want to add "/*" or "EOD" as data to the accumulator. If it's not the last card, we add the number from the card to the accumulator, add 1 to the counter, and go back to read another card. If it is the last card, we divide the count into the accumulated sum to find the average, print the average, and terminate the program. If a person were computing the average, it would be reasonable to assume a recording of the answer. With a computer, however, we can assume

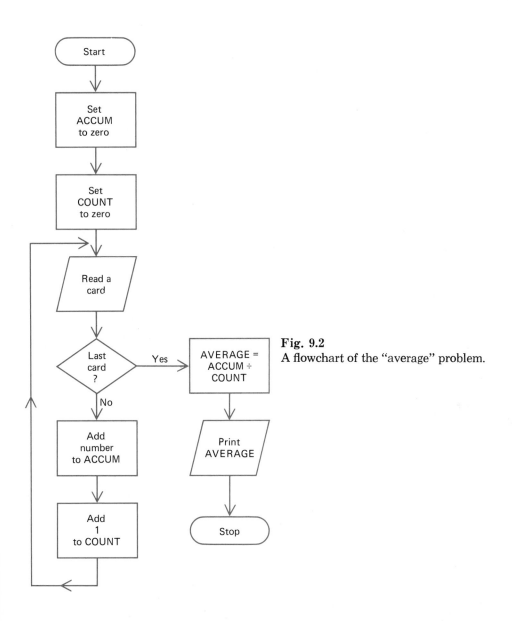

Fig. 9.2
A flowchart of the "average" problem.

nothing; thus the print instruction. And yes it *is* necessary to tell the computer to stop if there is nothing more to be done.

Now that the problem has been very carefully defined and thoroughly planned at a computer's level, we can begin to code it. Figures 9.3, 9.4, 9.5, and 9.6 show how the program might be coded in BASIC, FORTRAN, CO-BOL, and assembler, respectively. Compare each of these source programs to the flowchart shown in Fig. 9.2; you should be able to follow the logic easily.

```
100    LET A = 0
110    LET C = 0
120    INPUT X
130    IF X < 0 THEN 180
140    REM  THE < SIGN MEANS "LESS THAN"
150    LET A = A + X
160    LET C = C + 1
170    GØ TØ 120
180     M = A / C
190     PRINT ' AVERAGE = ';M
200    END
```

Fig. 9.3
The "average" program in BASIC.

```
       ACCUM = 0.0
       CØUNT = 0.0
30     READ (5,35) X
35     FØRMAT (F5.2)
       IF (X .LT. 0) GØ TØ 80
       ACCUM = ACCUM + X
       CØUNT = CØUNT + 1
       GØ TØ 30
80     AVG = ACCUM / CØUNT
       WRITE (6,95) AVG
95     FØRMAT (' AVERAGE = ',F6.2)
       STØP
       END
```

Fig. 9.4
The "average" program in FORTRAN.

Fig. 9.5
The "average" program in
COBOL.

```
IDENTIFICATION DIVISION.
  PROGRAM-ID. AVERAGE.
  AUTHOR. DAVIS.
  REMARKS. THIS PROGRAM READS A SERIES OF DATA CAR
           COUNTS THE CARDS, ACCUMULATES THE VALUE
           PUNCHED ONE TO EACH CARD, AND, AFTER TH
           LAST CARD HAS BEEN READ, COMPUTES THE
           AVERAGE VALUE.


ENVIRONMENT DIVISION.
  CONFIGURATION SECTION.
    SOURCE-COMPUTER. IBM-370-168.
    OBJECT-COMPUTER. IBM-370-168.
  INPUT-OUTPUT SECTION.
    FILE-CONTROL.
    SELECT CARD-FILE ASSIGN TO UT-S-SYSIN.
    SELECT PRINT-FILE ASSIGN TO UT-S-SYSOUT.
```

Figure 9.5 (continued)

```
DATA DIVISION.
 FILE SECTION.
  FD CARD-FILE, LABEL RECORD IS OMITTED,
                BLOCK CONTAINS 0 RECORDS,
                DATA RECORD IS INPUT-CARD.
   01 INPUT-CARD.
    02 NUMBR   PICTURE 999V99.
    02 FILLER  PICTURE X(75).


   FD PRINT-FILE, LABEL RECORD IS OMITTED,
                  BLOCK CONTAINS 10 RECORDS,
                  DATA RECORD IS OUTPUT-LINE.
   01 OUTPUT-LINE.
    02 FILLER   PICTURE X(14).
    02 MESSAGE  PICTURE X(10).
    02 AVERAGE  PICTURE 999.9999.
    02 FILLER   PICTURE X(100).


 WORKING-STORAGE SECTION.
  77 ACCUMULATOR PICTURE 99999V99 VALUE IS 0,
                 USAGE COMPUTATIONAL SYNCHRONIZED.
  77 COUNT       PICTURE 999 VALUE IS 0,
                 USAGE COMPUTATIONAL SYNCHRONIZED.




 PROCEDURE DIVISION.
       OPEN INPUT CARD-FILE.
       OPEN OUTPUT PRINT-FILE.


 LOOP.
       READ CARD-FILE, AT END GO TO QUIT.
       ADD NUMBR TO ACCUMULATOR.
       ADD 1 TO COUNT.
       GO TO LOOP.


 QUIT.
       MOVE SPACES TO OUTPUT-LINE.
       MOVE 'AVERAGE =' TO MESSAGE.
       DIVIDE ACCUMULATOR BY COUNT GIVING AVERAGE.
       WRITE OUTPUT-LINE AFTER ADVANCING 3 LINES.


       CLOSE CARD-FILE.
       CLOSE PRINT-FILE.
       STOP RUN.
```

Fig. 9.6
The "average"
program in as-
sembler language.

```
AVERAGE   STM    14,12,12(13)
          BALR   10,0
          USING  *,10
          ST     13,SAVE+4
          LA     13,SAVE
          B      BEGIN


CARDIN    DCB    DSORG=PS,MACRF=GM,DDNAME=SYSIN,EODAD=QUIT


PRINTER   DCB    DSORG=PS,MACRF=PM,DDNAME=SYSOUT


WORK      DS     D
SAVE      DS     18F


CARD      DS     0CL80
X         DS     CL5
          DS     CL75


LINE      DS     0CL132
          DC     CL14' '
          DC     CL10'AVERAGE ='
MEAN      DC     XL9'402021204B20202020'
          DC     CL99' '
```

The next step is assembly or compilation—our source program must be converted to an object module in the binary form required by the computer. The resulting program might contain instructions to perform the following functions:

1. Set ACCUMULATOR register to zero.

2. Set COUNT register to zero.

3. Read a card.

4. Test for last card.

Figure 9.6
(continued)

```
BEGIN      OPEN   (CARDIN,INPUT)
           OPEN   (PRINTER,OUTPUT)


           SR     3,3                ACCUMULATOR
           SR     7,7                COUNTER


LOOP       GET    CARDIN,CARD
           PACK   WORK,X
           CVB    9,WORK
           AR     3,9                ADD NUMBER TO ACCUMULATOR
           A      7,=F'1'            ADD 1 TO COUNTER
           B      LOOP


QUIT       M      2,=F'100'          ALIGN TO 4 DECIMAL POSITIONS
           DR     2,7                DIVIDE ACCUMULATOR BY COUNT
           CVD    3,WORK
           ED     MEAN,WORK+4
           PUT    PRINTER,LINE


           CLOSE  CARDIN
           CLOSE  PRINTER
           L      13,SAVE+4
           LM     14,12,12(13)
           SR     15,15
           BR     14
           END
                  =F'1'
                  =F'100'
```

5. If it is the last card, skip to instruction 10.

6. Convert the number of the card to numeric form.

7. Add this number to the ACCUMULATOR register.

8. Add 1 to the COUNT register.

9. Go back to instruction 3.

10. Divide ACCUMULATOR register by COUNT register.

11. Convert answer to coded form.

12. Move (copy) answer to output line.

13. Send a line of output to the printer.

14. Terminate the program.

We will use these "functional-level" instructions, rather than binary instructions, to discuss the execution of this program on the computer.

THE COMPUTER SYSTEM WITH A STORED PROGRAM

Fig. 9.7
The computer system with a stored program.

Figure 9.1 showed that our computer hardware system consists of a CPU, registers, main memory, a channel, control units, and I/O devices. Input and output data can also be seen. Figure 9.7 shows the completed system, with the addition of a stored program to provide control.

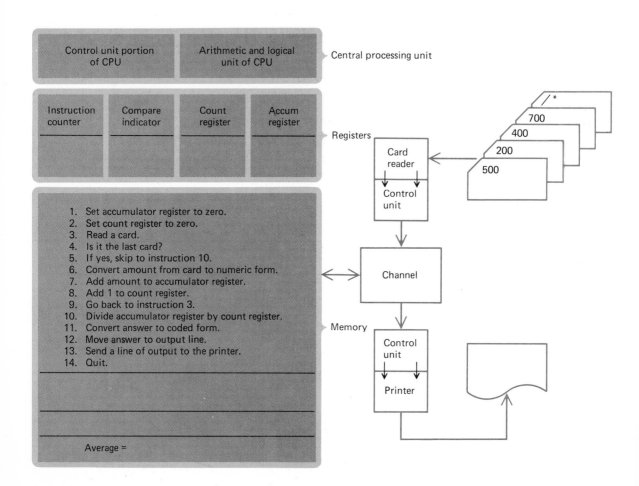

Let's take a close look at the computer itself (Fig. 9.7). Beginning at the top, we see the control unit and the arithmetic and logical unit. Moving down, we notice the registers. On the right, you'll see two registers identified as the ACCUMULATOR register and the COUNT register; their functions should be obvious. On the left are two registers called, respectively the INSTRUCTION COUNTER and the COMPARISON INDICATOR. These two registers are special, system registers which perform control and coordination functions, such as showing the CPU where to find the "next" instruction and allowing the program to test for the results of a comparison. As with most registers, these special registers can be found in many different places: in core, in the CPU, or in between, depending on the computer manufacturer. In this example, we'll show them in their logical position between the two primary pieces of the computer.

Main memory is shown at the bottom of Fig. 9.7. As you can see, our program is loaded into memory. Below the program are three other regions of memory. The first of these three regions will hold the contents of an input card as it is read into memory. The second area is a work space to hold intermediate results. The bottom region holds the contents of a single line of output data; we'll be building this line in memory prior to transferring its contents to the printer.

The balance of the system looks pretty much like the hardware system of Fig. 9.1. Note, however, the cards waiting to be read through the card reader. They contain data; our program will compute the average of the numbers punched into the first four cards. The last card has the characters "/*" in the first two columns; this is our "last card" or end-of-data marker.

GETTING STARTED

In Chapter 6, we discussed how the central processing unit (actually the control unit of the CPU), enters core and "fetches" one instruction, decodes this instruction, and passes control on to the arithmetic and logical unit, which executes the instruction. Following this cycle, control is returned to the control unit of the CPU, which repeats the same steps with the "next" instruction. How does the control unit know where to find the "next" instruction?

The answer is simple: The address (remember addressing—main memory locations are numbered sequentially) of the "next" instruction can be found in the special register called the INSTRUCTION COUNTER. As our program begins, the address of the first instruction is found in this special register (Fig. 9.8). How did it get there? The starting point may have come from an operating system, the program that preceded this program into memory, the operator, or any of a number of other sources. We will discuss this topic in detail in Part IV; at this point, it is important to remember that the

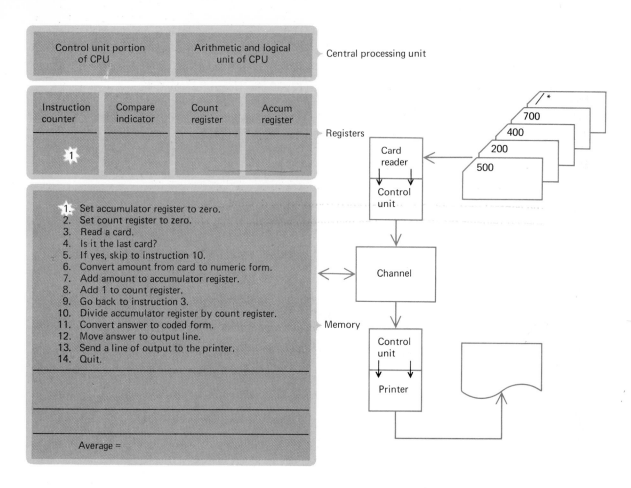

Fig. 9.8
As we begin our example, the INSTRUCTION COUNTER points to the first instruction.

INSTRUCTION COUNTER, as we begin this example, points to the first instruction in our program.

PROGRAM EXECUTION

Now we are ready to start. As we proceed through this example, we'll be following the computer through a series of memory cycles, watching the control unit of the CPU fetch and decode an instruction before turning control over to the arithmetic and logical unit. The instruction phase of this cycle, I-time, involves transferring an instruction from memory into the CPU. Although this occurs very quickly, there is still enough time for the CPU to "bump up" the instruction counter to point to the next instruction while waiting for the current instruction to arrive. This is how the control unit of the CPU knows where to find the next instruction.

Now, on to our example. To avoid possible confusion with the program instruction numbers, we'll use letters to identify the computer's cycles. Read carefully, being sure that you understand exactly what happens on each instruction before moving on to the next one. *Refer to the figures.*

STEP A   The control unit of the CPU, noting that the INSTRUCTION COUNTER points to the first instruction of the program, fetches this instruction from memory. While waiting for the instruction to arrive, the control unit adds 1 to the INSTRUCTION COUNTER, giving this special register the value "2." The instruction is decoded and control is given to the arithmetic and logical unit which, following orders, sets the ACCUMULATOR register to zero (Fig. 9.9). Control now goes back to the control unit of the CPU.

Fig. 9.9
After execution of instruction number 3.

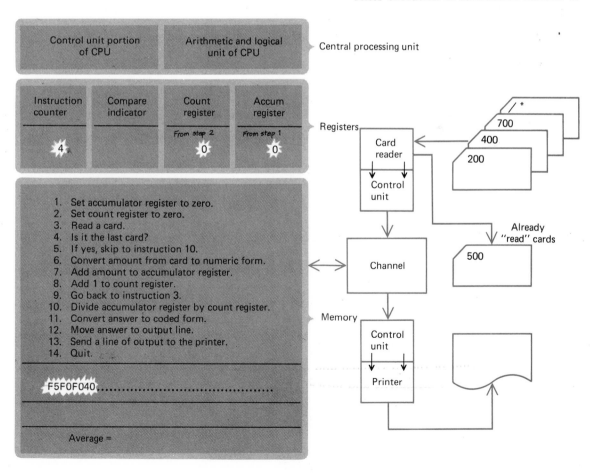

STEP B The control unit of the CPU, noting that the INSTRUCTION
COUNTER points to instruction 2, fetches this instruction from
memory. While waiting for the instruction to arrive, the control unit
adds 1 to the INSTRUCTION COUNTER, giving this special register
the value "3." The instruction is decoded, and control is given to the
arithmetic and logical unit which, following orders, sets the COUNT
register to zero (Fig. 9.9). Control now goes back to the control unit of
the CPU.

STEP C The control unit of the CPU, noting that the INSTRUCTION
COUNTER points to instruction 3, fetches this instruction from
memory. While waiting for the instruction to arrive, the control unit
adds 1 to the INSTRUCTION COUNTER, giving this special register
the value "4." The instruction is decoded and control is given to the
arithmetic and logical unit which, following orders, starts an input
operation (Fig. 9.9). (If this description is beginning to sound repetitive, good; that's the point. The computer functions by repeating this
same cycle over and over again. We'll cut down a bit on the verbiage
of each cycle from this point on.)

Let's stop for a minute and examine the process so far. An input operation has just been started. This operation involves physically reading a card,
converting the card code to an internal computer code through the control
unit, and physically transferring the data through the channel and into the
computer's memory. All this happens outside the computer, and it takes time.
The responsibility for actually controlling the I/O operation belongs to the
channel, not to the CPU. While the transfer of data is taking place, the computer waits, since it cannot possibly execute its next instruction without the
data. When the channel is finished transferring data, it signals the CPU with
an electronic message called an **interrupt.** The interrupt tells the computer
to begin another cycle.

Before resuming the processing of our program, let's take a look at the
contents of certain key components in our computer at the conclusion of the
input operation. The INSTRUCTION COUNTER points to instruction 4
(Fig. 9.9). The COUNT register and the ACCUMULATOR register both
contain zero (0) as a result of the first two instructions. The contents of the
first card have been transferred into main memory, where they reside in
coded form (using a hexadecimal shorthand for the EBCDIC code, F5 is the
digit 5, FO is the digit 0, FO is another 0, and 40 is a blank). We are now
ready to continue.

STEP D The control unit of the CPU fetches instruction 4 and, while waiting,
bumps the INSTRUCTION COUNTER up to 5. The instruction is
decoded and control is passed to the arithmetic and logical unit. Here,
the first two columns of the card are compared to the standard end-of-
data marker, "/ *." Since they are not equal, the COMPARISON
INDICATOR is set to zero (Fig. 9.10).

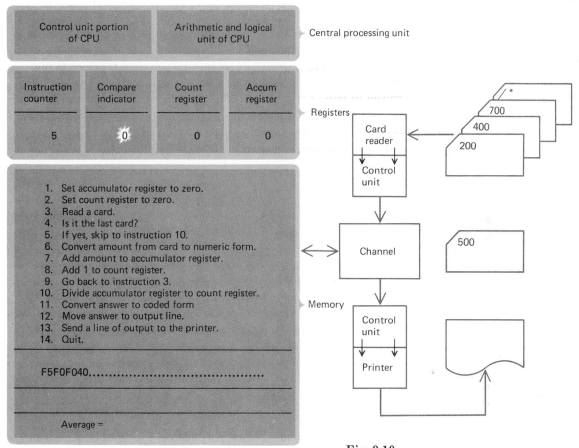

Fig. 9.10
After execution of instruction number 4.

Let's stop again and examine the COMPARISON INDICATOR. It is through this field that the computer's ability to perform yes/no logic is implemented. The fourth instruction ("Is it the last card?") is in the form of a question that has only two possible answers: yes or no. If the answer is yes, the COMPARISON INDICATOR is set to 1; if the answer is no, the COMPARISON INDICATOR is set to 0. In a subsequent instruction, the COMPARISON INDICATOR can be tested and action taken depending on the results of the test. The fifth instruction (Fig. 9.10) might, for example, be reworded as: "If the COMPARISON INDICATOR is 1, skip to instruction 10."

Since the COMPARISON INDICATOR is currently 0 (Fig. 9.10), we do *not* skip to instruction 10.

Now we'll resume the processing of our program.

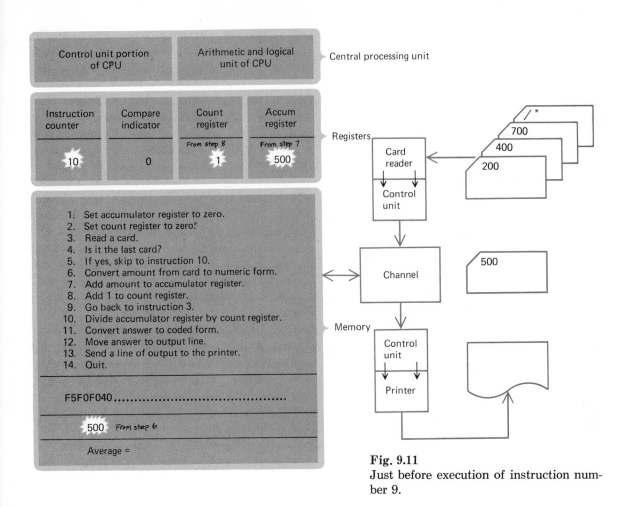

Fig. 9.11
Just before execution of instruction number 9.

STEP E   The control unit fetches the fifth instruction, bumping the INSTRUCTION COUNTER up to 6. Since, during the execution phase of the cycle, the COMPARISON INDICATOR is seen to be set to 0, no action is taken.

STEP F   The control unit fetches the sixth instruction, bumping the INSTRUCTION COUNTER up to 7. The instruction is decoded and passed along to the arithmetic and logical unit which, as ordered, converts the number to numeric form. The results of this conversion can be seen in Fig. 9.11. Following execution of the instruction, control is returned to the control unit of the CPU.

STEP G   The control unit fetches the seventh instruction, bumping the INSTRUCTION COUNTER up to 8. The instruction is decoded and passed along to the arithmetic and logical unit, which adds the number to the accumulator. (Again, refer to Fig. 9.11.)

STEP H   The control unit fetches the eighth instruction, bumping the INSTRUCTION COUNTER up to 9. The instruction is docoded and passed along to the arithmetic and logical unit, which adds 1 to the counter (Fig. 9.11).

STEP I   The control unit fetches the ninth instruction, bumping the INSTRUC-TION COUNTER up to 10. Note that the INSTRUCTION COUNTER does point to the tenth instruction (Fig. 9.11). If the system were to do "what comes naturally" next, it would divide the count (currently 1) into the accumulator (currently 500), print the result, and quit. This of course, is not what we want to do. Fortunately, the ninth instruction is an "unconditional" branch; in effect, it says, "No matter what the COMPARISON INDICATOR holds, go back to instruction 3." During the execution phase of this machine cycle, the arithmetic and logical unit replaces the current contents of the IN-STRUCTION COUNTER with the operand of this instruction—3 (Fig. 9.12).

Fig. 9.12
Following execution of instruction number 9.

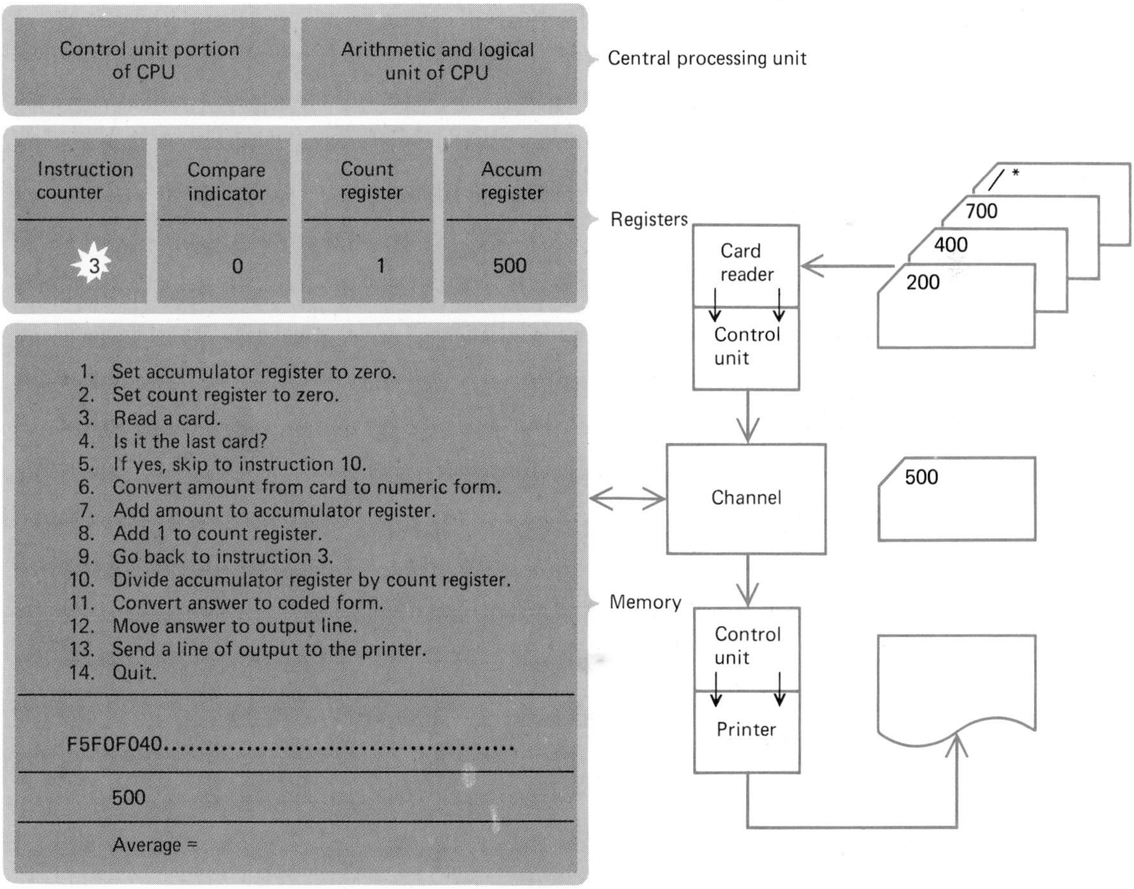

Control unit portion of CPU	Arithmetic and logical unit of CPU

Central processing unit

Instruction counter	Compare indicator	Count register	Accum register
3	0	1	500

Registers

Card reader

Control unit

700
400
200

1. Set accumulator register to zero.
2. Set count register to zero.
3. Read a card.
4. Is it the last card?
5. If yes, skip to instruction 10.
6. Convert amount from card to numeric form.
7. Add amount to accumulator register.
8. Add 1 to count register.
9. Go back to instruction 3.
10. Divide accumulator register by count register.
11. Convert answer to coded form.
12. Move answer to output line.
13. Send a line of output to the printer.
14. Quit.

F5F0F040.................................

500

Average =

Channel

500

Memory

Control unit

Printer

What will the computer do next? The current value in the INSTRUC-
TION COUNTER is 3 (Fig. 9.12); following the only rules that it knows,
the control unit of the CPU will fetch instruction 3, starting the process over
again. Another card will be read, a test for the last card will be made (negative again), the data from the card will be converted to numeric form and
added to the accumulator, 1 will be added to the counter, and the program
will branch back to read still another card. Rather than force the reader
through a series of increasingly dull repetitions of the same steps, the results
of processing the second, third, and fourth input cards have been shown in
Figs. 9.13, 9.14, and 9.15, respectively. In each case, the figure shows a "snap-
shot" of the computer just before the control unit once again fetches the "read
card" instruction.

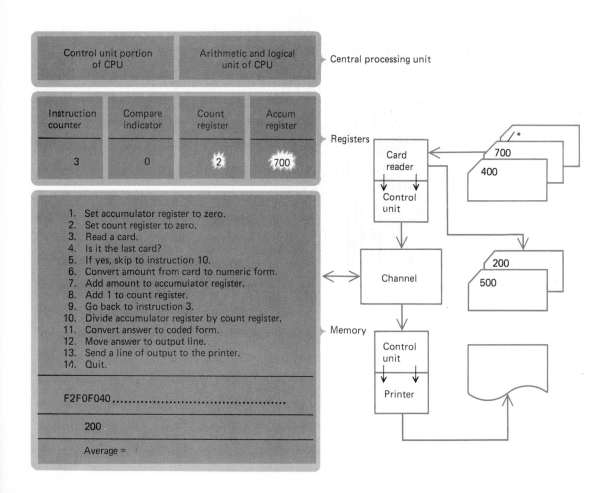

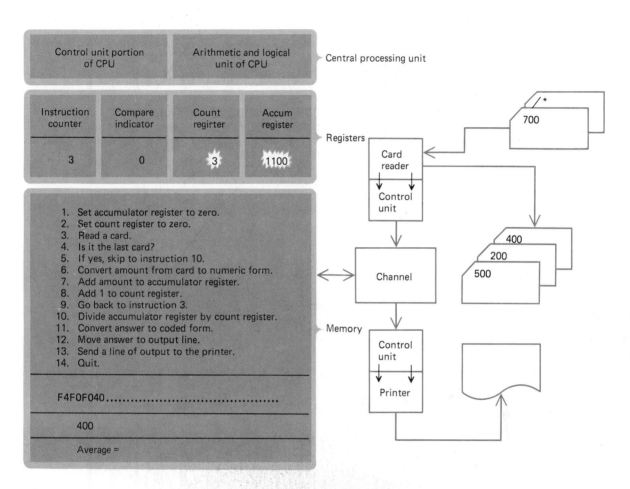

Fig. 9.14
After processing the third card.

◀ **Fig. 9.13**
After processing the second card.

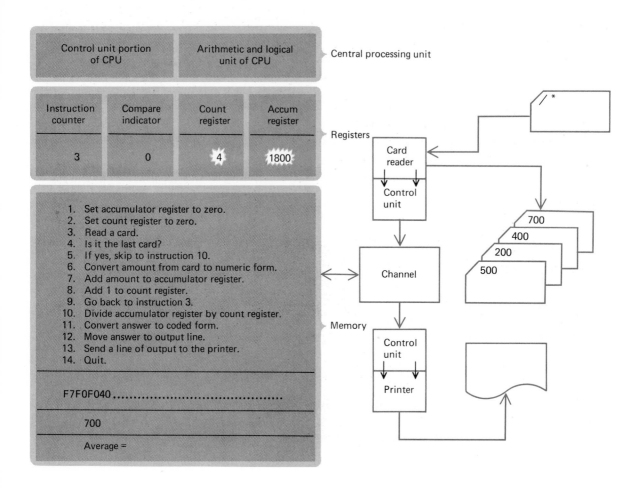

Fig. 9.15
After processing the fourth card.

FINISHING

As we resume processing, we note that the last card has just been read (Fig. 9.16), and we're about to fetch instruction 4. (Note: 615C is the EBCDIC code for /*.) To illustrate the idea that these instructions will represent the end of our program, we will use letters at the end of the alphabet to identify these steps.

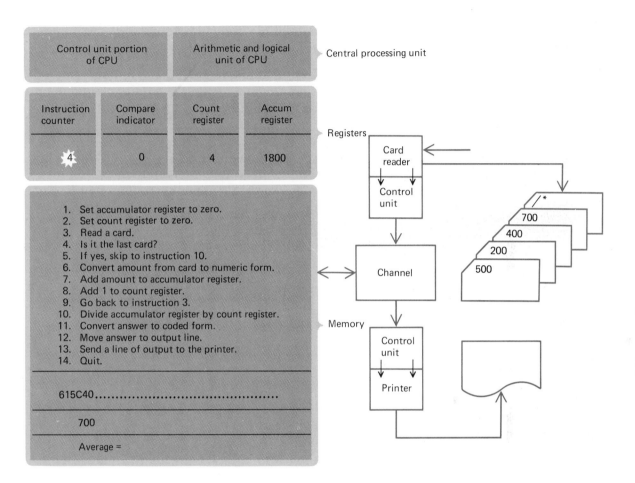

Fig. 9.16
The last card has just been read.

STEP T The control unit fetches instruction 4, bumping the INSTRUCTION COUNTER up to 5. The instruction is decoded and passed to the arithmetic and logical unit. Since this is the last card, the CPU sets the COMPARISON INDICATOR to 1 before passing control back to the control unit (Fig. 9.17).

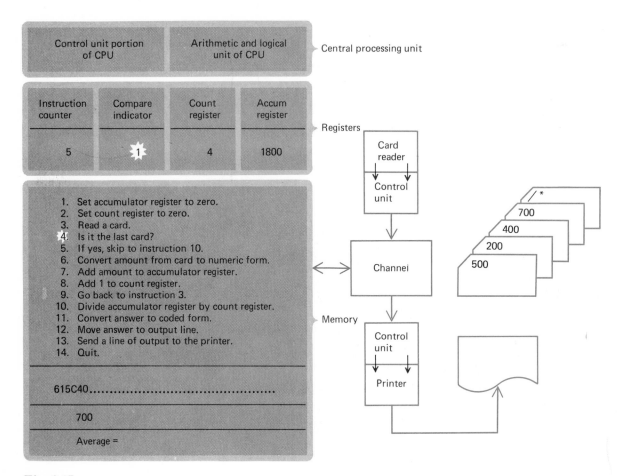

Fig. 9.17
Since the last card has been read, the COMPARI-
SON INDICATOR is set to 1.

STEP U Once again, the control unit "does its thing," passing the instruction along to the arithmetic and logical unit while leaving the INSTRUC-TION COUNTER pointing to instruction 6. This instruction (5) is a "conditional" branch. Up until this point, the computer has effectively ignored this instruction because the COMPARISON INDICATOR has been set to 0. Now, however, instruction 4, having encountered the last card, has set it to 1. Thus the arithmetic and logical unit replaces the current value in the INSTRUCTION COUNTER with 10 (Fig. 9.18) and returns control to the control unit.

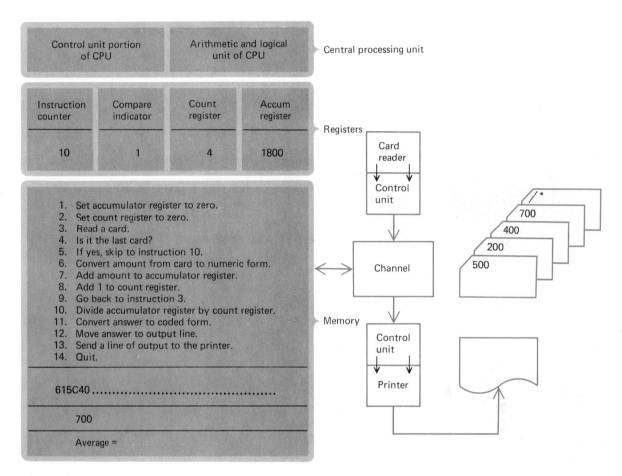

Fig. 9.18
Since the COMPARISON INDICATOR is "on,"
the next instruction will be number 10.

STEP V The current contents of the INSTRUCTION COUNTER point to the tenth instruction; thus the control unit fetches this instruction, bumping the INSTRUCTION COUNTER up to 11. The instruction is decoded and executed (it's a divide), and the answer is dropped into the ACCUMULATOR register (Fig. 9.19).

STEPS W, X, Y, and Z The answer is converted back from numeric to coded form (F4F5F0 is the EBCDIC code for 450) and stored in memory; a copy of the answer is placed in the output line being built in main memory;

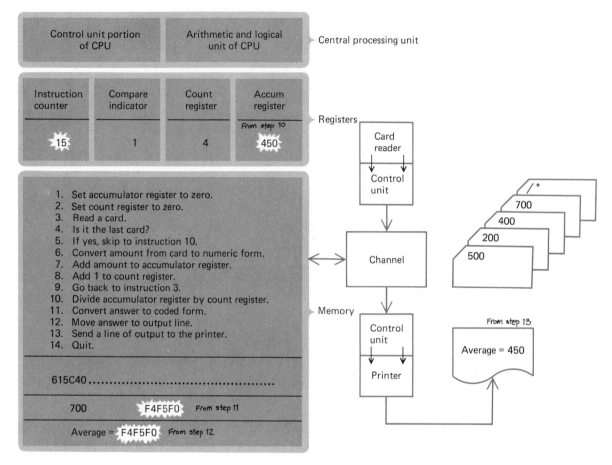

Fig. 9.19
The contents of the computer system as the program terminates.

the line of output is sent to the printer; and the program terminates. The results of these four steps are summarized in Fig. 9.19.

SOME FINAL COMMENTS

That's really all there is to it. The computer actually works in this "simple-minded" manner. The control unit of the CPU is capable of doing only one thing: fetching and decoding whatever instruction the INSTRUCTION COUNTER points to and bumping up the INSTRUCTION COUNTER during the process. Unless some outside force intervenes, the computer is restricted to processing instructions in strict sequence.

The outside force is provided by the other portion of the CPU, the arithmetic and logical unit. One of the functions available to this unit is copying; where appropriate, it can copy a new value into the INSTRUCTION COUNTER, causing the control unit to branch on the next cycle. The arithmetic and logical unit uses the COMPARISON INDICATOR in implementing this function, setting this special register in response to a comparison instruction and testing the indicator in response to a conditional branch.

If you feel that the material in this chapter was a bit repetitious after the first several pages, we made our point. A computer works by doing the same thing over and over again. It works very quickly and very accurately, but that's really all it can do.

Where are the special registers described in this chapter found in a real computer? On an IBM System/360 or System/370 computer, these fields are part of what is called the **Program Status Word,** or PSW, which occupies the first eight locations in main memory. On some computers, these special registers are a physical part of the CPU. On others, they actually float somewhere between the two primary computer components. Functionally, however, they serve to connect memory and the CPU, performing an essential coordination function. All computers contain something analogous to these two special registers.

In prior chapters, we have discussed input and output devices, the CPU, memory, and programs as independent entities, but they are *not* independent. The purpose of this chapter was to show how they fit together.

SUMMARY

This chapter summarized Part II of this book. We began with a hardware system consisting of a card reader, a printer, associated control units, a channel, and a computer. You should be familiar with the main features of each.

Once the hardware system was described, we planned and coded a program to compute an arithmetic average, discussing how this program might be compiled or assembled into an object module and loaded into main memory. We now had a complete computer system (rather than just a hardware system), with all the parts needed to execute this program and obtain an answer.

We then followed along step by step, as the computer executed our program. We saw how the control unit of the CPU looks to a special register called the INSTRUCTION COUNTER to find the next instruction to be executed. We saw how the value of this special register can be changed by the arithmetic and logical unit, thus implementing a branch; a conditional branch, as you may recall, involved the setting of another special register called the COMPARISON INDICATOR.

The intent of this chapter was to illustrate how, on a computer system, a group of hardware components can be made to function in a coordinated fashion under the control of a program. Having demonstrated this on a relatively simple "one computer/one program" system, we are now ready to move on.

EXERCISES

1. Explain what is meant by a complete hardware system.

2. Relate the process that we followed in planning and writing the average program of this chapter to the programming process described in Chapter 7.

3. How does the CPU know which instruction to execute next?

4. Describe a computer's memory cycle.

5. When the channel finishes an I/O operation, it sends an interrupt to the CPU. Why is this necessary?

KEY WORDS

central
processing unit

channel

comparison
indicator

control unit

data

hardware system

I/O device

instruction
counter

interrupt

machine cycle
(or memory cycle)

main memory

program

program status
word

record

register

File
Processing

Sequential File Processing and Magnetic Tape

OVERVIEW

Now that you have a basic idea of how a computer works, we can begin to discuss a number of more realistic examples of computer use. One of the most common applications of the computer is simply keeping records. We'll be examining this application throughout the chapter.

Computer record keeping often involves the processing of sequential files. Magnetic tape is a common medium for storing such files; thus we'll be covering a number of magnetic tape concepts. Finally, the idea of an access method will be introduced; look for it, because the concept is an important one.

CHARACTERS, FIELDS, RECORDS, AND FILES

The **character** is the basic building block of computer data. Letters, digits, and special symbols such as commas, periods, dollar signs, and other punctuation marks are all examples of characters.

By themselves, individual characters have little meaning; it's only when they are grouped together that they convey information. Consider the card shown in Fig. 10.1. Columns 6 through 20 contain an individual's last name. Columns 21 and 22 contain this individual's initials. Although it is not quite so obvious, the same person's hours worked and hourly pay rate are punched, respectively, in columns 31 through 33 and in columns 41 through 44. In computer terminology, a group of characters which forms a single, logical "chunk" or piece of data is called a **field**.

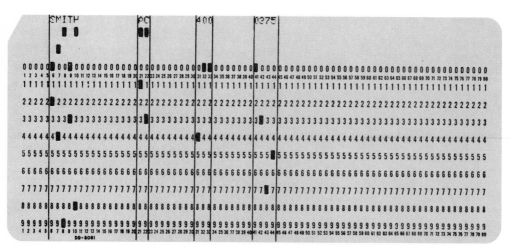

Fig. 10.1
A punched card record showing a number of fields.

Fields alone are not particularly useful either. You can't do very much with "SMITH". But these four fields, when combined, do serve a very useful purpose. They allow us to compute this particular individual's pay. The card contains one **record** of data; in other words, all the data needed to support one complete cycle of a program. A record is a collection of fields.

In our example, the next card would contain the name, initials, hours worked, and hourly pay rate of another person. The third card would contain the same fields for still another person. If "A. C. SMITH" works for a typical company, there are probably hundreds, perhaps even thousands, of similar records, one for each employee. Such a collection of similar records is called a **file**.

Files are very common, particularly in business applications. A firm's accounts receivable file is a collection of records, each identifying an amount due the firm; accounts payable is a file of bills to be paid. Payroll involves a number of files, including time cards, year-to-date earnings records, and personnel records for each employee. Banks maintain files of checking-account and savings-account balances. Most companies keep track of their inventories by keeping a record for each part number showing the amount currently in stock or on order.

The computer is often used to maintain these files; in fact, record keeping and **file processing** are probably the most common business applications of the computer. Let's take a look at a familiar file processing application: keeping track of the current balance of a number of checking accounts in a bank.

UPDATING CHECKING ACCOUNTS

Let's begin our analysis of this problem by considering how we might go about handling it manually. We have two files to work with. The first contains a list of all the active checking accounts in the bank, showing the old, or "start-of-day," balance for each. The second holds a collection of all the checks and deposits handled by the bank today. Our objective is to compute the new, or "end-of-day," balance for each account. To do this, we must use the old balance as a starting point and subtract all checks and add all deposits, account by account.

If there were only a few accounts, this would be a very simple process; we would merely read the transactions (checks and deposits) one at a time, find the old balance for the same account, and either add or subtract, depending on the type of transaction.

But what if we have thousands of accounts? Since the transactions are processed by different tellers at different times of day, they are not in any particular order. Trying to update the master file by looking up the proper account for each transaction would be a very time-consuming operation. Wouldn't it make sense to sort the transactions into account-number sequence first?

Consider the process of sorting for a moment. When you play cards, don't you group your cards by suit and, perhaps, within suit in sequence so as to better evaluate your hand? In examining your own checking account, don't you arrange cancelled checks into check-number sequence so as to simplify the task? When you are shopping in a supermarket or a department store, don't you expect to find similar products grouped together? Sorting is a very common human activity. We sort things to make it easier to keep track of them.

Sorting achieves two primary purposes. First, obviously, it places things in a known sequence. If both the master checking-account file and the transactions (checks and deposits) file are sorted in the same sequence by the same key (in this case, by account number) we know that we can start at the top of both files and go through them together, making the file update activity much easier. A second advantage of sorting is perhaps not quite so obvious. If the transactions are sorted into account-number sequence, we know that all checks and deposits against account number 0001, for example, will come before *any* transactions for account number 0002. (In other words, the process of sorting gathers together all records having the same key.) What this means to our master-file update application is that we can process all the checks and deposits for account number 0001 before moving on to account number 0002. Looking at it from another perspective, we know that we are finished with account number 0001 as soon as we encounter the first transaction against account number 0002.

If we were to try to update the checking-account master file by hand, we might begin by sorting the transactions into account-number sequence. Once this has been done, assuming that the master file is itself sorted into account-number sequence, the problem becomes one of simply starting with an old balance, adding all deposits and subtracting all checks drawn against the same account, and writing a new balance to the new master file before moving on to the next customer's records. The logic of the "program" assumes that both the old master file and the transactions file are in sequential order. In computer terminology, we would say that these two files are organized *sequentially* and that the activity we have been performing is **sequential file processing.**

Updating Checking Accounts on the Computer Using Cards

It is not at all unusual for a bank to have over 100,000 checking accounts. Although the calculations are no different from what we've already discussed, the tremendous number of additions and subtractions needed to update a master file of 100,000 records makes this job a candidate for automation.

A computerized version of the checking-account master-file update problem is shown in Fig. 10.2. First the checks and deposit slips are sorted into account-number sequence using a special machine called a MICR sorter (recall our earlier discussion of the magnetic characters imprinted on the bottom of a check). These sorted transactions are then read into the *master-file update* program and merged with the records from the old master-file card deck. Two output files are produced by this program: a printer listing showing the current end-of-day balance for each account, and a punched-card new master file.

A single box of cards measuring roughly 8″ by 3½″ by 15″ holds 2000 cards. For a master file of 100,000 records, we would need 50 boxes. That's 50 boxes for the old master file and another 50 boxes for the new master file—

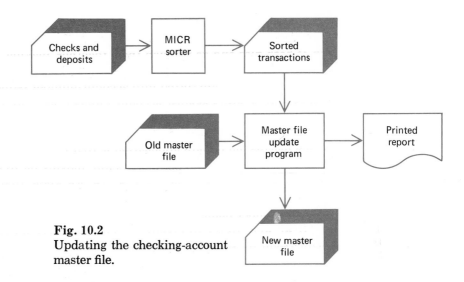

Fig. 10.2
Updating the checking-account
master file.

one hundred boxes of cards which must be handled by the computer operator
just to update the master file! The volume alone creates a serious problem.

Perhaps even more important than the physical bulk is the difficulty that
an operator would face in maintaining the sequence of 50 separate boxes of
cards. The master-file update program, as you may remember, assumes sequence; in fact, the program logic is written to take advantage of sequence.
Try maintaining the sequence of 50 boxes of cards (not to mention the cards
in each individual box) day after day after day. It's only a matter of time
before an all-too-human operator makes a mistake or drops a box.

By far the most serious problem with cards (as if the previous two weren't
enough) is the extreme slowness of card readers and card punches compared
to the internal processing speed of a computer. With card input and output,
the computer will spend most of its time waiting for I/O rather than accomplishing useful tasks.

A final problem with cards, one that is becoming more and more important these days, is the fact that cards are not reusable; there is no way to
fill up the holes and use the cards again. With a continuing activity like
record keeping, this tends to make punched cards a rather expensive storage
medium.

The ideal medium for this application would store a great deal of data
in a compact space, maintain this data in a tightly fixed sequence, support
very rapid data transmission between an I/O device and the computer, and
be reusable. Magnetic tape scores high on all these tests.

Updating Checking Accounts Using Magnetic Tape

Magnetic tape stores data at very high densities. A common density is 1600 characters per inch. If we assume an 80 character record (the capacity of a punched card), 20 of these records could be stored on a single inch of tape! Our 100,000-record file would require only 5000 inches of magnetic tape. A standard *reel* of tape holds 2400 feet, considerably more than is needed, and such a reel fits in a plastic case about the size of an imaginary, one-inch thick, long-playing record album. That is compact!

What about sequence? Data stored on tape is arranged in sequence along the surface of the tape. The only way to break the sequence is to physically break the tape. Magnetic tape is normally constructed of a very tough plastic called mylar, which is extremely difficult to break.

Magnetic tape is also fast—at least 100 times faster than punched cards. And magnetic tape is reusable. Anyone who has a reel-to-reel tape recorder will tell you that sound-recording tape can be reused simply by recording (or writing) new information directly over the old; magnetic computer tape is made from the same material as magnetic sound-recording tape.

Substituting tape for the card files we used before gives us a more typical version of the checking-account update problem (Fig. 10.3). Rather than simply sorting the transactions on a mechanical sorter and then reading them directly into the master-file update program, the transactions have been read, sorted, and copied to magnetic tape. The most obvious reason for using tape

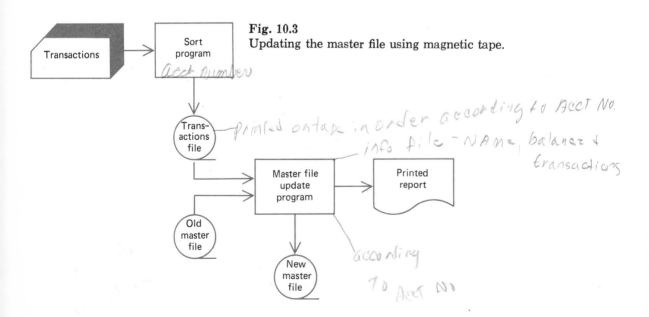

Fig. 10.3
Updating the master file using magnetic tape.

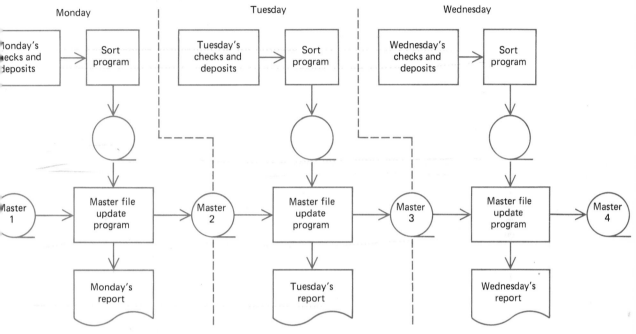

Fig. 10.4
The master file is updated on a daily basis.

to hold the sorted data is that tape can be read into the master-file update program at a higher speed than can the individual unit records of the transactions. A second advantage arises from the fact that most banks return checks to the customer; the magnetic tape allows the bank to keep a copy of the information.

Another important idea is the link between successive runs of this master-file update program (Fig. 10.4). Monday's output (or "new") master file becomes Tuesday's old master file; Tuesday's output becomes Wednesday's input, and so on. In effect, the balance of a checking account at the close of "today's" business is the same as the balance at the start of "tomorrow's" business.

OTHER EXAMPLES OF RECORD-KEEPING APPLICATIONS

Look back at Fig. 10.3, and note that it does *not* refer to checks and deposits or account balances. Instead, the figure has been generalized to refer to transactions, the old master file, the new master file, and a report. The reason for making this change is simple: Record keeping is a very common computer application that is not restricted to processing checks and deposits. In fact, the sequential master-file update application is, without a doubt, the most common business application of the computer. Let's take a look at a number of other examples.

In addition to checking accounts, a bank must also maintain savings-account balances. This application involves reading deposit and withdrawal slips, sorting them into sequence, and changing the old master file to reflect these transactions, creating a new master file in the process. Computing and adding interest to savings accounts is another example of a sequential file-processing activity, involving the multiplication of a field in each old master file record by a constant, adding the computed interest to compute the new balance, writing a new master file record, and preparing a written report showing interest earned by each account holder.

Banks also make loans, and loan payments are processed in much the same way. Usually a card or other record is prepared to accompany the payment. These "transactions" are sorted into loan-number sequence and processed against the old master file of loans "outstanding," producing a new master file reflecting current payments and overdue accounts. A written report often highlights such overdues.

As those of us who pay taxes know all too well, employers are required to keep track of our earnings throughout the year. This is yet another master-file update problem, with transactions being represented by time cards which are sorted into social security number (or employee number) sequence and used to compute pay for the current period. This current income (along with current deductions) is added to the year-to-date earnings from the old year-to-date file, and a new year-to-date file is generated. The report consists of paychecks. Other reports are usually prepared for accounting and budgetary purposes.

An inventory master file might show the stock-on-hand of various products or raw materials. Transactions (additions to and deletions from inventory) are used to update this master file. Credit card companies keep track of the "balance due" on each account in a master file. Current purchases and credits are used to update this file on a regular basis.

Accounting records are updated in a similar fashion, with the start-of-period balances being updated by receipts and expenditures. Another common business application is the maintenance of an order backlog, a list of pending customer orders; new orders and shipments are the transactions which are used to update this master file.

Even in the field of education, this program is common. Unless your school is very small, your academic record is kept on computer. The old master file holds student records as of the end of the previous marking period. Current grades are sorted into student-number sequence, and the master file is updated to reflect this new data. The written report, as you've probably already guessed, is a grade report. Dozens of other examples could be cited.

CHARACTERISTICS OF THE MASTER-FILE UPDATE PROBLEM

These applications all have a number of characteristics in common. First, consider their timing. Student records are updated at the end of each grading period; interest is added to savings accounts at regular intervals; billing and the updating of accounting records usually follow a monthly cycle; inventory and order backlog are updated on a regular basis with the period determined by the firm; payroll is computed weekly, biweekly, monthly, or quarterly. All of these activities can be scheduled. In each case, transactions are collected into a batch and processed at a predetermined, scheduled time. This type of information processing is called **batch processing.**

Another characteristic of this general category of application is high *activity*. When used in this context, activity means that a significant percentage of the records in the master file are accessed each time the program is executed. It would make little sense, for example, to update the checking-account master file each time a teller cashes a check; since the master file is sequential, the computer would have to go through half the records on the file (on the average) in order to find and update the correct one. It is much less expensive to collect a batch of transactions and process them all at the same time.

If we can afford to wait long enough to collect a sufficiently large batch of transactions to create enough activity to make sequential file processing economically justifiable, then we have a candidate for this type of master file update. But what if activity is "slow"? Or what if the data is so important that we cannot wait until an economical batch can be collected? In such cases, the file should not be organized sequentially; some examples and some alternative file organizations will be discussed in Chapters 11 and 12.

MAGNETIC TAPE

Its Physical Characteristics

We have already seen that magnetic tape is an ideal medium for sequential files. It is compact, holds data in sequence, can be read into or written from a computer at high rates of speed, and can be reused. What are the physical properties of magnetic tape that give it these advantages?

Magnetic computer tape is made from a $\frac{1}{2}$-inch wide ribbon of mylar coated with a magnetic material (Fig. 10.5); it's very much like reel-to-reel sound-recording tape. If you want to play the fifth song on a reel of recording

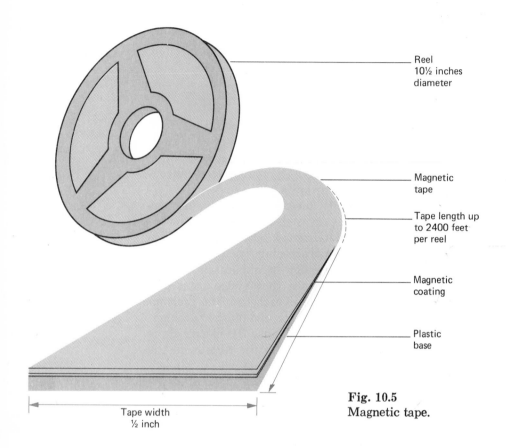

Reel
10½ inches
diameter

Magnetic
tape

Tape length up
to 2400 feet
per reel

Magnetic
coating

Plastic
base

Tape width
½ inch

Fig. 10.5
Magnetic tape.

tape, it is necessary to at least move the tape holding the first four songs past the recording head; likewise, to access the 500th record on a reel of magnetic computer tape, it is first necessary to move the first 499 records past the read/write heads. Both types of tape store data in a fixed sequence. Another similarity involves the reusability of the tape. To reuse a reel of sound tape, simply record new information on top of the old; computer tape works in the same way. Magnetic tape is both sequential and reusable.

The speed and compactness of tape are both factors of the tape's *density*. Data is normally stored on magnetic tape at a density of 800 or 1600 characters per inch. Even at the lower figure, a card containing 80 columns of information can be stored in only one tenth of an inch of ½-inch wide magnetic tape! A file of 100,000 records can be contained in less than 900 feet of tape, even at 800 characters per inch. A typical 10½-inch reel of tape holds about 2400 feet. That is compact!

Magnetic tape's density also leads to high data-transmission speed. A good card reader can handle roughly 600 cards per minute, a rate of ten (10) cards per second. If we were to lay these cards end to end, we would have

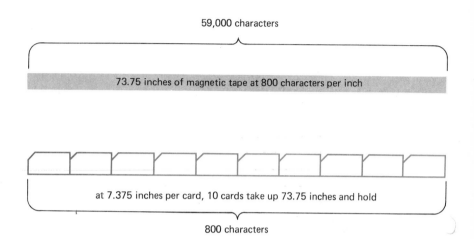

59,000 characters

73.75 inches of magnetic tape at 800 characters per inch

at 7.375 inches per card, 10 cards take up 73.75 inches and hold

800 characters

Fig. 10.6
Tape capacity vs. card capacity.

73.75 inches of card stock (each card is 7.375 inches long). Given that each card contains 80 characters of information, these 73-plus inches of card stock would hold a total of 800 characters of information (Fig. 10.6). Lay the same length of magnetic tape next to the cards (see Fig. 10.6 again). At 800 characters per inch, the tape would hold 59,000 characters of information, which is over 73 times as much as the cards. If the tape moves at the same physical speed as the cards, it's going to be 73 times as fast—59,000 as opposed to 800 characters per second. In fact, since the cards are separate pieces of paper while the tape is a smooth, continuous piece of plastic, the tape can move much faster. Tape can be processed at speeds of up to 800,000 characters per second!

We've been discussing characters of data on magnetic tape for some time now, and have not yet explained how these characters are actually stored. Data are stored on tape as a series of invisible magnetized spots, using the BCD, EBCDIC, or ASCII codes. Picture the upper surface of the tape divided into a gridlike pattern (Fig. 10.7). Each square on the grid represents one bit of data. If the spot is magnetized, it holds a 1-bit; if it is not magnetized, it holds a 0-bit.

Fig. 10.7
Data is stored on tape as a series of magnetized spots.

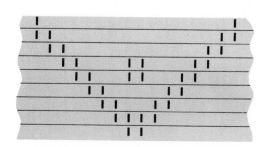

One common variety of tape is known as seven-track tape, which uses the six-bit BCD code, storing one character of data on a single cross-section of tape (Fig. 10.8). Even more popular is nine-track tape, which uses one of the eight-bit codes such as EBCDIC or ASCII (Fig. 10.9).

Note that seven-track tape uses a six-bit code and nine-track tape uses an eight-bit code; what about that extra track? Data on tape is stored at such high densities and is read at such speeds that something as simple as a piece of dust in the wrong place can cause an error. This extra bit is used to help catch such errors before they enter the computer. The extra track holds a *parity bit.* Under *even* parity, an even number of 1-bits will be stored for each character. In EBCDIC, the digit 1 is represented by $(11110001)_2$; the code for the digit 1 contains exactly five 1-bits. If the parity bit were set to 1, this particular cross-section of tape would contain six 1-bits, which would meet the requirements of even parity. The digit 3, $(11110011)_2$ in EBCDIC, would have a parity bit of 0. The parity bit is set when the data is written to tape. Later, assuming even parity, if a character with an odd number of 1-bits (including parity) is read, it is known to be an error. *Odd* parity is the exact opposite of even parity.

Parity checking is not restricted to magnetic tape; it is also used in main memory as part of the computer's internal error checking circuitry. Its ability to check and correct its own errors is one reason for the computer's unbelievable accuracy.

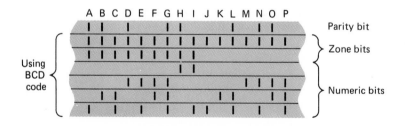

Fig. 10.8
Seven-track tape with even parity. (*Note:* The parity bit is shown in the top track to simplify visualization.)

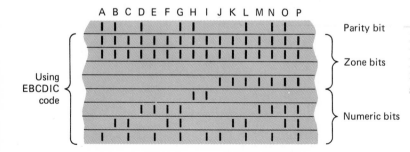

Fig. 10.9
Nine-track tape with even parity. (*Note:* The parity bit is shown in the top track to simplify visualization.)

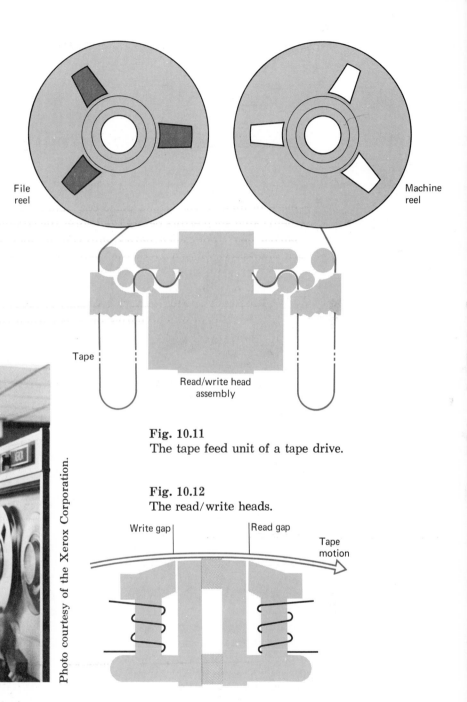

Fig. 10.10
Tape drives.

File reel

Machine reel

Tape

Read/write head
assembly

Fig. 10.11
The tape feed unit of a tape drive.

Fig. 10.12
The read/write heads.

Write gap

Read gap

Tape
motion

Photo courtesy of the Xerox Corporation.

Before reading or writing tape, a reel must first be loaded onto a tape drive (Fig. 10.10). The tape is passed from the initial reel, through a read/write head assembly, and onto a takeup reel (Fig. 10.11). Magnetic devices in the read/write assembly (Fig. 10.12) sense the magnetized spots (or create the spots on an output tape) as the tape moves over the heads.

Photo courtesy of the IBM Corporation.

Fig. 10.13
A data cartridge
about to be inserted
into an IBM 5100
portable computer.

A growing trend, particularly on small computers and some terminals, is toward the use of smaller tapes such as the *data cartridge* shown in Fig. 10.13. Even standard sound-recording cassettes are sometimes used.

Fields, Records, and Files on Tape

As with cards, the basic building block of data on tape is the character. On cards, one character is stored in each column; on tape, a single character is stored across the width of the tape.

A group of characters still forms a field, but a field can be different on tape. Within the computer, a series of two, three, or four storage locations might hold a single field in numeric rather than coded form. Such data could not be sent to the printer without conversion; a printer can print only certain characters. Although it is possible to send numeric data to a card punch, the resulting punched-card codes are tricky and require special handling on subsequent input; therefore, this is not normal practice. Sending numeric data to tape, however, creates no problem. The tape drive simply transmits or accepts a stream of eight-bit plus parity-bit characters (assuming nine-track tape) and, so long as the parity bit is correct, the fact that a particular combination might not be a valid EBCDIC or ASCII character does not matter. Thus, a field on magnetic tape might hold coded, pure binary, packed-decimal, or floating-point data.

As with cards, a logically complete collection of fields forms a record on tape. The physical nature of cards normally limits us to exactly 80 characters per record. No such natural limitation exists on magnetic tape; records can be of almost any size. The records within a single file can even vary in length. A perfect example of a variable-length record is an academic history file. As a first-quarter freshman, your record holds only personal and family data, but, as you progress, courses and grades are added at the end of each marking period, making the record longer and longer.

A collection of records of similar type forms a file. A very large file might span two or more reels of tape. It is also possible, at the other extreme, to store two or more smaller files on a single reel of tape. In data processing terminology, a single reel of tape is called a **volume.** A single file spanning two or more volumes is called a *multivolume file,* while a single volume holding two or more files is called a *multifile volume.* The concept of a file has nothing to do with a physical piece of tape or a physical box of cards; a file is simply a collection of similar records. A file is a logical, not a physical, concept.

There is no visible mark on the surface of magnetic tape—people cannot read tape. How then can we be sure that the correct tape is mounted? Normally, each tape volume is assigned a serial number which is affixed to the side of the reel. If we ask the operator to mount tape #IPS001, the volume with this serial number can be found and mounted on the tape drive.

But what if there are two files on the same volume? How do we tell them apart? And how can we be sure that the operator has in fact mounted the correct volume? Mistakes do happen. The answer is really very simple. Tape files are normally preceded on the tape by a header **label** (see Fig. 10.14) which identifies the file. Before file processing begins, this label can be checked by the program.

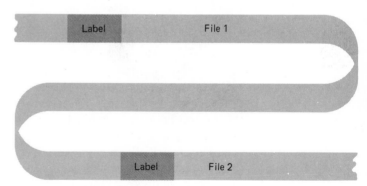

Fig. 10.14
Tape files are usually labeled.

Processing Tape Records: The Interrecord Gap

A program that processes tape data is like any other program. It reads a record of data from the input file, processes the data, and writes a record to the output file before going back to the beginning and repeating the cycle. This implies that there will be some delay between reading the first record and reading the second record (or between writing subsequent records).

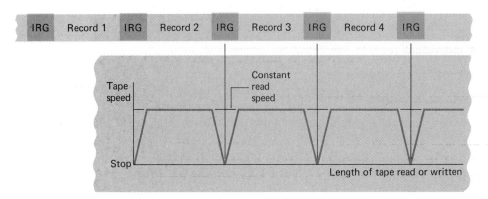

Fig. 10.15
The interrecord gap.

This delay creates a very real problem on a magnetic tape device. Tape drives are designed to read or write data at a constant speed. The fact that there is some time delay between the reading of adjacent records implies that the tape drive will stop between I/O operations, and this is in fact what it does. Imagine what would happen if records were jammed together at 800 characters per inch. After reading the first record, the drive mechanism would have to bring the tape from a constant speed to a dead stop within the 1/800 of an inch separating the last character in the first record from the first character in the last record, which would be something like an automobile running into a brick wall. The result would be destruction of the tape (and probably the tape drive). Reading the second record would be equally impossible; no physical device can go from a dead stop to full speed in "nothing flat."

The solution to this problem is to place a gap of unused tape between the records. Picture the read/write heads being located right in the middle of the gap between records 1 and 2 (Fig. 10.15). It is necessary to move the tape one-half gap in order to bring it up to speed. The record is read at a constant speed. When the end of the record is reached, the drive has one-half gap available to slow the tape to a safe stop, leaving it in position for the next read. The gap between records is called an **interrecord gap.**

How big is this gap? On nine-track tape, the usual length of the interrecord gap is six tenths (0.6) inch; on seven-track tape, the gap is even wider. Imagine an 80-character record being stored at 800 characters per inch. Given a file of such records, the tape would hold a series of 0.1-inch records separated by 0.6-inch gaps. That's like putting six blank cards for every data card in a deck! This is hardly an efficient way of utilizing the tape, but for physical reasons the gap must be there.

Blocking

One solution to making better use of the tape is to **block** the data. Rather than write a series of individual records separated by interrecord gaps, why not combine a number of records into a single block (Fig. 10.16)? If we use a **blocking factor** of 10 (that is, ten logical records per block), we could store ten 80-character records on one inch of tape, to be followed by a 0.6-inch gap, to be followed by another inch of data, and so on. Figure out the amount of tape needed to store 1000 records, each 80 characters long, assuming 800 characters per inch and a 0.6-inch gap, using no blocking. Then try using a blocking factor of 10. Do you begin to see the advantage of blocking? Now try it with a blocking factor of 20. By blocking data, we cut down on the amount of dead space.

Fig. 10.16
Blocking.

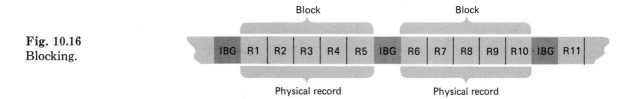

Of course, we can't call the gap an interrecord gap; when the data is blocked, the term **interblock gap** is used. An individual block of data lying between two interblock gaps is called a **physical record,** while the individual records within this block are called **logical records.**

A record has been defined as a collection of fields needed to support a single iteration of a program. To compute pay for employee number 0001, we need a record containing data for *only* employee number 0001. On the next iteration of the program, we would need a record for employee number 0002.

A single physical record on tape might contain individual logical records for employees 0001, 0002, 0003, 0004, and 0005. What is it our program expects? A program is written to process logical records. What is going to be transferred between the tape drive and the computer? Because of the physical nature of tape, the drive will read and transfer all the data lying between two gaps. We will get (or send) a physical record.

This creates a new problem for the programmer. A request for input data might result in the transfer of 5, 10, 15, 20, or any number of logical records depending on the blocking factor used. If the program is to work properly, these logical records must be separated and handled individually. On output, if blocked data is to be sent to the tape drive, the program must collect a series of logical output records in main memory before sending the physical record to the tape drive.

The process of building a physical record in main memory from a number of logical records is called **blocking.** The process of breaking a physical input record into individual logical records is called **deblocking.** The main-memory space needed to hold a block is called a **buffer.** Control units and channels contain buffers too; this one just happens to be in main memory.

SEQUENTIAL ACCESS METHODS

We began this chapter by discussing sequential file processing; lately, we have been concentrating on the characteristics of magnetic tape. Let's now pull together the application, the physical device, and the data that is accessed through this physical device.

The master-file update application involves reading a series of transactions, using these transactions to update an old master file, and creating a new master file. The individual who writes this program is not at all interested in the physical characteristics of the file. The real problem lies in making sure that the individual records are updated correctly. The fact that they are stored 10, 15, or 20 to the block is not important; it is a detail that the programmer really doesn't want to worry about. (Note that we haven't even used the terms logical and physical record; the programmer visualizes "good old-fashioned" records.)

But the data *is* stored on a *physical* file. A physical device *will* transfer *physical* records because it can do nothing else. And these records *must* be blocked and deblocked.

In most installations, the problems of blocking and deblocking are handled by an **access method.** An access method is a special **subprogram,** a collection of previously written, machine-level code that is grafted to the program. These instructions perform the functions of blocking and deblocking, allowing the programmer to "pretend" that only logical records must be handled.

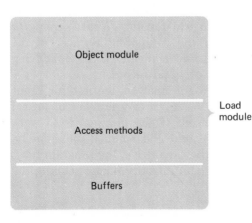

Fig. 10.17
A load module with access methods and buffers.

A program consists of three distinct parts (Fig. 10.17). At the top is the object module produced by a compiler from the programmer's object code. In the middle is the access method—in this case, a sequential access method. At the bottom are the buffers needed to hold blocks or physical records of data. Physical records are read, under control of the access method, into a buffer. Logical records, again under control of the access method, are made available to the main program one at a time. As the main program creates output records one at a time, these logical records are transferred by the access method to a buffer for eventual transfer to an output device. Where did the access method come from? How was it "grafted" onto the main program?

THE LINKAGE EDITOR

The first step in going from programmer source code to a machine-level program is, as you may remember, compilation (Fig. 10.18). A compiler produces an object module, which by itself (except in a few special cases) is incomplete, needing access methods and buffers before processing can begin.

Fig. 10.18
The compile, link edit, and execute sequence.

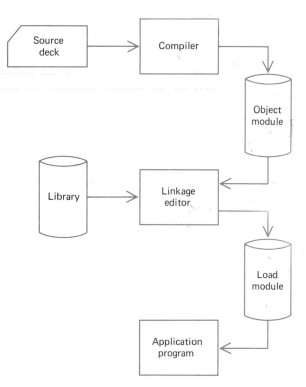

A special program called a linkage editor has, as part of its function, the responsibility for adding these necessary pieces. The linkage editor produces a load module (see Figs. 10.17 and 10.18), which can be executed by a computer.

The process of producing and then executing a load module is a good example of **bootstrapping.** First, a compiler must be loaded into the computer so as to produce an object module. Next, another program, the linkage editor, must be loaded so it can produce a load module. Finally the load module can itself be loaded and executed. The compile, link edit, and execute sequence is illustrated in Fig. 10.18.

Where does the linkage editor find the access methods and other subroutines that it needs to produce a load module? On a **library.** When most of us think of a library, we picture a place in which books are kept. A library, however, is much more; it is really a place in which books are carefully cataloged and stored in such a way as to make them easy to find again. A book that cannot be found is not very useful.

A program library is a place where computer programs are carefully cataloged and stored. Some libraries exist on magnetic tape; occasionally, decks of cards are used; more frequently, the library exists on a direct access device, the subject of Chapter 11. When the linkage editor program encounters a need for an access method or a subroutine, it checks the library *catalog*, finds the physical location of the needed routine, reads a copy into main memory, and adds it to the developing load module.

Sequential file processing implies the use of magnetic tape or some other bulk storage medium. Tape implies blocking. Blocking implies that such functions as blocking, deblocking, and buffering must be added to the application program. These functions are usually implemented through an access method. A compiler translates a source deck into object code. Since an access method is not normally part of the source deck, the compiler has nothing to translate; thus the access method is not part of the object module. It must, however, be added before the program can execute on the computer. As one of its functions, the linkage editor adds the access method and buffers to the object module in building a load module.

SECONDARY STORAGE

Magnetic tape is sometimes called **secondary storage** or **bulk memory,** a distinction that it shares with direct access devices. Like main memory, data on tape or a direct access device is stored as an electronic pattern (rather than as physical holes, as on cards). Data can be written to and retrieved from these devices quite rapidly. Any form of data valid within the computer—coded, pure binary, packed-decimal, or floating-point—can be stored without modification on tape or a direct access device; in effect, data or programs can be moved back and forth between tape or direct access devices and main memory with a minimum of difficulty; thus, the term *secondary storage*.

Why not put all data in main memory? Main memory is too expensive. Why not put it all on a secondary storage device? Even though these devices are fast, they are many times slower than main memory.

SUMMARY

We began this chapter with a discussion of characters, fields, records, and files, defining these terms. We then moved into the master-file update application, using checking-account maintenance as an example. Key characteristics of this application include the sorting of a number of transactions into sequence, followed by the merging of this transaction file with an old master file to produce a new master file and, usually, a report.

We demonstrated that cards are badly suited for this application. Magnetic tape, because of its compactness, speed, fixed-sequence mode of recording, and reusability, is superior. After discussing the checking-account update problem using magnetic tape as the storage medium, we mentioned a number of other examples of computer-based master-file updating; all are batch-processing applications involving highly active files.

We used magnetic sound-recording tape to explain the reusability and the fixed-sequence nature of computer tape. Density, typically 800 or 1600 characters *per inch*, can be used to explain both the speed and compactness of tape. Data was shown to be stored as a series of magnetized spots, with a single cross-section normally holding one coded character. Both seven- and nine-track tapes were discussed. The concept of parity was explained, as well as the physical nature of a tape drive.

Fields, records, and files have the same meaning on tape as they did on cards, with a few important differences. Because data is stored on tape as a pattern of electronic or magnetized spots, numeric fields can be stored without conversation. A single file might be spread over two reels (or volumes) of tape, or a single volume might contain two or more files. For this reason (plus the fact that people cannot directly read data on tape), most magnetic tape files are created with labels.

Because of the physical nature of a magnetic tape drive, individual records must be separated by an interrecord gap. To make more effective use of the tape, individual logical records are often combined into blocks called physical records. This creates problems for the programmer who must block and deblock logical records in main memory. Typically these problems are handled by an access method, a software module which is normally grafted onto the object module by a linkage editor as it creates a load module.

Magnetic tape is sometimes called secondary storage because it is fast and able to hold data in any format available to main memory. Direct access devices, the topic of the next chapter, are another example of secondary storage.

EXERCISES

1. Define once again the following terms: character, field, record, and file. Write the definitions in your own words *before* referring to the glossary.

2. In a file processing application such as updating checking accounts, why is sorting desirable?

3. Why is the computer used to maintain records?

4. Why is magnetic tape, rather than cards, used to hold the files in so many master-file update applications? What advantages does magnetic tape enjoy over cards?

5. What is meant by sequential file processing?

6. For what is the parity bit used?

7. What is the difference between a file and a volume?

8. Why is blocking desirable on magnetic tape?

9. What is an access method? What do access methods do? How is an access method added to a program?

10. What is a load module? Explain the difference between a load module, an object module, and a source module.

KEY WORDS

access method	bulk memory or storage	file processing	magnetic tape	secondary storage
activity		interblock gap	master file	
batch processing	cassette	interrecord gap	master-file update	sequential file processing
block	character	label	parity	
blocking	data catridge	library	physical record	sorting
blocking factor	deblocking	linkage editor	read/write head	subprogram
bootstrapping	density	load module	record	subroutine
buffer	field	logical record	reel	volume

File Processing
and
Direct Access
Storage Devices

OVERVIEW

Sequential processing is often inadequate. In this
chapter, we will examine a number of applications
that require quick response or access to specific
records, making sequential access unsuitable. We
will also examine a number of devices that support
direct access, primarily disk and drum. The chapter
ends with some comments on file processing
economics.

SEQUENTIAL FILES AND BATCH PROCESSING

Let's review briefly the characteristics of sequential files as presented in Chapter 10. On a sequential file, the individual records follow one another in a fixed sequence: To process record number 500, it is necessary to go through the first 499 records. Typically, these records are sorted into logical order by some **key** such as a part number, social security number, name, or some other "key" field. Magnetic tape is well suited for such files because tape, by its very nature, preserves this sequence.

For a master-file update, this type of organization makes a great deal of sense. A master file and a number of transactions can be sorted by the same key and, in essence, merged together, allowing the new master file to reflect all current activity: The sequential nature of the files makes the updating process much simpler than would be possible with transactions in random order.

This application is a good example of batch processing. The transactions are collected into a batch, and the master file is updated (usually) at regular intervals. There is a very strong financial reason for collecting a substantial batch of records: If only a few of the records on a file are updated each time the program is run, the cost per change becomes prohibitive. Let's examine this statement more closely. Do you recall the discussion of the breakeven point in Chapter 2? That's really what we're dealing with here. The cost of processing a sequential file (on magnetic tape) is essentially a fixed cost (Fig. 11.1). It costs x dollars to read and to update an entire tape, and the nature of a sequential file makes it necessary to read the entire tape. If we could find a technique that would allow us to update records one at a time, this approach would be less expensive until the number of record changes reached some critical point (Fig. 11.1)—in other words, the breakeven point.

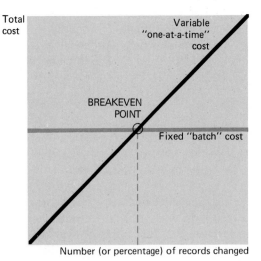

Fig. 11.1
"Breakeven" on the file update application.

For example, let's say that we have a deck of punched cards in alphabetical order, each one containing an individual's name and address. What is the easiest way to change one individual's address? The answer should be obvious: Select that individual's card, change it, and replace the corrected card in the deck. This is not sequential file processing. Would anyone seriously consider reading the old master file one record at a time, merging the transactions file (a single record) with it, and creating a complete new master file? No. Why not? Because it is so much easier and less expensive to select and change the single record.

Now let's change the problem. We'll go back a few years and assume that the post office has just decided to require zip codes on all addresses. If all the individuals on our name-and-address file live in the same general area, we could write a program that would read the old master file one record at a time, check the street address and figure out the zip code, and punch a new master file. Would it be simpler to automate this process or to have a group of clerks add the zip code to one record at a time? The answer depends, of course, on the size of the file. A thousand records or so could be updated by hand, but a few hundred thousand would probably make the cost of writing a program worthwhile.

Consider a magazine with one million subscribers, several thousand of whom change addresses every month. Given the size of the master file and the volume of change (or the activity), it would be quite unusual for such an operation to be performed manually. With most magazines, address changes and other subscription modifications (new subscriptions and cancellations) are collected into a batch and processed at regular intervals (which is why it takes several weeks for an address change to become effective).

THE NEED FOR ON-LINE SYSTEMS

Among the typical sequential file-processing applications discussed in Chapter 9 were the updating of checking and savings accounts. Checking accounts are generally quite active, but what about savings accounts? Although there are exceptions, most people do not maintain an extremely "active" savings account, making deposits and withdrawals perhaps only a few times a month. If the bank were willing to wait until the end of the month to update all savings accounts, an economically sound batch of transactions might be collected, but the bank cannot wait that long. What would happen, for example, if a customer intentionally overdrew and had a 30-day head start before the crime was even detected?

Have you ever been in a bank or a savings and loan institution that processed your deposit or withdrawal through a terminal? This is becoming a very common approach, with individual account records updated directly, one at a time. A sequential file organization just will not do for this application; the cost and time delay inherent in processing an entire file for each transaction would be prohibitive.

Why won't simple, sequential batch processing do in this case? For reasons involving such factors as risk, security, and control, the master file must be updated at least daily. There is not enough activity to economically justify a daily, sequential master-file update.

Let's look at another application in which sequential file processing just won't do, this time for quite different reasons. Our national air defense system is computer-coordinated. Information on regularly scheduled flights, non-scheduled charter or private flights, the weather, and wind conditions is kept in a massive *data base*. Radar, ground spotters, airborne units, and sea installations constantly feed current information to the system. If an unidentified aircraft is spotted, an attempt is made to identify it, starting with calculations to determine, for example, whether a known flight might have been blown off course and ending with the dispatching of interceptors and the alerting of responsible personnel.

An operation of this type cannot run in a batch mode. Imagine insisting that we wait until 5:00 P.M. to determine the identity of the aircraft because "5:00 P.M. is the scheduled time for our batch run." By 5:00 P.M., Chicago might not be there. This is a good example of an **on-line, real-time** application. It's on-line because the equipment providing or displaying the information is directly attached to the computer, with no keypunch operator or data-entry clerk involved. It is real-time because data is processed so as to influence a decision that must be made "right now" in "real time."

Air defense is an extreme example of an on-line, real-time system; let's take a look at a different one. Many airlines run an on-line, real-time reservation system. A ticket agent, using a terminal, requests a reservation for a customer. The information is sent to a central computer that checks the status of the desired flight and, in a matter of seconds, confirms or rejects the reservation. Transactions are processed one at a time. Obviously, transactions are not batched. Why? Most airlines are private organizations in business to make money. What if you, as a customer, were to approach "Tree Top Airways" to request a reservation on the next flight to New York and were told to wait until one half-hour before flight time (when the batch of reservation requests is run) for confirmation? While waiting, you walk across the aisle to the ticket agent for "Kamikaze Airlines" who gives you an immediate, firm reservation on a flight leaving only a few minutes after the "Tree Top" flight. Which airline are you going to choose? Ignoring any qualitative differences, you'd probably select the "sure thing" over the "come-back-later" response. Although there are other reasons for putting a reservation system on-line, such as minimizing the impact of "no-shows" and handling a last-minute rush, it is basically done for competitive reasons. This, of course, translates into money —lost customers mean lost revenue.

DIRECT ACCESS

The applications that we have just finished discussing have at least one characteristic in common: They require the processing of each transaction as it occurs, one at a time. Batch processing is not acceptable.

Sequential files leave a lot to be desired in such applications. We might get lucky and try to update the very first record on the master file, but we might get unlucky and try to update the last record. On the average, we would have to go through about half the file for each transaction. This is very time-consuming and very expensive.

What is needed is a storage medium that allows us to go directly (or almost directly) to the one record we need without going through all the intervening records. Consider a telephone book. It is organized sequentially, but we can bypass the sequence when looking for a specific phone number or address: When looking for Joe Smith's number, we do *not* start with the A's and read until we encounter the name we want. A deck of punched cards gives us this ability. We can pull, change, and replace selected cards, but cards are too slow and bulky, and provide this "direct access" capability only when processing is done manually. What we need is a device with the density and speed of magnetic tape.

What if we were to cut a volume of magnetic tape into strips (Fig. 11.2), each strip containing exactly 100 records? Assume that the file had been organized sequentially and that there are no missing records. Records 1 through 100 would be found on the first strip, records 101 through 200 would be on the second strip, and so on. Let's say that we wanted record 1132. It's a simple matter to figure out which strip holds this record; all we need do is find this strip, mount it on some magnetic I/O device, and search the selected strip for the desired record. This process is not quite direct, but we do get fairly close without going through all the intervening records.

Fig. 11.2
The direct access concept illustrated by a volume of magnetic tape cut into strips.

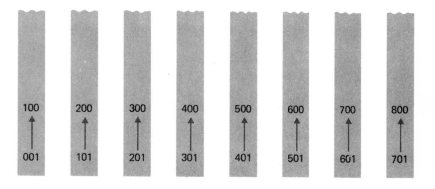

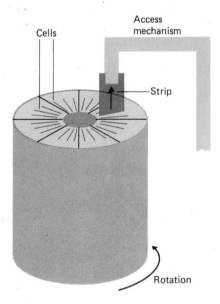

Fig. 11.3
A data cell.

This approach was actually tried at one time. The device was called a **data cell** (Fig. 11.3). Individual strips of tape were stored in a number of **cells** on top of the device. The programmer (through a program) simply asked for a given tape strip in a given cell. The device would then select the strip, wrap it around the outer surface of the data cell, and read or write it. At the conclusion of the I/O operation, the strip was returned to the proper location. The data cell never really became popular because of problems with reliability and access speed, but it does illustrate the basic idea of what is now called **direct access.**

MODERN MASS STORAGE SYSTEMS

Although the data cell was never a commercial success, a number of modern **mass storage systems** show greater promise. Everyone knows what a jukebox is; it's a device that plays records. After depositing some coins, you select a song by pressing some buttons. Once a song has been selected, an access arm in the jukebox moves across the stack of available recordings, pulls out the one you selected, and places it on a turntable to be played. Several newer mass storage devices work on much the same principle.

Rather than 45-RPM records, these devices use small reels of magnetic tape or small cylinders coated with magnetic material. These storage media are arranged in a matrix pattern (Fig. 11.4). If the data we want is on the data cartridge stored at location (3,5) and we know that the first number in the address indicates how far we must move to the right, while the second

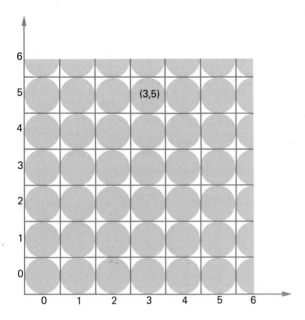

Fig. 11.4
A modern mass storage device; a section of the data storage matrix.

number indicates the number of cells we must move up, we can find the data cartridge holding our data. Once located, the tape on this cartridge can be mounted on a tape drive and processed.

Examples of mass storage systems that work pretty much as described above include IBM's 3850 Mass Storage System and Control Data Corporation's Mass Storage Facility. These systems are composed of at least three primary components: a bank of cells in which data cartridges can be stored, an **access arm** to move cartridges from the storage matrix to a read/write area, and a mechanism to read data from or write data to the cartridges. The operation of one of these devices begins with a request from the computer for a particular data cartridge. The access arm moves into position over the desired cartridge and removes it from the matrix, transferring it to the read/write mechanism. There the data can be read and transmitted into the computer. On output, information from the computer can be recorded on the magnetic surface. When the operation is finished, the access arm returns the data cartridge to its proper position in the storage matrix.

The process of transferring a data cartridge from the storage matrix to the read/write mechanism takes time. Control Data Corporation estimates that the average **access time** on its Mass Storage Facility is about 2.5 seconds. To a computer, this is a very long period of time; still, it's much faster than having a human operator walk into the tape room, select a tape, walk back to the computer room, and mount it on a tape drive.

The storage capacity of these devices is impressive. The CDC Mass Storage Facility can hold up to 2052 cartridges, each capable of storing as many as eight million bytes or characters of data. This means that there are close to eight billion bytes of data on-line at one time. IBM's 3850 can handle up to 472 billion bytes! The effective storage capacity of a mass storage device can be augmented by off-line storage, in that individual cartridges can be removed or inserted manually.

Data on a mass storage device such as the ones we've been discussing is accessible by the computer without human intervention. It is not necessary to begin at the data cartridge located at cell (0,0) and work through the cartridges one at a time until the needed record of data is located. It is instead possible to access directly the single data cartridge desired. In effect, we have taken the individual strips of tape discussed earlier and placed each one in its own little cell, thus allowing direct access.

MAGNETIC DRUM

The mass storage devices described above are relatively new to the marketplace. The first commercially important direct access device was the **magnetic drum.** The name is quite descriptive. Imagine a cylindrical drum-shaped device with the "strips of tape" wrapped around the outer surface. If we replace these individual strips with a continuous coating of the same material that coats magnetic tape, we have a magnetic drum (Fig. 11.5).

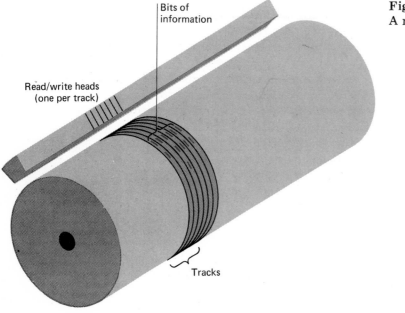

Bits of information

Read/write heads (one per track)

Tracks

Fig. 11.5
A magnetic drum.

Data is stored around the surface in a circular pattern called a track. Just as on tape, individual bits are represented by magnetized spots; these bits are grouped into characters which, in turn, form fields which, again in turn, form records. On tape, one cross-section holds one character; on drum, although it's possible to store the bits of a given character on parallel tracks, the individual bits are normally stored in series around the track, with the first nine (eight-bit code plus parity) holding the first character, and so on.

Most drums have one read/write head for each track. This makes data access very fast. The drum normally rotates constantly at a very high rate of speed. With one read/write head per track, all that is needed to access data is to specify a track, turn on the associated read/write head, and wait for the desired data to rotate under the head.

This does take time; even a drum is slower than the internal processing speeds of a computer. Turning on the proper head can be done electronically —it's very fast. The major delay involves waiting for the data to rotate beneath the head. We might get lucky and have the record just about to pass under the head as we turn the head on. We might get unlucky and have to wait for the record to come all the way back around. On the average, we'll wait for about one-half revolution for the data. This is called **rotational delay**.

The final component of a drum's total data access time involves the transfer of data between the device and main memory. **Data transfer time** is normally measured in microseconds.

A magnetic drum is a fixed storage medium in that the data storage cylinder cannot be removed. A typical drum can hold approximately four million bytes or characters of data.

MAGNETIC DISK

Today's most commonly used direct access device is the **magnetic disk**. In describing magnetic tape, we used the analogy of reel-to-reel sound-recording tape. A magnetic disk is analogous to a long-playing record album. It is a disk-shaped device with a magnetic coating on the flat surface (Fig. 11.6). Unlike the long-playing record album, data on a magnetic disk is not stored in a spiral pattern, but instead is stored on a series of concentric circles

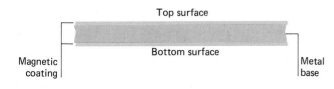

Top surface

Bottom surface

Magnetic coating

Metal base

Fig. 11.6
A cross section of a disk.

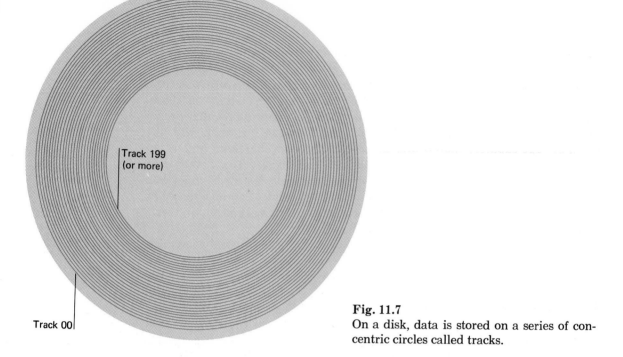

Track 199
(or more)

Track 00

Fig. 11.7
On a disk, data is stored on a series of concentric circles called tracks.

called **tracks** (Fig. 11.7). Individual bits are represented by magnetized
spots, bits are grouped to form characters, characters are grouped to form
fields, and so on.

On a long-playing record, it is possible to play the fourth song on the
first side by simply picking up the tone arm and placing it at the beginning
of the desired song. Since we can skip the intervening three songs, we have
a form of direct access. A magnetic disk is equipped with a movable read/
write head that works in analogous fashion, moving over the track holding
the desired data. (Fig. 11.8).

Fig. 11.8
A typical disk arrangement showing
a stack of individual disks and
movable read/write heads.

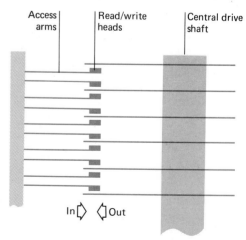

Access
arms

Read/write
heads

Central drive
shaft

In ▷ ◁ Out

Finding a specific record on a disk is a bit more complex than on a drum. On a drum, the first step is to simply turn on the proper read/write head, but on a disk, the head must be physically moved so as to position it over the proper track. The times for rotational delay and data transfer are roughly the same, but this physical motion, called **seeking**, does make disk somewhat slower than drum. Why use disk if it's slower? Because disk has greater storage capacity than drum. Let's explain.

A long-playing record album has two sides. Similarly, data can be stored on both sides of a magnetic disk. In fact, a **disk pack** normally consists of a stack of individual disks (10 to 20) rotating on a single spindle and accessed by a comblike set of read/write heads (Fig. 11.8).

Let's assume that we have a drum that is ten inches in diameter and ten inches high (Fig. 11.9). Data can be stored only on the outer surface. The formula for computing the outer surface area of a cylinder is

Area = $\pi\cdot$(diameter)$\cdot$(height),

which in our example figures out to be a little over 314 square inches.

Now let's assume that we have a stack of ten disk surfaces which just fits inside the drum we discussed in the preceding paragraph (Fig. 11.9). Data can be stored on each of ten surfaces. Each surface is a circle. The formula for the area of a circle is

Area = $\pi\cdot$(radius)^2.

Fig. 11.9
Disk vs. drum:
storage capacity.

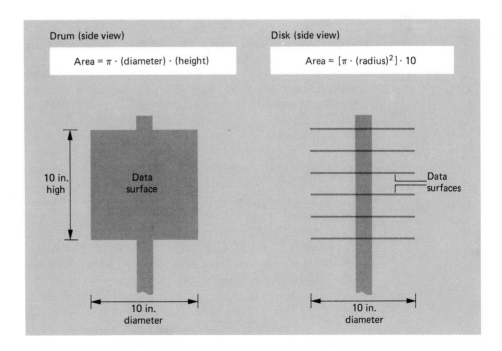

Drum (side view)

Area = $\pi \cdot$ (diameter) $\cdot$ (height)

Disk (side view)

Area = $[\pi \cdot$ (radius)$^2] \cdot 10$

10 in. high

Data surface

10 in. diameter

Data surfaces

10 in. diameter

With a radius of five inches, the area of each surface is 78.5 square inches; since we have ten such surfaces, the total area available for data is 785 square inches. That is $2\frac{1}{2}$ times as much storage capacity in the same physical space. Although the numbers used in this example are not precise, they are reasonably close and realistically reflect the capacity advantages of disk over drum. Drum is faster; disk has greater capacity.

We have seen how data is stored in concentric circles called tracks. We've also shown how a number of disks are typically stacked together, indicating how a single comblike set of read/write heads can be made to access one track in each of the surfaces at the same time (see Fig. 11.8). In other words, one position of the read/write mechanism gives us access to one track on each surface. This single access-arm position is called a **cylinder.** Accessing data on a disk involves three distinct steps:

1. Locate the read/write heads over the proper cylinder.

2. Turn on the head corresponding to the proper track and wait for the desired record to rotate beneath the head.

3. Transfer the data to (or from) the computer.

The time delay associated with the first step is called **seek time,** and is measured in milliseconds. The second step involves a rotational delay; although still measured in milliseconds, it is not nearly as slow as seek time. Finally, there is data transfer time, which is measured in microseconds.

As you can see in Fig. 11.7, the "outer" tracks on a disk surface are considerably bigger than the "inner" tracks. Does this imply that we can store more data on the outer tracks? No. Every track holds the *same* amount of data. No, it isn't an optical illusion. Have you ever played "crack the whip"? In this game, often played on ice skates, a group of people join hands, and the individual on one end begins turning slowly in a circle. Proceeding outward, each individual moves around the center in circles of increasing radius. Since the people further along the chain must travel in bigger circles, they must skate faster in order to keep up. The person at the end has to skate like mad just to stay even.

The same principle applies when using a disk. The surface rotates at a constant speed. If that speed is, for example, 1000 revolutions per second, then a particle on either the inner *or* the outer track would make exactly 1000 revolutions in one second. But the particle on the outer track would have to travel further, and therefore faster, in that second.

What if we were to place 100,000 particles on the inner track and another 100,000 particles on the outer track? Those on the inner track would be fairly tightly packed, while those on the outer track would be (relatively speaking) fairly spread out. But if the disk is rotating at exactly 1000 revolutions per second, a read/write head stationed on the inner track would

Fig. 11.10
A disk drive. Through the windows, you can see
two disk packs. The control unit is on top.

see 100,000 particles per millisecond. The same head moved to the outer
track would also see 100,000 particles per millisecond. The read/write head
is designed to read "so many" characters per second; timing, and not physical distance, is the controlling factor. Each track has the same capacity.

Typically, what is this capacity? Since there are many different types of
disk packs, there are many possible answers to this question. Some packs
have only two data surfaces, while others have ten; still others stack as
many as twenty surfaces on a single spindle. IBM's 3330 disk system uses
packs that hold 13,030 characters of data on each track. There are 404
tracks (plus seven alternate tracks) on each surface and 19 surfaces per
pack, giving a total of 7676 data tracks. Given the capacity of each track,
there is something in excess of 100 million characters of storage capacity
(100 **megabytes**) on each pack. IBM's 3330 is also available in a dual-
density version, yielding twice the capacity. Other manufacturers offer similar products.

Disk drives are often sold in clusters; Fig. 11.10, for example, shows a
drive housing two packs. As with any I/O device, a disk drive is attached

to a computer through a channel and a control unit. When several disk drives are housed in a single package, they usually share a control unit. Disk, being a high-speed I/O device, usually communicates through a selector channel in burst mode, meaning that only one disk can be communicating with the computer at any one time. Since only one drive can be active at a time anyway, it makes sense to share the control unit. A typical 3330 system might consist of a cluster of eight drives sharing a single control unit; this means that eight disk packs with a combined total of 800 megabytes of storage capacity are on-line with the computer.

Disk packs are normally removable; in other words, they can be taken off their drives and stored off-line (Fig. 11.11). An installation with eight disk drives might well have twelve to sixteen packs containing active data, switching packs to match the needs of the current programs. Switching disk packs does, however, take time—time during which the drive is not available for other use. As a consequence, many data processing centers frown on switching disk packs, preferring to keep the same packs spinning all day. It is possible to purchase fixed-head disks that cannot be removed.

Fig. 11.11
Disk packs can often be removed. Here the operator is removing a small disk pack from a minicomputer system.

Photo courtesy of Honeywell, Inc.

Incidentally, an individual disk pack, like an individual reel of magnetic tape, is sometimes called a volume.

Floppy Disks and Diskettes

Not all disk applications call for the massive storage capacity of a full-sized disk pack. In Chapter 4 we discussed key-to-disk data entry systems on which an operator entered data directly to disk; how many characters can the average terminal operator type in one day? This application calls for a smaller, more easily handled disk pack. A similar need can be found on smaller minicomputers, where the amount of data that must be stored is usually less than might be expected on a larger machine. In both cases, the answer is the floppy disk or the diskette.

A **floppy disk** usually consists of a single recording surface (sometimes two) with a capacity of roughly 250,000 bytes. It is called a floppy disk because the manufacturing tolerances are less tight. On a regular disk drive, the read/write heads ride on a cushion of air, never actually touching the surface of the disk pack. On a floppy disk system, the read/write heads ride directly on the surface, which means that a certain amount of up-and-down movement that would be intolerable on a regular disk drive is acceptable. In effect, the floppy disk can "flop" around. The term **diskette** is synonymous with floppy disk.

THE ECONOMICS OF DATA STORAGE

Core memory (or its modern equivalent) is a direct access device, allowing the programmer to directly access the data stored at any memory location. In fact, main memory is the ideal direct access device. It is very fast, and using it, we can go directly to the desired data rather than just get "in the ballpark," as is the case with disk and drum. Why not just use core or integrated circuit memories exclusively? It's a question of economics: Main memory is very expensive, and disk and drum are relatively inexpensive.

Let's examine this question of economics a bit more closely. All types of data storage have their advantages and their disadvantages; some of these are summarized in Fig. 11.12. Let's begin with punched cards. Cards are very inexpensive. If the actual cost of the medium were the only consideration, most computer data would probably be stored on punched cards. But cards are also quite slow, being limited to access speeds of approximately 1000 characters per second. A slow I/O medium wastes computer time, and computer time is very expensive; this tends to wipe out the apparent cost advantage of cards.

Next, there is magnetic tape. Some tapes are as slow as 20,000 characters per second, while some are as fast as 800,000 characters per second, but 300,000

Storage type	Access time to locate a record	Data transfer rate in characters per second	Storage capacity in characters for a typical configuration	Cost to store 1000 characters for one year
Punched cards	Minutes	1,000	-------	Pennies
Printer paper	-------	2,000	-------	-------
Magnetic tape	Minutes	300,000	------	Nickels
Mass storage	Seconds	800,000	16 billion	Dimes
Disk	Several milliseconds	800,000	100 million	Dimes (a few more)
Drum	A few milliseconds	1,200,000	4 million	Quarters
Core memory	Several microseconds	4,000,000	1 million	$100
Semiconductor memory	Several microseconds	8,000,000	1 million	$200 (but dropping)

Fig. 11.12
A comparison of the speed, storage capacity, and cost of a number of storage media.

characters per second is a reasonably typical figure. Under ideal conditions, as many as six million characters of data can be stored on a single tape volume, and, if you are willing to accept the argument that a tape file can be spread over as many volumes as necessary, it is possible to claim that the storage capacity of tape is limitless.

Tape is a bit more expensive than punched cards, but much of this added expense is offset by the fact that tape is reusable. As we discussed in Chapter 10, tape enjoys many advantages over punched cards, particularly on the master-file update application.

But tape has its problems too. It is a sequential medium, period. You can't store anything but a straight sequential file on magnetic tape. On some applications, this is fine. On others, however, this lack of flexibility is a definite handicap. The biggest problem in using tape, however, is its accessibility. Before a program can access a tape file, a human operator must first mount the volume on a tape drive. This takes time—often five minutes or more, which in the world of computers is an eternity.

To gain accessibility, we can utilize one of the newer mass storage devices. The data cartridges are on-line and can be accessed without human intervention in a matter of seconds. The data transfer rate of mass storage devices is much higher than standard magnetic tape. They do, however, cost more.

To a human being, the ability to locate a record within a few seconds is nothing short of phenomenal, but to a computer it is slow. By using disk, the time required to find the right record can be reduced to several milliseconds. Access speed is about the same as on the mass storage system, but look at storage capacity (Fig. 11.12). We dropped from 16 billion to 100 million characters, which is, to say the least, significant. We are paying a price for the ability to locate data quickly: We cannot store as much data in one place. The actual cost of data storage is a bit higher on disk too.

When very fast data access is essential, the use of a magnetic drum is a good choice. Since a drum has one read/write head for each track, there is no seek time with which to be concerned. Thus a record of data can normally be located in the few milliseconds needed to turn the drum. Data transfer time is faster too, averaging approximately 1,200,000 characters per second. But storage capacity is way down, and storage costs are much higher.

Tape is restricted to sequential files. Direct access devices are not so restricted in that both direct and sequential files can be stored on a direct access device. With every advantage, however, comes a cost; data storage on a direct access device costs more than data storage on tape.

Stop for a minute and evaluate what you've just read. Starting with punched cards, we moved through a series of data storage devices, eventually working our way up to drum. At each step (Fig. 11.12), the new device was able to locate a record more quickly and to transfer this data into the computer at a higher speed; in every sense of the word, as we moved from cards through tape, mass storage, disk, and drum, the speed of the device increased. At the same time, storage capacity dropped off, and the cost of storing data rose. What we are looking at is a trade-off. Sure we can have faster I/O devices, but they're going to cost more and they won't allow us to store as much data. Sure we can have low-cost data processing, but our response time is going to be very slow. There's an old saying, "What you get for nothing is nothing." This is as true in data processing as in any other field.

We might consider core memory next (Fig. 11.12). As expected, it is faster than anything we have seen to this point. But it is also more expensive and, largely because of the expense, there is less of it on most systems. Semiconductor memory is even faster but, once again, it's more expensive.

WHAT'S THE BEST DATA STORAGE DEVICE?

In Chapter 8, we considered the question, "What's the best programming language?" We answered that it depends on the application. Not surprisingly, the answer to the question, "What's the best data storage device?" is the same.

The selection of a storage device depends on a number of factors. Cards are inexpensive but slow; what is the cost, in terms of wasted computer time, of slow I/O? Semiconductor memory is very expensive but very fast; is the extra speed worth the extra cost? In general, the selection of a storage device depends on the answer to two crucial questions: How fast do we have to be and how much are we willing to spend?

A national air defense system must be fast. How much time do we have to react to a possible enemy attack in this nuclear age? Is cost a limiting factor? Yes, but it's not *very* limiting; our leaders are not willing to gamble our lives for a few hundred thousand dollars. Therefore, high-speed I/O will be used.

What about processing payroll? This job can be scheduled, so speed is not really essential. This, as we've seen, is a tape job, with tape being selected over cards for economic reasons.

The best data storage medium for a given job depends on the requirements of that job. The selection of a storage device involves a number of trade-offs, as we sacrifice speed for capacity and lower cost. There is no simple answer to the question: What's the best data storage device?

TRENDS IN DATA STORAGE

The major problem with existing bulk storage devices is the fact that all involve mechanical motion. Tape must be physically mounted on a drive, and the tape must be wound and unwound from reel to reel. On a mass storage device, an access arm must move in order to select the proper data cartridge. Disk and drum both rotate; on disk, the read/write heads move. This mechanical motion is a source of both delay and wear.

Core memory and modern semiconductor memories do not move. Data is stored as a pattern of electronic pulses, and can be written or read electronically without the need for rotation or movable read/write heads. As a result, main memory is much faster than any bulk storage device and does not wear out. Technically, this makes main memory the ideal data storage device.

The only problem with main memory is cost—it is expensive. There are, however, a number of new technologies that show promise of supporting economical, nonmoving bulk storage. Among the possible successors to disk and drum are magnetic domain "bubble" memories, charged-coupled semiconductor devices, electron beam devices, and laser beam devices.

SUMMARY

This chapter began with a discussion of a number of computer applications for which the batch processing approach is less than adequate. Direct access was presented as a solution.

The concept of direct access was introduced through the imaginary exercise of cutting magnetic tape into a number of strips and then selecting and mounting the strip containing the desired record of data. An unsuccessful attempt to implement this concept, the data cell, and an apparently successful attempt, the modern mass storage device, were then presented.

Magnetic drum was the first of the commercially successful direct access devices. A drum is a cylinder coated on the outside surface with a magnetic material. Data is stored around this surface in circular patterns called tracks. Drum normally has one read/write head for each track; thus the only delay involved in locating data is a rotational delay.

Magnetic disk is today's most popular direct access medium. A disk is a plate-shaped object with a magnetic coating on both flat surfaces. Data is stored on these surfaces in a series of concentric circles called tracks. A moveable read/write head allows access to any single track; the time required to move this head is called seek time. Frequently, several disks are stacked on a single spindle, with a single access mechanism simultaneously handling all surfaces. One position of this read/write mechanism defines a cylinder, which contains several tracks.

Small floppy disks or diskettes are growing increasingly popular on minicomputers and terminals.

The chapter ended with a discussion of the economics of storage device selection. Storage capacity and speed tend to be inversely related; as speed increases, storage capacity drops. Higher speed also costs more. In a final note, the possibility of future nonmoving bulk storage was discussed.

EXERCISES

1. What is meant by the term batch processing?

2. What do the terms on-line and real-time mean? How does an on-line, real-time system differ from a batch processing system?

3. Why is magnetic tape less than adequate on an on-line, real-time system?

4. What is direct access?

5. Briefly explain how a modern mass storage device accesses data.

6. How does a magnetic drum work?

7. Reading data from disk (or writing data to disk) involves three distinct steps: seek time, rotational delay, and data transfer time. Explain each of these three steps.

8. Explain the difference between a track and a cylinder on disk.

9. What is a floppy disk? Why is it used?

10. Compare magnetic tape, a mass storage device, disk, and drum in terms of their speed, storage capacity, and physical limitations (direct access, sequential access, etc.).

KEY WORDS

access arm	drum, magnetic
access time	floppy disk *251*
cylinder	mass storage device
data cell	
data transfer time	megabyte
	on-line
direct access	real-time
disk, magnetic	rotational delay
disk pack	seek time
diskette	track

Data Management

In Chapter 10 we discussed how data can be stored
on magnetic tape, while in Chapter 11 we covered
data storage on a direct access device. In both
chapters, we concentrated on the physical nature of
the I/O devices, using examples to illustrate main
points. In this chapter, we turn our attention to the
data that is stored on these devices, describing a
number of techniques for organizing and managing
files. Both sequential and direct files will be covered
in some detail, and brief discussions of indexed
sequential and virtual files are included. The key
ideas of data base management, one of the more
important trends in current information processing,
will be explained. The chapter ends with a discussion of the factors to be considered in selecting a
file organization.

DATA MANAGEMENT

In Chapter 10 we introduced the concept of a program library—a place in which programs are carefully cataloged and stored for future recall. A library is more than just a place where programs can be stored; careful cataloging to ensure retrievability is every bit as important as the physical fact of storage.

Data too must be retrieved. Once a file has been created, how can we be sure that we'll be able to find it when we need it again? Once a file has been located, how can we find the individual records we need? These are the kinds of questions with which **data management** deals.

The telephone book provides a number of excellent examples of what is meant by the term data management. First, how can you be sure that you have the correct phone book? (A New York City directory would not be very useful in Los Angeles.) The cover clearly identifies the city or area covered by that particular telephone book. Inside the book, data is arranged in alphabetical order; in other words, it is organized sequentially. Knowing the rules used by the telephone company in organizing the phone book, we can very quickly find the specific name and telephone number that we need.

Our first concern in the discussion of computer data management is one of locating the proper file. Once a file has been found, we must know the rules used to create that file if we want to be able to find individual records. Thus our second concern is to describe some of the more commonly used sets of rules: the access methods.

LOCATING FILES

A reel of magnetic tape is called a **volume.** Typically, each tape file consumes a single volume, although there are multivolume files and multifile volumes. Since people cannot read the data on tape, labels are used to identify files.

A single disk pack or a single drum is also known as a volume; the term volume is used to refer to a single physical unit of some data storage medium. The existence of multiple files on a single volume is the exception on magnetic tape; on a direct access volume, this is the rule rather than the exception. On tape, individual files are preceded by a label. Direct access files need labels too. Typically on a direct access volume, the labels of all the files on that volume are grouped at the beginning of the volume, usually on the first cylinder or two. This **volume table of contents** identifies each file and indicates where the file begins, in terms of the actual cylinder and track address.

If you refer back to the chapters on software (Figs. 8.11, 8.12, 9.5, and 9.6), you should be able to find an OPEN instruction in the COBOL and assembler programs. The function of the OPEN instruction is to get an I/O operation started. On magnetic tape, this means mounting the tape volume on a drive. On a direct access device, OPEN involves, among other things, finding the desired file in the volume's table of contents and positioning the read/write heads at the start of this file.

On most systems, however, there are many different direct access volumes; disk, for example, is typically installed in clusters, with several drives sharing a common control unit. Before finding a volume's table of contents, we must first find the correct volume. One approach is to search all the volume tables of contents until the one containing the desired file is located. This might work on a small system, but on a larger system with perhaps dozens of direct access volumes on-line, the task of searching each one in turn would be too time-consuming.

An alternative is to maintain a **catalog** or **index** listing the name and location of each file on the system. This catalog could be stored at a known location on one of the direct access volumes. When a programmer wants a particular file, this catalog can be read into main memory and searched by the computer; through this approach, the proper volume and the location of the file on that volume can be determined.

On some systems, magnetic tape files are cataloged too. Such catalog entries might tell an operator or a tape librarian exactly where a particular tape volume is located (for example, shelf 3, tape 14).

Having located our file, we are now ready to turn our attention to finding a particular record on the file. The key to understanding almost all file organization methods is the relative record address, our next topic.

THE RELATIVE RECORD ADDRESS

Imagine that you are looking for a house located at 838 Main Street. You have just passed 832 Main and are approaching 834 Main. Are you heading in the right direction? How many more buildings can you expect to pass before arriving at your destination? Assuming that standard street addresses have been assigned in this town, you are heading in the right direction, and you can reasonably assume that you are only a few buildings away from 838 Main Street.

Imagine that you are looking for the number of Robert Smith in a telephone book. At the top of a column you find the name "Smith, Jane." Do you move forward or backward to locate the entry for "Smith, Robert?" Knowing that the data in the phone book is in alphabetical order, you move forward.

In both these examples, you were dealing with the idea of relative location; in other words, how far you would need to move from your present location to get to where you wanted to be. The idea of relative location can also be applied to computer data files.

On magnetic tape, we know that records are stored in a fixed sequence. It might be reasonable to number the records, assigning the number "0" to the first record, "1" to the second, "2" to the third, "99" to the hundredth, and so on. We begin with zero because then the first record on the file is located at the start of the file plus "0" records, the second record is at the start plus "1" record, the third is at the start plus "2" records, and so on. We might refer to these numbers as **relative record numbers**; they give the position of a given record relative to the start of the file.

This relative record number, sometimes called a **relative record address**, is not particularly useful on magnetic tape, but it is tremendously useful on a direct access device. Let's assume that we are working with the drum shown in Fig. 12.1. Six of the tracks on this drum hold a file. There are exactly 100 records on each track; thus, records 0 through 99 are on the first track (*relative track* 0), records 100 through 199 are on relative track 1, records 200 through 299 are on relative track 2, and so on (Fig. 12.1).

Where would you expect to find relative record 432? It should be on relative track 4. How do we know this? Well, records 0–99 are on 0, 100–199 are on 1, 200–299 are on 2, 300–399 are on 3, and 400–499 are on 4. Since record 432 lies between records 400 and 499, it too must be on relative track 4. Also, since record 400 is the first record on track, its position relative to the start of the *track* is 0. Record 401 is relative record 1 on this track, and record 402 is relative record 2 on the track; thus record 432 must be relative record 32 on the track. By knowing a record's relative record number, we can determine its physical location.

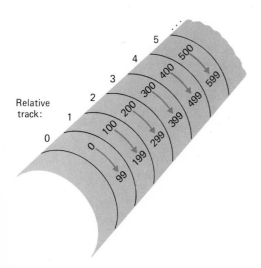

Fig. 12.1
A file on magnetic drum.

Relative track:

Given that there are exactly 100 records on each track in this imaginary file (Fig. 12.1), we might go about computing the address of record number 432 in a different manner. What do we get when we divide 432 by 100? The answer is 4, with a remainder of 32. We want the 32nd record on relative track 4. We can always compute a relative track location by simply dividing a relative record number by the number of records per track. This method works for any number of records per track, not just 100. If, for example, a file were stored with exactly 20 records per track, we would divide the relative record number by 20.

Let's refer again to the drum file shown in Fig. 12.1. We now know how to locate a record relative to the beginning of the file. How do we find the **absolute address**, in other words, the actual physical location of the record on the device?

Let's assume that our file starts on track number 50. The first track used by our file is number 50, the second track is 51, the third track is 52, and so on. (Don't forget that we start numbering relative tracks at zero.) Given this starting point, we can compile the following table.

Relative track	Absolute track
0	50
1	51
2	52
3	53
4	54
5	55

and so on.

Our file starts on absolute track 50. In every case, if we add the relative track to the address of the start of our file, we arrive at the correct absolute address.

For example, assume that we are driving from New York to Los Angeles. Our present position is 35 miles west of Kansas City. If we know the distance from New York to Kansas City, we can easily figure out how far away from New York we are. New York to Kansas City is the absolute address; 35 miles is our position relative to Kansas City.

Where does our relative address come from? Knowing the relative record number and the number of records on a track, we can compute it. Where does the absolute address of the start of the file come from? From the volume table of contents. Given these two numbers, the location of the actual track holding our data can be computed, the associated read/write head can be turned on, and the data can be accessed.

In this example, we computed a relative track address because we were working with a drum. If the file had been stored on a disk, we would have computed the relative track and relative cylinder addresses, since the physical nature of a disk drive requires both a track and a cylinder location. On a mass storage device, our objective would have been to compute the relative data cartridge. Using core, we would simply multiply the relative record number by the length of the record and compute the relative memory location. Our objective is to compute an address that is compatible with the physical device being used. In every case, however, the starting point is the relative record number.

In the above discussion, the relative record number was always known. Where did it come from? Over the next several pages, we will answer this question for a number of different file organizations.

SEQUENTIAL FILES ON A DIRECT ACCESS DEVICE

One of the biggest problems with using magnetic tape arises from the fact that a human operator must mount tape volumes on a tape drive. This is a source of error and, although the few minutes needed to mount a tape may seem insignificant to us, tape mounting represents a substantial waste of time to a computer capable of executing a million or more instructions per second.

Because of this cost, many firms maintain key sequential files on disk. An on-line direct access device also makes a great deal of sense when intermediate results must be stored on a secondary medium. As a result, even though disks and drums are called direct access devices, it is not at all unusual to find sequential files stored on them.

How do we access data sequentially when it's stored on a direct access device? Simple. The first record on the file is relative record 0, next we have relative record 1, then 2, then 3, and so on. Do you see the pattern? Just add the number 1 to the preceding relative record number. The starting point, the address of the beginning of the file, is in the volume table of contents.

We have not yet mentioned how the computer "knows" when there is no more data on a file. If you again refer back to the material on software (Figs. 8.11, 8.12, 9.5, and 9.6), you will notice a CLOSE instruction near the end of the COBOL and assembler programs. One of the functions performed by this CLOSE macro is the writing of an end-of-file marker. Later, when it is reading the file, the computer "knows" that there is no more data when this marker is encountered.

DIRECT ACCESS

Direct access means that we can go directly (or almost directly) to the single record we want without working through all the records that precede it in the file. The way we use a telephone book is a perfect example of what is meant by the term direct access.

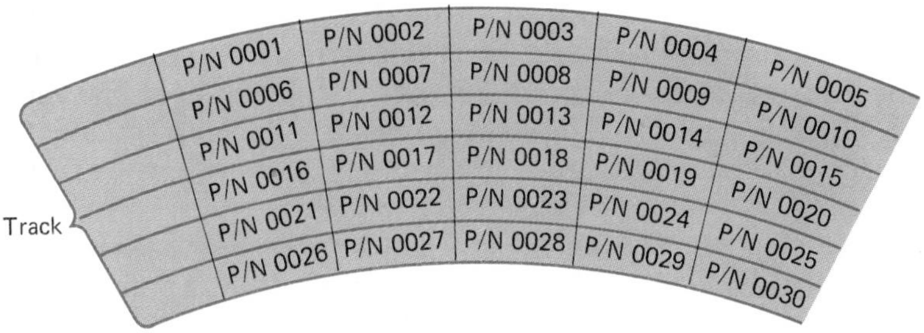

Fig. 12.2
Simple direct access with the actual key being (with limited modification) the relative record address. For simplicity, the individual records are shown as they might be arranged on a single-surface disk, with exactly five records on each track. The "P/N" stands for "part number."

To get a good example of a simple direct access file, let's take a look at a small store that stocks and sells 5000 different items. Each of these items is assigned a unique part number—0001 through 5000 would make sense. A file is created to hold records for each of these part numbers (Fig. 12.2); individual records might hold the part number, description, stock on hand, selling price, cost, source, and other information.

This file would probably be created sequentially. But look at the relationship between the part number (the **actual key**) and the relative record number (Fig. 12.2). Part number 0001 is relative record 0, part number 0002 is relative record 1, part number 0003 is relative record 2, and so on. The relative record number can be computed directly from the actual key (in this case, the part number) simply by subtracting one. Once we have the relative record number, we can compute the actual location of the record and move the read/write heads directly to the desired cylinder and/or track location, bypassing the intervening records. This is the simplest form of direct access. For this technique to work, there must be one record for every possible actual key; given this restriction, the actual key becomes the relative record number (with a possible slight adjustment, such as subtracting one).

Simple direct access does not always work. What if your school were to decide to create a file of every student's academic record? If the key to the file were the student's social security number (as is often the case), how many records would the school have to allow for in order to use the simple "actual-key equals relative-record-address" approach? Since the social security number is nine digits long, space for 999,999,999 records would be needed! Even if we were to identify carefully the lowest and highest social security numbers among the students in the school, we would still need 100,000 or more records (probably more) to cover even this limited range. If you compare the number of different records needed to the number of students actually attending your school, you will see that a great many record slots would be wasted.

Try a little experiment in your own class (or even your own home). Find the lowest and highest social security numbers in the class or group. How many different numbers lie between these two extremes? How many people are in the group? To use simple "actual-key equals relative-record-number" direct access, you must assign enough direct access space to hold one actual record for each possible key. What percentage of these keys is actually utilized by your group? What percentage of the direct access space would be wasted?

A common solution to this problem is to maintain an **index** showing the relative record number of each record. As the file is created, a table is built showing the actual key and the relative record number of the associated record of data (Fig. 12.3). Normally, this index is kept in sequence by actual key. Later, when a record is to be retrieved, the actual key can be looked up in the index, the matching relative record number found, the actual physical address computed, and the data accessed.

On large files, the index can become so big as to be difficult to maintain. When this happens, a technique known as **randomizing** is sometimes used.

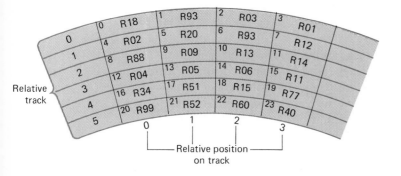

Fig. 12.3
Direct access using an index.

Index			Computed	
Actual key	Relative record number		Track	Record
01	3		0	3
02	4		1	0
03	2		0	1
04	12		3	0
05	13		3	1
06	14		3	2
09	9		2	1
11	15		3	3
12	7		1	3
13	10		2	2
14	11		2	3
15	18		4	2
18	0		0	0
and so on				

The basic idea of randomizing is to take the actual key and grind it through a number of mathematical computations so as to compute a relative record number.

For example, let's say that our actual key is a social security number. The social security number is nine digits long, much too long to use as a relative record number. But what if we were to create a new number by selecting only the second, fourth, sixth, and eighth digits? Social security number 123–45–6789 would, for example, become relative record number 2468. We now have a four-digit number, and there are only 9999 possible different four-digit numbers. This computed key could be used as a relative record number.

Although not too many people would be expected to have social security numbers with the same four digits in these four positions, some would. What happens when the actual keys of two different records compute to the same relative record number? Obviously, we cannot store both records at the same place on a direct access device. When two or more different actual keys produce the same relative record number, we have a **synonym**. Synonyms must be stored in an **overflow** area. Later, when the data is to be retrieved, a check of the record at the computed location might show that it is the wrong record. In such a case, the read/write heads must be moved to the overflow track or overflow area so that the proper record can be found.

The randomizing **algorithm** described above is a very simple one; most are far more complex, involving mathematical computations that are beyond the scope of this book. The whole purpose of randomizing is to produce relative record numbers that are evenly distributed throughout the space available to the file, with a minimum of synonyms.

INDEXED SEQUENTIAL FILES

A major problem with the index approach described above is the difficulty encountered in maintaining the index. Using an indexed sequential approach, special system software maintains the index.

To create an **indexed sequential file**, data must first be sorted into sequence by key. The individual records are then copied to successive locations on disk, with no space (except for the usual interrecord gaps) between records. As a track is filled, the key of the last record added to the track is placed on a **track index**. Later, when searching for data, if the actual key is found to be less than the key of the last record on this track, then we know that the record must lie on this track.

As more and more records are added to the file, more and more tracks will be filled, increasing the number of entries in the track index. Eventually all the space on an entire cylinder is filled. When this happens, the key of the last record added to the cylinder is placed in a **cylinder index**. A cylinder, remember, consists of several tracks.

Moving along to the next cylinder, a new track index is started, containing the key of the last record stored on each of the tracks in this second cylinder. When this cylinder is filled, another entry is made in the cylinder index, and the system moves along to the next cylinder. Note that there is one cylinder index for the entire file and one track index for each cylinder.

Once the file has been created, the records can be accessed either sequentially or directly. How sequential access is achieved should be obvious, since the file was created sequentially. To access a record directly is a three-step operation:

1. Get the cylinder index and locate the cylinder holding the desired record.

2. Get the track index associated with this cylinder and identify the track holding the desired record.

3. Move the read/write heads to the indicated cylinder, turn on the head associated with the indicated track, and search for the record with the correct key.

The ability to access data either directly or sequentially is the major advantage cited for the indexed sequential technique. This advantage, of course, also exists with the "actual-key equals relative-record-number" and the "programmer-maintained table-of-contents" approaches.

Because of the need to access both a cylinder and a track index prior to locating a record of data, direct access is relatively inefficient on an indexed sequential file. The indexes are normally stored on disk, along with the data. To find a given record means a seek and a read for the cylinder index, another seek and a read for the track index, and a final positioning of the read/write heads to get the data. Careful file design can help to minimize some of the time lost on these multiple I/O operations, but the fact remains that three I/O operations for each record is inefficient.

Since an indexed sequential file must be created in sequence, it is difficult to add and delete records using this approach. Every possible storage location is filled in creating the file; thus there are no blank spaces for new records. The need for absolute sequence creates other problems as well. Let's assume that on a particular indexed sequential file the last record stored on the first track has a key of 52. What this means is that all the other records on this track have keys of less than 52; if this were not true, the indexing method would not work. If we want to add record number 50, it must go onto this first track, but there is no room for it, making the process of adding *overflow* records to an indexed sequential file very complex. Such records complicate both direct and sequential file access, adding to the inefficiency of an indexed sequential file.

Perhaps the major disadvantage of the indexed sequential approach to file management is its "disk only" orientation. Cylinder and track indexes are maintained in support of an indexed sequential file. Cylinders and tracks exist on disk, and on no other input/output device. There are a number of new technologies which show promise of eventually supplanting disk. When these new devices become commercially available, they probably won't support indexed sequential files in quite the same way as on disk. On files using relative record numbers, a switch to one of the newer devices should be relatively transparent to the programmer. Programs accessing indexed sequential files may, however, require substantial revision.

FUTURE APPROACHES

By far the best of the available direct access devices is core memory or its modern equivalent. Since no mechanical motion is involved, it is very fast. Also, it is possible to go directly to the desired record (or even character), rather than just getting as close as the desired track. The only disadvantage to using main memory for bulk data storage is its high cost.

Future memory developments will probably try to copy the best features of main memory. Specifically, future bulk memory will involve less mechanical motion and will be addressed more like main memory than are the present disk and drum.

What does this mean in terms of the file organizations we have discussed in this chapter? These trends will really not create a problem for techniques using the relative record number approach to direct access. Main memory is addressed by numbering the memory locations sequentially. When relative record numbers are used, secondary memory is "addressed" by numbering the records sequentially. Let's assume that each of the records in some future file is 100 memory locations in length. The first record, relative record 0, is zero memory locations away from the start of the file (because it *is* the start of the file). The second record, relative record 1, is exactly 100 memory locations away from the start of the file. The third record, relative record 2, is 200 memory locations away from the start, and so on. The pattern should be obvious; relative record addresses are much like main-memory addresses.

The conversion is not quite as easy with an indexed sequential file. Cylinders and tracks exist because of, *not* in spite of, the physical mechanical nature of a disk drive. When disk is eventually supplanted by faster and more cost-effective secondary-storage devices, the indexed sequential technique will also change.

Many modern computers support a new type of file organization based on a **virtual storage** approach. Virtual storage is a technique for expanding the capacity of a computer by putting much of what would normally be in main memory on a secondary-storage device (we will be discussing this in more detail in a later chapter). To simplify the task of the programmer, virtual memory systems include special hardware or software that assumes the responsibility for converting the secondary-storage addresses into their main-memory equivalents. In other words, the programmer can program as though everything were in main memory, and the fact that portions of the program might actually be on secondary storage is completely transparent, with any necessary address translation being handled by the system.

This is a very important concept from the standpoint of data access too. Why not simply give the "system" a relative record number and allow it to do whatever is necessary in order to figure out the actual secondary-storage location of the data? Using this approach, the actual physical input or output device used by the system would be of no concern to the programmer; data access would be device-independent. If at some time in the future the actual physical device were to change, so what? Only the special system software or hardware, and *not* all the programs, would need to be changed.

The special software or hardware needed to implement virtual storage normally assumes a rather rigid organization of data on the secondary-storage device, usually requiring a series of fixed-length blocks. Given this restriction, such *virtual-storage access methods* are available (and widely used) today.

THE LINK TO SOFTWARE: THE ACCESS METHOD

Is it necessary that the programmer be aware of the intimate details of file access in order to write a program? No. Typically, the programmer states, in some formal way as part of the program, that either a sequential file, a direct file, an indexed sequential file, or a virtual file is to be used. The exact procedure for defining the file type varies from language to language and from manufacturer to manufacturer, but once a programmer learns the rules, it is a fairly straightforward procedure.

This definition is subsequently used by the linkage editor program in selecting an access method. Let's briefly review the functions performed by the linkage editor. A compiler program converts a programmer's source code to an object module (Fig. 12.4). The linkage editor adds such things as access methods and buffers to the object module to form a load module (Fig. 12.4). The resulting load module (Fig. 12.5) can then be loaded and executed.

There are many different kinds of access methods available. On an IBM machine, for example, there are two types of sequential access methods: a Queued Sequential Access Method (QSAM) which automatically performs blocking and deblocking, and a Basic Sequential Access Method (BSAM) which leaves these responsibilities to the programmer. The Indexed Sequential Access Method (ISAM) also has both Queued (QISAM) and Basic

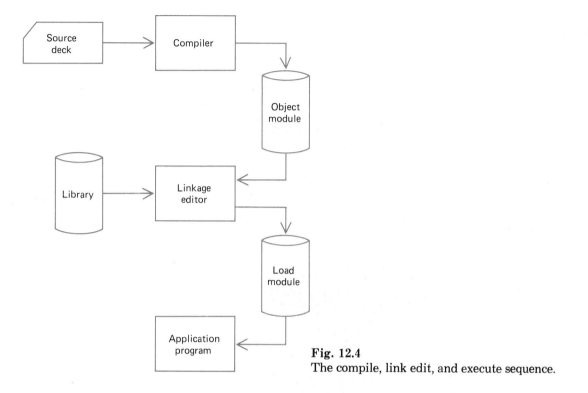

Fig. 12.4
The compile, link edit, and execute sequence.

Fig. 12.5
A load module.

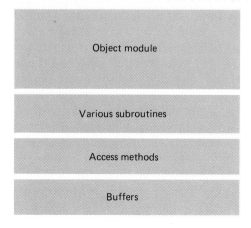

(BISAM) versions. Only a Basic version (BDAM) is provided for direct access. Virtual files are accessed through VSAM, the Virtual Storage Access Method. BTAM, QTAM, and VTAM allow the program to access files over telecommunication lines, a topic to be covered in Chapter 16.

DATA BASE MANAGEMENT

The fact that a computer is an information processing machine is what makes this machine so valuable. Information is the key to decision making in an organization, and the computer is a warehouse of information. Logically, this information should be available to management, but all too often it is not.

Files have historically been designed to match a specific application. Payroll files contained all the data neded to support the payroll application. Inventory files held only those fields which were necessary to the processing of inventory. The personnel department might maintain a different set of files to keep track of employee progress. This approach is not unique to business: At a university there are files for a student's academic record, different files for financial matters, and still other files for housing and financial aid.

On the surface, it makes sense to customize a file to an application, but this does cause problems. Your name and address, for example, probably appear on several different university files. What if you move, marry, or legally change your name? The chances are that the financial files will reflect the change quickly and accurately, but what about the other files? What we have here is **redundant data,** in other words, the same data appearing in several different places. With redundant data, a simple name change must be processed several different times in order to correct every copy; unfortunately, it seems that one or two of the versions are usually incorrect. Redundant data is difficult to maintain; hence it is often inaccurate.

Why not store just a single copy of each student's name and address and allow every program to access it from this single location? In this way, data redundancy would be minimized. Data accuracy would improve because a change, once made, would immediately be available to every program. This is one of the basic ideas behind a concept known as **data base management**.

Using the data base approach, data is treated as an important organizational resource, *not* as the property of an individual programmer or department. The emphasis is on the accuracy and the accessibility of the data. Often, to improve accessibility, logically related elements of data are linked together. Perhaps the best way to illustrate these ideas is through an example.

A university maintains a number of files on every student: academic records, financial records, financial aid records, housing records, and others. Under a data base management system, each student might be assigned a master record (Fig. 12.6) containing such key data as the student's ID num-

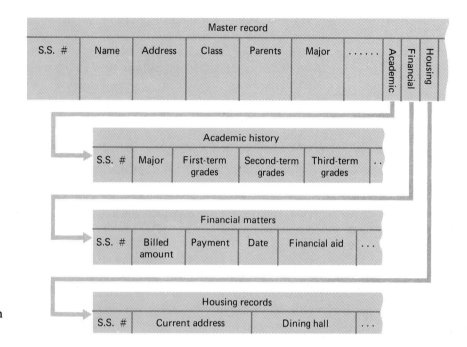

Fig. 12.6
Data relationships on an
integrated data base.

ber, name, address, class, parents' name and address, major, and so on. Also contained in this record are a number of **pointers** to other records (Fig. 12.6), including this student's academic, financial, and housing records. These pointers might be the relative record numbers of the related records that are located in other physical files on, perhaps, physically separate pieces of equipment.

Beginning with this master record, it is possible to collect all the data the university has on any one student. The secondary files can still be processed independently (the academic history file, for example, would be updated each term), accessing the master file record through its key (the social security number in this example) when data such as the student's name and address are required. Since all requests for a name and address will access the same copy, the chances are that the data obtained will be the most accurate and up-to-date information available.

When the records in a data base are connected in this way, they are said to be **integrated**. On a well-planned **integrated data base**, all relevant data can be tracked down and found; in other words, the data is accessible. Building such a data base is not an easy task. Data base design starts with a definition of all of an organization's data resources, identifies key interrelationships between individual elements of data, and then puts the pieces together as an integrated whole rather than as a collection of separate and independent files.

The whole point of a data base is to make the data resources of the organization available to whoever needs them.

Physically, the elements of a data base are the same records and files we discussed earlier; the only difference is the integration of these files. A data base management system might use sequential, direct, indexed sequential, or virtual files, actually accessing the data through one of the standard access methods. The physical devices are the same too—disk, drum, tape, and mass storage. The pieces are merely put together in a different way.

We will return to the concept of data base management in Chapter 15, when we discuss modern system software.

WHAT'S THE BEST FILE ORGANIZATION?

The best file organization for a given application depends on a number of factors, perhaps the most obvious of which is the available hardware. An installation with no direct access devices is rather obviously restricted to sequential files. VSAM makes little sense to the manager of a computer center if the computer does not have the special hardware and software needed to support virtual memory. Although hardware limitations may keep an installation from using the "ideal" organization, the cost of obtaining the extra equipment needed to support the ideal approach may make it uneconomical (hence, not ideal).

Another important and often overlooked restriction is the format of existing files. If an installation is using ISAM, for example, its programmers are trained in ISAM. Switching to a new or different access method would create a need for additional training and might require the reorganization of several existing files; both training and reorganization can be costly. The status quo can sometimes keep a programmer or system designer from using what is obviously the best approach.

Another important consideration is *file size*. It makes little sense, for example, to use a direct or indexed sequential organization on a file that consumes only a single track of a disk pack. The best approach is to organize the file sequentially and search for the desired key since you can't get closer than the nearest track anyway. On a small file, it is easy to maintain an index; as the file grows in size, however, this becomes a real problem. A huge file—a complete metropolitan telephone book, for example—might be just too big to keep on an expensive direct access device, thus leading to the choice of a sequential organization on tape.

What about sequential files on disk? Disk storage is more expensive than tape storage, but magnetic tape must be handled by an operator. On relatively small, frequently accessed sequential files, the cost of handling the tape may offset the added cost of disk storage. Again, file size is a key.

Activity is another important consideration. By activity, we mean two things: the frequency with which the records in a file are accessed, and the distribution of this access. A payroll year-to-date file is considered to be very active because almost every record in the file is accessed each time the payroll program is run. When a significant percentage of the records in a file are accessed frequently, that file is highly active. Such files are good candidates for the sequential master-file update application described in Chapter 10.

A bank's checking-account master file is quite active, but not nearly as active as a payroll file; every employee in a company gets paid, but in any given period of time there will be many bank customers who do not write a single check. Savings-account master files are even less active. Because of this lower activity, many banks and savings-and-loan institutions use direct or indexed sequential organizations for these files, feeling that it is less expensive to individually look up each of the relatively few records requiring modification than it is to read the entire file in order to update a small percentage of the records. As activity declines, sequential files become less and less attractive.

An airline reservation system calls for a file to hold records for each scheduled flight. Although there may be many transactions against the file on a given day (a few hundred requests for a seat on a particular flight, for example), these requests are generally not distributed throughout the file. Very few people really care about information on a flight scheduled to leave three months from now; the greatest emphasis is on flights leaving in the near future. This concentration of activity on a small number of records (localized activity) tends to favor a direct organization.

A file's *volatility* is a measure of the frequency of additions to and deletions from the file. It is possible for a file to be very active but not very volatile—a payroll file in a company with very little turnover is a good example. A list of the current prices of each of the firms currently being traded on the stock market would be quite active (the prices change frequently) but not very volatile (new firms and bankruptcies do not occur every day, at least not on the "big board").

The indexed sequential organization is not a good approach for highly volatile files. On a sequential file, volatility is simply handled as part of a regular master-file update. A well-designed direct access file encounters little trouble with additions or deletions.

Becoming more and more important as a file attribute is *response time*, which is a measure of the delay between making a request for information and receiving an answer. In an air defense system, quick response is essential for obvious reasons. In an airline reservation system, response time is important (though not quite as crucial) for competitive reasons. If quick response is needed, the sequential access method will not do. Direct access is probably the best alternative.

The term *integration* is used to refer to the relationship between files and between various applications. A payroll application might, for example, involve a number of related files, such as the time-cards file, the year-to-date earnings file, and a personnel file. Even though the rate of personnel turnover and other personnel changes (marriages, births, etc.) might argue for a direct access file, the fact that this file is so closely related to the payroll application (integration) might mean that sequential is the best choice.

Integration can also occur between different applications. A file of current income tax rates might be used by payroll, accounting, and financial applications. In such a situation, the file's organization might well be chosen by compromise.

More and more firms are beginning to recognize the true extent of the relationship between their various data files, and the question of file integration is thus gaining in importance. Data base management is an outgrowth of this concern.

Two other factors, *security* and file *backup*, are also growing in importance today. The computer is being used to house very sensitive and important information ranging from key operational data for a business concern to classified governmental and military secrets. The theft or loss of this information could prove to be disastrous. These factors must be taken into account when planning a file organization.

KEY WORDS	SUMMARY
absolute address	In Chapters 10 and 11, we considered a number of devices used to physically store data. In this chapter, we concentrated on the data itself, discussing how data can be organized, stored, and retrieved.
access method	
activity	The chapter began with the topic of data management. Next, techniques for locating a file were discussed, followed by a presentation of the relative record address concept, the key to understanding most file organization techniques.
actual key	
algorithm	
backup	A direct access device can hold both sequential and direct files; sequentially accessing records involves simply incrementing a relative record number. Several techniques for organizing a direct access file were then discussed, including the "actual-key equals relative-record-number" approach, the "programmer-maintained index" approach, and randomizing. Indexed sequential files can support both sequential and direct access.
catalog	
CLOSE	
data base management	
data management	Since main memory is the ideal direct access device, future hardware will probably be similar to main memory, with a form of straight sequential addressing. Files organized along relative record number lines will be easy to convert, but conversion to these new devices may
direct access	

be a problem for the indexed sequential file. The virtual-storage access methods that are currently available represent a move toward device-independent files, perhaps in anticipation of these trends.

Access methods added to a program by the linkage editor represent the link between an application program and its files.

Many organizations are moving in the direction of data base management. By treating the organization's information as the valuable resource that it is, and collecting all the information into a single integrated data base (as opposed to a series of independent files), data redundancy can be reduced, accuracy can be improved, and the data can be made more readily available to those who need it.

Several factors should be considered in selecting a file organization. The existing hardware of an installation is an obvious limiting factor. The format of existing files should also be considered. File size, activity, volatility, the need for response time, the degree of file integration, and the need for security and backup are other important factors.

file organization

file size

index

indexed sequential

integrated data base

integration

key

OPEN

overflow

pointer

randomize

redundant data

relative record address

relative record number

response time

security

sequential file

synonym

virtual storage access method

volatility

volume table of contents

EXERCISES

1. What is data management?

2. Explain how a file can be located on a direct access device.

3. Explain the concept of a relative record number.

4. How can data stored on a direct access device be retrieved sequentially?

5. Discuss several techniques for organizing a direct access file.

6. What is meant by an indexed sequential file organization?

7. Explain the concept of an access method. Why are there so many different kinds of access methods?

8. What is data base management? Discuss the advantages of this approach.

9. Why is it so difficult to select a single best access method?

10. Why are each of the following considered to be important in selecting a file organization?
    - a) file size
    - b) activity
    - c) volatility
    - d) integration
    - e) security
    - f) backup

Information Systems

IV

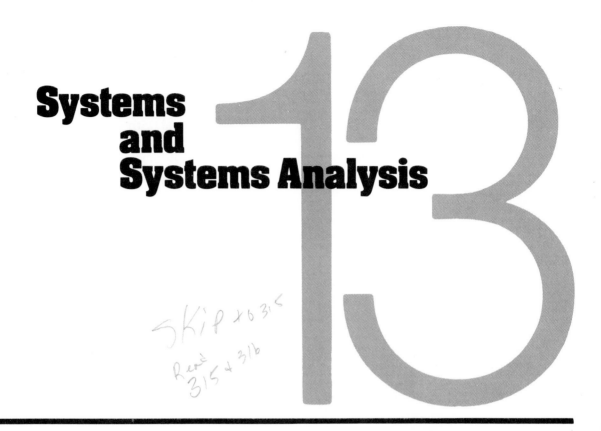

Systems and Systems Analysis

13

We have now covered the basic ideas of how a computer works and discussed a number of typical computer applications, especially file processing. Our studies have concentrated on one computer as it performed one task at a time. Actually, a computer's "real life" is much more complex than we have pictured thus far, but it is necessary to learn the basics before looking at the complexities.

In Part IV we will consider the actual environment in which modern computers work. Our first topic, the subject of Chapter 13, is the system. We'll introduce the idea of a total-system point of view and discuss the job of the systems analyst, stressing a top-down approach to systems analysis. Having introduced the system, we'll move along to the concept of operating systems (Chapter 14), using these software tools to demonstrate the dynamic environment of a modern computer. Chapter 15 expands on this information, dealing with a number of current system software topics. Part IV ends with a discussion of teleprocessing and distributed data processing (Chapter 16).

As you read this material, remember that the computer is still performing the functions that we have discussed in the first 12 chapters. What we are concerned with now is the environment in which these activities take place. **279**

WHAT IS A SYSTEM?

To the astronomer, a galaxy is a system of stars. The earth is part of our solar system. Here on earth, we are concerned with the ecological system, the economic system, and our system of government. Our nation is criss-crossed by an interstate highway system. An automobile has a cooling system and an electrical system (among others). Most of our younger citizens attend one of the schools that are part of our educational system. What exactly does the word *system* mean?

All these systems have a few things in common. They are all composed of a number of components, and these components are interrelated. Each system has a specific objective; in other words, each system performs a specific function. Some systems are planned and implemented by human beings (the automobile cooling system, for example). Other systems are natural or accidental; people do not, for example, plan ecological systems. But all systems are composed of a number of interrelated parts that work together to perform some function.

How can we gain a real understanding of the term system? We might start by stating an objective and defining the specific function to be performed. The system would then consist of all the components that must be assembled in order to achieve this objective.

Payroll is a good example of a system. The objective is obvious: to distribute a correct paycheck on time to each employee. What steps must be taken in order to achieve this objective? By combining the right steps and performing them in the right order, we arrive at a system that produces paychecks.

A Typical System: Payroll

Let's analyze a typical payroll system (see Fig. 13.1). It begins with the individual employee who punches a time card, thus creating a record of arrival, departure, and "off" times. This record is a source document. In many companies, a timekeeping department is responsible for collecting, analyzing, and correcting these time cards, thus ensuring that a reasonably accurate set of source documents is passed along to the next phase, key-punch, where the source data is converted to machine-readable form. Finally, a file of time cards, a transactions file, is ready to be read into the payroll master-file update program.

Before starting the payroll program, the operator must first mount the year-to-date earnings master file on a tape drive. This is not the simple task it might seem to be. What if an error is made? Incorrect checks might be distributed, which would upset just about everyone. The checks might be late, which would also upset everyone. Records might be destroyed. The point is that on a job as important as payroll, mistakes cannot be tolerated.

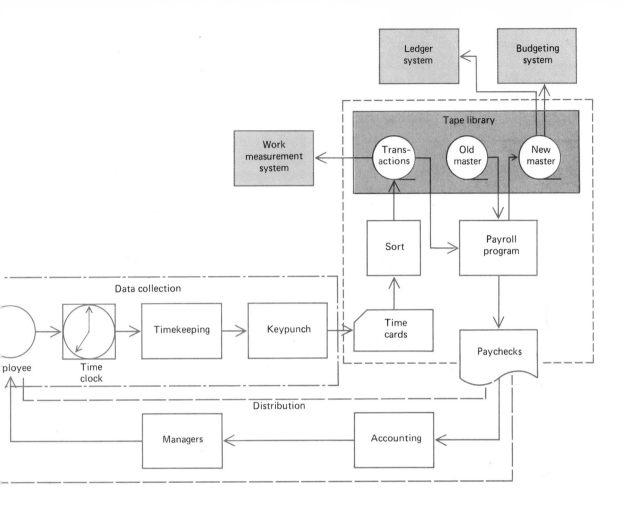

Fig. 13.1
A typical payroll
system.

So the process is controlled in order to minimize the chance of an error. Often master tapes are kept in a tape library, with a librarian responsible for storing and retrieving them. When a tape moves into or from the library, a written record is kept. On a job such as payroll, control is frequently even tighter than normal. In many companies, all but a few essential employees are cleared from the computer room prior to running the payroll, in order to minimize the possibility of accidental (or intentional) error. Such security precautions are a key part of the system.

During execution of the program, progress is carefully monitored by the operator. Often, normal processing is interrupted and a **checkpoint,** a copy of the current state of the program and all files, is taken. Checkpoints provide added protection against a program error or an equipment failure. If anything goes wrong, the error can be corrected and processing can resume at the last checkpoint, rather than at the beginning of the program (an important consideration in a long-running program).

The process does not end with the program. The new and old master-file tapes must be carefully labeled and returned to the tape library where, typically, the newly created, the old, and the prior period's old master tapes are kept. These old master files represent another hedge against error; should anything go wrong, the fact that these tapes exist allows the payroll program to be rerun.

Once printed, checks must be distributed. Normally, they go from the computer center to the payroll or accounting office where someone signs them. Why is a human being involved? One of the major problems with a computer is that it has no "common sense." If incorrect data had told the machine to compute an individual's net pay and print a check for $1,000,000, the computer would do exactly as it was told, seeing nothing wrong with such an obviously unreasonable answer. The accounting or payroll clerk is, of course, more apt to catch such an obvious error. Such errors are rare, but they do happen.

Once the checks have been signed, they are normally given to department managers for distribution to the employees. This is another carefully controlled process, with signed vouchers and other identification verification procedures helping to prevent the distribution of checks to unauthorized people.

Look at Fig. 13.1 again. It shows a series of individual functions connected by lines. Taking all these functions and interconnections together gives us a picture of the entire payroll system. Where is the programmer? He or she isn't there. The programmer's job was finished earlier when the payroll program was completed and released for production. But the programmer is a part of the system too, albeit an absent one.

Note that the computer itself and the payroll program are only parts of the system. They do not exist as ends in and of themselves. They exist because they provide a convenient, accurate, fast, and relatively inexpensive way of computing a payroll. It's the information that is important—the paychecks and year-to-date earnings files—and *not* the computer. Because paychecks are needed, the computer is needed. Computers do not create applications; they are merely tools.

You may have noticed near the top of Fig. 13.1 the presence of a number of other systems. Although it is possible to talk about a payroll system as a separate and independent entity, it really isn't. Accounting must enter the results of the payroll operation into the company ledgers. Industrial engineering or manufacturing might be interested in the hours-worked statistic for work measurement. The cost department might want actual production labor costs for its own purposes. Accounting uses these numbers to measure actual versus budget costs for the various manufacturing and indirect labor functions. Thus, individual systems are interrelated and integrated into a still larger system. In a modern business environment, nothing exists in a vacuum.

The Corporation as a System

The interrelationships in a system are very important. The higher up the managerial "ladder" one goes, the more important they become. At the bottom of a typical organization chart (Fig 13.2) are the workers who manufacture, service, or sell the company's product. A salesperson is rarely concerned with the problems of manufacturing. The individual who is responsible for inserting three screws in the bottom left-hand corner of a refrigerator is rarely interested in product design.

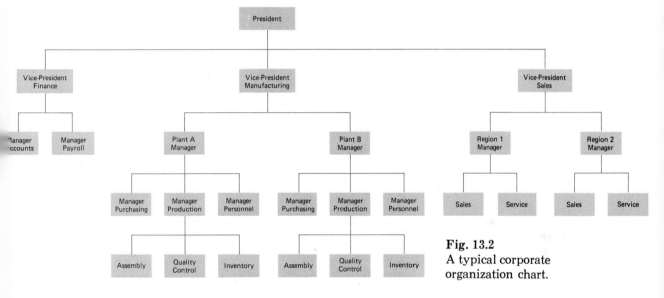

Fig. 13.2
A typical corporate organization chart.

A production manager is concerned with many different individual jobs. It makes no sense, for example, to produce thousands of engine blocks if there are only hundreds of automobile bodies in which to put them. This need to balance a number of functions gives the production manager a broader perspective than the worker has.

At the very top of the pyramid (Fig. 13.2) is the president who is responsible for coordinating the entire company. The president views manufacturing, sales, the warehouse, accounting, engineering, research and development, marketing, service, and the other functional parts of the organization as components in the total organizational system. All these functions must be performed if the organization is to be successful.

The corporate system is, of course, part of a still larger system—our economic system. The corporation impacts and is impacted by the government system, the stock market, the banking system, the monetary system, and many others. Lately we have been reading a great deal about how the corporation is part of the ecological system. The president of the corporation, however, has little control over these broader systems. For this individual, the total system is the corporation.

The University as a System

Not all systems are business systems. Assuming that most of the people reading this book are students, the university provides a relevant example of a similar broad system. Students tend to view the university from a very narrow perspective. Once each term, a schedule is published. Courses are selected from this schedule, and the student registers. Assuming no conflicts, the student pays tuition for these classes, attends lectures and labs, takes examinations, writes papers, and receives a grade. At the end of the term, a grade report is sent to the student's home.

These apparently simple activities involve the cooperation of many interrelated components. Individual departments must make a reasonable guess as to their likely student enrollment and develop a preliminary schedule. When the schedules of all the departments are combined, the inevitable conflicts must be adjusted before a final schedule is prepared, and students can register. But if too many or too few students register, additional adjustments must be made.

The registrar's office prepares a final list of the courses that each student is taking. Tuition bills are prepared or checked, and class lists are compiled for the benefit of the instructor.

Later, after final exams have been graded, grade reports must be compiled. This process starts with the instructor who prepares a grade form for each class. These grades must then be sorted into student order so as to prepare grade reports for each student.

All these activities must be carefully coordinated. The academic departments (all of them), the registrar, the bursar, the treasurer, and many other functional groups must work together if the university is to be successful. The university is a large, very complex system.

THE TOTAL-SYSTEM POINT OF VIEW

Every organization, every system, consists of a number of interrelated components. In order for the system to function properly, these components must work in harmony. Consider, for example, a football team. What good is a truly outstanding quarterback who throws so hard that none of the "just-average" receivers on the team can catch his passes? Of what use is the best defensive line in the league if the weaknesses of the secondary give opponents an opportunity to pass over the strength? Coordination and balance are crucial.

Unfortunately coordination and balance are easier to talk about than to achieve. We all have a natural tendency to believe that so long as each of the components performs at a peak level, all will be well. This may be true at a conceptual level, but all too often, "do your best" is translated to mean "do what's best for you," which is not always in the best interest of the team or the system.

A few simple examples might help to illustrate this point. What happens if manufacturing breaks all efficiency and production records during a time when sales are down? The company must keep the completed but unsold products in storage, and storage is expensive. What happens if the sales department breaks all sales records during a strike when delivery is not possible? The cost to the company arising from customer annoyance could be quite high.

Interrelationships are important and must be taken into account when decisions are made. This requires a broad point of view, a **total-system point of view.**

Let us again consider the payroll system. A decision to replace the time clock with an on-line data-entry terminal (Fig. 13.3) is not as simple a replacement as it might seem to be. Employees must be trained to use the new device. But how can the timekeeping department ensure the accuracy

Fig. 13.3
The payroll system with a data entry terminal replacing the timecard, timekeeping, and keypunch functions.

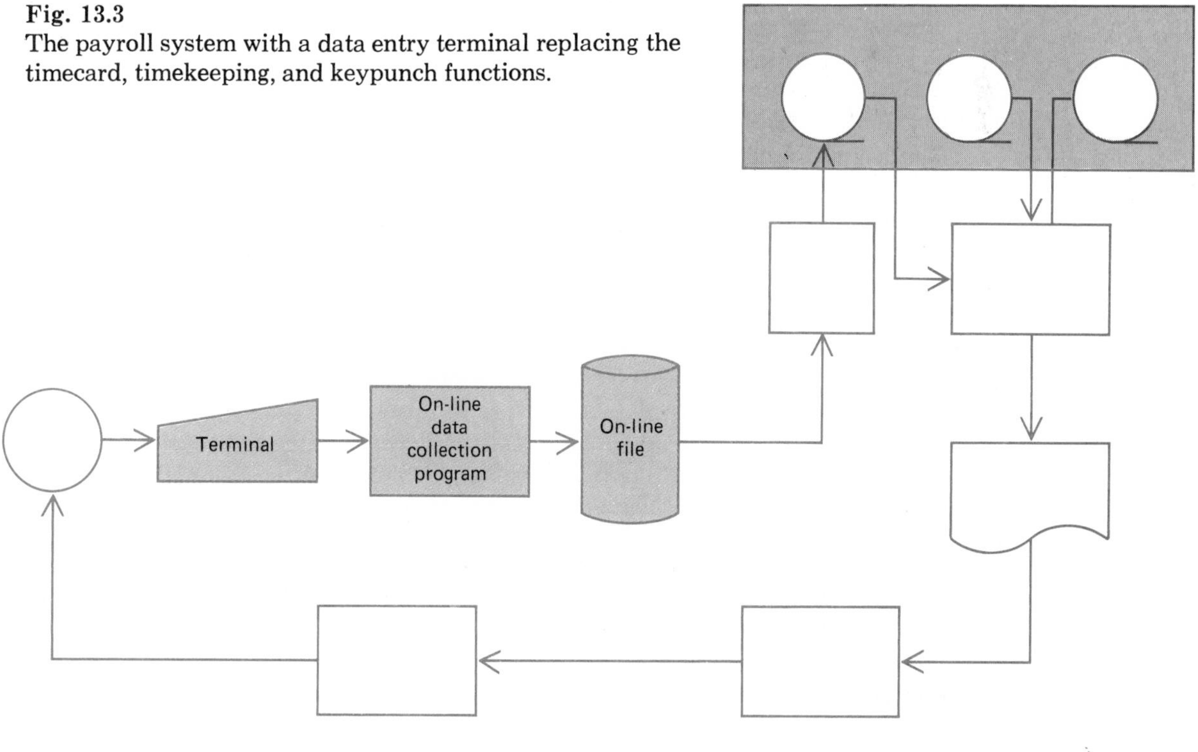

of data if it goes directly into the computer? Is the timekeeping function even necessary? If not, what can the union be expected to do about the displacement of these employees? The keypunching department will be eliminated in this new system; how will the union respond to this loss of jobs? What modifications must be made to existing payroll programs to allow the transactions to come from a different source? Do any nonpayroll programs use the old labor cards? If so, these programs will have to be modified too.

Remember the accounting, budgeting, work measurement, and other systems that depended on the output of the payroll system? All might be affected by a change in the payroll system. These "ripple effects" are very important, and must be considered. The cost of adjusting a related system can easily wipe out any benefits that might be gained from a change.

This is really the essence of the total-system point of view. It simply implies a recognition of the fact that all the functions of an organization are interrelated and that a decision made in one area can have an impact on another. An individual who realizes the importance of this broad viewpoint will attempt to identify and account for these ripples.

Baseball managers don't always play the best available hitters at every position, because they realize that defense is very important if the team is to win. Football coaches have been known to move an outstanding fullback to linebacker so as to improve the total performance of the team. In sports, the objective of the team is an obvious one—winning. The best team is not always the highest scoring team.

In business, the objective is a bit less precise; the firm is concerned with making a profit and continuing to make a profit in the future. In education, the objectives include factors that are difficult to quantify, such as maintaining knowledge, passing this knowledge along to a new generation, and creating new knowledge through research. The objective of the armed forces is to protect the country from foreign and domestic enemies. Every organization has an objective, perhaps even several objectives. The extent to which an organization meets its objectives determines that organization's level of success.

In a well-run organization, decisions and activities are undertaken with the best interest of the total organization in mind. The technical term for this is **optimization.** In a business organization with profit as an objective, optimization means to maximize total profit or to minimize total cost. Note that this does not mean to maximize profit or minimize cost within a given department or function. Cutting quality is a good way to minimize manufacturing cost, but such a move can have a negative impact on the total corporation; this is called **suboptimization.** Real optimization—doing what is best for the total organization rather than for just a single department— requires a broad, total-system point of view.

Why is the computer important in this context? Because the best way to attain this broad viewpoint is through information, and, at least in larger systems, the computer is the storehouse of information. Note that optimization and the total-system point of view are not *derived* from the computer and do not *require* the computer. Outstanding leaders have followed these basic principles for centuries. The computer is merely a tool that makes the analysis of a total system easier. And that makes the computer a very important tool. But it's just a tool.

SYSTEMS ANALYSIS

Unfortunately, the organization chart of the typical organization (see Fig. 13.2) only promotes the total-system point of view at the very highest levels. In most organizations, each individual member is given responsibility for a specific function and is rewarded (or punished) based on performance. Is it reasonable to tell a salesperson to stop selling a particular product because of manufacturing problems when that salesperson is paid on a commission basis and can be fired for failure to meet a sales quota?

High-level management is responsible for the coordination function but as modern organizations become more technical in nature, it becomes more difficult for management to be really aware of all the possible consequences of a given course of action. Thus a new field of specialization has come into being: **systems analysis.**

The **systems analyst** is not a manager, but a technical professional responsible for planning and implementing systems. The analyst's job is to study a complete system from a broad, total-system viewpoint, dealing with the details of each individual function (or subsystem) within the total system and considering the interrelationships with other systems. Based on this analysis, the systems analyst recommends a course of action to management. Ideally, management is given a number of clearly identified alternatives from which to choose. Once management decides on a course of action, the analyst helps to implement the decision. The analyst shares the broad viewpoint, but not the authority or responsibility, of the manager. Let us again consider the payroll system presented at the beginning of this chapter (Fig. 13.1). In attacking this problem, an analyst would probably begin by defining it. In this case, a management decision has already been made: paychecks will be printed and distributed to all employees. Thus the definition of the problem is a relatively simple task in this case—devise a system to produce paychecks. Problem definition is not always so easy.

Now the problem becomes one of analysis. How are the paychecks to be produced? Company policy and the union contract specify that pay is to be computed by multiplying the number of hours worked by an hourly pay rate. Federal, state, and local government income taxes must be withheld, along with union dues, credit union payments, and other deductions authorized by the employee. Records must be kept on all earnings and

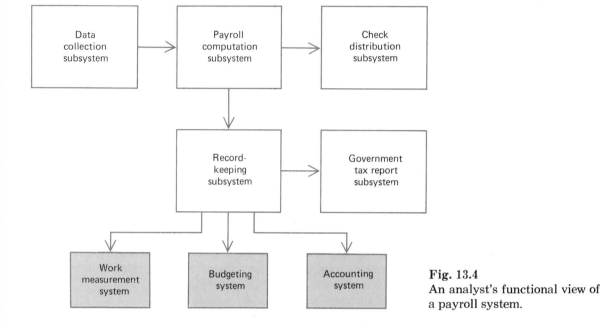

Fig. 13.4
An analyst's functional view of
a payroll system.

deductions. (Note that although we are covering a number of activities which must take place, we are concentrating on the details of none of them.)

The data to generate payroll must come from somewhere, so the analyst must consider data collection activities. After checks are prepared, they must be distributed to the individual employees, so a check distribution *subsystem* must be considered. At the end of the year, payroll records must be given to the federal, state, and local governments, so a subsystem to provide these reports must be devised. At this point, the analyst's "functional" view of the payroll system might look like Fig. 13.4.

Before moving along to the next lower level, a wise analyst would make it a point to check into the interrelationships between payroll and other systems while still working at a functional level. It is much easier to include such factors in the original planning than to change details later. In this example, for the sake of simplicity, we'll assume that there are none.

Now we're ready to begin planning the details of each of the individual subsystems. Where do we start? First let's think about the objectives of this organization. If it is a profit-making concern, our objective should be to maximize profit, but there is no profit to be made in computing payroll. Since profit is computed by subtracting costs from incomes, we can still have a positive impact by attempting to minimize cost. Thus, keeping cost at the lowest possible level becomes our objective.

Most of the cost of our payroll system is tied up in the payroll computation subsystem, making this an excellent place to start. We might very well do the same kind of breakeven analysis that we discussed in Chapter 2, comparing the cost of a manual system to the cost of a computer-based system and choosing the less expensive alternative. Note that the systems analyst does not automatically decide to put the system on the computer. The analyst deals with systems that cut across traditional departmental boundaries. Coordination of such systems implies the processing of information, and the computer is an excellent tool for processing information. Thus although the analyst is a general problem solver, he or she must be quite knowledgeable in the area of computers.

Let's assume that a breakeven analysis clearly shows that a computerized system is by far the best (meaning the least expensive) alternative. Having made this choice, we are now ready to turn our attention to the other subsystems.

How should records be maintained? As analysts, we might consider a number of alternatives, including magnetic tape, disk, drum, punched cards, or written or printed forms. Since we have already decided to computerize, we will, of course, gravitate toward some computer storage medium. We'll certainly consider the requirements of other related systems in making our choice. It is also possible that the high cost of computer data storage might cause us to reconsider the decision to computerize the payroll computation subsystem. Assume that magnetic tape is our choice after careful consideration of the alternatives.

The government tax-report subsystem is fairly simple after the decisions on computerization and magnetic tape have been made: All we need do is copy the master year-to-date earnings file at the end of each year and send it to the appropriate governmental agency. (We have, of course, already asked the Internal Revenue Service if magnetic tape is acceptable).

Let's now turn our attention to the data collection subsystem, where we have many alternatives to consider. The objective is to produce records that are ready for input to the payroll computation subsystem. We want the alternative which will produce these records at the lowest possible cost. A traditional time card and keypunch approach, an on-line data collection terminal, the traditional system with CRT terminals replacing the keypunch, even an "honor" system requiring the reporting of only deviations from a normal schedule might be considered. From these alternatives, the least expensive will be chosen. We must be careful here, however; "least expensive" implies "from a total-system point of view." Although an honor system might well be the least expensive data collection approach when only the data collection costs are considered, the risk of inaccurate data, employee cheating, and lack of control might make this alternative totally unacceptable. Let's assume that our choice, after careful evaluation of all the alternatives and consideration of all the costs, is an on-line data collection terminal.

The check distribution subsystem is fairly straightforward, with tradition and company policy being very important considerations. Typically, a payroll or accounting department signs the checks and distributes them to managers who, in turn, distribute them to the employees. An expanded view of the payroll system might now resemble Fig. 13.5.

Now we are ready to begin working on the details. We might start by specifying the exact format of the transactions and master file records. Why start here? Because the subsystems are interrelated, and like any set of interrelated functions, this fact is reflected in the information that must pass from one subsystem to another. By defining the interrelationships first, we avoid the problem of making changes after details have been "cast in cement."

Once record formats have been defined, the functions of the programs in the payroll computation subsystem can be specified: Given these two input records, we must match them by social security number and produce, according to a set of rules, a check and a new master file entry for each employee. The programmer can now begin to write a program to implement this subsystem.

Fig. 13.5
A more detailed system flow diagram.

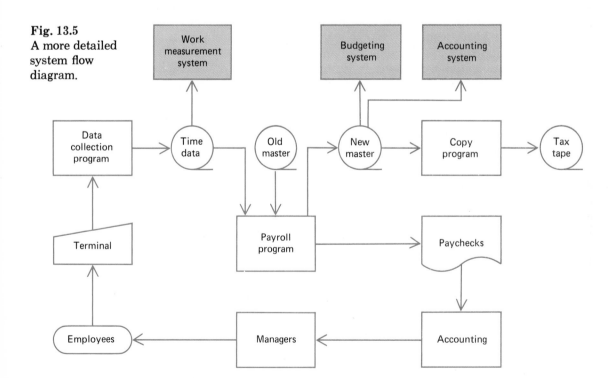

Procedures for the operator, including such things as security precautions and checkpoints, can be generated. The tape librarian can be given a set of procedures for maintaining records. Specifications for the copy program in the government tax-report subsystem can be prepared, and programming on this function can begin. Security precautions and other procedures for distributing the checks can be prepared. Much activity remains in the data collection subsystem, with input procedures to be defined and specified, a data collection program to be written, and employees to be trained.

The final step in the system development process is testing. Each of the subsystems must be carefully tested; the total system must also be put together and successfully tested before the system can be used. This is a very important part of the process. If the system has been carefully planned, testing should be relatively easy, but poor planning can come back to haunt the analyst at this stage.

The approach we took in planning and implementing this system is called a **top-down** approach. Basically, this means that we started at the top with as broad a view of the system as was possible and gradually, step by step, worked our way down to the details of implementation. The temptation is to begin immediate work on the details. Such an approach often leads to disaster, as the belated discovery of the requirements of some other system force major modifications in work that has been completed. Top-down systems analysis implies a total-system point of view; it is a highly recommended approach.

The systems analyst is responsible for planning and implementing a system. He or she brings a wide, "total" viewpoint and a solid understanding of the functions of a number of different parts of the system to bear on the problem. The interrelationships between the various parts of the system are important considerations; since these interrelationships are usually reflected in information flows, a knowledge of the computer is essential to the analyst, but he or she is not restricted to computerization. To gain an appreciation of a broad problem, the analyst often finds it necessary to construct mathematical models or to simulate various processes; these mathematical and simulation tools are also important to the analyst. In addition to these rather technical skills, the analyst must be capable of dealing with people by conducting interviews and making presentations. It's a very interesting and demanding job.

THE TOP-DOWN APPROACH

In the previous example, the systems analyst used a top-down approach to arrive at a solution. The steps in this process were as follows.

1. Problem definition
2. Analysis
3. Planning
4. Detailed planning
5. Implementation
6. Testing

Other books and other instructors (perhaps even your own instructor) may use other words to describe these steps. Some lists are longer, and some are shorter. The precise words used to describe the steps in the systems analysis process are not as important as the underlying idea of working from the top down.

We began with a very broad definition of the problem, a definition which, to the best of our ability, reflected the total-system point of view. We then proceeded to determine what had to be done, ignoring the details of exactly how these steps would be implemented. Gradually, step by step, more and more detail was introduced until finally a solution was generated. The idea of starting at the top and introducing details layer by layer, postponing hard and firm decisions on specific hardware or software until absolutely necessary, is a key to the top-down approach.

WHERE DO WE GO FROM HERE?

To this point we have been following a decidedly "suboptimum" approach to the computer, concentrating on a single program running on a single machine with no consideration being given to the rest of the system. Actually, the real environment in which a computer works is considerably more complex. Now that you have a solid understanding of how a computer works, we can begin to put these machines into perspective and spend some time discussing the environment in which they work. Rather than concentrating on the details of a particular application, we'll be taking a much broader point of view, examining the relationships between the various programs and applications running on a given computer and showing how the computer can be used to tie (physically) the pieces of an organization together.

Modern large computers are too powerful to allow individual programs to dominate them. Largely because of the tremendous speed disparity between computers and their I/O devices, these machines are normally shared by a number of programs. In Chapter 14, we will introduce the basic ideas of how these computer systems work, expanding on some of these ideas in Chapter 15. New technology has made very powerful minicomputers and microcomputers available at very reasonable prices, leading to a strong trend toward distributing or decentralizing data processing functions throughout an organization. In Chapter 16, we'll consider how teleprocessing can be used to tie such a distributed network of computers together.

As you read this material, remember that the computers we will be presenting are still performing the same functions as those we discussed earlier. Our concentration, however, will be shifting from the individual applications and toward the environment in which these applications are performed.

SUMMARY

The chapter began with a brief discussion of the meaning of the word *system*. We then developed a complete payroll system, showing how a group of related functions must be carefully coordinated in order to achieve the objective of producing valid paychecks on time. The computer is one of the components of this system. Next we considered the entire corporation as a system, stressing the importance of coordinating and balancing its parts.

We then moved into a discussion of the job of the systems analyst, emphasizing the importance of a total-system point of view and illustrating the main ideas behind the top-down approach to systems analysis. We illustrated these ideas by showing how an analyst might define, analyze, plan, detail-plan, implement, and test a system, working from the top down.

KEY WORDS

analysis

checkpoint

detailed planning

implementation

optimization

planning

problem definition

suboptimization

subsystem

system

systems analysis

systems analyst

testing

top-down approach

total-system point of view

EXERCISES

1. What is a system? You may want to define it by citing an example.

2. Why is the total-system point of view so valuable?

3. Several times in this chapter the "ripple effect" of a decision or a change has been mentioned. Explain what this means.

4. What does a systems analyst do?

5. Why is it so important to fully define a task before beginning work?

6. Why is breakeven analysis so important to the analyst?

7. What is meant by a top-down approach to problem analysis?

8. One of the topics covered in this chapter was the steps involved in the systems analysis process. Relate these steps to the top-down approach.

9. What is meant by optimization? Contrast optimization and suboptimization.

Multiprogramming, Time-Sharing, and System Software

14

OVERVIEW

In this chapter, we begin our analysis of the computer's environment. Starting with smaller computers, we'll introduce such concepts as the importance of scheduling, the use of compilers, program libraries, and access methods. Moving along to more modern machines, we'll consider the extreme disparity between the speed of the computer and its I/O devices, presenting the concepts of multiprogramming and time-sharing as solutions to this problem. The fact that a multiprogrammed computer works on a number of different programs concurrently creates a distinct risk of interference. Thus we will also examine how collections of systems software called operating systems have been developed to deal with these problems.

FIRST-GENERATION COMPUTERS

During the first generation, computers were brand-new and completely un-tried. They were very expensive and quite rare. Only a few large companies and research centers used them. These early computers were largely regarded as very powerful calculators, and were used to solve scientific, mathematical, and military problems that were too lengthy or too complex for manual solution.

This early phase of computer development was a veritable "do your own thing" period. Only a few experts knew how to program the computers (in binary, initially), and only a very dedicated (or very interested) individual was willing to tolerate the difficulties inherent in the programming task. Typically, a programmer scheduled a block of time, took over the computer room, wrote a program on the machine, executed and tested the program, made necessary modifications, and kept at it until the problem was solved (or the programmer became totally frustrated).

For our purposes, perhaps the most important development of the first generation was the basic idea of an assembler or a compiler program. Assembler language and FORTRAN were in use by the end of this period— this is not surprising when you consider the fact that one of the prime purposes of a computer was to save the time of talented human beings.

THE SECOND GENERATION AND MODERN MINICOMPUTERS

The second generation of computers began when the electronic tubes of the first generation were replaced by transistorized components. These machines were faster, more reliable, and less expensive (on a cost per transaction basis) than their predecessors. This made second-generation machines attractive to business and meant that computers began to be used to solve more general problems such as computing payrolls, keeping track of inventories, and main-taining accounting records.

Business was willing to convert to computers for these applications simply because with the declining cost and increasing speed and reliability the computer was able to perform these functions at a lower cost than human labor, a factor we considered in some detail earlier. Since computers were selected to minimize cost, it is reasonable to assume that business management would be quite concerned with controlling computer costs. For example, why spend $10,000 per month on a computer when a smaller machine, costing perhaps $7500 per month, can do the job?

A computer may save a company money, but it is still a very expensive piece of capital equipment—a fixed-cost item. If the machine costs $7500 per month it will cost that much whether it is used one hour a day or 24 hours a day. It's only natural to try to get as much work from an expensive machine as you possibly can—in other words, to try to keep the computer as busy as possible.

The term **throughput** is used as a measure of the amount of work going through a computer. Usually it is expressed in terms of time (for example, last week the computer was busy for 142 of the available 168 hours, giving 85-percent throughput). Throughput is a measure of how efficiently the computer is being used.

Suppose we are running a supermarket and decide to increase the throughput of our checkout clerks. One way of improving throughput would be to keep only a single checkout line open, forcing all our customers to wait. This tactic would, of course, keep that one checkout clerk very busy. However, it would not work for the obvious reason that too many of our customers would find another store in which to shop. Throughput is not the only measure of efficiency.

Since early second-generation computers were still quite expensive, the cost of the equipment tended to dominate the total-cost picture. The fact that programmers had to wait to have their jobs run was irrelevant, since human time was less costly than computer time. Gradually, as computers became even faster and computer costs continued to drop, this emphasis began to change. **Turnaround time**, a measure of how long an individual must wait to get the results of a computer run, and **response time**, a measure of how quickly the computer responds to a request for information or service, have become very important today. But we are digressing. Let's concentrate for the moment on throughput and consider a number of techniques which can help to increase the amount of work going through a computer.

SETUP AND THE VALUE OF SCHEDULING

Before you start to bowl, it is necessary to spot the pins. Before a play is begun, the stage must be set. Before you begin a school term, it is necessary to register for courses. These are examples of an activity known as **setup**. They describe functions that must be performed before actually beginning an activity.

Setup is present in all areas of human activity. A supermarket must stock its shelves. A bank teller's cash drawer must be prepared. Fires must be started before a steel mill can be put into operation. Apparatus must be made ready before a scientific experiment can begin. To the businessperson, setup time is nonproductive time. No steel is made when the fires are being started. No cars are made when the new tools needed to produce a new model are being installed. Since setup time is "wasted" time, it is highly desirable to minimize it.

Setup occurs on the computer too. Paper must be loaded into a printer; disk packs must be mounted; cards must be loaded. Let's take a look at one common setup activity—loading paper on a printer.

Just as a typist can make multiple copies of a letter by using carbon paper, a computer printer can produce multiple copies by using what is called multi-part paper—several sheets of paper bonded together at the edges with carbon paper between them. Imagine that you are an operator and have programs calling for the following.

Program	Paper requirements
A	four-part
B	two-part
C	four-part
D	two-part

It takes about five minutes to change the paper in a printer and, for simplicity's sake, we'll assume that each of the four programs takes exactly five minutes to run.

What would happen if we were to run the four jobs in exactly the order given? First we would set up job A, putting four-part paper into the printer (Fig. 14. 1). After the program was finished, we would set up job B, and so on. During the time in which we are setting up the printer, the computer does nothing. In the 40 minutes needed to complete these four programs, the computer actually works for only 20 minutes: The throughput rate is 50 percent.

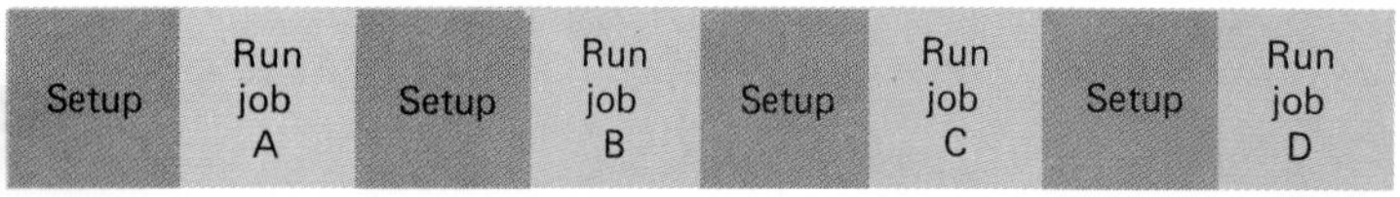

Fig. 14.1
The impact of setup.

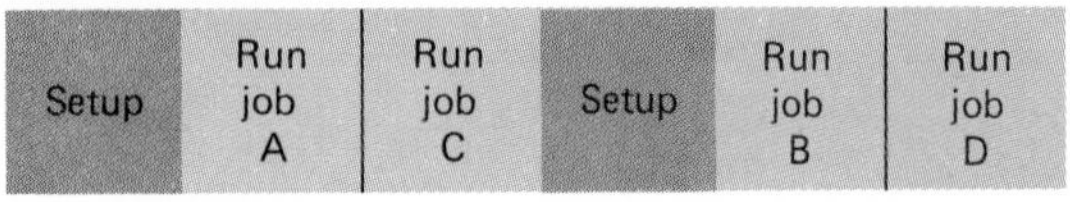

Fig. 14.2
The impact of setup can be minimized by scheduling.

What if we were to use a little intelligence and run job A first, followed by job C, and then jobs B and D? We would only need two setup operations (Fig. 14.2). The total time needed by all three jobs would be reduced to 30 minutes; the computer would be "doing something" for 20 of these 30 minutes; and the throughput rate would rise to 66.7 percent, just from a little intelligent planning. There are other instances in which **scheduling** and planning can help. Tapes and disk packs can be mounted during the execution of programs not needing these facilities. Paper can be changed during the running of a tape-to-tape program.

Scheduling is not, however, easy or automatic. It's one thing to tell an operator to run all the four-part paper jobs together; it's quite another for the operator to select all the "four-parters" from the thousands of jobs that might be in the computer room at any one time. What is needed is a system— a set of rules and procedures designed to simplify the identification of jobs by type.

In many early computer centers, the system used was a very simple one. All jobs requiring only card input and single-part paper output were thrown on table A; jobs requiring tape were thrown on table B; those requiring multipart paper went on table C, and so on. Once the jobs had been grouped according to their setup requirements, it became a simple matter for the operator to run all the similar jobs together, resulting in a minimization of the time lost to setup. Modern computers rarely use such simple scheduling systems. Rather than allowing a programmer simply to toss his or her program onto the proper table, most computer centers insist that each program be preceded by a **JOB card** (Fig. 14.3) which very clearly indicates the job's class, either through a keypunched parameter such as CLASS = A, through color coding, or through some other technique. In effect, the JOB card allows the operator or the computer itself to determine the job's setup requirements and decide where it fits in the scheduling system.

Scheduling helps to improve throughput by minimizing the time lost to setup.

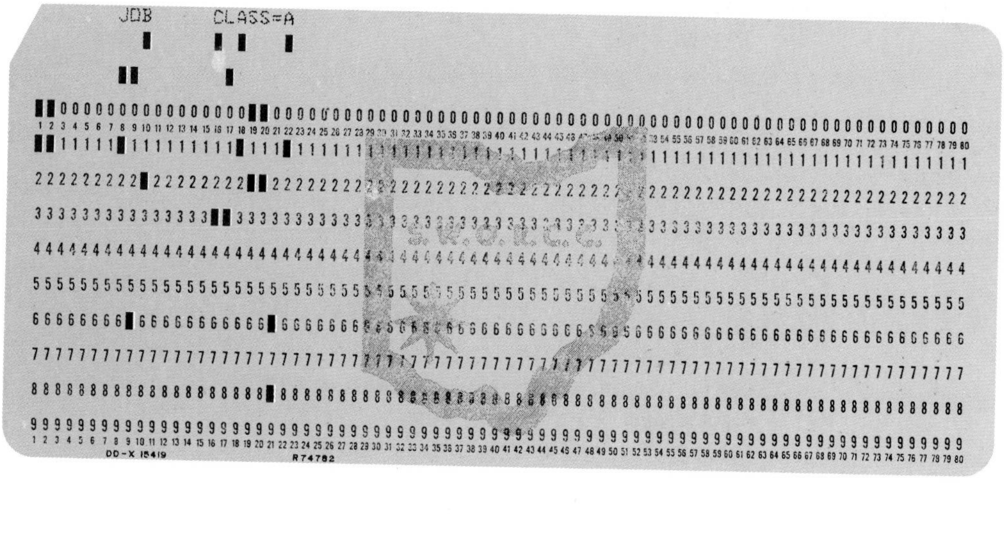

Fig. 14.3
A JOB card.

COMPILATION AND THE USE OF LIBRARIES

The fact that a computer is active does not necessarily mean that it is doing useful work. Consider, for example, what happens during the compilation process. A source module is "translated" into an object module (Fig. 14.4), which usually is subsequently converted into a load module by a linkage editor. The compile and link-edit steps take time. But is any useful work performed during these operations? Are any checks printed? Are any inventory records updated? No. Why not make a copy of the load module? Disk, tape, or even cards could be used. Once this is done, the program can be executed by simply loading a load module, bypassing the compile and link-edit steps.

In a regular computer center, this is what is usually done. A program goes through the compile and link-edit steps until it is successfully debugged. At this point, a copy of the current load module is cataloged and placed on a library for future use. From this point on, the program can be retrieved and executed by simply copying the library entry into main memory.

A library is not created and maintained simply by discussing it. Librarian programs and storage space are needed, and both are expensive. On a program

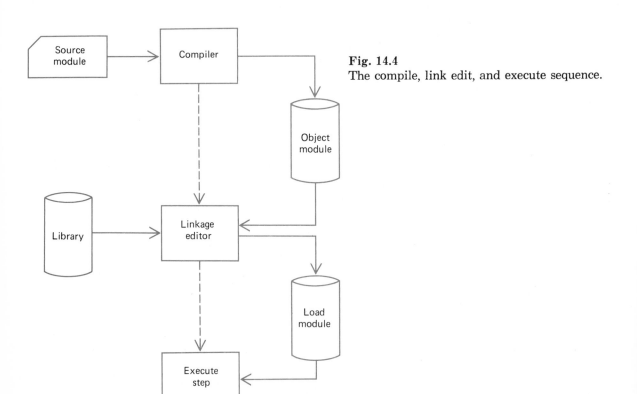

Fig. 14.4
The compile, link edit, and execute sequence.

library, the storage space is usually on a direct access device, although tape and cards are sometimes used for less frequently accessed programs. The functions of a librarian are carried out by a series of service programs that control the addition of programs to and the deletion of programs from the library, maintain the catalog needed to retrieve a program, and keep track of things in general.

I/O DEVICE SPEEDS VERSUS COMPUTER PROCESSING SPEEDS

A good card reader is capable of handling 1000 cards per minute; if a card holds 80 characters, the rate is approximately 1333 characters per second. A good tape drive can transmit 100,000 characters per second. Main memory is capable of moving 4,000,000 characters per second, and modern noncore memories are capable of doing even better. The speed disparity between a computer and its I/O devices is significant.

Consider the typical data processing pattern (Fig. 14.5) in which we read one record of data, process that data, write a record of output information, and go back to the top to repeat the cycle. What does the computer do during the "read" portion of the cycle? Is it possible to process data that has not yet gone into the computer? No. During the input operation, the computer waits for the I/O device. This also happens during output.

Since cards are quite slow, relatively speaking, it makes a great deal of sense to eliminate the reading of cards as much as possible. It is better to make the computer wait for a record from tape or disk, because they are faster. Speed of data transmission was one of the primary considerations in the decision to use tape rather than cards to store a master file. The speed of the magnetic media, tape and disk, represents another advantage of the use of libraries; copying a load module from disk to main memory is much faster than reading a source deck through a card reader.

Still, some data must be read from cards. Source programs must be written. Time cards must be processed. How can the time lost in reading this data be minimized? One technique that has proven quite effective in minimizing card reading (and printing) time is called **spooling**. During the computer's second generation, spooling was often implemented off-line (Fig. 14.6). Cards were read into an inexpensive "controller" which simply copied the card images to tape. When a tape was filled, it was hand-carried over to the "real" computer and read in. Output from the computer went to tape. Full tapes were hand-carried to another off-line controller, which dumped logical records to the printer.

What advantages are to be gained from this approach? During the input stage, the data is copied from cards to magnetic tape. Since it is impossible to copy data faster than the data can be read, this process is paced by the rather slow card reader. On eventual output, information is dumped from magnetic

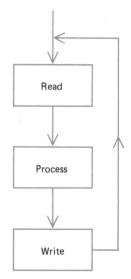

Fig. 14.5
The typical data processing pattern.

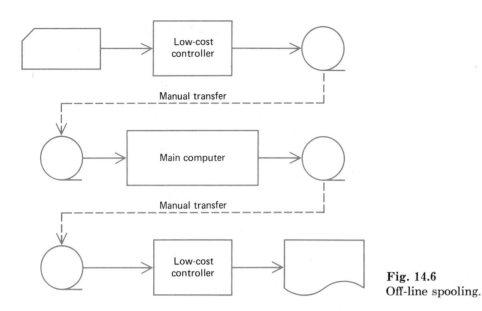

Low-cost
controller

Manual transfer

Main computer

Manual transfer

Low-cost
controller

Fig. 14.6
Off-line spooling.

tape to the printer where, once again, the slower device (the printer) sets the pace.

With a card reader and a printer attached directly to the computer, the speed of the computer is limited by these slow devices. With spooling, however, all data has been transferred to magnetic tape before being input to the computer and all data is transferred to magnetic tape (or a direct access device) before being dumped to the printer. Thus the computer always reads and writes high-speed magnetic tape. High-speed I/O means that the computer wastes less time waiting for its input and output devices, leaving more time for useful work.

There is, of course, an added expense: Special card-to-tape and tape-to-printer equipment must be purchased. Such devices are, however, considerably less expensive than computers are. It is better to waste the time of such inexpensive devices than to waste the time of a very costly computer.

Card readers and printers function in the range of from 1000 to 2000 characters per second; on magnetic tape, speeds in excess of 80,000 characters per second are common. It might take a minute or more to copy 1000 cards to tape; at 80,000 characters per second, these card images could all be read into a computer in about one second. At these speeds, the computer could easily keep up with several card-to-tape and several tape-to-printer devices. Imagine three or four input controllers feeding and three or four output controllers being fed by a single computer—this is the basic idea of spooling. Picture the computer as a superhighway, with the spooling devices being the on/off ramps that allow plenty of time for acceleration and deceleration.

In this example, the slow I/O operations took place off-line. Later we'll see how spooling can be performed on-line on a faster, more modern computer.

SYSTEM SOFTWARE

All this efficiency is not, of course, without cost. Scheduling requires highly trained operators and tightly controlled procedures. The use of libraries implies extra storage space and a number of librarian programs. The use of magnetic tape and disk means that data will often be blocked; we can expect to use access methods and may require the resources of a linkage editor. Spooling requires additional equipment and special access methods.

Several of these extra costs are really extra programs. Let's take a brief inventory of this special software. We already know about compilers and the linkage editor. We also considered the existence of sort routines and other "utility programs" in prior chapters; these are nothing more than programs that are used so frequently and in so many different applications that, rather than requiring the programmer to recode them each time they are needed, a single copy is made available to everyone, usually through a library. We covered access methods earlier; generally speaking, access methods are kept on a library and added to the load module by the linkage editor. Librarian programs are also needed.

What do all these programs have in common? They do not participate directly in any application. They are support programs, helping the "real" application programs to read data, to write data, to access a library, or to create a load module. They do not compute payroll, or update inventory, or figure out a grade point average. They support the programs that actually perform these primary functions.

In a business environment, these programs would be called **overhead**. In a manufacturing operation, the people who actually put products together are known collectively as direct labor. Everyone else—the people who prepare payroll, manage, keep track of inventory, run the computer, program the computer, keep the books, type letters, answer the telephone, purchase raw materials—is considered indirect labor. This is not to say that these functions are unimportant, since the president of the company is an indirect worker. It just means that they are not *directly* involved with building the product.

An application program performs a direct function, taking data and processing it into information of greater value. Compilers, the linkage editor, utility programs, librarian programs, access methods, and similar software packages are more indirect, functioning in a support role. The term **system software** is sometimes used to describe such programs and program modules; they belong to the entire system, rather than to any one application or programmer. This system software represents an early form of operating system, a topic we will consider in more detail shortly.

In the next section of this chapter, we'll be taking a look at larger, third-generation computers that require larger and more complex system software packages. Before we begin, it might be wise to mention the fact that many modern minicomputers still function in much the same way as a second-generation machine did, and even the larger machines continue to use most of these techniques.

THE THIRD GENERATION

Advances in electronics, most notably the development of the modern integrated circuit, have made possible a third generation of computers. These machines are faster, more powerful, and less expensive than their earlier counterparts. As a result, the use of computers continues to increase because as costs drop, the breakeven point also drops.

The beginning of the third generation is generally considered to be the mid-1960s when IBM announced its System/360 series of computers. Since that time, additional improvements and refinements have convinced many observers that we have moved into a fourth generation, with IBM's System/370 as the chief example. In the past, the change from one generation to another was abrupt and rather extreme, with modifications in program structure and file access creating significant problems for users. Since the mid-1960s changes in technology have been implemented much more smoothly, with most modifications being largely transparent to the user. Rather than become involved in an argument over which generation we are in, we will simply refer to these newer machines as the "current" generation.

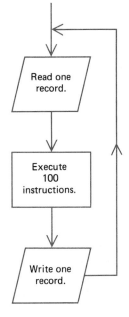

CPU VERSUS I/O SPEED IN THE CURRENT GENERATION

Modern computers are very fast, easily handling 1,000,000 instructions per second (and more)! During the second generation, a speed disparity between the computer and its I/O devices was recognized, causing the cost-conscious manager to switch as much I/O as was possible to faster devices such as tape and disk. Although I/O devices have been improved, their essentially physical nature puts a limit on their speed. Computers—electronic devices requiring no physical motion—have advanced much further. As a result, the speed disparity is much more significant today.

An example might help to explain this point. Let us assume that we have a program that (1) reads a record, (2) executes 100 instructions in processing that record, and (3) writes a record of output before going back and repeating the process (Fig. 14.7). Let's take a look at this program with card input and printer output (Fig. 14.8). Our computer is a modern machine capable of executing 1,000,000 instructions per second.

Fig. 14.7
A simple program.

A typical card reader can handle 100 cards per minute—a rate of 10 per second or 0.10 second per card. On a machine capable of executing 1,000,000

Read one record .... 0.1000 seconds
Execute 100 instructions........... 0.0001 seconds
Write one record .... 0.0500 seconds

Total cycle time .... 0.1501 seconds

Effective utilization = $\dfrac{0.0001}{0.1501}$ = 0.000666 or 0.0667%

Fig. 14.8
The program with card input and
printer output.

instructions per second, how long will it take to execute 100 instructions? Simple division tells us 0.0001 second. Printers (at least the normal line printer) normally operate in a range of from 1000 to 1500 lines per minute. If we use a speed of 1200 lines per minute (which makes our computations easy), we can calculate 20 lines per second, or 0.05 second per line. What does the computer do during the card read and print operations? Nothing. It sits and waits. Thus the time needed to read, process, and write one record can be obtained by adding the three components of the cycle; in this case, it takes 0.1501 second.

If the computer does nothing during the card read and print operations, how much time does it spend on productive activities during each cycle? The answer is 0.0001 second. In other words, if we were to read cards and print lines for 1501 seconds (a little less than 30 minutes), we would get exactly one second of work from our computer, which is less than one minute of work in a 24-hour day! No businessperson will buy or lease a piece of capital equipment which can only be used for one minute per day.

High-speed I/O devices solved this problem back in the second generation; let's take a look at tape as the input and output medium (Fig. 14.9). Tape is much faster than cards; a typical drive can easily handle an 80-character record in 0.001 second or so. Since an output line is a bit longer than a card (120 rather than 80 characters, for example), the output opera-

Fig. 14.9
The program with tape input and output.

Read one record .... 0.0010 seconds
Execute 100 instructions........... 0.0001 seconds
Write one record .... 0.0015 seconds

Total cycle time .... 0.0026 seconds

Effective utilization = $\dfrac{0.0001}{0.0026}$ = 0.03846 or 3.846%

tion will take a little longer—0.0015 second. Have we done anything to change the computer? No, we have just changed the input and output devices, so the time required to execute 100 instructions doesn't change. Our cycle time (Fig. 14.9) is now 0.0026 second. During each cycle, the computer is performing useful work for only 0.0001 second—slightly less than four percent of the time. This works out to roughly one hour per day, which is better than a rate of one minute per day but still not enough to excite the average controller.

Picture yourself as a salesperson trying to sell a computer. "I have a great machine for you, Charlie. It's a thousand times as fast as your old machine, costs only ten times as much, and does almost twice the work." Unless Charlie is unbelievably naïve, he will point out that by spending only *twice* the money, he can do twice the work by purchasing another of his old machines. Extra power is useless if it cannot be used. Why build a 200-mph train when road-bed conditions in many parts of the country restrict the engineer to 20 or 30 miles per hour? Before the current generation of computers could be effectively marketed, something had to be done to make more of the computer's power available to the user.

MULTIPROGRAMMING

Fig. 14.10
During an I/O operation, the computer waits.

The problem with which we are trying to deal arises from the extreme speed disparity between a modern computer and its I/O devices. Since a computer can't process data that it does not yet have, processing must wait for the completion of an input operation. Normally, to avoid possible errors, the computer also waits for an output operation. When computers were slow this was no problem, but today a computer might process data for a few microseconds, wait for several hundred microseconds as an input or output operation takes place, process for a few microseconds, wait for a few hundred microseconds, and so on (Fig. 14.10).

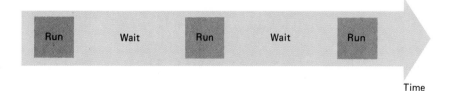

Imagine yourself running a telephone answering service. You have one customer. Over the course of your eight-hour shift, you expect, on the average, to handle three or four calls. Your job would be much like the computer's, with brief periods of activity surrounded by long periods of waiting.

What would you do with your **wait time**? Would you simply sit and wait? Probably not. You would find something else to do—read, listen to the radio,

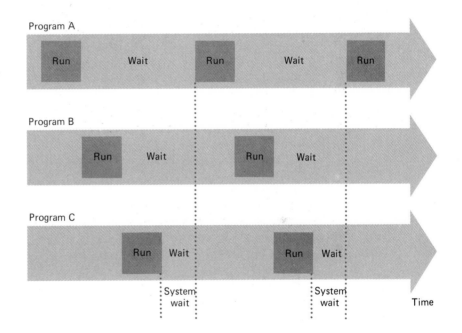

Fig. 14.11
With two programs in main memory, the CPU can switch its attention to program B when program A is waiting for I/O.

Fig. 14.12
More programs in main memory means that even more "wait" time can be utilized.

do homework, watch television, work on a hobby. If you were ambitious, you might consider taking on another client. Surely, six to eight calls a day could be handled with a minimum of interference. Why not three extra clients? Or four? Or even more? Eventually, the number of clients might climb so high that your telephone would always be busy; this inability to "get through" would tend to defeat the purpose of the answering service, so there is a limit to the number of clients you could have. But the idea of doing other work during time that would otherwise be wasted is still solid.

Why not apply the same idea to the computer? Why not put two different programs in the computer's memory? Then, when program A is waiting for the completion of an input or output operation (Fig. 14.11), the computer can work on program B. And why stop at two programs? With three, even more of the otherwise wasted time can be utilized (Fig. 14.12).

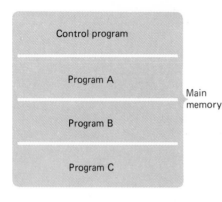

Main memory

Fig. 14.13
Under multiprogramming, main memory contains several different programs, with the CPU switching its attention from one, to another, to another, and back again, in turn.

This technique is known as **multiprogramming.** Basically, a number of programs (10, 15, 20, and even more on some modern computers) are placed in memory (Fig. 14.13) and the central processing unit switches its attention from one program to another to another, taking advantage of time that would otherwise be spent waiting for I/O.

Have you ever seen (or heard about) a chess master taking on 25 concurrent opponents? The master starts with the first board, quickly sizes up the situation, and makes a move. Then he or she moves on to the second board where the pattern is repeated, and so on. Eventually, the chess master comes back to the first board to begin a second cycle. If the expert is good (and those who participate in such exercises usually are), opponent number one has had just about enough time to analyze the board situation, decide on a move, and make it. The chess master has probably forgotten about the first move made on this first board, but has the skill and experience to recognize the board situation quickly and to make an intelligent decision.

The central processing unit on a multiprogrammed computer works in much the same way. Let's say that we have three programs in main memory (Fig. 14.13). The CPU begins working on program A. A few microseconds later, A requests the start of an I/O operation and drops into what is called **a wait state.** Since nothing can be done in support of program A for the time being, the CPU can turn its attention to program B. A few microseconds later, B needs some input data and drops into a wait state. Thus the CPU turns its attention to program C. Eventually the I/O operation requested by program A will be completed, and control can be returned to this program.

Take careful note of a few very important points. The CPU works on only *one program at a time.* We may have a number of programs in memory at the same time, but the CPU can work on only one at a time. Do you recall (Chapter 9) our discussion of how a computer works? A special register or control field (we called it the instruction pointer) contains the address of the next instruction to be executed. The CPU fetches this instruction during the first phase of the machine cycle and then executes it. In other words, the central processing unit is designed to execute *one instruction* at a time, and modern computers are no exception to this rule. How can the computer possibly work on more than one program at a time?

Thus it is not correct to say that multiprogramming means executing several programs at the same time or simultaneously. Like the chess master playing several opponents, a computer (more specifically, the central processing unit of a computer) implements multiprogramming by switching its attention from one program to another, in turn. The word **concurrent** is sometimes used to describe activities of this type. Although the words *simultaneous* and *concurrent* are very close to being synonymous, there is a very subtle difference in meaning, at least so far as computer-related usage is concerned. Simultaneous means "at the same instant of time." A central processing unit cannot execute two or more programs simultaneously. Concurrent means "over the same period of time"; the fact that, on a computer, this period of time might consist of mere fractions of a second might explain why the term concurrent is used in this sense. A central processing unit can certainly execute two or more programs concurrently.

OPERATING SYSTEMS

The advantages of multiprogramming are obvious; more programs can be run in the same amount of time and, since the cost of a computer is fixed, this means that we can do more work for the same amount of money. But where do we pay for this gain?

Multiprogramming causes a number of problems that did not arise in the old one-program-at-a-time serial batch days. These problems occur because of the conflicts that are inevitable whenever we try to do too many things at the same time.

Let's say that we have two programs in main memory: programs A and B. Some time ago, program A requested a record from tape (Fig. 14.14).

Fig. 14.14
When two programs are both ready to resume processing, which one goes first?

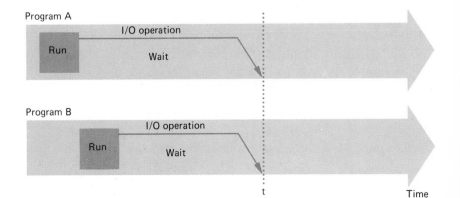

Program A

I/O operation

Run   Wait

Program B

I/O operation

Run   Wait

t

Time

After the input operation had been assigned to a channel, the CPU turned its attention to program B which, shortly thereafter, requested a record from disk. Disk is somewhat faster than tape. All of a sudden the CPU receives interrupts from both channels at the same instant in time (Fig. 14.14). Which program goes first? Two I/O operations ending at precisely the same instant is unusual. More realistically, what happens when a computer is working on one of a dozen programs currently in memory and an I/O operation for one of the other programs is completed? Two programs are ready to go. Which one goes first?

One possible solution to this problem would be to print a message on the operator's console identifying the two (or more) programs that are ready to go and requesting a decision. Assuming that the operator is alert and ready, the response might take a second or two. But in a second or two, the computer could easily have taken *both* programs to their next I/O point and probably handled several more. Even if the computer were to make a totally arbitrary and incorrect choice and simply choose one, the result would be better than having a human being make the "right" choice. Computers are so fast that human beings cannot possibly react quickly enough to effectively control them at this level. The priority decision must be made automatically and internally.

How do we do this? By writing a special program and keeping it in main memory at all times—in other words, by creating a **core resident priority module** (Fig. 14.15). Whenever internal priority conflicts occur, control is given to this special program, which makes a decision. It might use a "biggest first" rule, or it might use a "smallest first" rule. Maybe the first program in memory will be allowed to go first; maybe the last program will go first; or perhaps a more elaborate priority scheme will be implemented. The point is that the question of who goes first is handled by a program on the computer at computer speeds.

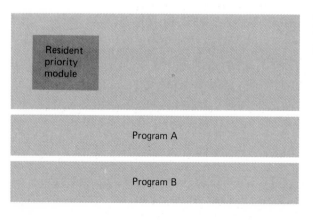

Fig. 14.15
The internal priority decision can best be made by a core-resident software module.

Memory management and **memory protection** are other important problems. What happens if program A were to read a record of data into the memory space assigned to program B? With only one program active at a time this was not a problem, but with several programs sharing main memory, it could be. The system must be capable of assigning space to programs, protecting these programs from one another, and keeping track of where all these programs are. Can a human operator possibly stop program 8 from taking over program 13's space? Consider the fact that the problem might occur during any given microsecond, and it is easy to see that this task is beyond a human being (one blink would be more than enough time to wipe out the entire system). Again, memory management and core protection are best implemented through core resident programs (Fig. 14.16).

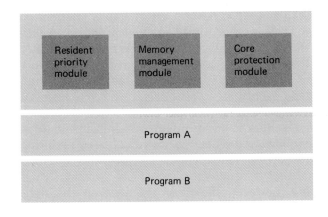

Fig. 14.16
Modules to take care of memory allocation and to provide core protection should also be resident.

What about **I/O device allocation?** What would happen if two programs were allowed to take turns writing data to the same printer? Or what would happen if program A was reading data from a tape at the same time that program B was writing new data to that same tape? Chaos! This cannot be allowed to happen. Again, can a human operator be expected to control the allocation of dozens of I/O devices among dozens of different programs? No! Once again, a special resident program is needed (Fig. 14.17).

The number of special system programs is beginning to grow, with modules to handle and control internal priority, memory management, memory protection, and device allocation clearly being needed. In Fig. 14.17, all these modules have been grouped together in a single region of the computer's memory and the term **operating system** has been used to describe this region. Depending on the computer, such terms as **supervisor, nucleus, monitor,** and resident operating system are sometimes used to refer to this collection of core-resident program modules which serve to handle the prob-

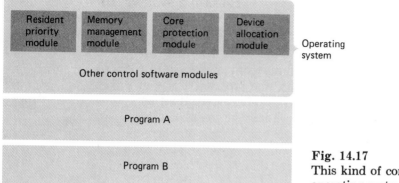

Fig. 14.17
This kind of control software is often called an
operating system.

lems resulting from the interference that is certain to occur when a number
of different application programs share the resources of a computer.

Scheduling is another problem that is beyond direct human control on
a multiprogrammed computer. This was relatively easy when only one program ran at a time, but with 10, 15, or even more programs concurrently
active it becomes very difficult, especially when (as is often the case) many
of the programs require only a few seconds of computer time. If you picture
yourself judging ten concurrent events at a track meet, you will have an
idea of the problem.

Recall that in the second generation scheduling was implemented by
grouping similar jobs, thereby allowing the operator to run all jobs requiring
only, say, single-part paper together. The grouping of programs by their
setup and equipment requirements is equally important on a modern computer. With multiprogramming, however, the "toss the jobs on the right
table" approach is not at all adequate.

Instead jobs are frequently queued to an on-line file for later processing.
Source decks and data cards are read by a job queueing program module
(Fig. 14.18) which copies them to (usually) a direct access file. Later, a

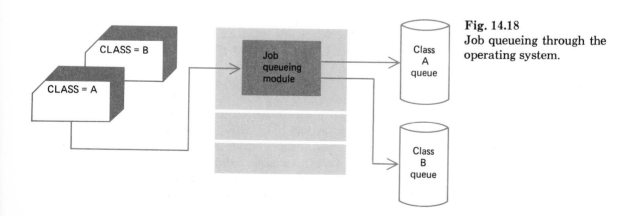

Fig. 14.18
Job queueing through the
operating system.

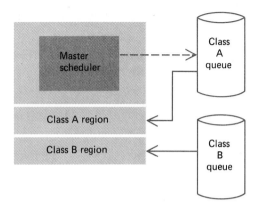

Fig. 14.19
Job scheduling through the operating system.

master scheduler program loads these application programs from the queue into main memory (Fig. 14.19). The **queueing module** and the master scheduler are two more pieces of the operating system.

Note in Fig. 14.18 that jobs are often queued to several different files. The class A queue might hold all card reader/printer jobs; the class B queue might hold all tape jobs; other job classifications might have their own queues. Generally, a field on the JOB card tells the queuing module where to put a program.

Do you recall our discussion of spooling? Earlier in this chapter, we talked about how cards could be copied off-line to tape. The tape could subsequently be transferred to the computer and read at high speed. Output could be written to tape, and the tape could later be dumped, again off-line, to the printer. On a modern multiprogrammed computer, spooling can be done on-line. Implementation of this idea is really quite simple. Even with several programs sharing main memory, the computer will frequently encounter periods when all programs are in the **wait state**. During these periods, a card can be read and a line can be printed. Application programs can thus get their card images from and send their output lines to a high-speed device such as tape or disk. The spooler is another operating system module.

Communicating with the Operating System: Interrupts

When a program requests input, a channel assumes control of the I/O operation, and the CPU turns its attention to another problem. The channel and the CPU work independently, each "doing its own thing" without reference to the other; in computer terminology, we say that they function **asynchronously.** Later, the program requesting the I/O will want to resume processing. How does the computer know whether or not the requested operation has been successfully completed?

The channel assumes full responsibility for controlling the I/O operation. When the operation is finished, the channel notifies the computer through an electronic signal known as an **interrupt.** An interrupt, as the name implies, is a signal to the computer to stop what it is doing and to make a note of what has just happened. A computer must have instructions if it is to do anything. The instructions that handle interrupts are part of the resident operating system.

There are also other types of interrupts. What happens, for example, when an application program attempts to perform an illegal operation such as division by zero? The program is normally cancelled, and the cancellation is carried out through a type of interrupt. The operator communicates with the computer through a different type of interrupt. In effect, the operator says, "Stop what you are doing. I have something to tell you." Application programs can get help from the operating system through a supervisor call interrupt. A program caught in a loop, endlessly repeating the same instructions, is often cancelled through a timer interrupt. An interrupt is nothing more than an electronic signal that causes the computer to stop whatever it might be doing and give control to the operating system. Special program modules to handle these interrupts must be core-resident; they represent an important part of an operating system.

Operating Systems: A Summary

An operating system is a collection of support programs. Most experts consider the old, second-generation system software (compilers, linkage editors, access methods, utilities, librarian programs) to be part of the operating

Fig. 14.20
The functions of
an operating
system.

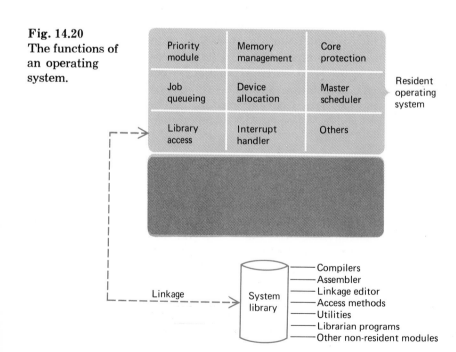

system; these software packages are still in common use. In addition to these system programs, multiprogramming creates a need for software to perform such functions as making the "who goes first" decision, managing main memory, protecting programs from each other, allocating I/O devices, scheduling jobs, queueing jobs, spooling, and handling interrupts. Many of these functions must be performed on-line by software modules that are resident in the computer's main memory—that is the only way these functions can be handled in a reasonable (computer) time frame. The resident portion of the operating system goes by such names as the supervisor, the monitor, the resident operating system, and the nucleus; each computer manufacturer seems to use a different set of words. The various functions performed by an operating system are summarized in Fig. 14.20.

An operating system is a collection of system software programs and program modules. These programs are written in the same languages (usually assembler) and use the same instructions as any application program. The only characteristic that sets operating system modules apart is the fact that they perform a support rather than a direct function. The basic idea of an operating system is crucial to understanding how a modern, large computer works. The environment is considerably more dynamic than was the case in the old, one-program-at-a-time days.

TIME-SHARING

Many of you have undoubtedly seen a computer terminal that is connected to a computer via telephone; perhaps your school has such terminals. Typically the person working at a terminal can write programs in languages such as BASIC, FORTRAN, or PL/1, or execute previously written programs. How can we possibly limit a high-speed computer to the typing speed of a human being? A card reader is considered too slow, although it can handle 600 cards per minute, or 10 cards per second, or 800 characters per second! How fast can you type?

A person sitting at a terminal can economically be given access to a computer only if there are many such terminals (and persons) attached to the same machine. That way, while one terminal user is thinking, the computer can turn its attention to another. Thus a number of terminals might be attached to a single computer, some via telephone lines and some locally over regular wires (Fig. 14.21). The term used to describe such arrangements is **time-sharing**. Since time-sharing involves a number of users (programs) sharing the time of a single central processing unit, it is, at least from the computer's point of view, much like multiprogramming.

There is, however, one important difference. Multiprogramming is essentially passive, in that the means of transferring control from one program to another depends on the individual programs. The CPU can switch its atten-

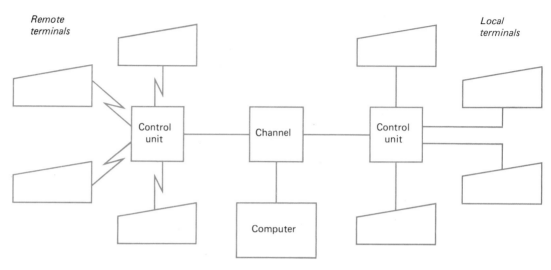

Fig. 14.21
A typical time-shared network.

tion to another program only when the program in control issues a request for input or output. The CPU cannot normally obtain control itself. This is what we mean when we say that multiprogramming is a passive technique.

What happens when one program takes control and will not give it up? This might happen in a complex mathematical or statistical problem in which significant amounts of computation are required to produce a single answer; such programs are said to be compute-bound. Under regular multiprogramming, this application can simply take control of the computer until it is finished, forcing all the other programs to wait. This will never do on a time-shared system. Imagine 49 of the 50 current users waiting 30 minutes or more while the 50th user runs a statistical analysis. The whole purpose of time-sharing is to make the computer accessible to the individual. If wait times become too long, the user will do just as well to keypunch a source deck and submit it to the computer center for a batch processing run.

On a time-shared system, this problem is minimized by restricting each user to a tiny "slice" of time. This might be done through the computer's internal timer—a type of clock. As the program begins, the time is checked. If the program quickly requests input or output, another program can be given control. If, however, after a few fractions of a second the program has not voluntarily given up its control of the CPU, control is taken away from it, the "offending" program is placed at the end of the waiting line (or queue), and the CPU switches its attention to another program. This is called **time-slicing.**

THE IMPORTANCE OF A CHANNEL

Throughout our discussion of multiprogramming and time-sharing, we have implied that during an input or output operation the central processing unit could perform some other task. The CPU is in fact free during I/O because a channel assumes responsibility for controlling the input or output operation.

A channel is a device that sits between a control unit and the computer. Actually, it is more than just an empty box that "has to be there." A channel is a minicomputer of sorts. It performs a number of logical functions, such as counting the number of characters which have been transferred between the computer and the I/O device and keeping track of where, in main memory, the next character goes (or comes from). If it were not for the channel, the CPU would have to perform these functions. If the CPU had to control an I/O operation, it would not be able to give its full attention to some other task, and multiprogramming would be difficult to implement. Channels, by accepting this responsibility, free the CPU to do other work, hence channels are important to multiprogramming.

CYCLE STEALING

Not all computers use channels. On many smaller, less expensive machines, the cost of a channel (a minicomputer in its own right) might rival the cost of the main processor itself, making this approach economically unacceptable. On such computers, the central processing unit controls the input or output operation. Since I/O devices are significantly slower than even a small inexpensive CPU, this control does not require the full attention of the central processor. Instead, the input or output operation can be controlled by stealing an occasional machine cycle or two from the CPU's other activities. This is known as **cycle stealing,** a process that is very common on modern minicomputers.

SUMMARY

We began this chapter with a brief discussion of the computer's first generation, a period of expensive machines used primarily for mathematical and scientific problem solving. Second-generation computers were faster, more reliable, and, in terms of what they could do, less expensive. These improvements made the machines attractive to business, and with business use came a concern for cost. Throughput, a measure

KEY WORDS

asynchronous

concurrent

core resident

cycle stealing

interrupt

I/O device allocation

JOB card

memory management

memory protection

monitor

multiprogramming

nucleus

operating system

overhead

priority

queueing

response time

scheduling

setup

spooling

supervisor

system software

throughput

time-sharing

time-slicing

turnaround

wait state

wait time

of the amount of work going through a computer, became the accepted standard of computer efficiency.

We explored a number of techniques for improving throughput including scheduling, the use of libraries, and spooling. The system software needed to support these activities represents the beginnings of modern operating systems.

The computers of the current generation are even faster than their second-generation counterparts; the tremendous disparity between the speed of these machines and their I/O devices led to a need for solutions such as multiprogramming and time-sharing, techniques that allow the computer to work concurrently on a number of different programs. To handle the inevitable interference, resident operating systems were developed. Among the problems handled or resolved by the resident operating system are the determination of internal priority, memory management, memory protection, I/O device allocation, scheduling, queueing, spooling, and interrupt processing. Channels were shown to be important on a multiprogrammed machine.

The term operating system is sometimes used in a broader sense to refer to the collection of *all* the system software. In addition to the resident portion (called the supervisor, monitor, or nucleus), this broader concept of an operating system includes such system software as compilers, the linkage editor, access methods, librarian programs, and utilities.

EXERCISES

1. Define throughput and turnaround time.

2. How can scheduling help to reduce the time lost to setup?

3. From the standpoint of throughput, why is magnetic tape so much better than punched cards?

4. What do we mean when we refer to system software?

5. What is multiprogramming?

6. Why is a technique such as multiprogramming necessary on a fast, modern computer?

7. What is a time-sharing system? What is meant by time-slicing?

8. What is an operating system?

9. Why is a channel so important to a modern multiprogrammed computer system?

10. Discuss some of the functions performed by an operating system.

Modern
System Software

OVERVIEW

In Chapter 14 the basic ideas of multiprogramming,
time-sharing, and system software were introduced.
In this chapter we will expand on that discussion
and discuss some modern system software. The
chapter begins with an analysis of a number of
different types of operating systems, starting with
those that assign main memory in fixed-size increments and then proceeding through a number
of more dynamic memory management techniques
to the idea of virtual memory. We'll then discuss
data communications software, data base management systems, spooling packages and other
commercially available system software. The chapter
ends with an analysis of the impact that this software
has had on the application programmer and some
comments on probable future trends.

MEMORY MANAGEMENT

The basic principle of multiprogramming is to load several different programs into main memory and allow the CPU to switch its attention from one to another. By doing this, the computer system is able to use for a productive purpose what would otherwise be wasted time. The result is that more work is done in the same amount of time; in other words, throughput is increased. Since the cost of the computer is relatively fixed, this means that more work is done for the same total cost.

Generally, the more programs we can get into main memory at any one time, the more efficient we become. Let's assume, to cite a simple example, that each of a number of programs requires exactly 10 microseconds of run time and is then followed by a 90-microsecond I/O operation. With one program in main memory, the computer will be waiting 90 percent of the time. With two programs in core, once the I/O operation is started for the first program the computer can switch its attention to the second one for another 10-microsecond burst of productive activity before dropping into a wait state. The total wait time now represents only 80 percent of available time. A third program gives the system something to do with more of this wasted time; waiting drops to 70 percent. Each additional program decreases wait time and increases throughput. Of course, there is a limit; in our example, ten programs would consume all available time and program interference would probably have an impact long before we reached this point. But, generally speaking, the more programs we can "shoehorn" into main memory, the more efficient our system becomes.

The amount of available main memory imposes a limit on the number of programs. If we have 1000K memory locations, our absolute limit is ten 100K programs. (K means 1024 and is taken from the Greek word kilo, meaning 1000.) Usually this limit is well below the CPU's saturation point.

What this means is that if we want to use our computer efficiently, we must get as many programs as possible into our available main memory. **Memory management** is very important.

Fixed-partition Memory Management

In a **fixed-partition memory management** system, main memory is divided into a number of fixed-length **partitions.** In a typical example, memory might be divided into three such partitions (Fig. 15.1), one to hold the operating system and the other two, called the **foreground** and the **background** partition, respectively, to hold application programs. The partitions need not be the same length, but once the length of a given partition is set, it stays the same.

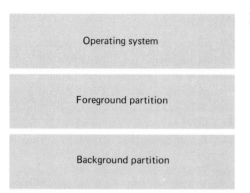

Fig. 15.1
Fixed-partition memory management.

An operating system designed to work in a fixed partition environment will have a number of predictable features. First, let's consider how such a system would allocate main memory to application programs. This should be obvious: Each application program is assigned to one of the partitions. The memory allocation decision has really been made ahead of time; the operating system simply assigns a program to a free partition.

Core protection is implemented in an equally straightforward manner. Each program is simply restricted to its own partition; any attempt to modify memory locations outside the partition will result in the cancellation of the program.

What about the internal priority decision? How would such a system determine which program goes first in the event that two are ready to run? Again, the answer is simple. The program in the foreground partition always goes first. The background partition gets control only when the computer has nothing else to do.

The answers to questions involving such problems as device allocation, queueing, scheduling, and interrupt handling are not quite so simple, and vary from manufacturer to manufacturer and from installation to installation. Basically, however, these functions are handled by a program located in the operating system's partition.

Not all fixed partition systems are limited to three partitions, of course. IBM's Disk Operating System (DOS), for example, can handle the operating system plus five application programs. The application program partitions are called foreground-1, foreground-2, foreground-3, foreground-4, and background, and are listed in priority order. Another IBM system, OS/MFT (Operating System/Multiprogramming with a Fixed Number of Tasks), can handle the operating system plus up to 15 different application programs.

Other manufacturers market similar systems. The fixed partition approach is the simplest way to manage memory on a multiprogrammed system, and these operating systems continue to enjoy great popularity.

Dynamic Memory Management

There is, however, one problem with the simple fixed-partition approach to memory management: It wastes space. Consider what might happen on such a system when a common compile, link edit, and execute job is run. The job consists of three steps—three different programs. A typical compiler needs 60K to 120K of main memory; to make our example more dramatic, let's assume that we are using an assembler program and need only 60K. The linkage editor might require 120K. Our application program, once it is converted to load module form, will need only 20K of main memory in this example. How big must our partition be if we are to run the assembler followed by the linkage editor followed in turn by our load module? The linkage editor needs 120K and the assembler and the load module can both run easily in a 120K partition. Since the linkage editor cannot run in anything less than 120K, we need a 120K partition.

Under a fixed partition system, if a 60K assembler program runs in a 120K partition, a full 60K of the partition space will be wasted (Fig. 15.2a). The linkage editor needs the full 120K, so no space is wasted during the execution of this step (Fig. 15.2b). During the execution of our load module, which needs only 20K, a full 100K of main memory will be wasted (Fig. 15.2c). This is hardly efficient memory management.

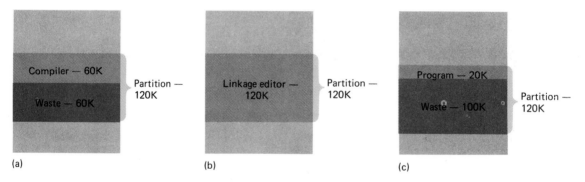

(a)   (b)   (c)

Fig. 15.2
A fixed-partition memory management system can waste main-memory space:
(a) the compile step; (b) the link edit step; and (c) the execute step.

One common solution to this problem is to allocate to each program exactly the amount of main memory that it needs. Under such a variable partition approach, our assemble, link edit, and execute job might run as shown in Fig. 15.3. First (Fig. 15.3a), 60K would be allocated for the

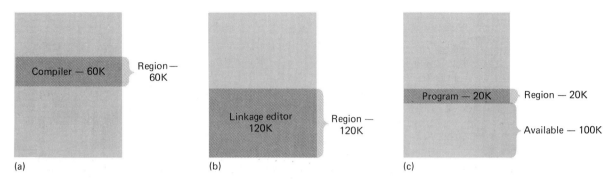

Fig. 15.3
Under dynamic memory management, main memory is allocated as needed:
(a) the compile step; (b) the link step; and (c) the execute step.

assembler step. Once an object module had been generated, the operating system would look for a 120K chunk of free core to hold the linkage editor, eventually loading and executing this program (Fig. 15.3b). After the load module is generated, it can be loaded into the first 20K of the region that previously held the linkage editor (Fig. 15.3c). We still have 100K of space left over, but the difference is that the operating system can allocate this space to another program, thus getting one more program into main memory. More programs means greater efficiency.

A variable-partition or *variable-length region* operating system is inherently more complex than a fixed partition system. Rather than simply loading programs in already assigned locations, the operating system must assign space "on the fly" as the programs enter the computer. At times there may be four applications in core; a few microseconds later, there may be six or eight or two. The beginning and ending locations of programs are constantly shifting. It's much more difficult to keep track of just exactly where everything is when everything keeps moving around and changing. Consequently, an operating system to support a variable system will be more complex than an operating system to support a fixed system. A more complex operating system will be bigger, taking up more main memory and leaving less for the application programs. IBM's OS/MVT is an example of a variable-task operating system.

Fragmentation

Although the more dynamic, variable-length region approach does a better job of managing main memory than the simpler fixed partition approach, it isn't perfect. Let's say that we have an 80K program which is followed, subsequently, in memory by a 70K program (Fig. 15.4). Getting the 70K

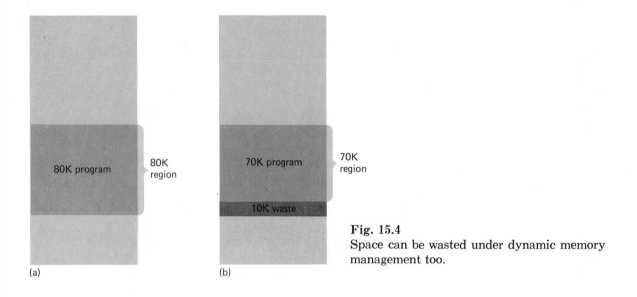

Fig. 15.4
Space can be wasted under dynamic memory management too.

(a)   (b)

program in is no problem—it fits and we have 10K left over. But if we don't have any 10K programs, the space is wasted.

This happens frequently on a variable system. In fact, it is not at all unusual to have unusable 5, 10, 15, and 20K chunks of unused space spread throughout memory. This is called **fragmentation.** There might be a total of 30K of free space spread throughout core, and we might have a 30K program all ready to go, but the fact that the free space is not **contiguous** means that we cannot use it.

Dynamic Memory Relocation

Why not do something to gather all the free memory in one place? It has been tried, and done successfully. The technique is called **dynamic memory relocation.** Basically, this means that when core becomes fragmented (Fig. 15.5), the active programs are simply moved up in memory to fill in the empty space (Fig. 15.6). As a result, all the free space is gathered together at the end of main memory and can be used to hold another program.

Dynamic memory relocation also has its cost. It takes time to move all those programs around, time that could be spent on more productive activities. Also, because of the addressing approach used on some computers it can be difficult to implement. This type of dynamic memory relocation is not commonly used today.

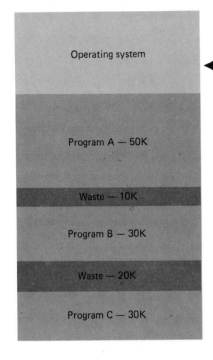

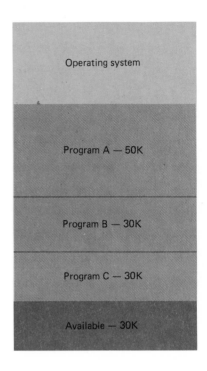

◀ **Fig. 15.5**
The fragmentation problem.

Fig. 15.6 ▶
Dynamic memory relocation.

Program Segmentation

In discussing fragmentation, we mentioned that because the free space is not contiguous (in other words, gathered in one place) we cannot use it. Why not? Why must an entire program be loaded into contiguous memory before it can run? Good question. It doesn't have to be.

As an alternative, a program can be broken into logical segments, locations within each segment can be addressed relative to the start of the segment, and the segments can be loaded into noncontiguous memory locations (Fig. 15.7). No dynamic memory relocation is needed, and we can still take advantage of the small pieces of available memory.

Programmers tend to segment their programs anyway, with key functions viewed as separate problems to be solved and linked together, so **segmentation** makes sense. In a payroll program, for example, one segment might hold the instructions that compute gross pay and prepare a check for output, while the computation of income tax, a fairly complex activity, might be performed in a separate segment.

Closely related to segmentation is the concept of paging. Using this technique, a program is divided into a number of fixed-length pieces called **pages.** The memory locations within a page are addressed relative to the start of the page. Under **paging,** a program can be loaded, page by page, into noncontiguous memory and executed. The basic difference between segmentation and paging is that under segmentation a program is broken into

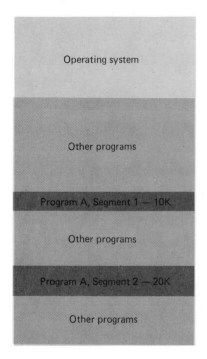

Fig. 15.7
Program segmentation.

pieces that follow the logic of the program, while under paging a program is divided into fixed-sized pieces with the page size being selected for the computer's convenience. Common page sizes are 2K and 4K.

Note that the programmer does not directly control paging. A page is "so many" memory locations, period. Wherever a page break occurs, it occurs without regard for the logic of the program. Paging is imposed by the compiler or by the operating system. The size of a segment, on the other hand, is variable, and a good programmer can designate where a segment is to begin and end, thus matching the physical loading of a program into memory with the actual logic of that program. This is the essential difference between segmentation and paging.

Virtual Memory Systems

Now that we have successfully questioned the need for contiguous memory before a program can run, let's ask another question. Why must the entire program be in main memory before execution can begin? If you remember the step-by-step example of how a computer works as presented in Chapter 9, you know that a computer, more specifically the central processing unit, can execute only one instruction at a time. Why should it be necessary for the entire program to be present if the computer can execute only one instruction at a time?

It isn't necessary. Under a memory management technique known as **virtual memory,** an entire program is stored on a secondary storage device such as disk or drum. This program is divided into pages or segments. A few of these pages or segments are moved into main memory (Fig. 15.8) with the bulk of the program remaining on the secondary storage device. As the instructions contained in the **real-memory** pages are executed, eventually control will pass to one of the pages or segments still on the secondary device. When this happens, a copy of the needed page is moved into real memory, and processing continues. Pages or segments that are no longer needed in real memory are copied back to the secondary device.

The computer's main memory is referred to as real memory. Since the secondary device that holds the major part of the program isn't "real" memory (at least not in this context), we need another name for it. The term used to describe this bulk memory is virtual memory. The word virtual means, according to Webster, "being in essence but not in fact." Virtual memory is "in essence" just like real memory, but "in fact" it is not real memory.

The idea of keeping something less than the full program in main memory has been around for quite some time. In the second generation, tight core

Fig. 15.8
Virtual memory.

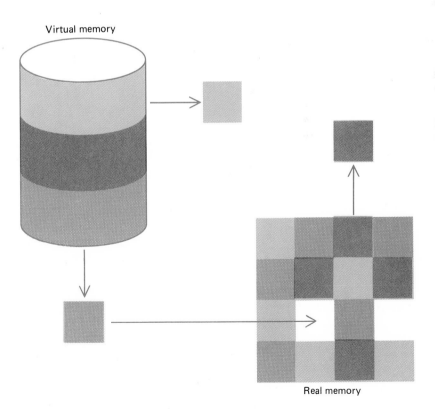

Virtual memory

Real memory

limitations sometimes forced a programmer to literally write a 16K program on an 8K machine. This could only be done by breaking the program into segments. Through very careful planning, the programmer determined the most crucial 8K of the program and arranged to have this portion in main memory, with the rest of the program remaining on disk. When a need for one of these less-used modules occurred, the module was read into core, overlaying (and thus destroying) a part of the program that was in core. Later, when this new module had finished, the program was restored to its initial condition.

Operating systems incorporating many of the concepts of virtual memory have existed since the mid-1960s. The term "virtual" came into common use in the early 1970s when IBM announced a new series of operating systems incorporating this concept to support their System/370 computers.

What is the advantage of the virtual memory approach? Since only part of any given program must be in main memory at any one time, it is possible to get more different programs into the same amount of main memory. More programs mean greater efficiency.

What is the cost? Since programs are located partly in real memory and partly in virtual memory, keeping track of the location of a program is much more difficult than it is in the simpler operating systems. Thus a virtual operating system is more complex, larger, and more expensive than an operating system designed to keep track of programs stored in contiguous memory. Also it takes time to transfer pages between virtual and real memory.

TIME-SHARED SYSTEMS

In the last chapter, the basic idea of time-sharing was introduced. A time-sharing system, as you may recall, is characterized by a number of terminals, each connected to the central computer. The individuals using these terminals can typically write original programs in such languages as BASIC, FORTRAN, PL/1, and APL and can execute existing programs. The users of such a system expect quick response time; in fact, the whole purpose of the time-slicing approach that we discussed in Chapter 14 is to prevent any single user from dominating the system at the expense of everyone else.

The characteristics of a time-shared system create some unique problems. First, consider the number of users who might be active at any given point in time. Some smaller time-shared systems are designed to handle eight to ten; many larger systems can handle well over one hundred. Why so many?

The relative slowness of a card reader and other I/O devices forced us into multiprogramming. A card reader, the slowest of the "regular" I/O devices, can handle 600 to 2000 cards per minute. A card is one record. On a terminal, a single typed line often represents one record. Can you imagine typing 600 lines per minute? That's 10 lines per second! The way most of us type, one line every ten seconds might be a more reasonable speed estimate, and this doesn't even take into account the "thinking" time of the terminal user.

If a card reader is too slow and a manual terminal is, depending on the skill of the typist, 10 to 100 times slower, then we have a problem. A partial solution is multiprogramming. For terminals, the obvious solution is even more multiprogramming.

Let's take a look at the typical program run by a time-sharing user. First, can we say anything about the original programs that this individual might write? Of course. Original programs will probably be fairly short. Why? How long would you be willing to spend sitting at a terminal typing statements? If a program is really long, the chances are that the programmer will write the program by hand on a coding sheet and give it to the keypunch department for conversion to punched cards.

What about the amount of data processed by a typical time-shared program? There probably won't be a great deal. Once again, it's a question of time. Each element of data going into a time-shared program must be typed, one line at a time. When a significant amount of data must be processed, it is much easier and much faster to have the data keypunched or placed on tape or disk and read into a batch program.

So we're dealing with small programs designed to process relatively small amounts of data. Small programs processing small amounts of data will run quickly.

Another characteristic of programs on a time-shared system is the very significant time delay between processing activities. The programmer might, for example, type in a record of data, get a quick response from the system, and then think about the answer for a while before going on to the next step. In other words, the typical time-shared program is characterized by brief shots of computation separated by extremely long periods of idleness during which the user thinks, composes an answer, and types in the next request. These periods of contemplation can range from a few seconds to several minutes. From the computer's point of view, each user represents a series of brief computational activities spaced at long, irregular intervals; each burst of activity is called a **transaction.**

Now let's put the pieces together. We have a number of very small programs. A terminal, the device providing input and accepting output data, is extremely slow. Transactions arrive from a terminal at irregular, widely spaced intervals and normally involve a brief period of computation. How can we implement an efficient system to handle such activities?

With multiprogramming, but with a difference. Previously we were dealing with 5, 10, or 15 concurrent programs; we'll want more on a time-shared system. Let's say that the average transaction requires 1/10 second of computer time and that the average user can provide transactions at the rate of one every 10 seconds. Each user would need 1/10 second every 10 seconds. How many users could we accommodate, in theory, without interference? If each user needs 1/10 second, then ten users would need a full second every ten seconds (leaving nine seconds unused). We would need a full 100 terminal users to saturate the available time! The numbers we have used in this little example are very conservative; the typical program probably uses significantly less than 1/10 second per shot and the typical user rarely maintains a pace of one transaction every ten seconds. Thus our estimate of 100 potential users is probably low.

Where is all of this leading us? We are about to consider how we might implement such a system on a computer. We have a number of small, short-running programs. The fact that input and output are extremely slow means that we want to be able to handle large numbers of users concurrently. What we have is a special case of multiprogramming.

On a typical time-shared system, the available memory is broken into a number of small regions, often called work spaces, each big enough to hold one of the (typically) small programs. Main memory is a limited and rather expensive resource. The time between transactions, at least from the computer's point of view, is very long. It makes little or no sense to keep inactive programs in expensive main memory; thus, a process known as **roll-in** and **roll-out** is frequently used (Fig. 15.9). Using this technique, the program is normally kept on a secondary storage device such as disk or drum. As a transaction is received, the program needed to process that transaction is found and "rolled in" to main memory. Once the transaction has been processed and a response sent back to the terminal, the program can be "rolled out" to the secondary device, thus freeing the main memory space for another program.

Fig. 15.9
Roll-in and
roll-out.

How does all this activity affect system performance? It takes time to transfer programs between main memory and a secondary storage device. This time delay, however, is measured in, at worst, milliseconds. The person sitting

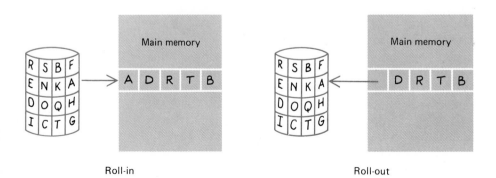

Roll-in   Roll-out

at the terminal probably considers a response time of three to five seconds fantastic; the few milliseconds of delay on the computer are insignificant.

Thus we have a system that breaks available main memory into many small pieces. This system must be capable of handling a very large number of different programs, keeping track of such things as where in main memory each resides, where on secondary memory each resides, which terminal is associated with each program, the identity of the next instruction to be executed in each program, and so on. Add the time-slicing requirement that we discussed in Chapter 14, and you have the makings of a very complex operating system. (Incidentally, does roll-in and roll-out remind you of paging and virtual memory? If it does, you are very observant.)

DATA COMMUNICATION MONITORS

There are computers which are designed specifically to support time-sharing. On these machines, special operating systems and/or hardware features are used. Frequently, however, it is desirable to have time-sharing capability on a general-purpose computer. In many companies, terminals are used for data entry, with the individual who is responsible for creating a record of data also being held responsible for entering it into the computer. Management is beginning to use terminals more and more to *query* the computer for an answer to a managerial problem. Engineers and research and development personnel use terminals to solve mathematical and statistical problems. Most general-purpose operating systems were not designed with the unique characteristics of time-sharing in mind. How can time-sharing be implemented on a general-purpose computer?

Why not use a special-purpose software package specifically designed with time-sharing in mind? Such packages are commercially available and are called **data communication monitors.**

A typical data communication monitor works as follows. One partition or region of a system is turned over to the data communication monitor (Fig. 15.10); note that, so far as the main general-purpose operating system is concerned, the "communications" partition is just another application program partition. Within this region, the data communications software package takes control, subdividing the available space into smaller chunks, controlling the roll-in and roll-out of programs, keeping track of the relationship between individual programs and individual terminals, and supervising things in general. In effect, the data communication monitor performs many of the functions normally attributed to an operating system; it is merely restricted to its own partition. This is sometimes called **partition management**. In effect, the data communication monitor is a little operating system working under the control of a bigger operating system.

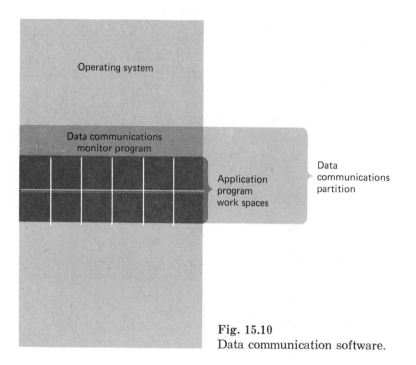

Operating system

Data communications
monitor program

Application
program
work spaces

Data
communications
partition

Fig. 15.10
Data communication software.

Most commercially available data communication monitors have additional features as well. Consider, for example, the problems of compilation on such systems. If, let's say, BASIC is available to the users and the system can support up to 50 users, it is possible that 50 copies of the BASIC compiler might be in memory (or active on the secondary storage device) at the same time. Why carry all those copies of the same program? It seems wasteful, and is.

To get around this problem, a data communication monitor capable of supporting compilation will usually keep a single copy of the compiler in the monitor (as opposed to application) area of the partition and make this single copy available to any and all of the application programs (Fig. 15.11).

On some monitors, the compilation process is performed in a unique manner. We've learned that a compiler reads a source module one statement at a time, and generates an object module. We've also learned that the complete object module (actually load module) must be available before the program can begin. But the computer is capable of executing only one instruction at a time. Why not design a special compiler that reads a single statement, translates this statement to machine language, and immediately does what the instruction tells it to? For languages like BASIC and APL, such special compilers not only can be, but have been, developed. This special type of compiler is called an **interpreter**.

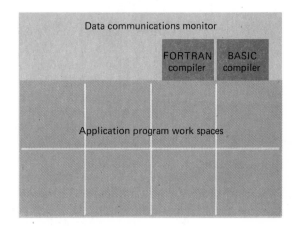

Fig. 15.11
Data communication software packages often
contain their own compilers which can be used by
any (or all) of the active programs.

Some data communication monitors are designed to make it easy for a clerk to enter data, or for a manager to retrieve data selectively. It would be great if the manager or clerk could take a look at a record just by asking for it: "Give me the current stock status of part number 183519." On many systems of this variety, requests for data can be made in just such a straightforward and logical manner. These data communication monitors are built around what is called a **query** language. Using this query language, a nonprogrammer can compose requests for specific types of data by following a few simple rules. It's a nice feature.

In addition to managing the partition and providing special services, most commercially available data communication managers include a **logging** feature. Essentially, logging means keeping track of what every user of the system does. Often a tape showing the start time, stop time, and features used by each and every user is maintained. This log serves two important functions. First, it gives accounting a basis for charging users for services rendered. Second, logging provides a significant amount of security (would you do anything illegal if you knew someone were taking notes?) and, in the event of system failure, helps to identify what went wrong.

DATA AS A RESOURCE

Throughout the preceding discussion of data communication monitors, the idea that a manager might want to access selectively the information stored on a computer was mentioned. The information stored on an organization's computer is a very valuable organizational resource.

Historically, data files were planned to meet the requirements of specific programs. This was a natural outgrowth of the emphasis placed on throughput: Make the program run as quickly as possible. Thus the payroll program, which needed an individual's name, social security number, and number of dependents, but not his or her home address, had a personnel file that contained the individual's name, social security number, number of dependents, and little more—why waste time waiting for the address to be read in when it isn't needed? The company's publications department, in order to support the mailing of a quarterly employee newsletter, would have to maintain a completely independent personnel file containing each employee's name, home address, and little more. The education department might have still another personnel file, as would the union, the employee's credit union, the recreation association, and various other groups.

In Chapter 12, we discussed the concept of an integrated data base. Using this approach, the data resources of an organization are treated as though they belong to the entire organization and not just to a single department or a single application. Typically, a master record contains pointers to related records, thus linking all the pieces of the data base. A key advantage is reduced data redundancy, making the data easier to maintain. As a result, the data is generally more accurate than was possible in the old private-file days. Another major advantage of the integrated data base approach is data accessibility. Private ownership tends to restrict access; the ideal data base is organized in such a way that any member of the organization who has a need for a particular type of data can get it without restrictions or impediments.

Data Base Management

A data base is a collection of carefully integrated files. The data in these files must be managed. Special software packages are available for managing a data base, and the term **data base management** system is often used to describe such packages.

Data base management actually begins with the physical organization of the data itself. We already discussed some of these basic ideas in Chapter 12, including the key concept of linking related records through pointers. A detailed analysis of the physical organization of any single data base is, however, beyond the scope of this book.

Most data base management systems work by requiring all requests for input or output to go through a data base manager, a special system software module that acts much like an operating system module. Take a look at Fig. 15.12, which shows main memory divided into a number of partitions. One contains the operating system. Two others hold, respectively, a data base manager and an application program. When the application program wants some data, it transfers control to the data base manager which starts the actual I/O operation (with the help of the operating system and a channel, of course). Every application program follows the same set of rules; the only way to access the data base is through the data base manager.

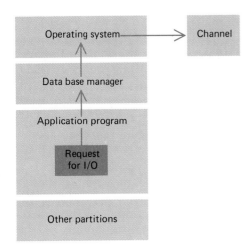

Fig. 15.12
Data base management software.

Not all data base managers work in exactly the same way. In some cases, particularly on smaller computers that cannot afford to assign a separate partition to the data base manager, this software module is treated much as an access method and added to an individual program load module (Fig. 15.13). Within this program, all requests for access to the data base must pass through this single module. Note the difference: In the first case (Fig. 15.12), all requests from all programs were filtered through a single module, while in the second case (Fig. 15.13), the control imposed by the data base manager functions on the level of a single program only.

What are the advantages of requiring all input and output operations against the data base to filter through a single module? Let's consider a few.

On most data base management systems, the programmer doesn't have to pay attention to the physical nature of the file, ignoring such factors as the actual input or output device and the organization of the records (QSAM, ISAM, etc.). The programmer simply asks instead for the specific elements of data needed by the program ("Give me the name and address of employee number 3341267," for example), and the data base manager assumes responsibility for getting the data and assembling the desired record.

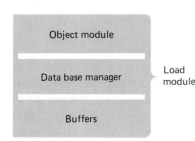

Fig. 15.13
The data base manager as an access method.

Why is this important? What happens when an I/O device is changed or the format of a physical file is modified? What happens, for example, when a zip code must be added to every mailing address? On systems using the old, independent-file approach, all the files are changed and all the programs using these files (whether they need the zip code or not) must be recoded. With data base management, the entire change can be absorbed by the data base manager, and only those programs that actually need the zip code must be changed. This can save a tremendous amount of recoding and program maintenance. Data base management allows application programs to be independent of the actual physical structure of the data.

Data base management also helps to improve data security and file protection. Let's consider file protection first. As more and more users access the information stored on the computer, the possibility of interference also arises. For example, what would be the outcome of the following case study? Data entry clerk A accesses record number 52 to make a change. While clerk A is working on the modification, clerk B comes along and gets record number 52 —the same record—in order to make still another change. While B is making the change, A puts an updated version of the record out on the master file, overlaying the old copy. Shortly thereafter, B puts out his or her changed record, wiping out A's change. This is a very real problem on any on-line data entry system.

With data base management, all I/O passes through the data base manager routine. Since A and B must both pass through this same module, the data base manager can prevent this problem by simply denying clerk B access to record 52 until clerk A is finished with it. The data base manager functions much as a traffic policeman, preventing accidents by exercising centralized control.

Another problem is security. As computer use grows (and the growth rate continues to be nothing short of amazing), more and more individuals will want to access the organization's data. Most requests are legitimate, and no one wants to miss out on a great opportunity just because data on a computer is unavailable. Yet what if a competitor were to gain access to the data? What if an employee were to access salary information for his or her manager? Data access is essential, but it must be controlled.

Once again, the data base manager is the perfect place to implement such security controls. Since every request for access to the data base must pass through the data base manager, it is possible to simply check the identity of the requester before granting the request.

On an old second-generation computer, these problems existed, but were not considered very important. Even on a modern batch processing system these problems are not serious. Redundancy, security, and protection really were not recognized as problems until the idea of the computer's information base being an organizational resource began to take hold. If information is a key resource, it must be available. If the information is made available to the manager as an aid to decision making, it must be accurate, current, secure, and protected.

Until recently, the high cost of the computer itself made computer efficiency extremely important. The cost of the hardware is dropping, while the cost of human labor continues to rise. Competition continues to become tougher and tougher, and such factors as timeliness and quick reactions grow in importance. From a total-system point of view, computer efficiency begins to become less important, and organizational efficiency more important. Thus the image of information and the computer, the storehouse of information, is beginning to shift. No longer is the computer viewed as just an inexpensive way of doing payroll. No longer can the computer be viewed as a repository for a number of private single-function files. A company's information resources are valuable and of interest to the entire organization. Data base management allows this information to be treated as the valuable resource that it is.

MANAGEMENT INFORMATION SYSTEMS

Many larger organizations, taking advantage of the combined potential of data communications and data base management, have created what is often called a **Management Information System** (MIS) on their computers. Let's take a brief look at how a typical management information system might work (Fig. 15.14).

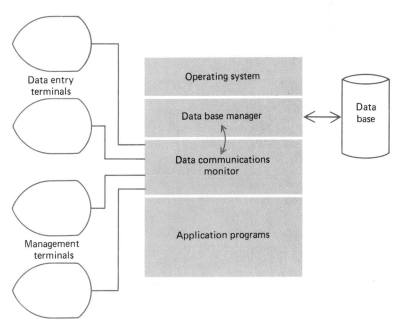

Fig. 15.14
The software supporting a typical management information system.

Data entry terminals

Management terminals

Operating system

Data base manager

Data communications monitor

Application programs

Data base

Data entry, in this example, is done on-line via CRT terminals. The data entry clerks type data directly into the computer under control of the data communication monitor. This software package, in turn, passes the data along to the data base manager, which immediately updates the data base. As a result of this on-line data entry capability, the organization's data base is as current and as up to date as possible.

The data is now on-line, and management can access it. Taking advantage of the query capability of many data communication packages, the manager can enter a request for specific data through perhaps a desktop terminal (Fig. 15.14). The data communication monitor would interpret this query, obtain the help of the data base manager to locate the requested data, and return an answer to the manager.

Under such a management information system, an organization's data base can be accurate, current, and accessible; thus the data becomes a usable organizational resource. The software keys to implementing such a system are data communication and data base management.

COMMERCIAL SOFTWARE

Where do things such as compilers, operating systems, data communication monitors, and data base management software come from? Compilers and operating systems are usually supplied by the manufacturer of a computer; in fact, since a modern large computer can be said to be almost incapable of functioning without its operating system, this particular software package is often considered to be a part of the standard configuration and is thus included in the purchase or lease price of the machine.

Data base management and data communication monitors are different. These programs were developed in response to a specific need; the earliest data base and data communication packages were customized to fit a single application. It has only been recently that such software has been generalized and sold as a commercial software package. Several of the major computer manufacturers do have the ability to provide customers with an excellent data base management or data communication package, but a number of independent software vendors are also active in this field. It's a highly competitive market.

OTHER COMMON SOFTWARE PACKAGES

The spooling and queueing performed by most operating systems is very basic. Many users want more than is normally provided. Features such as the ability to separate jobs onto several different queues, the ability to load jobs from a queue in priority order, the ability to spool data in blocked form, several accounting functions, and many others are considered important.

The user can have these capabilities by purchasing or leasing any of a number of commercially available spooling packages. Typically, these spoolers consume a single partition.

Commercial software is rapidly becoming one of the real growth markets within the information processing field. Software packages to perform such functions as maintaining libraries, converting shorthand code into regular compiler-level source statements, generating flowcharts and other documentation from a source program, creating files and data bases, and performing almost any other imaginable function are available. Not even application programs are immune; packages to take care of a significant number of common applications can be purchased.

ASSIGNING PARTITIONS

The operating system needs its own partition. So do the spooling package, the data base manager, and the data communication monitor. How should these partitions be assigned? Does it make any difference?

Yes, it does. The operating system almost always occupies the first or top priority partition—only fitting for the program in charge. Normally, the spooling package is given the partition with the second highest priority (Fig. 15.15). Why? Because the spooling program does little or no actual process-

Fig. 15.15
Assigning software to partitions.

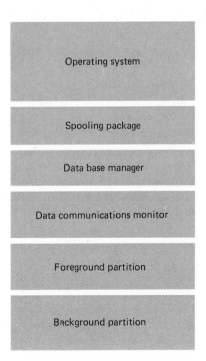

Operating system

Spooling package

Data base manager

Data communications monitor

Foreground partition

Background partition

ing. Its function is to read cards and transfer them to disk or to read disk and transfer records to the printer. The spooling package is almost exclusively I/O-bound. This means that soon after the spooling program gets control it will start an input or output operation and give control right back to the operating system. The spooler cannot possibly tie up the system.

Next, in order of priority, we will usually find the data base monitor (Fig. 15.15). This is another "pure I/O" module that will not grab control and keep other programs waiting. The data base monitor (if present) is usually followed by the data communication monitor. Although this module is largely I/O-bound, occasional shots of serious computation are common, justifying the slightly lower priority of this module.

At the bottom are the application programs. Ideally, any compute-bound jobs are identified and assigned to the low-priority background partition (Fig. 15.15). Other, less compute-bound jobs are assigned to the remaining partitions.

This intelligent approach to laying out main memory yields a number of significant advantages. Every program, no matter what its characteristics may be, gets a shot. The I/O-bound programs near the top willingly surrender control to the other programs. The compute-bound program down at the bottom is prevented from taking over because whenever anything happens, including an I/O interrupt from a channel or operator intervention through the operator's console, the operating system goes back to the top again.

CONSTRAINTS ON THE PROGRAMMER

Historically, the programmer was held responsible for writing the most efficient possible programs. An efficient program was defined as one that ran in the smallest possible amount of main memory space and that used the least possible CPU time.

With operating systems, compilers, data base management packages, data communication, and spooling, the definition of a good program changes. Consider Fig. 15.16. It shows a COBOL program which is constrained by a number of system software packages. The programmer can't do anything directly. I/O is beyond his or her control; the programmer cannot even read a card without the intervention of the spooling package. All that's left to the programmer is the basic program logic—the addition, subtraction, multiplication, division, copy operations, and comparisons required by the application. How can the programmer possibly shave time or space from an arithmetic operation if the application *requires* that arithmetic operation? With the programmer so tightly constrained, there is very little that he or she can do in order to make the program more "efficient."

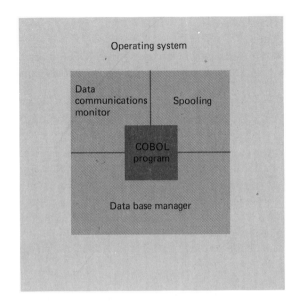

Fig. 15.16
System software tends to limit and constrain the application programmer.

This trend is being accelerated by another trend, this one toward something called structured programming. Although this term means many different things to many different people, at its core it means that programmers are required to write their programs using a common standard style that stresses program documentation and readability. The old "creative programmer" philosophy is replaced by a rigidly structured approach to programming; since every programmer working in a given installation is required to program according to the same set of rules, the programs written by one individual tend to look much like those written by anyone else.

There are advantages to this. Do you remember our discussion in Chapter 8 of the total cost of writing a program? Included in this total cost are such factors as definition, planning, coding, documentation, debugging, execution, and maintenance. The old "creative programmer" approach was aimed at minimizing execution costs by making the program as efficient as possible on the computer. But computer costs are dropping, and labor costs continue to rise (programming is, after all, a labor-intensive activity). Structured programming has as its objective the writing of easily read, easily maintained programs. The costs associated with program debugging and program maintenance tend to drop when structured programming practices are followed, and, generally speaking, these factors have come to be recognized as the most significant components of total program cost. Again, we are taking a total-system point of view.

SOME FINAL COMMENTS ON HARDWARE

The functions discussed in this chapter are system functions. The application programmer asks the system for support; where this support comes from doesn't matter so long as the job gets done. It is possible to design hardware to perform these functions; since the application programmer doesn't care how they are performed, a hardware approach presents no technical problems.

In the past, the use of hardware to perform the functions of the system software described in this chapter has proven to be much too expensive for practical use. But just as the costs of pocket calculators and digital watches have dropped over the past several years, the cost of computer hardware, which is constructed from similar electronic circuits, is also dropping. As hardware costs continue to drop (and every indication is that they will), we can expect more and more of these "system software" functions to be incorporated into the hardware of the computer.

SUMMARY

This chapter began essentially as an extension of Chapter 14, with a discussion of the memory management techniques used in various operating systems. We first looked at fixed-partition memory management. We then moved on to discussions of dynamic memory management, dynamic memory relocation, segmentation, and paging, eventually covering the basic concepts of virtual memory.

We saw how the unique problems of time-sharing create a need for data communication management, sometimes called partition management. The trend toward treating information as a valuable organizational resource has resulted in many firms creating an integrated data base and has sparked a demand for data base management software. Other typical system software, most notably spooling packages, was also discussed. Guidelines for assigning priority to software and the constraints that modern system software place on the programmer were also considered.

EXERCISES

1. What is meant by fixed-partition memory management?

2. What is the major weakness of fixed-partition memory management?

3. How does variable-region memory management differ from fixed-partition memory management? Which technique would you expect to require the bigger, more complex operating system? Why?

4. What is fragmentation?

5. What is dynamic program relocation (or dynamic memory relocation)?

6. What is segmentation? What is paging?

7. Explain how virtual memory works.

8. What is a data communication monitor? Why is this type of software needed on a time-shared system? A data communication monitor is sometimes called a partition manager. Why?

9. Contrast the independent "matched-with-the-program" approach to file organization with data base management. What are the advantages of data base management?

10. Assume that you have an I/O-bound application program, a compute-bound application program, a spooling program, a data base manager, a data communication monitor, and a resident operating system, each of which must be assigned to a separate memory partition. List the programs in priority order. Why did you select the particular priority order you did?

11. System software constrains the programmer. Explain this statement.

KEY WORDS

background	foreground	partition management
contiguous	fragmentation	
data base management	interpreter	query
		real memory
data communication monitor	logging	roll-in
	management information system	
dynamic memory management		roll-out
	memory management	segmentation
dynamic memory relocation		transaction
	page	variable-length region
fixed-partition memory management	paging	
	partition	virtual memory

Distributed Information Processing and Telecommunications

16

OVERVIEW

In this chapter, we'll consider the phenomenon of distributed information processing—the trend toward moving computer access away from the exclusive control of those who run the main computer, and out into the "real" world. This trend involves terminals, minicomputers, microprocessors, and communication facilities.

The chapter begins with a discussion of data communications, concentrating on communication lines and services, data sets or modems, and the need for buffering. Next we'll move on to remote job entry terminals, gradually building up to the idea of an intelligent terminal. A number of special-function terminals designed to support such activities as data entry, supermarket checkout, and banking will be illustrated. The trend toward declining hardware costs will be shown as the key factor behind these trends. Multiprocessing, a term that refers to two or more computers (or processors) working together, will be the final topic of the chapter. **345**

TERMINAL NETWORKS

In discussing time-sharing in Chapter 14, we mentioned the idea of a time-shared network (see Fig. 14.21). The network consisted of a number of terminals, some "remote" and some "local"; the **remote** terminals were attached to the computer via telephone lines, while the **local** terminals were attached directly to a control unit. These terminals were used to support a number of activities, such as data entry, scientific or engineering problem solving, and managerial information retrieval.

A local terminal, though it's quite slow, is much like any other input or output device. It can be connected directly to a control unit that is connected directly to a channel that, in turn, is connected to the computer (Fig. 16.1). A remote terminal is different in that a telephone line or other communication link is involved. What is it about data communications that makes a remote terminal different?

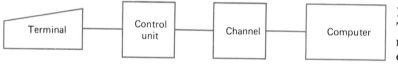

Fig. 16.1
The hardware involved in connecting a local terminal to a computer.

DATA COMMUNICATION: MODULATION

Within a computer, data can be represented as individual pulses of electricity; a pulse of current is a 1-bit and "no" pulse is a 0-bit. Since the individual components of a computer system are generally pretty close to one another, this does not present a problem. When we attempt to send information over a long distance, however, several things happen. First, the signal tends to drop in intensity, to "die down," due to the resistance of the wire, much as a bicycle coasts to a stop on a level surface. The second problem is that the signal tends to pick up interference. If you've ever tried to listen to a distant radio station, or if you've ever heard other voices in the background on a long-distance telephone call, then you have experienced this interference, called **noise.**

An electronic signal traveling along a wire or a radio signal traveling through the air will lose strength and pick up noise. As it gets further and further away from the source, the signal gets weaker and weaker, and the noise becomes more intense until eventually the noise overwhelms the signal and the signal is lost. When this happens, no information can be transmitted.

But, you say, our telephone system allows us to talk from coast to coast and even halfway around the world, and we see television programs from virtually every spot on earth (not to mention the moon and Mars). If signal loss and noise create problems for long-distance data communications, how can we explain these obvious discrepancies? Data *can* be transmitted over long distances. In order to transmit information over long distances, however, it is necessary to boost the signal occasionally. It's a bit like swinging on a swing; in order to keep going high, we must pump every so often.

Boosting an electronic signal is, however, not quite that simple. Some signals are easier to boost than others. As it turns out, the easiest signal to boost is in the form of a sine wave (Fig. 16.2). The "electronic pulse" approach within the computer (Fig. 16.3) is one of the most difficult patterns to boost. Thus, in transmitting computer data over any communication facility, it's highly important that the data first be converted from the computer's internal "pulse of current" form to a wave pattern.

In determining how we might make this conversion, we must first spend some time examining the wave shown in Fig. 16.2. Note that the wave starts at point zero, goes up for a while, drops back down to the zero point and

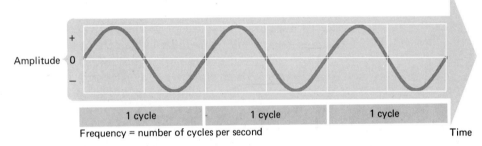

Fig. 16.2
A typical sine wave.

Fig. 16.3
Data within a computer is represented as a series of electrical pulses. Current either is or is not present.

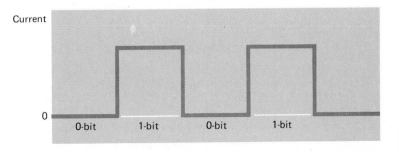

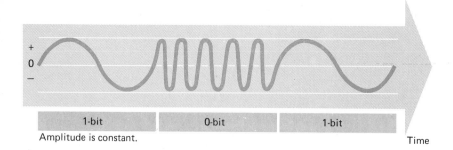

+
0
—

| 1-bit | 0-bit | 1-bit |

Amplitude is constant.   Time

Fig. 16.4
Frequency
modulation.

continues down, and then after reaching its low point comes back up to the zero line again. One complete "S-on-its-side" pattern is called a **cycle;** the rest of the wave pattern is nothing more than a repetition of this cycle. We can measure the height of a single wave (cycle) from its lowest to its highest point; this measurement is called the wave's **amplitude** (Fig. 16.2). Since the wave is moving, we would like to know how fast. The simplest way to measure the speed of a wave is to count the number of cycles that occur in one second; this is known as the wave's **frequency** (Fig. 16.2).

How can we use these wave properties to encode and transmit binary data? Simple. We'll start with a standard wave of known frequency and amplitude (the wave shown in Fig. 16.2 will do nicely). We'll let each cycle represent a single bit. If we want to send a 1-bit, we'll leave the pattern alone; a normal cycle holds a 1-bit. If we want to send a 0-bit, we'll mess up the frequency of a cycle (Fig. 16.4). A cycle at the regular frequency is a 1-bit; a cycle at any other frequency is a 0-bit. This is called **frequency modulation,** better known as **FM.**

As an alternative, we might send a 1-bit with a normal cycle but interfere with the *amplitude* of a cycle holding a 0-bit; this is called **amplitude modulation,** or **AM** (Fig. 16.5). The whole point is that binary data can be converted to a wave pattern for data transmission over any significant distance. The process of converting from a binary pattern to a wave pattern is called **modulation.**

Fig. 16.5
Amplitude
modulation.

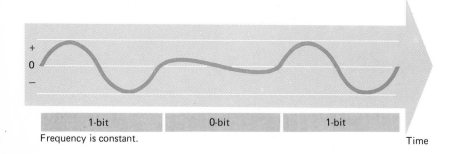

+
0
—

| 1-bit | 0-bit | 1-bit |

Frequency is constant.   Time

Data Sets or Modems

Let's stop for a minute and think about what happens when a computer communicates with a remote terminal. First, the data is in the computer in "pulse" form. Next it enters the communication system—telephone or radio—where it must be modulated or converted to a "wave" form. Finally, it arrives at the terminal where, since most terminals are designed to be used locally as well as remotely, it must be converted back to a "pulse" form.

The device that performs the conversion from pulse to wave and back to pulse form is called a **data set or modem** (Fig. 16.6); the word modem is an acronym that stands for *mo*dulator/*dem*odulator, a name that accurately describes the functions performed by this device. Normally, there is a data set or modem on each end of the communication line (Fig. 16.7).

Photo courtesy of
Anderson Jacobson, Inc.

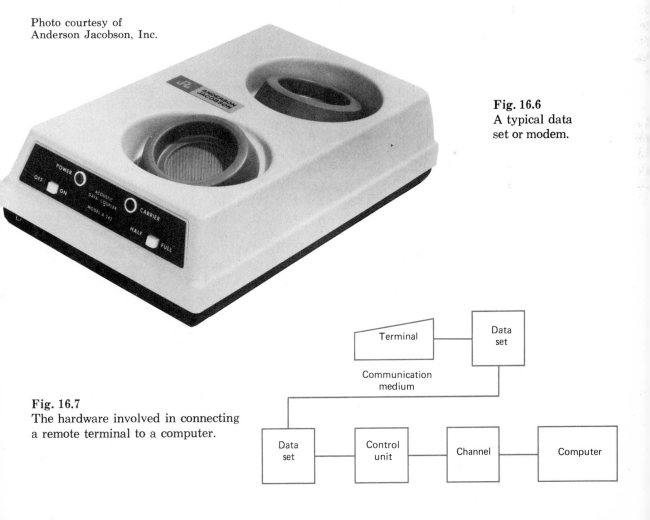

Fig. 16.6
A typical data
set or modem.

Fig. 16.7
The hardware involved in connecting
a remote terminal to a computer.

These devices must be present because of the electronic incompatibility between a computer and communications.

A typical data set for telephone communication is composed of two basic parts (Fig. 16.6). Near the top, you can plainly see what looks like a set of earphones; this part of the data set is called an **acoustical coupler,** and is used to hold the telephone receiver. Inside the device are a number of electronic circuits that perform the modulation and **demodulation** functions; this is the modem.

COMMON COMMUNICATION FACILITIES

Now that we have identified the various parts of a remote terminal network (terminal, data set, communication medium, data set, computer system) let's turn our attention to the communication facilities. We'll start with the telephone system. Our national **telephone network** connects just about every point in the world, and it's extremely reliable and dependable.

The type of telephone **line** that we all use for voice communication is called a **voice-grade line.** It can also be used for data communication. A voice-grade line normally transmits between 2000 and 2400 bits of data per second. A man named Emile Baudot was an early pioneer in the data communication field; in his honor, the basic unit of *data transmission* speed, one bit per second, is called a **baud,** making a voice-grade line a 2400-baud line.

If 2400 baud isn't enough, it's possible to combine a number of voice-grade lines and use them in parallel. Two 2400-baud lines working together can transmit data at a rate of 4800 baud. Three lines gets up to 7200 baud. Combine four, and we have a 9600-baud line, with other **wide-band channels** being treated separately.

One major difference between transmitting data over a 2400-baud line and over a 4800-baud line is the data set that must be used. On the surface they are identical, but inside there are some differences. A data set designed for 2400-baud data transmission sends bits along the line in serial fashion, one after another. Since a 4800-baud line is essentially two 2400-baud lines in parallel, a data set designed for 4800-baud transmission splits the data, sending odd-numbered bits along line A and even-numbered bits along line B. The 4800-baud data set at the other end of the lines puts the bits back together.

In many cases, the need for data communications is not continuous; short occasional bursts of **connect time** are all that is needed. In such cases, the user will typically take advantage of the regular public telephone system, dialing the computer, making a connection, and hanging up the phone when the work is finished. This approach is called **dial-up.**

Dial-up can get expensive if the call is long distance. Even if the call is local, many data communication users are not willing to accept the noise, interference, occasional busy signal, and other problems that are inherent in the dial-up approach. As an alternative, it's possible to lease a *private line*. This is a very common solution when line speeds in excess of 2400 baud are involved.

If 9600 baud is not enough, it's possible to lease a wide-band channel with data transfer rates ranging from 19,200 baud to one million baud. If 2400 baud is more than is necessary, telegraph channels ranging from 75 to 300 baud are available. There really is a broad range of alternatives.

Data communication is not, however, inexpensive. Although rates do vary from place to place, a single voice-grade line will typically rent for about one dollar per mile per month. It doesn't take long before that cost begins to add up.

Alternatives are available. Data can be transmitted between two points via radio waves, and many organizations doing a significant amount of data communication have installed private **microwave** relays. When microwave is used, transmission is restricted to a "line of sight"; in other words, if any large solid object gets in the way, microwave transmission will not work. The earth, as we all know, is round; it curves. The curvature of the earth limits the maximum distance of data transmission, making expensive relay stations necessary (Fig. 16.8). In an attempt to circumvent this problem, there is talk of a special data communication satellite that will allow installations located anywhere within the United States to send data, via microwave, to any other spot (Fig. 16.9).

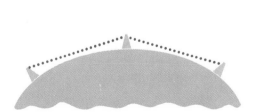

Fig. 16.8
Since microwave data transmission is limited to a "line of sight," relay stations must be used to compensate for the curvature of the earth.

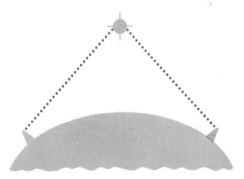

Fig. 16.9
Satellites can also be used for microwave data communication.

DATA COMMUNICATION SERVICE BUREAUS

Another development is the emergence of the data communication **service bureau.** A typical communication service bureau leases a network of wideband channels connecting a number of major cities (Fig. 16.10). Customers sublease portions of these communication channels. A typical customer might utilize regular telephone lines to get from a local office to the communication center in city A, have the message transmitted to city B over the wide-band facilities of the service bureau, and return to regular telephone lines to get the message from the communication center in city B to the local city B office. Getting to and from a communication center involves regular lines and regular rates; the city-to-city leg involves private wide-band lines and a lower-than-normal cost.

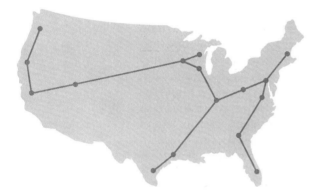

Fig. 16.10
The leased-line network of a typical data communication service bureau.

A key problem in operating such data communication service bureaus is keeping track of the source and destination of each of the messages passing through the system. Consider a simplified **network** linking two cities as an example. In city A, perhaps 100 or more different customers use the facilities of the service bureau. At any given instant in time, messages from dozens of these customers may be descending on the communication center. The service bureau is responsible for accepting all these messages and funneling them through a single wide-band line toward city B. The communication center in city B must, in turn, accept a continuous stream of data from the wide-band channel, separate this data into individual messages, and route each message to its proper destination along regular telephone lines. It's a very complex operation even on a two-city network; imagine how complex this **message switching** task becomes on a network connecting 20 or 30 cities.

Message switching, at least at this level, is so complex and requires such speed of response that unaided human beings cannot do it. Thus a communication service bureau typically has a computer located in each city served by the network; the sole purpose of this computer is to keep track of the source and destination of each message going over the line. The telephone company uses similar computers to handle regular telephone communications; that's why a direct-dial call is less expensive than an operator-assisted call.

THE SPEED DISPARITY PROBLEM

Let's return to a typical keyboard terminal/data set/voice-grade line/data set/computer system network. At the computer's end, data can be manipulated at speeds of four million characters per second and more. A voice-grade line is rated at 2400 baud; if we assume an eight-bit code, we get 300 characters per second, which is significantly less than four million. What about the terminal? Typical terminals are rated in the range of from 20 to 30 characters per second and, given the typing speed of most people, the rated speed is probably an exaggeration.

We have a 20-characters-per-second device attached to a 300-characters-per-second line which, in turn, is attached to a four million-characters-per-second computer. That's quite a range!

How can we possibly deal with this speed incompatibility? We can use buffers and we can handle a number of terminals at the same time. Let's deal with the first part of the solution first.

Most terminals contain a buffer (Fig. 16.11). Typically, a terminal's buffer is just big enough to hold one line of data. As the user types at a certain rate of speed, the individual characters go into the buffer. The RETURN key

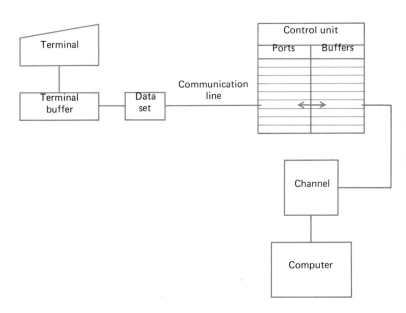

Fig. 16.11
On a typical data communication network, buffering takes place at both the terminal and the control unit ends of the line.

usually signals the end of a line, be it a partial or a full line. When the RE-TURN key is depressed, all of the data is in the buffer in an electronic form. This means that it can be transmitted at electronic speeds—300 characters per second is easy. Output data can be written into the buffer at a rate of 300 characters per second and transferred to the printed page at a rate of 20 or 30 characters per second. With a buffer in the middle, both the terminal and the telephone line can work at peak speed.

What happens at the other end of the line? Once the data has passed through a modem, it enters a control unit to begin its trip into the computer. A modern **transmission control unit,** often called a **front-end device,** is made up of a series of **ports** and associated buffers (Fig. 16.11). A port is nothing more than a connection point for a communication line, and we already know what a buffer is. Data enters the control unit at a rate of 300 characters per second and is moved into the buffer associated with the "port of entry." Once all the data is in the buffer, the transmission control unit can signal the channel which in turn can signal the computer (an interrupt, remember?) that data is available for transfer into the computer. As soon as the computer is ready, the data transfer can be achieved at close to the computer's internal speed. Going back out, data can be dropped in one of the transmission control unit's buffers at four million characters per second, parceled out to the communication line at 300 characters per second, dumped into the terminal's buffer at this rate, and printed at a rate of 20 characters per second.

But this is only half the story. If the computer supplies data to the transmission control unit at a rate of four million characters per second and the communication lines at the other end of the control unit can accept only 300 characters per second each, how many lines can the front-end transmission

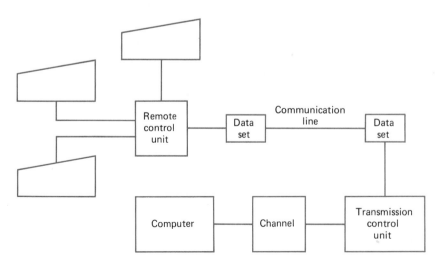

Fig. 16.12
It is possible to improve the utilization of a communication line by placing a control unit responsible for concentrating the transmission activities of several terminals at the remote end of the line.

control unit handle? At 4,000,000 per second in and 300 per second per line out, the transmission control unit could, in theory, take care of a full 13,333 lines at the same time (or at least concurrently)! Most front-end machines do not operate nearly this high—25 to 100 lines is a more reasonable range. But the idea that a single control unit can easily keep pace with a number of lines should be obvious to you. Buffering makes it possible.

Getting back to the terminal end of the line, we might note that attaching a single 20- or 30-character-per-second terminal to a 300-character-per-second line represents a bit of a speed mismatch, too. It's possible to put another control unit at the terminal end (Fig. 16.12) and assign to this piece of hardware the responsibility for controlling several terminals, concentrating their data transmission requirements, and getting closer to full utilization of the communication line.

HANDSHAKING AND POLLING

One of the basic skills of a computer is, as you may recall, the ability to request the start of an I/O operation. Many computers, strangely enough, are not particularly good at dealing with I/O operations that they did *not* request. On a terminal network, it's very difficult to predict exactly when any given user will complete a line of input data and hit the RETURN button, and a totally unexpected I/O operation can "drive a computer bananas."

Even though the data really originates "out there somewhere," the computer must be led to believe that *it* really started things. This is done through a process known as **polling,** which works as follows.

1. The computer, being ready to accept some data, asks the channel if it has any.

2. The channel, being little more than a data path anyway, asks the transmission control unit.

3. The transmission control unit asks the first terminal on the network if it is ready to transmit data.

4. If the terminal is ready (in other words, if there is data in the buffer and the user has already hit the RETURN key), the terminal sends a message (essentially, "yes") back to the control unit and:

   a) The control unit tells the terminal to send it;
   b) The terminal sends it;
   c) The control unit tells the channel it has data;
   d) The channel tells the computer it has data;

    e)   The computer tells the channel to send it;
    f)   The channel tells the control unit to send it;
    g)   The control unit sends the data through the channel;
    h)   The channel signals the computer when it has finished;
    i)   The process starts all over again.

5. If the terminal is *not* ready (i.e., the user is still typing), no message is returned to the control unit which, apparently feeling ignored, goes on to the next terminal.

6. If *no* terminals are ready, the process starts all over again.

That was not a comedy routine; polling really works that way. The signals that pass back and forth between the various machines are, as you probably assumed, in binary. The term given to this exchange of signals is, believe it or not, **handshaking.**

Many modern transmission control units have been designed to simplify this task a bit. Rather than wait for the computer to start things, they continuously poll their terminals, transferring data into the control unit's buffers as soon as a terminal makes it available. Later, when the computer asks for data, it's already in the control unit and can be quickly transferred. A front-end control unit with this kind of logical capability is a very complex piece of electronics in its own right, approaching minicomputer status. Such front-end controllers are quite expensive.

While we're on the subject of transferring data, it might be wise to mention a few points that students sometimes find confusing. In our discussion of terminals and communications, we have consistently pictured a terminal as working from a buffer—data is typed, character by character, into a buffer and then transferred over the communication line. However, not all terminals work this way. Some transmit each character as it is typed. When buffers are used, we have what is called **synchronous** data communication. When individual characters are transferred one at a time, we have **asynchronous** data communication.

Let's start at the terminal and try to visualize what happens during data transmission. First the modem at our end takes the binary code of a character and modulates it into a sine-wave pattern. At the other end of the line, another modem must demodulate the sine wave back into a binary form. But how does that modem know exactly when to expect that data? Is it possible to predict the precise instant at which a user will depress a key? No.

Since predicting the exact time of arrival of data is impossible, the modem must be given some warning. This warning is provided by placing special **message characters** in front of and behind the data (Fig. 16.13). Now, just before the data hits the modem, the modem gets a message that says, in effect, "Here comes the data." This gives the modem time to react and get itself

Fig. 16.13
When transmitting data, message characters are normally placed in front of and behind the data.

aligned and "in synch" with the incoming signal. The data can then be demodulated, with the end-of-message characters marking, as you may have guessed, the end of the message.

Under asynchronous communication, message characters surround each character of data. This means that more total bits must be transferred than is necessary under the synchronous mode, where a single set of start- and end-message characters might do for 80 or more characters of data. Since the speed of a line is limited to so many bits per second, asynchronous communication, with its need for more bits per character, will be able to transfer fewer characters per second. On the other hand, the modem that handles synchronous communications, since it must stay "in phase" with the incoming signal for a longer period of time, will be more complex and more expensive than the asynchronous modem—another tradeoff.

PROTOCOLS

Handshaking involves an exchange of prearranged signals. Message characters follow a prearranged pattern. Together, the signals associated with handshaking and the pattern of message characters define a very specific set of rules for exchanging information over a communication line. Many different sets of rules are used, with the "correct" rules being dependent on the computer manufacturer, the front-end device, the modem, the telephone company, and every other device or organization involved in the data transmission. In connecting a specific terminal to a specific computer (or front-end device) over a specific communication medium, however, a specific set of rules must be used. This specific set of rules governing handshaking and message characters is called a line **protocol.**

REMOTE JOB ENTRY TERMINALS

The only real difference between a remote terminal and a local terminal is the fact that there is a communication line and associated hardware involved with the remote terminal. Otherwise the link to the computer is identical—device, control unit, channel, and computer.

Keyboard terminals are not the only devices that can be located away from the mainframe. What's wrong with taking a card reader or a printer, breaking the line connecting the device to its control unit, inserting a telephone line and a pair of data sets, and teleprocessing card data? Nothing.

In fact, the use of remote card readers and printers is very common today. Typically, rather than simply dropping the device out there on its own (which would involve some major modifications to the equipment), a small control unit accompanies the card reader and printer (Fig. 16.14). The resulting collection of hardware is called a **remote job entry** terminal (Fig. 16.15). With such a terminal, cards can be entered from a remote site and placed on one of the computer's regular batch job queues. When the job's turn comes, the printed output can be routed directly back to the remote site. In effect, the remote location gets many of the advantages of a computer at the cost of a

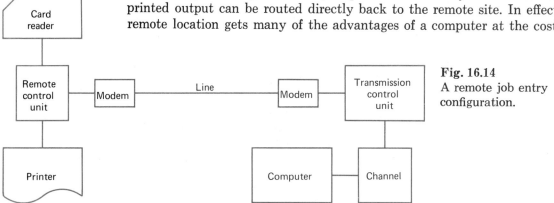

Fig. 16.14
A remote job entry configuration.

Fig. 16.15
A remote job entry terminal.

Photo courtesy of Data 100 Corporation.

terminal. Jobs that are much too big or too complex for a keyboard terminal can be run without the long delays that a courier system might entail.

Typically, the control unit associated with a remote job entry terminal performs blocking and buffering functions. A number of cards are read into the controller's buffer and then transmitted in a block to the transmission control unit at the computer end of the line. While this buffer is being emptied, data that is in the printer buffer can be printing, in parallel. Later, while the card-read buffer is once again being filled by the card reader, the terminal's controller can be accepting another buffer full of output data from the computer. By overlapping input and output in this way, the line is kept as busy as possible.

HALF DUPLEX AND FULL DUPLEX

Some terminals are capable of transmitting data in both directions at the same time, accepting output data from the computer at the same time that input card data is being sent to the computer. When data transmission takes place in both directions at the same time, we call it the **full duplex** mode. **Half duplex** or **simplex** means that data is transferred in only one direction at a time.

LINE SPEED AS A BOTTLENECK

A card reader can handle 600 cards per minute, which is 10 per second. At 80 columns per card, this reader handles 800 characters per second.

A 2400-baud line can transmit only 300 characters per second. If we were to attach a 600-card-per-minute card reader to a 2400-baud line, the card reader would spend a considerable amount of its time waiting for the transmission line. On a remote job entry terminal, the transmission line often becomes the limiting factor on speed.

It is essential that the input and output devices attached to a remote job entry terminal be carefully matched with the line speed. At 2400 baud, with an eight-bit code for each character, a total of 300 characters per second can be transmitted. A card reader or a printer capable of going faster than 300 characters per second represents wasted, unusable power. For a card reader, a reasonable upper limit is about 225 cards per minute; for a printer, 150 lines per minute. These speeds can be doubled for a 4800-baud line, tripled for 7200 baud, and so on. Wasted capacity is worthless.

Go To 363

TERMINAL INTELLIGENCE

There are things that can be done to improve the performance of a remote system. One such technique is called **data compression**. The typical card contains quite a few blank columns. The typical output line contains even more, since spacing for readability is considered important. Why transmit these blanks? With data compression, the terminal controller strips blanks from the input cards, replacing them with a control field telling the transmission control unit at the other end how many blanks to put back in. Coming the other way, the transmission control unit strips the blanks from a line of output, and the terminal's controller puts them back in.

What's the advantage of this? Fewer characters must be transmitted over the line. At 120 characters per print-line, a 2400-baud line can drive a printer at 150 lines per minute. If, through data compression, we could reduce the average print-line as actually transmitted to 100 characters, we could drive the printer at 180 lines per minute.

Data compression is a logical function. It requires some intelligence. A terminal that can support data compression will be somewhat more complex and a bit more expensive than a terminal that doesn't have this feature.

Some terminals are even more "intelligent," being locally programmable. It's possible on terminals of this type to write a program to "edit" input cards for accuracy, eliminating obvious errors before they are transmitted. After all, why send bad data to the computer? An important part of most printed output is information that serves only to identify the data, such as page headings and column headings. On a programmable terminal, only the "raw" data need be transmitted; the column headings, page headings, and spacing can be added locally. By eliminating the transmission of unneeded information, it's possible to get more performance from the terminal.

As we begin to add more and more logical functions to the terminal, it begins to look less like a terminal and more like a small computer in its own right. These devices are called **intelligent terminals**. The dividing line between an intelligent terminal and a minicomputer is nebulous at best. Many of these terminals contain such features as cassette tape storage and floppy-disk drives.

For many years, the high cost of the central processing unit and other mainframe components forced firms into centralization, concentrating all information processing in one or two large, expensive machines. Today, however, the declining cost of minicomputers and intelligent terminals is forcing these same organizations to take another look at this decision. What seems to be developing is a trend toward what is now known as **distributed data processing**.

At its core, distributed data processing doesn't seem to be too different from the centralized approach of the recent past — we still have a large, cen-

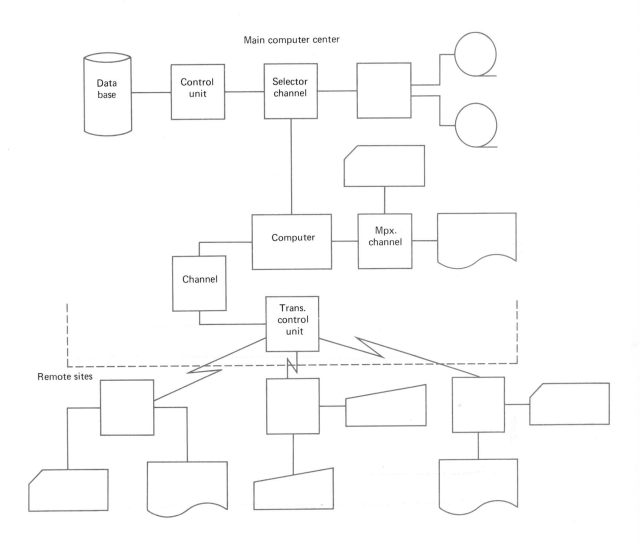

Main computer center

Remote sites

tral computer (Fig. 16.16). Typically, this computer houses the organization's data base and handles key corporate-wide functions. The difference lies in all the intelligent terminals spread throughout the organization. Given this widely distributed intelligence, the individual functional groups of the organization can do most of their information processing locally, dialing the central computer at the beginning of the day (to get current information), at the end of the day (to report activity to the central data base), and only as required at other times. The local groups enjoy the flexibility of having their own computer at a very reasonable cost, with the central machine being available to

Fig. 16.16
Distributed data
processing.

handle an occasional large job. The organization still enjoys the advantages of a centralized data base.

The term distributed data processing is not restricted to systems with a large centralized computer. A network of interconnected minicomputers might be considered a distributed system too.

SPECIAL SINGLE-FUNCTION TERMINALS

The use of single-function terminals is another interesting trend. One variety, mentioned in Chapter 4, is an on-line data collection terminal used to collect data from manufacturing employees. These terminals typically contain a card reader, a badge reader, and a very limited manual entry keyboard. To report on progress, the employee might enter his or her own badge, a card that identifies the activity just completed, and, via the keyboard, the number of units of work completed; the resulting record goes directly into the computer. The terminal is designed to perform one and only one function—in this case, data collection.

Fig. 16.17
An automatic
bank-teller
terminal.

Many banks have installed automatic teller terminals (Fig. 16.17), which allow the customer to handle everyday banking transactions at any time of

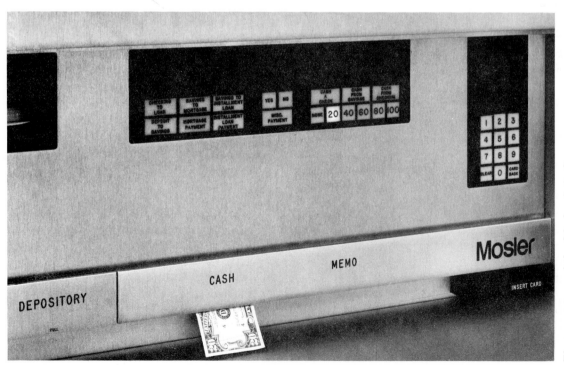

Photo courtesy of the Mosler Safe Company,
an American Standard Company.

day without human intervention. Supermarkets are experimenting with automatic computer-controlled checkout systems capable of reading a bar-code printed on the side of a package. Many department stores installed special terminals to check on a customer's credit rating. Though single-function in nature, these terminals can be quite sophisticated, approaching the status of minicomputers.

The fact that minicomputers are continuing to drop in cost will tend to lead to more and more such examples. Do you remember our discussion of a breakeven point? As the cost of the computer drops, what happens to the breakeven point? It becomes possible to economically justify automation for applications with fewer and fewer repetitions. As recently as the early 1970s no one really believed that the job of the bank teller would begin to fall to computerized automation. It has, because computer costs are dropping while labor costs are rising.

Of particular importance in the world of single-function terminals is the rapid development of **microcomputers**. A microcomputer or **microprocessor**, as the name implies, is an extremely tiny processor, usually consisting of a single integrated-circuit chip. Microprocessors are found in pocket calculators and digital watches, to cite two of their more common applications. They can also perform more complex functions, and they are inexpensive—*very* inexpensive. Look at the current cost of pocket calculators and digital watches.

In addition to being inexpensive, microprocessors are very flexible. A chip can be designed to perform a myriad of functions, and the individual design can be mass-produced. Even more important, these microprocessors can be combined to perform even more complex functions. In the future, look for such things as a full-function computer in a briefcase weighing perhaps 20 pounds, microprocessor control of pacemakers and other medical equipment, an inexpensive box that will convert your television set into an electronic ping-pong game—an almost endless list can be compiled.

MULTIPROCESSING

Multiprogramming involves a single computer working concurrently on a number of different programs. **Multiprocessing** involves a number of different computers working together. Since we have discussed distributed intelligence, it's only fitting that we should now introduce the topic of multiprocessing.

One of the earlier attempts at multiprocessing involved the control of a remote time-shared network similar to the one that we discussed in the beginning of this chapter. Recognizing the fact that the big central computer was not too good at dealing with transactions arriving at random intervals from a number of different sources, the designers of this system placed another computer, a smaller machine (the master), specifically designed with data communications in mind, in front of the larger one (the slave) (Fig. 16.18). The

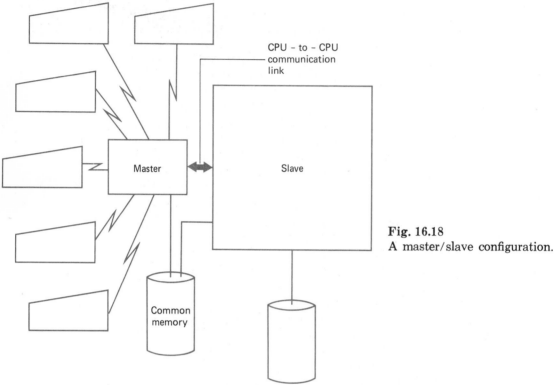

Fig. 16.18
A master/slave configuration.

small computer accepted all responsibility for coordinating the terminals and scheduling the big machine. The big machine did most of the heavy work, but ran under the direct control of the smaller one. Such configurations are called **master/slave systems**, and represent a good example of multiprocessing.

Control Data Corporation markets a computer that, in addition to the central processing unit, contains a number of peripheral processors. These peripheral processors handle such functions as the control of I/O operations, operator communication, scheduling, and handling interrupts. They can work in parallel with (i.e., at the same time as) the main processor. On a regular computer equipped with a single processing unit, interrupt handling is an operating system function. The processor must stop what it's doing to execute the instructions in the interrupt handler routine. On a CDC computer this job can be handled by the peripheral processor while the main processor goes about its other work. The CDC approach makes a lot of sense.

But is this multiprocessing? The peripheral processors are much smaller and less powerful than the main processor, and this fact puts the CDC approach right on the border; some call it multiprocessing, some do not.

What about the relationship between a computer and its channels? The channels are minicomputers that work in parallel with the computer. Both the channel and the computer have access to the same memory. They obviously work together. But due to the very low level of intelligence evidenced by the channel, most experts do *not* regard this as multiprocessing.

What then is multiprocessing? Multiprocessing occurs when two or more processors of roughly comparable power are able to communicate with each other and share a common memory. The shared memory can be main memory (Fig. 16.19) or any on-line direct access memory (Fig. 16.20).

Why is this important? Many experts believe that the computer of the future will be radically different from today's single-processor machines, consisting perhaps of a bank of independent microprocessors which, whenever necessary, can be combined to attack a problem. Most of the time each of these processors will be working independently on its own problems, using a pool of available memory. When one of these processors encounters a problem that is beyond its capabilities, other processors could come to its aid. The declining cost of the microprocessor might actually make this approach possible.

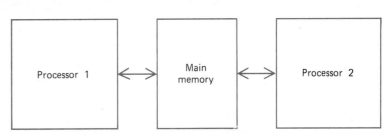

Fig. 16.19
Multiprocessing with the two processors sharing main memory.

Fig. 16.20
Multiprocessing with the two processors sharing on-line secondary memory.

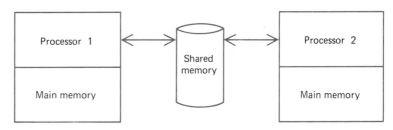

KEY WORDS	SUMMARY

KEY WORDS

acoustical coupler

amplitude

amplitude modulation

baud

connect time

cycle, wave

data compression

data set

data transmission

demodulation

dial-up

distributed data processing

frequency

frequency modulation

front-end device

full duplex

half duplex

handshaking

intelligent terminal

line

local

master/slave system

message characters

SUMMARY

The chapter began with a discussion of a terminal network. The unique problems of transmitting data over any distance were pointed out, and the need for converting the electronic pulses of the computer into a wave for data transmission was established. We also discussed the concept of modulation and demodulation and the need for a modem or data set to bridge the electronic incompatibility.

We then moved into a discussion of data communication facilities, starting with the standard voice-grade telephone line. Combinations of two, three, and four voice-grade lines can be used. Higher transmission speeds can be obtained from wide-band channels. A major alternative to the telephone is microwave; special satellites are planned.

Keyboard terminals are very slow, creating a serious speed disparity problem. The line transmission speed is also quite slow when compared to the computer's internal processing speed. Buffering and the assignment of multiple terminals to a single control unit are two techniques that help to minimize the impact of this speed disparity.

Because of the fact that most computers are not very good at handling unexpected I/O operations, terminals are coordinated through a process known as polling. The exchange of electronic signals that usually accompanies polling is called handshaking. A specific set of rules for handshaking and message characters is called a protocol.

Keyboard terminals are not the only devices that can work over data communication lines; a remote job entry terminal is often used to control a card reader and a printer. If data transmission takes place in only one direction at a time, it is known as half duplex; a full duplex system allows for transmission in both directions at the same time.

The speed of the transmission line is frequently a bottleneck, limiting the speed of the attached devices. Data compression and intelligent terminals can allow the user to get more performance from the system. Special-function terminals with intelligence limited to a single area of application are also growing in popularity. There is a very strong trend toward the use of intelligent terminals, both single-purpose and general-purpose; this trend toward distributing computing power throughout the organization is known as distributed data processing.

The chapter ended with a brief discussion of multiprocessing.

EXERCISES

1. What is a communication line? What is a communication network?

2. What is meant by modulation and demodulation?

3. What is a data set or modem? Why is it necessary?

4. What is a voice-grade line? What does the term baud mean?

5. What is the difference between microwave data transmission and telephone data transmission? Why is microwave transmission limited as to distance?

6. Why is buffering so important in communicating between a computer and a terminal?

7. What is handshaking? What is polling? What is a line protocol?

8. Often a transmission control unit or a front-end device is used at the computer's end of a communication line. What functions are performed by this device?

9. Contrast synchronous and asynchronous data communication.

10. Contrast half duplex and full duplex.

11. What is remote job entry? What is an intelligent terminal?

12. What does the term distributed data processing mean?

13. What is multiprocessing?

message switching

microcomputer (microprocessor)

microwave

modem

modulation

multiprocessing

network

noise

polling

port

private (leased) line

protocol

remote

remote job entry

service bureau

simplex

synchronous

telephone network

transmission control unit

voice-grade line

wide-band channel

Where Do We Go from Here?

V

The Impact of the Computer and Automated Information Processing on Our Society

---

17

OVERVIEW

This book began with a presentation of "a few days in the life of Bob Smith," following Bob and his family as they performed their daily activities and highlighting their interactions with the computer. Next we discussed the use of the computer in a number of other areas of modern American life. Hopefully, this material convinced you that computers are relevant and worth learning about.

Since that first chapter, we've concentrated on the more technical aspects of computers and information processing, including such topics as how the computer works, why computers are used, how some typical classes of applications are actually implemented, how files are stored and retrieved, the computer's own environment, the value of information, and systems analysis. Now that you have a solid understanding of what a computer is and what it can

371

and cannot do, we can return to a discussion of the impact of the computer on our society. We'll be a bit more specific this time; your newly acquired background should give you an appreciation for more detail.

The chapter starts with a brief review of why computers are used. Next, typical computer applications in a multitude of different fields are presented in tabular form. We'll then take a look at several specific computer applications given in case-study form. Although it's obvious from just looking at the list of applications that the computer has come to permeate all areas and all levels of our society, there are costs associated with computer use. The computer does create or at least contribute to some problems. In the second part of this chapter, we'll examine some of these problems, including unemployment, depersonalization, privacy, power and the misuse of power, computer crime, computer errors, and the tendency of people to believe anything coming from a computer.

A note of caution is in order here. To this point we've concentrated largely on factual material; in this chapter, we'll be moving into the area of opinion. All opinion is of course presented with a bias, and the author is mildly optimistic.

WHY COMPUTERS ARE USED

One of the key ideas introduced in Chapter 2 was breakeven analysis. In using this approach, we compared a fixed-cost solution, such as a computer, to a variable-cost alternative. We discovered that as the number of repetitions increased, we eventually approached and passed the breakeven point, after which the fixed-cost solution became the lower-cost alternative. This is one of the primary reasons for using the computer. It can do a job at a lower cost than any other alternative.

In business, this means that such highly repetitive activities as payroll computation and inventory maintenance will be computerized in all but the smallest of firms. In the areas of science and mathematics, it means that large-scale mathematical problems will be programmed and solved on the computer; the alternative, perhaps years of paper-and-pencil computation, is much too costly in terms of effort and time delay. The most common activity in this general category is record keeping. People can compute payroll, solve complex mathematical problems, and keep records without the aid of the computer, of course; it's just that the computer can do it at a lower cost.

In addition to this category of applications, the computer can also be used to allow people to perform otherwise impossible activities. The space program provides a good example. One of the more suspenseful real-life dramas of modern times occurred when one of our lunar modules developed a technical problem and three astronauts were threatened with being lost in space. NASA was able to provide a set of alternative plans, resulting in a safe return. Where did these plans come from? A team of NASA people used a number of computers to simulate possible strategies. Without the computer, the computations needed to figure out a solution would have taken weeks, perhaps even months, which would have been much too late.

This is but one example; many others could be cited. The entire space program would have been impossible without the computer; the problems are just too complex for manual solution, and speed and accuracy beyond the skill of any human being is required. Traffic control around major airports would be next to impossible without the computer's aid. Research in many areas of science, including physics, astronomy, chemistry, genetics, and many others, depends on the computer to help work with, predict, and measure things that are just too big, too small, or too quick for the unaided human being.

As you read the rest of this chapter, consider why the computer is used for any given application.

COMPUTER APPLICATIONS

The use of computers is widespread; the following pages present a list of applications by functional area. Scan this list; the diversity of applications is amazing. Find the applications cited for your own major field or your area of employment and examine these in a bit more detail. See if you can determine why the computer is used in each case. Within your own field, you should be able to find evidence of even more specific applications.

Over the next several pages, we'll be examining a number of interesting computer applications, concentrating on why the application is valid and how the computer solution to the problem is implemented. We'll be going into detail, but you should have little trouble following these discussions given a reasonable understanding of the material in Chapters 1–16.

Agriculture
financial records
crop planning
scheduling fertilizer applications

scheduling sprinkler systems
inventory

Banking and Finance
checking-account maintenance
savings-account maintenance
24-hour teller
maintaining loan and mortgage records
bank credit card billing
investment advice
bill-paying services
electronic funds transfers

Business: Management and Administration
payroll
billing
inventory
invoicing
account ledgers
accounts receivable
accounts payable
budgeting
budget analysis
auditing

order entry
personnel records
scheduling
credit control
purchasing
planning
facilities planning
market research
recruiting
management information

Construction
design analysis
stress computations

scheduling labor and materials
administration

Defense
air defense early warning system
weapons development
strategic planning

war games
tactics
intelligence analysis
weapons guidance
simulation
administration

Education

registration
student records
grade reports
classroom assignments
scheduling
budgeting
payroll
administration
examination grading
research
simulation
mathematical modeling
data analysis
computer-aided instruction

Entertainment and Sports

scoreboard control
computation of odds (horse racing)
player analysis for professional football draft
analysis of opponents' past trends
statistical analysis and computation
strategy analysis
timing events
computer dating
computer games
horoscopes

Fishing Industry

analysis of aerial photographs to locate schools of fish

Forestry

analysis of aerial photographs to identify diseased trees
analysis of aerial photographs to aid in fighting fire

Government

income tax records
social security records
military records
court records
unemployment statistics
automobile registrations
driver registrations
medicare records
administration
budgeting
planning
counting votes
economic analysis
intelligence records
social services records
index of government publications
payroll
voter registrations

Home Use (Future Applications)

electronic calculators

doing homework

computer games

shopping by telephone

security

Hotels and Motels

reservation systems

inventory

administration

Insurance

policy records

risk analysis

estate planning

administration

Law and Law Enforcement

data base

fingerprint files

"modus operandi" files

scheduling court cases

dangerous-criminal files

status checks on criminals via telephone

court records

dispatching police

analysis of crime statistics

laboratory tests

Liberal Arts

data analysis

cryptology

analysis of writing style

art

music

poetry

analysis of style, in general

data base applications

research

Libraries

book circulation control

circulation analysis

key-word-in-context indexing

addressing overdue notices

Manufacturing

industrial robots

production control

order tracking

planning

scheduling

expediting

inventory control

work-in-process inventory control

auditing

quality control

physical inventory

numerical control

Medical and Hospital Administration

bed inventory
drug inventory
record keeping
billing patients
laboratory tests

analysis of electrocardiograms
medical research
medical diagnosis
administration
patient monitoring in intensive care

Mining
mapping
aerial photograph analysis

Post Office
reading zip codes
electronic mail

Printing and Magazines
typesetting
maintaining subscriber records
billing

addressing subscriber copies
administration

Refining (Petroleum)
data analysis
sampling
control of the refining process

Restaurants
billing
auditing
inventory control

Retail Sales
credit checks
computerized checkout
inventory control
auditing

market analysis
billing
administration
point-of-sale terminals

Science, Engineering, and Research & Development
space program
engineering design
stress computations
drafting

simulation
mathematical models
complex calculations
measuring and timing experiments

Secretarial
word processing
filing
record keeping

Social Sciences
research
data analysis
mathematical analysis
statistical analysis

economic forecasts
artificial intelligence
mathematical modeling
mapping

Stock Market
record keeping
tracking prices
market analysis

Transportation
air traffic control
airline reservation systems
automated bus and railroad systems (future)
automated highways (future)
traffic signal control
inventory of freight cars

Television
voter analysis
election predictions
market analysis

ratings
demographics

Utilities
billing
administration
forecasting
scheduling

message switching (telephone)
data analysis
rating

Computer-Controlled Checkout at the Supermarket

Have you ever noticed the little black and white bar-code printed on most of the products offered for sale in the supermarket (Fig. 17.1)? It's called the **Universal Product Code** (UPC), and it uniquely identifies the product and the manufacturer. If you'd like to get a feel for how the UPC works, go to the desserts section of the supermarket and look at the gelatin packages. Each package of gelatin bearing the same brand name will have the same first few digits, but the last few digits will vary by flavor and package size. Shifting to another brand, you'll find a different first few digits; again, these digits will remain constant for all products carrying this brand, but the last few digits will vary by flavor and size. The Universal Product Code uniquely identifies the manufacturer and the specific product.

This code is the key to computer-controlled supermarket checkout. Using an electronic **bar-code scanner**, a checkout clerk can electronically read the UPC, eliminating the need to manually key each price into a cash register.

Fig. 17.1
A Universal Product Code is
printed on most products for
sale in a modern supermarket.

Let's take a quick look at how this system might work within a typical supermarket.

Essentially, two pieces of equipment are needed within the supermarket:
a bar-code scanner and a minicomputer (Fig. 17.2). The scanner is built into
the checkout counter. As the customer places the purchases on the counter,
the clerk locates the bar-code and passes it over the scanner. Typically, an
audible beep is used to signal a successful read; if the signal does not sound,
the clerk repeats the process, finally entering the code by hand only if two
or three tries prove unsuccessful.

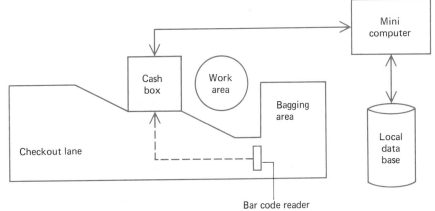

Fig. 17.2
A computerized
checkout system.

From the bar-code scanner, the code is read into the minicomputer which
(1) looks up the code in a table, (2) finds the current price and the description of the product, (3) adds any necessary tax, (4) adds the total cost of
this product to the customer's bill, and (5) sends the description and the
price to the checkout station's printer where a complete, detailed list of the order is prepared. All this happens in a fraction of a second, long before the
clerk has had enough time to move the next item over the bar-code scanner.

This process is repeated for each item in the order. When the entire order
has been entered, the minicomputer computes and prints the total bill, the
clerk enters the amount of payment, and the minicomputer computes the
amount of change due. Manual keyboard entry is still provided for those few
products that do not have the Universal Product Code or for the sale of items
on which the code has been destroyed. Other manual entry functions are designed to cover the problems that might be caused by a customer who changes
his or her mind.

Why are supermarkets using this approach, and what are its advantages?
One advantage often claimed for the customer is faster checkout. Have you
ever been forced to wait while a stock clerk checks on the price of an item or
while a checkout clerk struggles with a badly smudged, almost unreadable
price? Have you ever felt mild anger rising as you waited for a hopelessly
clumsy clerk to enter prices with one finger? These delays disappear under
computer-controlled checkout. Even with a dozen or more checkout stations
attached to a single minicomputer, a computerized checkout system is capable
of compiling an order just as quickly as the clerk can slide products over the
bar-code scanner; the complete checkout operation takes only a little longer
than the bagging operation used to take. To the customer, that means faster
checkout. To the supermarket, it means that fewer clerks are needed to handle the same workload.

Another big advantage is accuracy; there will be fewer errors on a computer-controlled system than on a manual system. Mismarked product and
checkout-clerk typing errors disappear. Contrary to popular belief, supermarkets lose more than they gain due to human errors; most customers will correct an error in the store's favor, while ignoring an error in the customer's
favor.

These benefits seem almost insignificant when compared with the potential for labor savings and inventory control made possible by computer-
controlled checkout. Let's consider labor savings first. How do you think
prices get on all the packages you buy? Someone stamps them on. At several
dollars per hour, the cost of stamping prices on product packages is very high.
With computer-controlled checkout, the price of each product is entered onto
a direct access file attached to the computer. Prices are entered once; any
change in price requires changing the price only once. No prices need be
stamped on individual items; the computer, using the product code as a key,

looks up the price. The elimination of labor represents a tremendous saving in cost.

The potential for better inventory control is another very significant benefit of computer-controlled checkout. A store must control its inventory so as to know what products must be reordered. Without the computer, inventory control within the store often takes the form of inaccurate manual counting of selected items; counting errors or incorrect guesses as to what to count can lead to overstocking or understocking. With the computer, as each item is passed over the bar-code scanner, the value "1" can be subtracted from the product's inventory level, giving management an up-to-the-second status of the stock on hand of each product in the store. Physical counts can be performed on a sample basis to provide checks on the accuracy of the system and to allow the store to estimate shoplifting losses.

Typically, a supermarket with computer-controlled checkout is tied into a distributed network (Fig. 17.3), with all the stores in a chain linked to a large central computer. At the beginning of a business day, the central computer supplies current prices for all products from the central data base. Once the file has been initialized, the store manager can make changes to reflect store specials. At the end of the business day, the store sends current inventory balances and sales data to the central computer, which handles the corporate data base, prepares corporate reports, and plans the distribution of products to the individual stores.

Why not use the central computer for all logical activities, putting only data entry terminals in the stores? One computer controlling hundreds of stores might be possible and might seem to be a good low-cost solution to the problem, but what if the central computer breaks down or for some reason

Fig. 17.3
A distributed network of computer-controlled supermarket checkout systems.

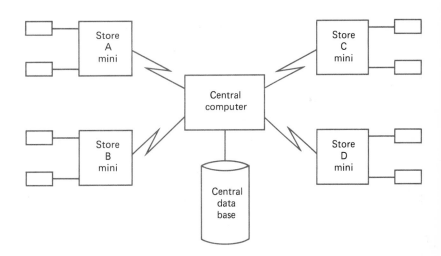

fails to operate properly? Hundreds of stores are temporarily out of business. If each store has its own computer, a computer failure impacts only one store. Another reason for distributing intelligence is communication costs; the cost of maintaining an open telephone line to each store during business hours would be prohibitive. By allowing each store to function on its own, dialing up the central computer twice a day, communication costs are kept at a minimum.

Why not do the whole job on the minicomputers? Distribution is a corporate function. It's a very complex problem, often involving mathematical techniques such as linear programming. Such activities are beyond the capacity of a minicomputer.

There are, of course, problems with computer-controlled checkout. Many customers do not like the fact that prices are not marked on individual items. Stores try to counter these objections by posting unit prices on the shelves or by setting up special bar-code scanners that allow customers to read the UPC on a package and obtain the current price of the item, but the lack of prices on the individual packages is still a major concern. Will customers be willing to shop in a supermarket that does not mark prices on every item? Only time will tell.

The main justification for computer-controlled checkout is a reduction in the need for supermarket labor. By eliminating the stamping of prices on each item and the physical counting of products for inventory purposes, the need for stock clerks is reduced. By allowing faster checkout, fewer checkout lines can be used to serve the same number of customers, meaning that fewer checkout clerks will be needed. But what is to be done with the people who are displaced by a computer? We'll consider this question in detail a bit later in the chapter.

Computer-controlled supermarket checkout does reduce the amount of labor needed to run a supermarket. Labor costs represent a significant part of the total cost of running a supermarket. If a computer can do the same job at a lower cost, the computer will be used. In spite of its problems, it would appear that computer-controlled checkout is here to stay, unless consumers reject the idea.

Monitoring Patients in Intensive Care

One of the most pressure-packed operations in any hospital is the intensive care unit. Almost by definition, patients in intensive care are in very critical condition, requiring minute-by-minute 24-hour surveillance; a sudden worsening of condition leading perhaps to death is possible at any moment.

In many hospitals, one nurse is assigned to one patient in intensive care, monitoring this single individual for any change in vital signs. Often, the shortage of nurses forces a hospital to double up or even triple up, assigning one nurse to a number of patients. As a result, even under the best of conditions, minutes might pass before a change in condition is recognized and corrective action taken, and these few minutes could spell the difference between life and death. Even the very best of nurses are human, suffering occasional periods of inattention or distraction.

At an increasing number of hospitals, the function of monitoring patients under intensive care has been assigned to a computer. Equipment designed to check breathing, pulse rate, and other critical life signs is plugged into the computer, often a stand-alone minicomputer. The computer samples the readings of each patient on a regular basis, perhaps several times a second, comparing actual readings with critical limits and sounding an alarm whenever one or more life signs deviates significantly from normal. At the sound of the alarm, a nurse responds, usually in a matter of seconds, and summons help.

There are several advantages to computer-controlled patient monitoring. Even with dozens of patients hooked into a single computer, the monitoring rate—several times per second—is much better than even the very best of nurses could possibly accomplish. The computer does not suffer from fatigue. Periods of inattention do not exist. Computers do not require coffee breaks or restroom stops. One or two outstanding nurses, with the computer to help them, can easily manage an intensive care unit, helping to overcome the shortage of qualified nurses.

The advantages cited above result from the computer's speed and accuracy. The computer does a better job of the tedious second-by-second monitoring of a patient than could any human being. Cost really isn't a factor; it probably costs more to use a computer to monitor patients than it would to assign one nurse to each patient. But what is the value of a human life? If a few split seconds might make a difference, isn't the extra cost worth it?

Incidentally, the technology that supports computer-controlled patient monitoring is a spinoff of the space program. Our astronauts were monitored in much the same way.

A Data Base for *The London Stage*

One of the more interesting computer-related books of the past several years was written by an English professor named Ben Ross Schneider and is called *Travels in Computerland or Incompatibilities and Interfaces* (Reading, Mass.: Addison-Wesley, 1974). In his book, Dr. Schneider describes the problems he encountered in creating a massive data base of *The London Stage*, a compilation of the casts of characters for every play presented in London between the years 1660 and 1800.

Why is such a data base desirable? English researchers are very interested in this data. With only the written form of *The London Stage* as a reference, a researcher might spend years extracting the information needed to prove or disprove a hypothesis, leafing through this multivolume work page by page. Even the most careful of researchers might miss that one piece of critical data. With a computerized data base, a researcher can have the computer extract relevant data, leaving the researcher with the task of analysis, a task more suited to human beings. The computer data base saves research time, and time is money.

Industrial Robots

When we think of robots, we tend to picture the almost-human, mechanical marvels of science fiction. Industrial robots are not nearly so fascinating, but they're still very interesting.

Cincinnati Milacron, an Ohio-based manufacturer of machine tools, electronic controls, and other industrial products, includes a number of computer-controlled industrial robots in its product line. One of the more interesting varieties is the 6CH Arm (Fig. 17.4). As the name implies, this robot is designed to function much like a human arm. Its hydraulic controls support motions that simulate the human shoulder, elbow, and wrist, with an ability to roll its "hand" almost 240° giving it an extra dimension. The arm can move at 50 inches per second and can lift, at full extension, up to 175 pounds. Its reach extends over eight feet in either direction, and over twelve feet high.

Fig. 17.4
Cincinnati Milacron's
6CH Arm, a computer-controlled robot.

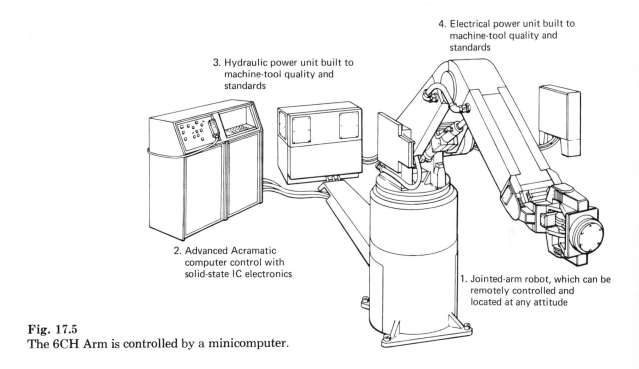

4. Electrical power unit built to machine-tool quality and standards

3. Hydraulic power unit built to machine-tool quality and standards

2. Advanced Acramatic computer control with solid-state IC electronics

1. Jointed-arm robot, which can be remotely controlled and located at any attitude

Fig. 17.5
The 6CH Arm is controlled by a minicomputer.

What can the robot do? Let's quote briefly from a Cincinnati Milacron advertising brochure:

> A wide variety of interchangeable "hands" and inexpensive "fingers" can be applied to the robot's jointed arm. This permits it to carry out the programmed commands required to "pick-and-place" many different sizes, shapes, and weights of objects, or to handle attachments that can hold and operate hand tools, spray guns, welding heads, power tools, etc. . . . (Cincinnati Milacron, Publication No. A-221, 1975)

In a demonstration, the author has seen the 6CH Arm assemble components on a moving assembly line, perform spot welding on a moving assembly line, load and unload two automatic drilling machines concurrently, clean engine blocks, and wire control panels. In industrial settings it might be used to perform such highly dangerous functions as inspecting the inside of a nuclear generator.

The 6CH Arm is controlled by a minicomputer (Fig. 17.5). The minicomputer is programmed (Cincinnati Milacron prefers to say that the machine is "taught") by an operator using a simple hand-held "teach unit." This teach

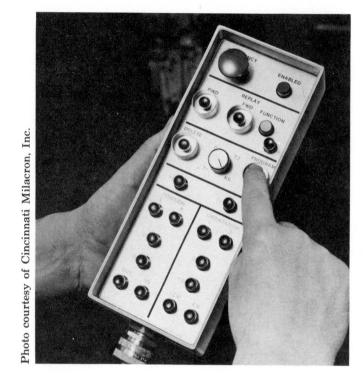

Fig. 17.6
The controls for programming or "teaching" the 6CH Arm.

unit is really a set of push-buttons (Fig. 17.6) that allow the operator to move the arm step by step through a process. Key points in this step-by-step walkthrough are recorded by the computer; later, during actual use, the computer guides the arm by moving it from programmed point to programmed point. Programming (or teaching) requires no computer experience and no mathematics; any individual who knows the physical job to be performed can teach the 6CH Arm.

Today the major market for such robots is in supporting jobs that must be performed in places which are unfit for human beings: inside a nuclear reactor, for example. But what about tomorrow? The 6CH Arm can perform many of the jobs on a modern assembly line. The cost of such robots is dropping as technology improves, and the cost of labor continues to rise. The robot is a fixed-cost item; human labor is a variable cost. Although a takeover is not imminent, look for increasing use of robots for purely economic reasons.

The Computer-Controlled Scoreboard

It's the bottom of the eighth inning. The score is 3 to 2, but the first two Cincinnati hitters have singled, putting runners on first and third. Out marches the visiting manager; it's time for a pitching change, and the fans settle back to enjoy (?) one of baseball's duller moments as the relief pitcher ambles slowly in from the bullpen and takes his allotted eight warm-up pitches.

Suddenly, out in center field, the scoreboard springs into action. An animated crane reaches out and bodily removes the cartoon caricature of the opposing pitcher from the game. As he leaves, the scene shifts to the bullpen where the designated relief pitcher, in obvious terror, begs not to be brought in to face the "Big Red Machine." A bull (what else would you expect to find in the bullpen?) chases the poor guy across the field and onto the mound, where he finds himself standing with the ball in his mouth. His first pitch, delivered with what could only be called a lack of confidence, is hit for an apparent home run. As the brief cartoon ends, the fans are left chuckling, and an otherwise dull break in the action has been converted into an enjoyable interlude by the computer-controlled scoreboard at Cincinnati's Riverfront Stadium.

Externally, the scoreboard looks just like an ordinary scoreboard. It displays runs by inning, hits, errors, the uniform number of the next hitter, the current batting average of each player as he comes to the plate, and other pertinent information. On the left side of the scoreboard is a bank of lights shaped much like a television set. This bank of lights allows word messages and animations to be displayed. Remember matrix printers? On these devices, characters were formed by printing a pattern of dots. Information is displayed on the scoreboard in much the same way, with selected lights being turned on to form a pattern. On an animation, the pattern of lights forms one frame, the lights are quickly turned off, and another pattern forming a new frame is displayed; the changing pattern of lights gives the illusion of motion much as in a moving picture.

This scoreboard is of interest to us because it's controlled by a computer, an early third-generation machine known as the General Automation 1830. The computer has 20K words (each 16 bits) of core storage, two drums totaling three million characters of secondary storage, and a tape drive. A typewriter terminal is also available for entering batting orders, the names of groups attending the game ("the Reds welcome the Bevis Beavers"), and other alphabetic information.

Main memory is divided into four partitions, one of which holds the operating system, a real-time control module known as the RTX18 operating system. This software module controls the transfer of messages or animations from drum or tape into main memory for subsequent display on the scoreboard.

Word messages such as the batting order, the names of the various groups in attendance, the "scoreboard stumper" (a baseball trivia question), and others are entered into the system via the keyboard terminal just before the game begins and stored on drum. Each message is assigned a number; later, during the game, the operator can cause the message to be retrieved from drum, read into core, and displayed on the scoreboard. Information such as the name and number of a new pitcher, a pinch hitter, defensive replacements, scores of other games, and emergency messages can be entered, stored, and displayed as the game progresses.

Another interesting feature is the way in which the system handles a player's batting average. The average is actually recomputed and displayed just prior to each time at bat, reflecting the latest possible statistic—a simple task for a computer.

Animations are stored both on drum and tape. Some of the cartoons, celebrating such "real-time" happenings as a home run or a stolen base (by the home team, of course), must be displayed as the action is happening; it would look a bit silly to play the home-run animation as the next hitter is striking out. Such real-time animations are stored on drum where they can be quickly retrieved and displayed. Others, such as the relief pitcher cartoon described earlier or the victory celebration at the end of a game, take place during slack periods when a little time can be spent in searching for the program without affecting the impact; such animations are stored on tape.

The animations are, of course, programmed ahead of time. The scoreboard in Cincinnati was built and installed by the American Sign and Indicator Corporation, and this firm did much of the animation programming, calling on the skills of Hanna-Barbera Productions for help. Animation programs are written on another computer, transferred to magnetic tape, and subsequently added to the scoreboard's repertoire.

Why go to all this trouble just to keep track of the score? Actually, the computer-controlled scoreboard does much more than keep score. It fills slow spots in the game with interesting action, adds a bit to the excitement of high spots, keeps the fans informed, and, in general, makes the game a bit more interesting. It's also great for public relations, allowing the Reds (and the Bengals, who use the stadium during football season) to offer nice little extras such as displaying the name of each group attending the game. These little extras (combined with the appeal of an outstanding team, of course) help to bring people back, and in the world of professional sports, that is the name of the game.

THE COMPUTER: A MIXED BLESSING

Even the most cursory review of the first several pages of this chapter should convince you of the extent to which the computer has come to permeate all levels of our society. Let's put it another way. It doesn't much matter what you plan to major in or what you plan to do for a living; unless there is another major revolution roughly equivalent to the barbarians sacking Rome, you *will* encounter the computer. Its impact is analogous to that of the automobile and television. Computers are a part of our society; things would be quite different without them.

We hear that the automobile is largely responsible for the air pollution and congestion of our major cities. And television has been accused of literally "rotting our minds." Technology is usually a bit of a mixed blessing, and the computer is no exception. In the next several pages, we'll examine some of the problems caused by or associated with the computer.

Computers and Unemployment

The image of a human being replaced by a computer is a common one. We see an automated bank-teller terminal and know that somewhere a human teller is out of work. Computerized supermarket checkout certainly has an impact on the jobs of supermarket clerks. In fact, one of the major reasons for using the computer is that it can do a job at a lower cost than its human competition can, but what happens to that human competition? There is little question that the use of computers does in fact displace some human workers.

How many? What is the real impact of this problem? The answer depends a great deal on the attitude of the respondent. Trade unions consider worker displacement to be a very serious problem, part of what they see as a general trend toward automation in this country. The union leader might look at a decision to computerize payroll and point out the five or ten people who would be replaced immediately. Should the company double in size as projected, the number of clerks who might have been employed would be twice the number being displaced today.

Management and the computer industry tend to look at the problem differently. From their point of view, the use of computers creates new jobs—keypunch operators, computer operators, programmers, systems analysts, and a new management group. Not only that, but without the computer the increase in paperwork would tend to swamp the growing concern, thus slowing growth; the use of computers, according to this group, creates jobs simply by allowing growth to proceed at a more rapid rate.

Just as there is little question regarding the fact that the computer does displace some people, there is little question that the computer creates new jobs. In a recent survey of the top 50 companies in the data processing industry (*Datamation*, June, 1977), the number of people employed in only the data processing areas of these companies is estimated to be in excess of 570,000. These are people who build, sell, and service computers; without the computer, these jobs would not exist. This survey certainly does *not* count the people who program, operate, or manage computer operations for almost every medium-sized to large-sized organization in the country.

Dire prophecies of the impact on employment have accompanied the arrival of almost every technological advance in history—none have come true.

Major technological breakthroughs tend to create growth, leading to additional jobs in the long run. The computer, at least in the opinion of the author, is no exception.

There is, however, one potentially very serious problem with the computer. The jobs that can be automated are highly repetitive and require little or no advanced training; the jobs that are created tend to be more sophisticated, requiring training, experience, or special skills. Given this shift toward skilled jobs and away from the low-skilled, entry-level positions, we can see a very real potential shift in the job mix. Without special technical training, the young person just entering the job market will have a difficult time "cracking" the computer field. Some form of training will be necessary.

This creates a companion problem in retraining those people who are displaced by the computer. Given the fact that the computer can best be applied to relatively simple, repetitive tasks, the army of the displaced will tend to include a disproportionate number of the unskilled and low-skilled. Is it reasonable to assume that an individual who has been working on an assembly line for 20 years and who has not attended any school during that time can be retrained as a computer programmer? The problem is that the very people who are displaced tend to be the most difficult to retrain. There is no easy answer to this problem.

Depersonalization

Have you ever felt that society in general or some organization to which you belong treats you like a number rather than a person? Does it bother you that such things as your social security number, your savings account number, your checking account number, your employment number, your telephone number, your automobile registration number, and your zip code have become as much a part of your identity as your name? Do you become annoyed when a clerk in a store asks for one of your numbers, in preference to your name, as identification? If so, you've probably commented on the increasing trend toward **depersonalization** in our society, and you've probably blamed the computer.

The fact that identification numbers and codes are coming into wider and wider use is undeniable. The reasons behind this trend are, however, not too difficult to understand and certainly not at all sinister. Look in the telephone book of any metropolitan area and count the number of entries for "John Smith." It has been said that there may be thousands of John Smiths, but there is only one 184–55–2238. Identification numbers are assigned because they make record keeping easier and more accurate.

Still, this annoys some people. It *is* somewhat dehumanizing to be known by your credit account number rather than your name. The alternative of disdaining the use of credit cards and other documents that impose a numerical identification is unrealistic today.

How is the computer involved in this controversy? The computer has become the primary record keeper; an identification number is sometimes called a computer code, implying that the computer somehow "demands" the use of such impersonal numbers. It doesn't. A computer could use an individual's name and street address as its key for storing data. The use of unique identification numbers is, however, more efficient and less expensive; this is a human, managerial decision, not a computer imposition. Personalization is possible, but it's more expensive. Are you willing to pay the extra price? Many people are, as evidenced by the continuing success of the small speciality shops that do provide personal service, though they may charge higher prices than the discount house around the corner.

What of the future? It's highly likely that the depersonalized numbers of today will be replaced by better, more personal methods of identification; numbers are too prone to theft and other criminal misuse. We all know that each one of us has a unique set of fingerprints, and equipment to identify fingerprints electronically is technically feasible. Unfortunately, when we think of fingerprinting, we think of a criminal, and many of us might balk at having our fingerprints taken for identification (after all, we are not common criminals). This could doom popular acceptance of fingerprinting as a means of identification. Handprinting is almost as accurate as fingerprinting and easier to implement, but it too shares fingerprinting's negative image. Perhaps the most promising identification scheme is built around **voice printing**. Voice printing is very accurate, and most of us would probably not consider a request to whisper "I'm the real John Smith" into a microphone at all depersonalizing. Using a computer to analyze a voice print may lead to the day when rather than causing depersonalization, the computer eliminates it.

Computers and Privacy

In his classic novel *1984*, George Orwell envisioned a future society in which the lives of human beings were tightly controlled and structured by an absolute dictatorship personified by "Big Brother." These controls were implemented by a fantastic array of electronic *surveillance* devices. Today, many fear that the combination of modern electronic "bugs" and the computer provides all the technology needed to make Orwell's nightmare come true.

Consider the data that is today held in computer data banks. Let's start with the federal government, where many agencies and bureaus maintain files containing personal information (Fig. 17.7). Add to this the files maintained by local and state governments and by private concerns (Fig. 17.7), and you have an imposing array of personal information in the hands of others. Have you ever done anything wrong? Have you ever made a mistake that you would rather forget? The changes are that it's on a computer file somewhere, and the computer never forgets. The potential for blackmail, particularly political blackmail, is enormous.

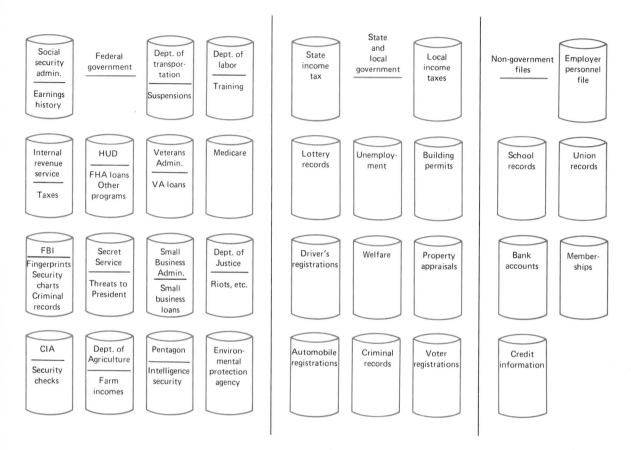

Fig. 17.7
Personal data is
maintained by
many groups.

Fortunately these files are not interrelated, belonging to a number of independent and often hostile groups. The possibility of combination does, however, exist, probably with the social security number as a key. This was suggested several years ago, and the idea of a **national data bank** was widely discussed. Among the strongest opponents were the members of the data processing profession. The potential for a misuse of *power* and the invasion of personal *privacy* was just too great. In effect, the slow wheels of bureaucracy serve to protect us from excessive misuse of existing files.

We continue, however, to be deluged by requests for computer data. Questionnaires and polls solicit our reactions, opinions, and attitudes on just about everything. Even the Census Bureau has ben accused of asking unnecessary and excessively private questions "under penalty of law." Would this kind of information even be requested, were it not for the ready availability of computers to digest and process it? We do have a right, after all, to be left alone. We do have a right to grant or withhold our consent. We must be guaranteed our confidentiality and anonymity when desired. Any data bank that cannot make these guarantees should not be allowed to exist.

Computers and the Misuse of Power

What would Adolf Hitler have done with a national data bank providing detailed personal information on every citizen? Are our leaders capable of misusing information? Ask those who were subjected to income tax audits in the Watergate era.

The control of information represents power. What if the government had the ability to compile, at the push of a button, a complete dossier on each and every one of us? Even for those who have absolutely nothing to hide, the possibility is a bit terrifying.

It's not enough to simply assume that our leaders will be ethical. We must have the right to control, correct, and question that which is on file about us. Exactly how these rights can be ensured has yet to be determined.

Crime and Sabotage

There once was a programmer who was assigned the task of writing a program to compute the interest due on savings accounts. Very early in his work, he recognized the fact that interest did not always compute exactly to the penny; frequently, fractions of a cent were involved. "What," he asked, "is the rule I should use for rounding?" "You don't round," he was told, "you truncate. We (the bank) keep those fractions of a cent."

Being well-versed in mathematics, it didn't take our programmer very long to realize that this "unpaid" interest amounted to an average of one-half penny per account. On 100,000 accounts, that's $500.00! "Why," he reasoned, "should the bank get all that money? I want some for myself."

So he wrote the program to add these fractions of a penny to his own account. It worked, for several years, but eventually he was caught and convicted of theft—one of the very first computer crimes.

Computer crime is an increasing problem. Recently a large insurance company was found guilty of creating and selling (to other insurers) bogus insurance policies. The key to making this scheme work was the computer; the fraudulent policies were simply added to the list of good policies on the company's data base. The crime was so well implemented that a well-known national auditing firm verified the accuracy of the insurance company's financial records, detecting nothing wrong. It took the testimony of a disgruntled employee to expose the scandal.

As more and more of our financial dealings take place on the computer, the possibility of computer crime will soar. The problem is security. To the average person, the computer is so complex that any data stored on the machine is bound to be safe. To the computer professional, breaking the security codes of a computer-based system is little more than a mental exercise. Given enough time, almost any modern security system can be broken.

The fact that so much of modern data communication takes place over telephone lines adds to the problem; any telephone line can be tapped. Illegal access to a computer can be gained from almost any telephone. Such things as passwords, identity checks, and data "scrambling" do help to prevent "accidental" access, but the determined professional who wants access can usually figure out how to get it. The computer manufacturers are aware of this problem and are attempting to deal with it.

Computer Errors

We tend to believe whatever the computer says. We have accepted, almost as part of our culture, that computers never make mistakes; hence, "if it's on the computer, it must be right." This belief is responsible to a large degree for many of the computer's problems.

A young quality control engineer walked into my office one day with a notebook full of the results of statistical computations that he had performed on a desk calculator. He asked me if I could write a program to print his results on computer paper. He did not want any data analysis or any computations performed; he just wanted a direct, one-for-one copy of his notes on green-and-white striped paper with holes in the sides. I asked why. His reply was a classic: "If I walk into my meeting with this notebook in my hand, they'll throw me out; but if I hand them the same results on computer paper, I'll be a hero." People tend to believe anything that comes from a computer, but computers are not infallible.

The computer can make mistakes. Occasionally, the hardware will fail, although this is unusual. When we speak of the computer's accuracy, this is what we generally refer to, and computer hardware is remarkably error-free.

One common source of computer errors is the programs. Ideally, a programmer carefully debugs a program before releasing it for general use, hopefully subjecting the program to thorough testing. Often, however, little bugs slip by unnoticed, showing up days, months, and even years later when some unusual set of circumstances arises. Problems of this type have been known to occur on system software too, although bugs are more common in application programs which, typically, are less thoroughly tested.

Operators cause errors. Incorrect tapes are sometimes mounted. Boxes of cards are sometimes dropped, changing their sequence. The wrong button pushed at the wrong time can destroy a computer system. Operators generally do a pretty good job, but they are in daily contact with the computer. This fact tends to make operator-caused errors more common than software errors.

Incorrect data is another common source of error. The accuracy of a key-punch operation, to cite one example, is generally estimated to be in the neighborhood of 95 percent, meaning that, on the average, 95 of every 100 cards keypunched will match the data on the coding sheet. In other words, 5 of every 100 cards will be wrong—and this is considered normal. Since data entry is the responsibility of human beings and human beings make errors, any data system will generate errors. A well-designed data entry system should be able to anticipate these errors and either correct them or at least shunt them aside for later correction.

Even more serious is the problem of poor program design. This is not quite the same as the software errors described above; poor program design implies that a program might do the wrong thing with perfect accuracy. Perhaps an example might help to explain this. A customer of a large department store once received a bill for $0.00; the bill was naturally ignored. One month later, another bill arrived, this one with a 50¢ service charge for nonpayment. The customer took the bill to the store, the mistake was admitted, and a credit granted. One month later, another bill arrived showing an old balance of 50¢, a credit of 50¢, another 50¢ service charge, and a new balance due of 50¢. The bill also contained a mildly threatening letter.

This cycle of complaint, credit, bill, and complaint, with each bill accompanied by an increasingly "nasty" letter, continued for several more months. An attempt was made to cancel the credit card. "Cancellation illegal—outstanding balance," said the computer. Finally, in desperation, the customer mailed a check for $0.00. The bank's computer refused it.

This little story illustrates a number of computer errors. Since we're considering the problem of poor program design, let's analyze how this whole problem started. The individual who wrote the billing program designed the program to send a bill if (a) there was an old balance greater than zero, or (b) there were any purchases made during the current period. The victim had an old balance of zero, but made a single purchase, which was subsequently returned for full credit. Under these conditions, the program told the computer to mail a bill, so a bill was mailed. A well-designed program would have made this decision on the basis of the *ending* balance.

A computer will do exactly what it is told to do. If a program instructs the computer to calculate and print a check for one million dollars, the computer will calculate and print a check for one million dollars. If the computer is told to mail a bill for $0.00, it will mail a bill for $0.00. If the computer is told to include a note demanding payment with bills more than 60 days overdue, it will. A computer has no sense of the ridiculous; it will do exactly what it is told to do no matter how absurd. If a badly designed program tells the computer to do something wrong, the computer will do it perfectly wrong.

Even more serious than poor program design is poor system design. It's possible to design a perfect data collection system with accompanying programs to analyze the data, but what if no one has any use for the results? A great deal of time and money has been wasted. Hardware errors, software errors, operator errors, data errors, and program design errors can be annoying and costly, but system design errors can sink a company.

Have you ever heard someone say, "I can't do anything about it because it's on the computer"? It's strange that in spite of our tendency to give the computer credit for omnipotence, we've also made it the modern "fall guy," blaming the computer for all sorts of problems.

Actually, it's almost never the computer's fault. It's the program's fault. Or the programmer's. Or the operator's. Or the system designer's. But rarely the computer's. The computer, being only a machine, has no emotions; it doesn't really care. Maybe that's why we blame it.

COMPUTERS AND SOCIETY: FINAL COMMENTS

It would be pretentious to pretend to offer solutions to these most serious problems in a few pages; therefore, no solutions are offered. We'll leave that to the psychologists, sociologists, political scientists, and others expert in dealing with the problems of society. The author hopes that the material in this book has provided a solid technical base against which to develop solutions.

A few comments are, however, in order. No major technological advance has ever been without its social cost. Mass production is probably responsible for bringing us up to our present high standard of living, but mass production brings drudgery into the lives of the assembly-line workers. The automobile provides us with unparalleled mobility, but automobiles pollute and take up precious space for parking and roads. Television provides entertainment, putting us in touch with the entire world, but television has been accused of creating a generation of passive followers.

We must deal with these problems. Solutions must be found. But in solving the problems arising from technological achievement, we must be careful not to destroy the advantages we derive from technology. Technology is not always right, nor is it always wrong.

SUMMARY

In this chapter we reviewed a number of typical computer applications in a variety of fields. We then moved into a brief discussion of a number of problems created or augmented by the computer, dealing with unemployment, depersonalization, privacy, power, computer crime, and computer errors. Like any technological achievement, the computer, while solving many problems, has created some of its own.

REFERENCE

Rothenbuecher, Oscar H., "The Top 50 Companies in the Data Processing Industry," *Datamation* (June 1977): 61–74.

EXERCISES

1. Why are computers used?

2. Do some outside reading on the use of the computer in your major field and write a short paper on your findings.

3. Select a possible area of future employment (for yourself) and do some reading to determine the impact of the computer on this field.

4. Do computers lead to unemployment? What do you think?

5. Is the computer responsible for the apparent depersonalization of our modern way of life?

6. How can computers be used to invade your privacy?

7. Relate the risk of the misuse of the data stored on a possible national data bank to our recent government scandals.

8. Find a few articles on computer crime, and write a short paper summarizing them.

9. Have you ever encountered a case in which an individual assumed that a computer "just had to be right"? Have you ever heard someone blame the computer for having made a stupid mistake? What's wrong with both points of view?

10. At the end of Chapter 1, you were asked to read a novel or short story and make a note of your reactions. Reexamine your reactions now.

KEY WORDS

bar-code scanner	power, political
computer crime	privacy
computer errors	surveillance
depersonalization	unemployment
labor displacement	Universal Product Code (UPC)
national data bank	voice print

Trends and Opportunities

In this chapter, we'll attempt to point out a number of trends in the information processing field, and then try to translate these trends into possible future employment opportunities.

TRENDS IN HARDWARE

Computers and computer-related equipment are electronic in nature. Modern integrated electronic devices have been declining in cost for some time now; pocket calculators and digital watches are two good commercial examples. This trend toward declining cost continues unabated. Computer hardware, being electronic, benefits from this trend. The declining cost of information processing equipment will be a very important factor in the future, allowing this equipment to economically compete for more and more new applications.

Along with cost, the size and weight of this equipment is also dropping. At the same time, speed, reliability, and computing power are increasing. Except for the computer, very few products offered by our modern industrialized society have shown such marked improvement as their cost declined.

Another important improvement in modern electronic computers is the lifting of *environmental constraints*. Until recently, a computer, to ensure reliable performance, had to be kept in a climate-controlled room, maintaining constant temperature ($72°F \pm 2°$) and relative humidity ($50\% \pm 5\%$). Newer computers, especially minicomputers, are designed to work almost anywhere. This represents another cost reduction, saving the customer the expense of special climate-control equipment.

The claim that the cost of computers is dropping may seem a bit strange to the manager contemplating the purchase or lease of a large machine; they always seem to cost more than the big machines of the prior generation. What changes is the capacity of the newer machine: A System/370 computer might cost $1\frac{1}{2}$ times as much as a System/360 computer at the same relative spot in the product line, but might be capable of doing three or four times the work. The customer contemplating the addition of another early-third-generation machine may well find that a newer model, more expensive than one but cheaper than two earlier models, provides more than enough extra power.

The cost decline is most obvious in the minicomputer market. Machines every bit as powerful as a second-generation computer can be *purchased* today for what would have been a few month's *rental* cost for the old machine. We even have personal computers today—about as big as a suitcase, powered by electrical current from a standard wall outlet, fully programmable in languages like APL and BASIC, and costing less than $20,000. This may seem like a great deal of money, but consider the fact that the UNIVAC I, a considerably less powerful machine, sold for over two million dollars as recently as the early 1950s. Eventually, if current trends continue (and there is no reason to believe that they won't), look for very powerful personal computers in about the same price range as a compact automobile.

Microprocessors—very small, often single-function computers—represent another remarkable growth market. Using microprocessors, special-function computers can be designed to perform almost any imaginable task. The manufacturing process for these devices (see Chapter 6) is highly automated; the big cost factor is concentrated in designing, building, and testing the first unit, with subsequent copies being produced at a nominal cost. This is why, as the demand continued to grow and more and more units were produced, the cost of pocket calculators and digital watches has shown such a marked decline. Pocket calculators and digital watches are controlled by special microprocessors.

What happens as a particular special-function computer begins to decline in cost? More and more are demanded; this is the basic law of supply and demand. As more and more are demanded, even more are built, and the cost per unit drops even further, fueling even greater demand. This is a tremendous potential growth area. Many experts foresee the day when even the small grocery store on the corner has a small, inexpensive computer dedicated to the tasks of billing, maintaining tax records, paying bills, and tracking inventory.

Another area where the potential for technological change is tremendous is in memories. Current bulk memories (disk, drum, and tape) move; this movement limits the speed and storage capacity of these devices and makes them susceptible to wear and eventual failure. It's only a matter of time before economically competitive static memories are developed. Numerous technological approaches, none of which we'll discuss in any detail, are under active study today.

These newer memories will probably be addressed much like main memory by simply counting memory locations in sequence. No longer will the programmer be forced to consider tracks, cylinders, and other factors that relate to physical efficiency. This will have a significant impact on the use of traditional access methods, causing a probable decline in the indexed sequential approach and tending to favor sequential access and techniques which are based on the relative record number concept.

The programmer will also be significantly affected. Today one of the most valuable individuals in any computer center is the programmer who fully understands the intricacies of physical I/O and can advise the other programmers as to the most efficient approach. With bulk memory addressed much like main memory, the complexity disappears, and with it the need for this individual. In effect, those who are today considered to be at the very top of their profession will be among the "first to go."

Probably the biggest potential growth area in the entire information processing field is in terminals of all types—keyboard typewriters, CRTs, remote job entry, intelligent terminals, and special-function terminals. More and more banks will begin to use the automatic teller terminal. Supermarkets will tend to increase the pace of checkout automation. Retail stores will place the credit-checking function on-line more and more. Schools will use terminals for instruction and administrative problem solving. Even personal terminals, roughly analogous to a pocket calculator but making a powerful computer as close as the nearest telephone, will come into general use. (Already it's possible to purchase a terminal, complete with communications equipment, for less than $2000.) The growth potential here is just tremendous!

TRENDS IN FIRMWARE

Traditionally the designer of a computer system was forced to choose between hardware and software for performing key logical functions. Hardware is highly reliable and very fast, software is slower and more prone to error, but it's also much more flexible and less expensive. Until recently, economics has tended to dictate a software solution for most logical functions.

Modern trends in electronics have tended to change this picture. It's possible, for example, to design a single circuit chip to find a square root. Traditionally, square roots have always been estimated by using a software algorithm. It was not implemented through hardware because the cost was too high. Today, however, with the tremendous growth of calculators with a square root function built in, the development cost of this piece of hardware has been spread over so many copies that the cost per unit has declined, making the hardware solution both faster *and* less costly than the software solution. Look for built-in square root functions (and other common mathematical functions) on many future computers.

Typically these electronic circuits are assembled on a single card or two and can be installed or removed from a computer almost at will. Where do they fit? They are obviously not software, but from the standpoints of cost and flexibility, they are different from traditional hardware too. The term **firmware** has been coined to describe these electronic circuits, which fall somewhere between traditional hardware and software.

Almost any function can be implemented through firmware. The big cost is in developing and building the first copy; subsequent copies are relatively inexpensive. What this means in practical economic terms is that a firmware solution to an information processing problem is only viable when a significant number of copies can be sold.

On a large computer, expect to see many of the system software functions (operating systems, I/O control, data base management, data communications management, utility programs and sorting) implemented through firmware. At the other extreme, the small, single-function minicomputer (the device used to control checkout at each of hundreds of supermarkets, for example) will be totally controlled by firmware programs. Supermarket employees will probably view the minicomputer in their store as a "magic sealed black box," never to be tinkered with or modified. Along the same lines, a small business can even today purchase or lease a minicomputer with "built-in" firmware programs to perform such typical business functions as payroll, accounts receivable, accounts payable, and inventory analysis. These computers look much like a normal piece of office furniture and require no professional operators and no programming staff.

TRENDS IN SOFTWARE

The trend in software is toward simplicity. Although some experts believe that a new, human-like language is about to take over, this does not seem to be the case. Instead, a few languages—COBOL, FORTRAN, BASIC, PL/1, APL, RPG, and, at least in Europe, ALGOL—seem to be gaining stature as "de facto" standards. Although the "perfect" language, perhaps even spoken language, is not beyond the realm of possibility, the trend toward simplicity will probably be seen in other ways first.

The first and perhaps most obvious trend is away from assembler-level languages and toward the higher-level compiler languages, at least for application programming. The major advantages of assembler language are related to computer efficiency; an assembler program usually runs faster and needs less main memory than an equivalent program written in a compiler language. New technology won't change this basic fact. Why then is the use of assembler-level languages expected to decline?

As the computer becomes faster and less expensive, the value of efficiency on the computer begins to decline. In the middle 1950s, eliminating 1000 instructions from a program might have amounted to a savings of a second or two each time that the program was run. On a modern high-speed computer, the same saving might yield a few microseconds at best and, given the fact that we might only be using 35 percent of the available time, who cares?

Even more important is the growing awareness of the true cost of writing a program. Debug, documentation, and maintenance are key components of this total cost, and programs written in a compiler language are much easier and much less expensive to debug, document, and maintain than are programs written in assembler. With declining "on-the-computer" costs, a program must be used with great frequency before the "on-the-computer" economies catch up with the much higher debug, documentation, and program maintenance costs arising from the use of assembler language.

One approach that should tend to simplify programming is the trend toward structured programming. Structured programming is implemented through a series of rules, restrictions, and guidelines for writing programs in a simple, straightforward, easy-to-read, and easy-to-maintain manner. Tricky programming is out. The simplified approach is in.

Purchased software also has an impact. Once a programmer becomes used to the syntax of a data base management package, the writing of application programs is greatly simplified because the programmer can forget about the details of input and output and concentrate on the logic of the program. With purchased, vendor-supplied system software, the modern programmer need do little more than sequence a series of add, subtract, multiply, divide, compare, move, read, and write statements, paying absolutely no attention to such details as physical I/O or converting coded data to numeric form. He or she can concentrate on solving a problem rather than fitting the solution to a particular computer.

Not only system software but also application software can be purchased today. Look for an acceleration of this trend as more and more managements begin to realize that what they do really isn't that much different from what many others do and decide to stop "reinventing the wheel."

DATA COMMUNICATIONS

Data communications is a major bottleneck today. The cost is very high, tending to limit the use of terminals and intelligent terminals. Line speeds limit the speed of the entire remote system.

Although the American telephone system is without a doubt the best in the world, it was not designed with data communications in mind. The telephone company is, of course, aware of the present limitations and is taking steps to deal with them; recent advertising tends to stress new technology. Look for major changes in the area of digital data transmission, with laser technologies, glass fibers, and other new approaches beginning to carry messages.

Other changes will come in the area of rate structures. Look for new data transmission rates, and don't be surprised if the new structures make overnight, "off-prime-time" data transmission very attractive. Many major firms manage to save a great deal on their long-distance communications by leasing special WATS lines which allow any number of long-distance calls for a fixed fee; in the future, there will be a similar arrangement on data communications.

The trend toward the use of intelligent terminals or minicomputers feeding a large centralized computer is partially due to existing telephone rate structures. It's much cheaper to allow a remote computer to handle its own load, dialing up the central computer only when necessary, than to attach a less expensive but less intelligent terminal directly to the main machine. The cost of telephone time is a function of connect time.

There are, of course, competitors. Microwave radio can be used for data transmission, and there are plans to launch a private communications satellite to support a national microwave network. Such a system would probably be designed to transmit data from city to city, with local telephone lines being used from the transmission station to the customer's installation. Given the fact that the demand for data communications is almost certain to continue to grow, new technologies are equally certain to be developed.

A growing submarket of the data communications field is the private leased network. Such networks are set up by private companies that lease wide-band facilities (similar to the cables that carry television programs from the network to its stations) connecting major cities, and then sublease the use of these lines to a number of customers. Generally, these communication service operations use special-purpose computers at the terminal points of the line; these computers control the transmission of data, making certain that messages get to the proper party.

COMPUTER NETWORKS

Distributed data processing implies a number of different computers interconnected by communication lines. Such configurations are often called computer networks. Some networks are composed of a number of minicomputers. Others are centered around a large "maxi" computer which houses the organizational data base and performs organizational data processing activities. Terminals of all kinds are attached to this central computer, including keyboard terminals, simple remote job entry terminals, intelligent terminals, and single-function terminals. The communication facilities, including perhaps special computers whose sole responsibility is message concentration or message switching, are also considered to be part of the computer network. Planning and balancing such networks has become a discipline of its own.

NEW MARKETS

Traditionally, a relatively small number of mainframe manufacturers supplied their customers with both hardware and software support. Independent software and "foreign" hardware did, of course, exist but was relatively rare.

Today one of the major markets within the information processing field is supplying **peripheral hardware,** primarily input/output devices, memory, control units, and terminals. Such devices are said to be **plug-to-plug compatible** with the mainframe of a given supplier; this term means that the equipment can simply be plugged into the mainframe. Plug-to-plug peripherals succeed mainly because they are quite cost-competitive, often selling or leasing for considerably less than equivalent peripheral equipment supplied by the mainframe manufacturer. As the use of computers grows, so will this market.

Probably the biggest growth potential, at least in the hardware area, can be found in the manufacture and sale of terminals, all types of terminals.

Closely associated with terminals is the equipment needed to support data communications—data sets, modems, acoustical couplers, data communications control units, and teleprocessing line controllers. This is another potential growth market.

With the advent of small, inexpensive, special-purpose minicomputers, many small firms that have never even considered the possibility of computer use before will "take the plunge." These firms will need help getting started. There is a growing market for people who are able to provide this service. The market is presently served by a number of independent consultants who purchase equipment from the various manufacturers and assemble a number of what are called **turnkey systems;** ideally, the customer should merely have to "turn the key" to make the system work. These consultants install the systems at customer locations, get things started, and provide follow-up support when necessary. The first-time user needs this kind of service. With the declining cost of minicomputers, there will be more and more first-time users entering the market, and that translates again into growth potential.

Closely related to the development of small, inexpensive computers, particularly microcomputers, has been the emergence of the computer hobbyist and the whole new field of **personal computing.** "Build-your-own-computer" kits are available at prices ranging from a few hundred to several thousand dollars. Computer hobby clubs are springing up all over the nation. There is even a possibility of nationally franchised personal computing centers along the lines of the more popular electronics and hardware chains.

Not only computers but terminals are beginning to have an impact on the hobby market. By constructing or purchasing a small, low-cost keyboard, it's possible to convert a regular black-and-white television set into a CRT terminal which can in turn be connected to a computer via telephone lines. We already have firms that, for a fee, will allow the terminal owner to access a computer and play computer games such as Star Trek, chess, electronic football, and countless others until his or her interest (or money) runs out.

System software has been supplied by private concerns for quite some time now, and this will continue. By using standard operating systems and vendor-supplied data base management, data communication, and spooling packages, many companies have, in effect, given full responsibility for maintaining all system software to outsiders. In fact, there are **independent software vendors** who will gladly accept full responsibility for a fee. Given this approach, programmers at the customer's location write only application programs. As more and more system functions are taken over by hardware or firmware, this trend will become more and more pronounced. If you want to be a **system programmer** working on operating systems and data base managers, you should plan to work for one of the mainframe manufacturers or for a large software vendor.

Many companies have "gotten out" entirely, assigning full responsibility for all systems and application programs and even the operation of the computer center to an outside vendor. In other cases, a firm will decide not to even own or lease a computer, sending all work to an **information processing utility.** There is a growing demand for services of this type.

Systems analysis and design is another growing field. Organizations are just now beginning to become aware of the value of a total-system approach to system planning. A particularly strong subfield within this general market involves the planning and implementation of data communications networks.

EMPLOYMENT OPPORTUNITIES

As the computer field goes through what seems to be an almost continual period of change, employment opportunities are certain to shift too. Let's take a look at some of the traditional jobs within this field and comment on the probable future of these jobs; then we'll consider some of the newer employment opportunities. The comments which follow are based to a large degree on the opinions of the author.

One traditional data processing job is that of keypunch operator. Don't look for any significant growth here. The newer data entry terminals and the trend toward on-line data collection via special terminals will, if anything, decrease opportunities in this area. Punched cards will not disappear, of course, and many former keypunch operators will find work operating one of the newer keyboard data entry devices. But this is *not* a growth field.

The traditional job of computer operator is another which will probably tend to stabilize or even decline in the future. The trend toward distributed data processing should reduce the emphasis on the large machines while increasing the use of minicomputers; a minicomputer does not require as many operators as a big machine does. Continued growth in the computer field will probably create enough new jobs to offset the expected job loss and thus maintain some stability, but operations is not a real growth field.

The demand for programmers will grow, but there will be changes in this job category. The trend toward implementing many system functions in firmware, coupled with changes in the way in which bulk memory is addressed and the switch to purchased software, will tend to cut the demand for the systems programmer, the person who traditionally has been at the top of the programmer "pecking order." The mainframe manufacturers and the independent software houses will still need good system programmers, of course; stability or a mild improvement in the employment opportunities for these individuals can be expected.

Application programming should grow simply because more and more organizations will be using the computer. Here again, however, there will be changes. As programming is simplified, the emphasis will shift from clever coding to problem solving. Perhaps we will someday be able to say that an accountant with a reasonable amount of computer training can be expected to write better *accounting* programs than a programmer with no accounting experience. Programming skill will become a valuable "companion skill" to go along with solid preparation in almost any major field. This may become the entry-level skill needed to get that first post-college or post-technical school job.

Systems analysis will be a real growth area. Individuals who can attack problems from a broad total-system point of view will always be in demand. The increasingly technical world of the future will only increase this demand.

The trend in hardware design—electronics, specifically—is a bit more difficult to pin down. While it is true that more and more computers and related electronic devices will be manufactured and sold, it's also true that the economics of modern integrated circuitry insist that a great many copies of a circuit be manufactured in order to recover the development costs. In the past, the designer could always concentrate on redesigning a circuit to make it better. To justify the redesign and replacement of a modern integrated circuit demands a potential for a really significant improvement before it becomes economically viable. This factor might tend to limit employment opportunities for newly minted computer designers. Look to the mainframe manufacturers and the major electronics firms for possible positions.

Sales and service will be affected too. As the sale of computer equipment increases, the impact on these two groups should be obvious. The fact that modern electronic devices are significantly more reliable than their predecessors could tend to dampen the growth in service a bit. The fact that these modern machines are electronically very complex will certainly increase the amount of training required of these people.

Where there are employees, there are managers. As the number of computer installations increase, so will the demand for installation managers.

Current trends are creating a number of new positions, too. As more and more small computers and intelligent terminals are installed, there will be an increasing demand for professional *programmer/operators*. As the name of the position implies, these individuals will be responsible for both operating and programming a machine. Typically, the demands placed on the operator of a minicomputer or intelligent terminal amount to something less than a full-time job. By effectively "wearing two hats," the programmer/operator becomes a very valuable employee. Current and potential operators should strongly consider learning a programming language or two—RPG and BASIC are good ones—to improve their own marketability.

Data communications is potentially a very strong growth market. The data communications consultant will find increasing demands for his or her services in the future.

One of the relatively unseen new markets is related to the anticipated growth in first-time computer users, the small "neighborhood" business establishment which, due to the rapidly declining cost of minicomputers, has decided to move into computer-controlled record keeping, accounts receivable, accounts payable, payroll, and inventory control. Such organizations rarely have ny technical expertise and don't really want any. What the small, first-t..ne user needs is a pure turnkey system. Someone must design and install these systems. The demand for people capable of doing this kind of work is bounded only by the number of small businesses in this country. If you want to succeed in this market though, solid training and experience are essential.

One traditional occupation that is bound to undergo some change as a result of all these trends is the position of the office secretary. Typing and shorthand skills used to be enough, but the secretary of the future may also have to know how to use a word processing terminal and how to operate an intelligent terminal. In the office of the future, the person who can handle more than one job will be more than welcome.

The growth of personal computing spells opportunity too. Personal computing franchises and personal computing services are certain to grow in the near future. This could well be another of those "ground-floor" opportunities.

Finally, with more and more people being exposed to the computer, the demand for computer-related training is certain to grow. In spite of the fact that the computer can, in some cases, be used to teach, the expected increase in the demand for such training is welcome to those who teach (and write books) in the field.

To summarize this author's view of the employment potential for those who have trained themselves for computer-related jobs, the prospects look solid.

SUMMARY

In this chapter we summarized a number of trends in the computer field. Hardware costs are dropping, particularly in the minicomputer area. Size and weight are also dropping, while speed, reliability, and computing power are increasing. These trends are opening the possibility of computer use to a number of brand-new markets. Memory is also changing, with the trend growing away from "moving" memory and toward electronic memories that are addressed much like main memory. Perhaps the biggest area of potential hardware growth is in terminals.

Firmware is a name given to certain modern integrated circuits that can be manufactured at a very low cost and used within a computer in a very flexible manner. These circuits combine the speed of hardware with the relatively low cost and flexibility of software. Firmware is being used to perform many system functions on larger computers, and this use should grow. These circuits are also used for controlling applications on smaller, special-purpose computers.

KEY WORDS

data
communications
consultant

environmental
constraints

firmware

independent
software vendor

information
processing utility

peripheral
hardware

personal computing

plug-to-plug compatible

programmer, system

programmer/ operator

purchased software

turnkey system

Software is becoming easier to use. More and more of the computer's details are being hidden in system software and in hardware, allowing the programmer to concentrate on the application.

Data communications is a major bottleneck; improvements are almost certain to occur. Information processing networks, with a number of computers interconnected by communication lines, are becoming common. Some networks are composed of a number of minicomputers; on others, various types of terminals and minicomputers are connected to a centralized "maxi" computer.

These trends are creating a number of new markets. The sale and support of traditional mainframes continues to be strong. Plug-to-plug compatible equipment and terminals are examples of new and growing segments of the computer hardware market. The growth of minicomputers creates a demand for people who can plan and install turnkey systems for the first-time or unsophisticated user. The demand for personal computers is growing too; a brand-new hobby is beginning to develop.

Independent software vendors are very important in the modern computer marketplace. These organizations sell both system and application software. Systems analysis, systems consulting, and communications consulting are other examples of new and growing market activities.

The chapter closed with an analysis of the potential for job opportunities in computer-related fields. Generally speaking, the outlook is optimistic.

EXERCISES

1. Why will the declining cost of hardware have an impact on software?

2. Why will the declining cost of firmware have an impact on software?

3. Why does the high cost of data communications tend to push users in the direction of distributed data processing?

4. What is a turnkey system?

5. Do some research on your own and write a paper on the future job opportunities in the information processing field.

Appendix:
A Payroll
Program

INPUT ONE RECORD

1.

   Push input button.

MEMORY AFTER STEP 1

					S	M	I	T	H						·					A	C			
001	002	003	004	005	006	007	008	009	010	011	012	013	014	015	016	017	018	019	020	021	022	023	024	025
4	0	0	·											0	3	7	5							
026	027	028	029	030	031	032	033	034	035	036	037	038	039	040	041	042	043	044	045	046	047	048	049	050
051	052	053	054	055	056	057	058	059	060	061	062	063	064	065	066	067	068	069	070	071	072	073	074	075
					I	J	K	L	M	N	O	P	Q	R	S	T	U	V	W	X	Y	Z	A	B
076	077	078	079	080	081	082	083	084	085	086	087	088	089	090	091	092	093	094	095	096	097	098	099	100
C	D	E	F	G	H	I	J	K	L	M	N	O	P	Q	R	S	T	U	V	W	X	Y	Z	1
101	102	103	104	105	106	107	108	109	110	111	112	113	114	115	116	117	118	119	120	121	122	123	124	125
2	3	4	5	6	7	8	9	0	A	B	C	D	E	F	G	H	I	J	K	L	M	N	O	P
126	127	128	129	130	131	132	133	134	135	136	137	138	139	140	141	142	143	144	145	146	147	148	149	150
Q	R	S	T	U	V	W	X	Y	Z	1	2	3	4	5	6	7	8	9	0	A	B	C	D	E
151	152	153	154	155	156	157	158	159	160	161	162	163	164	165	166	167	168	169	170	171	172	173	174	175
F	G	H	I	J	K	L	M	N	O	P	Q	R	S	T	U	V	W	X	Y	Z	1	2	3	4
176	177	178	179	180	181	182	183	184	185	186	187	188	189	190	191	192	193	194	195	196	197	198	199	200
5	6	7	8	9	0	A	B	C	D	E	F	G	H	I	J	K	L	M	N	O	P	Q	R	S
201	202	203	204	205	206	207	208	209	210	211	212	213	214	215	216	217	218	219	220	221	222	223	224	225
T	U	V	W	X	Y	Z	1	2	3	4	5	6	7	8	9	0	A	B	C	D	E	F	G	H
226	227	228	229	230	231	232	233	234	235	236	237	238	239	240	241	242	243	244	245	246	247	248	249	250

COMPUTE GROSS PAY

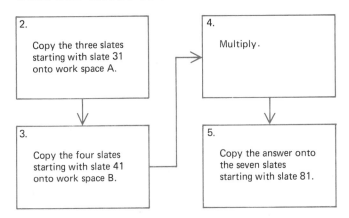

2.

Copy the three slates starting with slate 31 onto work space A.

3.

Copy the four slates starting with slate 41 onto work space B.

4.

Multiply.

5.

Copy the answer onto the seven slates starting with slate 81.

MEMORY AFTER STEP 5

					S	M	I	T	H												A	C		
001	002	003	004	005	006	007	008	009	010	011	012	013	014	015	016	017	018	019	020	021	022	023	024	025
					4	0	0								0	3	7	5						
026	027	028	029	030	031	032	033	034	035	036	037	038	039	040	041	042	043	044	045	046	047	048	049	050
051	052	053	054	055	056	057	058	059	060	061	062	063	064	065	066	067	068	069	070	071	072	073	074	075
					0	1	5	0	0	0	0	P	Q	R	S	T	U	V	W	X	Y	Z	A	B
076	077	078	079	080	081	082	083	084	085	086	087	088	089	090	091	092	093	094	095	096	097	098	099	100
C	D	E	F	G	H	I	J	K	L	M	N	O	P	Q	R	S	T	U	V	W	X	Y	Z	1
101	102	103	104	105	106	107	108	109	110	111	112	113	114	115	116	117	118	119	120	121	122	123	124	125
2	3	4	5	6	7	8	9	0	A	B	C	D	E	F	G	H	I	J	K	L	M	N	O	P
126	127	128	129	130	131	132	133	134	135	136	137	138	139	140	141	142	143	144	145	146	147	148	149	150
Q	R	S	T	U	V	W	X	Y	Z	1	2	3	4	5	6	7	8	9	0	A	B	C	D	E
151	152	153	154	155	156	157	158	159	160	161	162	163	164	165	166	167	168	169	170	171	172	173	174	175
F	G	H	I	J	K	L	M	N	O	P	Q	R	S	T	U	V	W	X	Y	Z	1	2	3	4
176	177	178	179	180	181	182	183	184	185	186	187	188	189	190	191	192	193	194	195	196	197	198	199	200
5	6	7	8	9	0	A	B	C	D	E	F	G	H	I	J	K	L	M	N	O	P	Q	R	S
201	202	203	204	205	206	207	208	209	210	211	212	213	214	215	216	217	218	219	220	221	222	223	224	225
T	U	V	W	X	Y	Z	1	2	3	4	5	6	7	8	9	0	A	B	C	D	E	F	G	H
226	227	228	229	230	231	232	233	234	235	236	237	238	239	240	241	242	243	244	245	246	247	248	249	250

COMPUTE SOCIAL SECURITY TAX

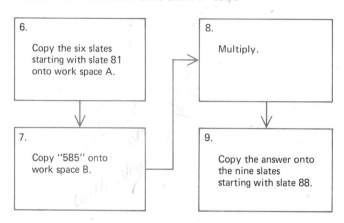

6. Copy the six slates starting with slate 81 onto work space A.

7. Copy "585" onto work space B.

8. Multiply.

9. Copy the answer onto the nine slates starting with slate 88.

MEMORY AFTER STEP 9

001	002	003	004	005	006 S	007 M	008 I	009 T	010 H	011	012	013	014	015	016	017	018	019	020	021 A	022 C	023	024	025
026	027	028	029	030	031 4	032 0	033 0	034	035	036	037	038	039	040	041 0	042 3	043 7	044 5	045	046	047	048	049	050
051	052	053	054	055	056	057	058	059	060	061	062	063	064	065	066	067	068	069	070	071	072	073	074	075
076	077	078	079	080	081 0	082 1	083 5	084 0	085 0	086 0	087 0	088 0	089 8	090 7	091 7	092 5	093 0	094 0	095 0	096 Y	097 Z	098 A	099 B	100
101 C	102 D	103 E	104 F	105 G	106 H	107 I	108 J	109 K	110 L	111 M	112 N	113 O	114 P	115 Q	116 R	117 S	118 T	119 U	120 V	121 W	122 X	123 Y	124 Z	125 1
126 2	127 3	128 4	129 5	130 6	131 7	132 8	133 9	134 0	135 A	136 B	137 C	138 D	139 E	140 F	141 G	142 H	143 I	144 J	145 K	146 L	147 M	148 N	149 O	150 P
151 Q	152 R	153 S	154 T	155 U	156 V	157 W	158 X	159 Y	160 Z	161 1	162 2	163 3	164 4	165 5	166 6	167 7	168 8	169 9	170 0	171 A	172 B	173 C	174 D	175 E
176 F	177 G	178 H	179 I	180 J	181 K	182 L	183 M	184 N	185 O	186 P	187 Q	188 R	189 S	190 T	191 U	192 V	193 W	194 X	195 Y	196 Z	197 1	198 2	199 3	200 4
201 5	202 6	203 7	204 8	205 9	206 0	207 A	208 B	209 C	210 D	211 E	212 F	213 G	214 H	215 I	216 J	217 K	218 L	219 M	220 N	221 O	222 P	223 Q	224 R	225 S
226 T	227 U	228 V	229 W	230 X	231 Y	232 Z	233 1	234 2	235 3	236 4	237 5	238 6	239 7	240 8	241 9	242 0	243 A	244 B	245 C	246 D	247 E	248 F	249 G	250 H

COMPUTE INCOME TAX

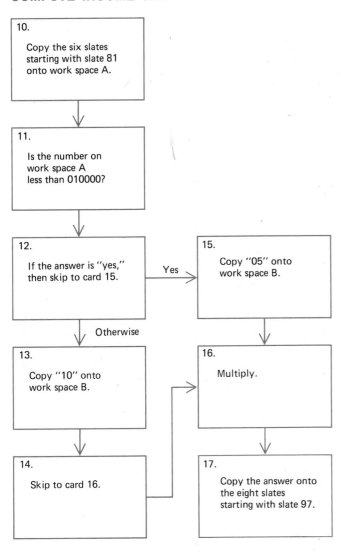

MEMORY AFTER STEP 17

001	002	003	004	005	006	007	008	009	010	011	012	013	014	015	016	017	018	019	020	021	022	023	024	025
					S	M	I	T	H											A	C			

026	027	028	029	030	031	032	033	034	035	036	037	038	039	040	041	042	043	044	045	046	047	048	049	050
					4	0	0									0	3	7	5					

051	052	053	054	055	056	057	058	059	060	061	062	063	064	065	066	067	068	069	070	071	072	073	074	075

076	077	078	079	080	081	082	083	084	085	086	087	088	089	090	091	092	093	094	095	096	097	098	099	100
					0	1	5	0	0	0	0	0	8	7	7	5	0	0	0	0	0	0	1	5

101	102	103	104	105	106	107	108	109	110	111	112	113	114	115	116	117	118	119	120	121	122	123	124	125
0	0	0	0	G	H	I	J	K	L	M	N	O	P	Q	R	S	T	U	V	W	X	Y	Z	1

126	127	128	129	130	131	132	133	134	135	136	137	138	139	140	141	142	143	144	145	146	147	148	149	150
2	3	4	5	6	7	8	9	0	A	B	C	D	E	F	G	H	I	J	K	L	M	N	O	P

151	152	153	154	155	156	157	158	159	160	161	162	163	164	165	166	167	168	169	170	171	172	173	174	175
Q	R	S	T	U	V	W	X	Y	Z	1	2	3	4	5	6	7	8	9	0	A	B	C	D	E

176	177	178	179	180	181	182	183	184	185	186	187	188	189	190	191	192	193	194	195	196	197	198	199	200
F	G	H	I	J	K	L	M	N	O	P	Q	R	S	T	U	V	W	X	Y	Z	1	2	3	4

201	202	203	204	205	206	207	208	209	210	211	212	213	214	215	216	217	218	219	220	221	222	223	224	225
5	6	7	8	9	0	A	B	C	D	E	F	G	H	I	J	K	L	M	N	O	P	Q	R	S

226	227	228	229	230	231	232	233	234	235	236	237	238	239	240	241	242	243	244	245	246	247	248	249	250
T	U	V	W	X	Y	Z	1	2	3	4	5	6	7	8	9	0	A	B	C	D	E	F	G	H

COMPUTE NET PAY

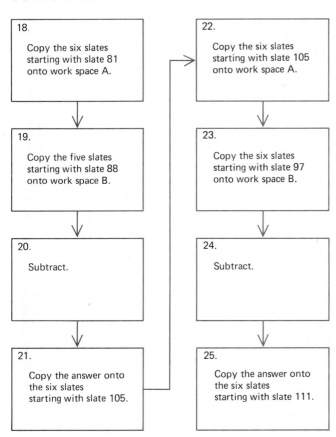

18.

Copy the six slates
starting with slate 81
onto work space A.

19.

Copy the five slates
starting with slate 88
onto work space B.

20.

Subtract.

21.

Copy the answer onto
the six slates
starting with slate 105.

22.

Copy the six slates
starting with slate 105
onto work space A.

23.

Copy the six slates
starting with slate 97
onto work space B.

24.

Subtract.

25.

Copy the answer onto
the six slates
starting with slate 111.

MEMORY AFTER STEP 21

001	002	003	004	005	006 S	007 M	008 I	009 T	010 H	011	012	013	014	015	016	017	018	019	020	021 A	022 C	023	024	025
026	027	028	029	030	031 4	032 0	033 0	034	035	036 .	037	038	039	040	041	042 0	043 3	044 7	045 5	046	047	048	049	050
051	052	053	054	055	056	057	058	059	060	061	062	063	064	065	066	067	068	069	070	071	072	073	074	075
076	077	078	079	080	081 0	082 1	083 5	084 0	085 0	086 0	087 0	088 0	089 0	090 8	091 7	092 7	093 5	094 0	095 0	096 0	097 0	098 0	099 1	100 5
101 0	102 0	103 0	104 0	105 0	106 1	107 4	108 1	109 2	110 3	111 M	112 N	113 O	114 P	115 Q	116 R	117 S	118 T	119 U	120 V	121 W	122 X	123 Y	124 Z	125 1
126 2	127 3	128 4	129 5	130 6	131 7	132 8	133 9	134 0	135 A	136 B	137 C	138 D	139 E	140 F	141 G	142 H	143 I	144 J	145 K	146 L	147 M	148 N	149 O	150 P
151 Q	152 R	153 S	154 T	155 U	156 V	157 W	158 X	159 Y	160 Z	161 1	162 2	163 3	164 4	165 5	166 6	167 7	168 8	169 9	170 0	171 A	172 B	173 C	174 D	175 E
176 F	177 G	178 H	179 I	180 J	181 K	182 L	183 M	184 N	185 O	186 P	187 Q	188 R	189 S	190 T	191 U	192 V	193 W	194 X	195 Y	196 Z	197 1	198 2	199 3	200 4
201 5	202 6	203 7	204 8	205 9	206 0	207 A	208 B	209 C	210 D	211 E	212 F	213 G	214 H	215 I	216 J	217 K	218 L	219 M	220 N	221 O	222 P	223 Q	224 R	225 S
226 T	227 U	228 V	229 W	230 X	231 Y	232 Z	233 1	234 2	235 3	236 4	237 5	238 6	239 7	240 8	241 9	242 0	243 A	244 B	245 C	246 D	247 E	248 F	249 G	250 H

MEMORY AFTER STEP 25

001	002	003	004	005	006	007	008	009	010	011	012	013	014	015	016	017	018	019	020	021	022	023	024	025
					S	M	I	T	H											A	C			
026	027	028	029	030	031	032	033	034	035	036	037	038	039	040	041	042	043	044	045	046	047	048	049	050
					4	0	0								0	3	7	5			.			
051	052	053	054	055	056	057	058	059	060	061	062	063	064	065	066	067	068	069	070	071	072	073	074	075
076	077	078	079	080	081	082	083	084	085	086	087	088	089	090	091	092	093	094	095	096	097	098	099	100
					0	1	5	0	0	0	0	0	0	8	7	7	5	0	0	0	0	0	1	5
101	102	103	104	105	106	107	108	109	110	111	112	113	114	115	116	117	118	119	120	121	122	123	124	125
0	0	0	0	0	1	4	1	2	3	0	1	2	6	2	3	S	T	U	V	W	X	Y	Z	1
126	127	128	129	130	131	132	133	134	135	136	137	138	139	140	141	142	143	144	145	146	147	148	149	150
2	3	4	5	6	7	8	9	0	A	B	C	D	E	F	G	H	I	J	K	L	M	N	O	P
151	152	153	154	155	156	157	158	159	160	161	162	163	164	165	166	167	168	169	170	171	172	173	174	175
Q	R	S	T	U	V	W	X	Y	Z	1	2	3	4	5	6	7	8	9	0	A	B	C	D	E
176	177	178	179	180	181	182	183	184	185	186	187	188	189	190	191	192	193	194	195	196	197	198	199	200
F	G	H	I	J	K	L	M	N	O	P	Q	R	S	T	U	V	W	X	Y	Z	1	2	3	4
201	202	203	204	205	206	207	208	209	210	211	212	213	214	215	216	217	218	219	220	221	222	223	224	225
5	6	7	8	9	0	A	B	C	D	E	F	G	H	I	J	K	L	M	N	O	P	Q	R	S
226	227	228	229	230	231	232	233	234	235	236	237	238	239	240	241	242	243	244	245	246	247	248	249	250
T	U	V	W	X	Y	Z	1	2	3	4	5	6	7	8	9	0	A	B	C	D	E	F	G	H

SET UP LINE AND PRINT NAME

26.

Erase 120 slates starting with slate 130.

↓

27.

Copy the 17 slates starting with slate 6 onto the 17 slates starting with slate 180.

↓

28.

Push output button.

MEMORY AFTER STEP 27

001	002	003	004	005	006	007	008	009	010	011	012	013	014	015	016	017	018	019	020	021	022	023	024	025
					S	M	I	T	H											A	C			

026	027	028	029	030	031	032	033	034	035	036	037	038	039	040	041	042	043	044	045	046	047	048	049	050
					4	0	0									0	3	7	5					

051	052	053	054	055	056	057	058	059	060	061	062	063	064	065	066	067	068	069	070	071	072	073	074	075

076	077	078	079	080	081	082	083	084	085	086	087	088	089	090	091	092	093	094	095	096	097	098	099	100
					0	1	5	0	0	0	0	0	0	8	7	7	5	0	0	0	0	0	1	5

101	102	103	104	105	106	107	108	109	110	111	112	113	114	115	116	117	118	119	120	121	122	123	124	125
0	0	0	0	0	1	4	1	2	3	0	1	2	6	2	3	S	T	U	V	W	X	Y	Z	1

126	127	128	129	130	131	132	133	134	135	136	137	138	139	140	141	142	143	144	145	146	147	148	149	150
2	3	4	5																					

151	152	153	154	155	156	157	158	159	160	161	162	163	164	165	166	167	168	169	170	171	172	173	174	175

176	177	178	179	180	181	182	183	184	185	186	187	188	189	190	191	192	193	194	195	196	197	198	199	200
					S	M	I	T	H											A	C			

201	202	203	204	205	206	207	208	209	210	211	212	213	214	215	216	217	218	219	220	221	222	223	224	225

226	227	228	229	230	231	232	233	234	235	236	237	238	239	240	241	242	243	244	245	246	247	248	249	250

SET UP LINE AND PRINT AMOUNT OF CHECK

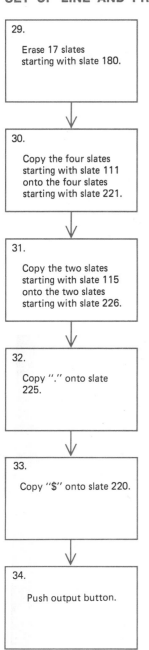

29.

Erase 17 slates
starting with slate 180.

30.

Copy the four slates
starting with slate 111
onto the four slates
starting with slate 221.

31.

Copy the two slates
starting with slate 115
onto the two slates
starting with slate 226.

32.

Copy "." onto slate
225.

33.

Copy "$" onto slate 220.

34.

Push output button.

MEMORY AFTER STEP 33

001	002	003	004	005	006 S	007 M	008 I	009 T	010 H	011	012	013 .	014	015	016	017	018	019	020	021 A	022 C	023	024	025
026	027	028	029	030	031 4	032 0	033 0	034	035	036	037	038	039	040	041	042 0	043 3	044 7	045 5	046	047	048	049	050
051	052	053	054	055	056	057	058	059	060	061	062	063	064	065	066	067	068	069	070	071	072	073	074	075
076	077	078	079	080 0	081 1	082 5	083 0	084 0	085 0	086 0	087 0	088 8	089 7	090 7	091 5	092 0	093 0	094 0	095 0	096 0	097 1	098 5	099	100
101 0	102 0	103 0	104 0	105 0	106 1	107 4	108 1	109 2	110 3	111 0	112 1	113 2	114 6	115 2	116 3	117 S	118 T	119 U	120 V	121 W	122 X	123 Y	124 Z	125 1
126 2	127 3	128 4	129 5	130	131	132	133	134	135	136	137	138	139	140	141	142	143	144	145	146	147	148	149	150
151	152	153	154	155	156	157	158	159	160	161	162	163	164	165	166	167	168	169	170	171	172	173	174	175
176	177	178	179	180	181	182	183	184	185	186	187	188	189	190	191	192	193	194	195	196	197	198	199	200
201	202	203	204	205	206	207	208	209	210	211	212	213	214	215	216	217	218	219 $	220 0	221 .	222 1	223 2	224 6	225
226 2	227 3	228	229	230	231	232	233	234	235	236	237	238	239	240	241	242	243	244	245	246	247	248	249 H	250

REPEAT THE PROGRAM OR QUIT

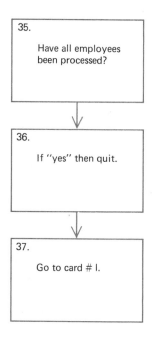

35.

Have all employees been processed?

36.

If "yes" then quit.

37.

Go to card # I.

Glossary

Sources

1. *American National Standard Vocabulary for Information Processing.* American National Standards Institute (1970), Publication number ANSI X3.12-1970.

2. *A Data Processing Glossary.* IBM Publication C20-1699.

3. *Webster's New World Dictionary of the American Language*, College Edition. Cleveland, Ohio: World Publishing.

The sources are listed in order of preference: A definition was first sought in the ANSI standard, with the other sources being consulted only when no definition was present in this primary source. The source of each definition is indicated as follows: (ANSI), (IBM), or (Webster). If no source is indicated, the definition is the author's.

Absolute address (ANSI) (1) An address that is permanently assigned by the machine designer to a storage location. (2) A pattern of characters that identifies a unique storage location without further modification. (3) Synonymous with machine address, specific address.

Access arm (ANSI) A part of a disk storage unit that is used to hold one or more reading and writing heads.

Access method (IBM) Any of the data management techniques available to the user for transferring data between main storage and an input/output device.

Access time (ANSI) (1) The time interval between the instant at which data are called for from a storage device and the instant delivery begins. (2) The time interval between the instant at which data are requested to be stored and the instant at which storage is started.

Accumulator (ANSI) A register in which the result of an arithmetic or logic operation is formed.

Acoustical coupler The portion of a data set that actually holds a telephone receiver.

Acronym (IBM) A word formed from the first letter or letters of the words in a name, term, or phrase; for example, SAGE from semi-automatic ground environment and ALGOL from algorithmic language.

Activity (IBM) A term used to indicate that a record in a master file is used, altered, or referred to.

Actual key (ANSI) In COBOL, a data item that may be used as a hardware address and that expresses the location of a record on a mass storage device.

Address (ANSI) (1) An identification, as represented by a name, label, or number, for a register, location in storage, or any other data source or destination such as the location of a station in a communication network.

(2) Loosely, any part of an instruction that specifies the location of an operand for the instruction.

Algorithm (ANSI) A prescribed set of well-defined rules or processes for the solution of a problem in a finite number of steps, e.g., a full statement of an arithmetic procedure for evaluating sin x to a stated precision.

Alphabetic data Data which is composed exclusively of letters of the alphabet and the blank character. Occasionally, the period and the comma are also used.

Alphanumeric (ANSI) Pertaining to a character set that contains letters, digits, and usually other characters such as punctuation marks.

Amplitude (IBM) The size or magnitude of a voltage or current waveform.

Amplitude modulation (IBM) Variation of a carrier's signal strength (amplitude), as a function of an information signal.

Analysis (ANSI) The methodical investigation of a problem and the separation of the problem into smaller related units for further detailed study.

AND (ANSI) A logic operator having the property that if P is a statement, Q is a statement, R is a statement . . . , then the AND of P,Q,R . . . is true if all statements are true, false if any statement is false.

Application program A program which performs a user function. Contrast with system program.

Arithmetic and logical unit The portion of a central processing unit in which arithmetic and logical operations are performed.

ASCII (American National Standard Code for Information Interchange) (ANSI) The standard code, using a coded character set consisting of 7-bit coded characters (8 bits including the parity check), used for information interchange among data processing systems, communication systems, and associated equipment.

Assemble (ANSI) To prepare a machine language program from a symbolic language program by substituting absolute operation codes for symbolic operation codes and absolute or relocatable addresses for symbolic addresses.

Assembler (ANSI) A computer program that assembles.

Assembler language The source language for an assembler.

Asynchronous (IBM) Without regular time relationship.

Automation (ANSI) (1) The implementation of processes by automatic means. (2) The theory, art, or technique of making a process more automatic. (3) The investigation, design, development, and application of methods of rendering processes automatic, self-moving, or self-controlling. (4) The conversion of a procedure, a process, or equipment to automatic operation.

Auxiliary storage (ANSI) A storage that supplements other storage. Contrast with main storage.

Background (author's definition, based on ANSI) The partition or region of a multiprogramming system holding lower priority programs which are executed only when higher priority programs are not using the system.

Backup A procedure, technique, or hardware intended to be used in an emergency to help recover lost or destroyed data or to keep a system running.

Bar-code scanner A device used to read a bar-code by means of reflected light, such as the scanners that read the Universal Product Code on supermarket products.

Base (ANSI) (1) A reference value. (2) A number that is multiplied by itself as many times as indicated by an exponent. (3) Same as radix.

BASIC Acronym for Beginners All-purpose Symbolic Instruction Code; a programming language.

Batch processing (ANSI) (1) Pertaining to the technique of executing a set of computer programs such that each is completed before the next program of the set is started. (2) Pertaining to the sequential input of computer programs or data. (3) Loosely, the execution of computer programs serially.

Batch processing (IBM) A systems approach to processing where a number of similar input items are grouped for processing during the same machine run.

Baud (ANSI) A unit of signaling speed equal to the number of discrete conditions or signal events per second. For example, one baud equals one-half dot cycle per second in Morse code, one bit per second in a train of binary signals, and one 3-bit value per second in a train of signals each of which can assume one of eight different states.

BCD (ANSI) Binary-coded decimal notation.

Binary (ANSI) (1) Pertaining to a characteristic or property involving a selection, choice, or condition in which there are two possibilities. (2) Pertaining to the number representation system with a radix of two.

Binary coded decimal (ANSI) Positional notation in which the individual decimal digits expressing a number in decimal notation are each represented by a binary numeral, e.g., the number twenty-three is represented by 0010 0011 in the 8-4-2-1 type of binary-coded decimal notation and by 10111 in binary notation.

Binary number system (ANSI) Fixed radix notation in which the radix is two.

Bit (ANSI) A binary digit.

Block (ANSI) (1) A set of things such as words, characters, or digits, handled as a unit. (2) A collection of contiguous records recorded as a unit. Blocks are separated by block gaps and each block may contain one or more records. (3) A group of bits or n-ary digits, transmitted as a unit. An encoding procedure is generally applied to the group of bits or n-ary digits for error-control purposes. (4)

A group of contiguous characters recorded as a unit.

Block gap See Interblock gap.

Block multiplexer A type of data channel which multiplexes or overlaps the operation of a number of high-speed I/O devices.

Blocking (IBM) Combining two or more records into one block.

Blocking factor The number of logical records in a single physical record or block.

Boolean logic (ANSI) (1) Pertaining to the processes used in the algebra formulated by George Boole. (2) Pertaining to the operations of formal logic.

Bootstrap (ANSI) A technique or device designed to bring itself into a desired state by means of its own action, e.g., a machine routine whose first few instructions are sufficient to bring the rest of itself into the computer from an input device.

Branch (ANSI) (1) A set of instructions that are executed between two successive decision instructions. (2) To select a branch as in (1). (3) A direct path joining two nodes of a network or graph. (4) Loosely, a conditional jump.

Breakeven point The point at which the total cost of a fixed-cost alternative and the total cost of a variable-cost alternative are equal.

Buffer (ANSI) A routine or storage used to compensate for a difference in rate of flow of data, or time of occurrence of events, when transmitting data from one device to another.

Buffered keypunch A keypunch containing a buffer. In typical operation, data is keyed as rapidly as the operator can type into the buffer, and punched into the card from the buffer, thus allowing the operator to work at a pace somewhat faster than that imposed by the punch mechanism. On some buffered keypunches, the operator can check data for accuracy before punching a card.

Bug (ANSI) A mistake or malfunction.

Bulk memory See Auxiliary storage.

Bulk storage See Auxiliary storage.

Burst mode Transferring data between a single high-speed I/O device and main memory via a selector channel.

Byte (ANSI) A sequence of adjacent binary digits operated upon as a unit and usually shorter than a computer word.

Card column (ANSI) A single line of punch positions parallel to the short edge of a $3\frac{1}{4}$ by $7\frac{3}{8}$-inch punched card.

Card punch (IBM) A device to record information in cards by punching holes in the cards to represent letters, digits, and special characters.

Card reader (IBM) A device which senses and translates into internal form the holes in punched cards.

Card row (ANSI) A single line of punch positions parallel to the long edge of a $3\frac{1}{4}$ by $7\frac{3}{8}$-inch punched card.

Cassette A small, self-contained volume of magnetic tape used for data storage. Similar to a sound-recording cassette.

Catalog (ANSI) An ordered compilation of item descriptions and sufficient information to afford access to the items.

Cathode ray tube terminal (IBM) A device that presents data in visual form by means of controlled electron beams.

Central processing unit (ANSI) A unit of a computer that includes the circuits controlling the interpretation and execution of instructions. Synonymous with main frame.

Chain printer (ANSI) A printer in which the type slugs are carried by the links of a revolving chain.

Channel (ANSI) (1) A path along which signals can be sent, e.g., data channel, output channel. (2) The portion of a storage medium that is accessible to a given reading or writing station, e.g., track, band. (3) In communication, a means of one-way transmission.

Character (ANSI) A letter, digit, or other symbol that is used as part of the organization, control, or representation of data.

Character printer (ANSI) A device that prints a single character at a time. Contrast with line printer.

Checkpoint (ANSI) A place in a routine where a check, or a recording of data for restart purposes, is performed.

Chip (IBM) In microcircuitry, a single device, either a transistor or a diode, that has been cut from a larger wafer of silicon.

CLOSE An instruction or macroinstruction, common to many languages, whose function is to perform end-of-program activities on a given file and to return the physical device to the use of the system.

COBOL (ANSI) (COmmon Business Oriented Language) A business data processing language.

Code (ANSI) (1) A set of unambiguous rules specifying the way in which data may be represented, e.g., the set of correspondences in the standard code for information interchange. Synonymous with coding scheme. (2) In telecommunications, a system of rules and conventions according to which the signals for representing data can be formed, transmitted, received, and processed. (3) In data processing, to represent data or a computer program in a symbolic form that can be accepted by a data processor. (4) To write a routine.

Coded data Data in coded (EBCDIC, ASCII) form.

Coding The act of actually writing program statements in a source language.

Comments Verbal explanations added to a program for purposes of documentation.

Communication link (ANSI) The physical means of connecting one location to another for the purpose of transmitting and receiving data.

Communication medium See Communication link.

Comparison indicator A special register or other field used to hold the result of a comparison.

Compile (ANSI) To prepare a machine language program from a computer program written in another programming language by making use of the overall logic structure of the program, or generating more than one machine instruction for each symbolic statement, or both, as well as performing the function of an assembler.

Compiler (ANSI) A program that compiles.

Compute-bound A program or a computer system which is restricted or limited by the speed of the CPU.

Computer (ANSI) A data processor that can perform substantial computation, including numerous arithmetic or logic operations, without intervention by a human operator during the run.

Computer crime Criminal activity involving or utilizing a computer.

Computer errors Incorrect results, for whatever reason, produced by a computer.

Computer network (ANSI) A complex consisting of two or more interconnected computers.

Computer operator An individual who operates a computer.

Computer program (ANSI) A series of instructions or statements, in a form acceptable to a computer, prepared in order to achieve a certain result.

Computer system The hardware, software, and procedural components which must function together in order that a computer might actually process data into information.

Concurrent (ANSI) Pertaining to the occurrence of two or more events or activities within the same specified interval of time.

Connect time The time interval from the initial connection to the final breaking of a communication.

Constant (IBM) A fixed or invariable value or data item.

Contiguous (Webster) (1) In physical contact; touching. (2) Near; adjoining.

Control unit An electronic device, intermediate between a computer and an I/O device, that performs such functions as buffering and standard interface.

Control unit portion of CPU (ANSI: instruction control unit) In a digital computer, those parts that effect the retrieval of instructions in proper sequence, the interpretation of each instruction, and the application of the proper signals to the arithmetic unit and other parts in accordance with this interpretation.

Core memory (IBM) A form of high-speed storage using magnetic cores. See also Magnetic core.

Core resident Software which is permanently located in main memory.

Core storage See Core memory.

CPU (ANSI) Central processing unit.

CRT See Cathode ray tube terminal.

Cycle (ANSI) (1) An interval of space or time in which one set of events or phenomena is completed. (2) Any set of operations that is repeated regularly in the same sequence. The operations may be subject to variations on each repetition.

Cycle stealing Taking an occasional machine cycle from a CPU's regular activities in order to control such things as an input or output operation. Commonly used on minicomputers.

Cylinder One position of a disk access arm, allowing access to a number of tracks.

Data (ANSI) (1) A representation of facts, concepts, or instructions in a formalized manner suitable for communication, interpretation, or processing by humans or automatic means. (2) Any representations such as characters or analog quantities to which meaning is or might be assigned.

Data bank Synonymous with data base.

Data base (ANSI: data bank) A comprehensive collection of libraries of data.

Data base management Software, hardware, and organizational techniques designed to manage a data base.

Data cartridge A small, self-contained reel of magnetic tape used to store data.

Data cell A mass storage device which utilizes strips of magnetic tape housed in a rotating cylinder.

Data communication (IBM) The transmission of data from one point to another.

Data communication consultant An expert in the design, planning, and implementation of a data communication system.

Data communication monitor A software package designed to concurrently control communications with a number of terminals. Often includes partition management and query functions.

Data compression A technique for minimizing the amount of data actually transmitted over a communication line by removing blanks at the sending end of the line and replacing blanks at the receiving end.

Data entry Introducing data into a data processing or information processing system.

Data entry terminal A terminal for entering data.

Data format A position-by-position description of each of the data fields in a record.

Data management (IBM) A general term that collectively describes those functions of the control program that provide access to data sets, enforce data storage conventions, and regulate the use of input/output devices.

Data processing (ANSI) The execution of a systematic sequence of operations performed upon data. Synonymous with information processing.

Data processing system (IBM) A network of machine components capable of accepting information, processing it according to a plan, and producing the desired results.

Data set (IBM) A device which performs the modulation/demodulation and control functions necessary to provide compatibility between business machines and communications facilities.

Data set A general term for a data file or program library.

Data transfer time The time required to transfer data from point A to point B.

Data transmission (IBM) The sending of data from one part of a system to another part.

Deblocking Separating blocked data into individual logical records.

Debug (ANSI) To detect, locate, and remove mistakes from a routine or malfunctions from a computer.

Decimal number system (ANSI) A fixed radix notation where the radix is ten.

Decision table (ANSI) A table of all contingencies that are to be considered in a description of a problem, together with the actions to be taken.

Demodulation (IBM) The process of retrieving intelligence (data) from a modulated carrier wave; the reverse of modulation.

Density (ANSI: recording density) The number of bits in a single linear track measured per unit of length of the recording medium.

Depersonalization Tending to remove or to deemphasize personal identification.

Detailed planning In the program development or systems analysis process, the step dealing with the planning and definition of a specific, detailed solution to a problem.

Dial-up (IBM) The use of a dial or pushbutton telephone to initiate a station-to-station telephone call.

Digit (ANSI) a symbol that represents one of the non-negative integers smaller than the radix.

Digit-times-place-value rule A rule for determining the value of a number written in any number system by summing the products of each digit and its place value.

Digital computer (ANSI) (1) A computer in which discrete representation of data is mainly used. (2) A computer that operates on discrete data by performing arithmetic and logic processes on these data.

Direct access (ANSI) (1) Pertaining to the process of obtaining data from, or placing data into, storage where the time required for such access is independent of the location of the data most recently obtained or placed in storage. (2) Pertaining to a storage device in which the access time is effectively independent of the location of the data. (3) Synonymous with random access.

Disk, magnetic (ANSI: magnetic disk) A flat circular plate with a magnetic surface on which data can be stored by selective magnetization of portions of the flat surface.

Disk pack A stack of magnetic disks.

Diskette A small disk pack.

Distributed data processing Decentralized data processing.

Documentation (ANSI) (1) The creating, collecting, organizing, storing, citing, and disseminating of documents or the information recorded in documents. (2) A collection of documents or information on a given subject.

Drum, magnetic (ANSI: magnetic drum) A right circular cylinder with a magnetic surface on which data can be stored by selective magnetization of portions of the curved surface.

Duplex See Full duplex.

Dynamic memory management See Dynamic storage allocation.

Dynamic memory relocation The shifting of programs and data in main memory so as to concentrate free areas into a single contiguous region.

Dynamic storage allocation (ANSI) A storage allocation technique in which the location of computer programs and data is determined by criteria applied at the moment of need.

EBCDIC (Extended Binary Coded

Decimal Interchange Code) An eight-bit code for representing characters.

Environmental constraints Temperature and humidity limits that must be maintained for the proper operation of a computer.

Execution The act of carrying out an instruction or performing a routine.

Execution time (E-time) The portion of a CPU's cycle during which an instruction is executed.

Feedback (IBM) The return of part of the output of a machine, process, or system to the computer as input for another phase, especially for self-correcting or control purposes.

Field (ANSI) In a record, a specified area used for a particular category of data, e.g., a group of card columns used to represent a wage rate, a set of bit locations in a computer word used to express the address of the operand.

File (ANSI) A collection of related records treated as a unit.

File maintenance (ANSI) The activity of keeping a file up to date by adding, changing, or deleting data.

File organization (1) The physical arrangement of records on a data storage device. (2) The logical set of rules used to physically arrange data. (3) Loosely, the access method used to read or write a file.

File processing Creating, utilizing, or maintaining files.

File size The number of records in a file.

Firmware Electronic circuits, typically arranged in the form of a card or a board, which can easily be added to or deleted from a computer's electronics. Firmware is often used to house the computer's instruction set.

First generation (IBM) A computer utilizing vacuum tube components.

Fixed cost A cost which remains the same for all levels of activity.

Fixed-partition memory management A memory management technique in which main memory is subdivided into a number of fixed-length partitions.

Floating-point data (ANSI: floating-point representation) A numeration system in which each number equals one of the numerals times a power of an implicit fixed positive integer base where the power is equal to the implicit base raised to the exponent represented by the other numeral.

Floppy disk A small disk of relatively limited storage capacity often used on a minicomputer or an intelligent terminal. See also Diskette.

Flowchart (ANSI) A graphical representation for the definition, analysis, or solution of a problem, in which symbols are used to represent operations, data flow, equipment, etc.

Foreground The partition in a multiprogramming system containing the high-priority application program.

FORTRAN (ANSI) (FORmula TRANslating system) A language primarily used to express computer programs by arithmetic formulas.

Fragmentation The presence of small increments of unused main memory space spread throughout main memory.

Frequency (IBM) Rate of signal oscillations in cycles per second.

Frequency modulation (IBM) Variation of a carrier frequency in accordance with an information signal.

Front-end device A transmission control unit capable of controlling polling and buffering independent of the CPU.

Full duplex (ANSI: duplex) In communications, pertaining to a simultaneous two way independent transmission in both directions. Contrast with half duplex.

General-purpose computer (ANSI) A computer that is designed to handle a wide variety of problems.

Half duplex (ANSI) In communications, pertaining to an alternate, one way at a time, independent transmission. Contrast with duplex.

Handshaking (IBM) Exchange of predetermined signals when a connection is established between two data sets.

Hardware (ANSI) Physical equipment, as opposed to the computer program or method of use, e.g., mechanical, magnetic, electrical, or electronic devices. Contrast with software.

Hardware system A collection of hardware devices capable of being used to process data.

Hexadecimal number system (ANSI: sexadecimal) Pertaining to the numeration system with a radix of sixteen.

IF ... THEN ... ELSE logic A form of logical test supported in many languages and consisting of three parts: a condition, a first conditional statement or series of statements usually preceded by the word THEN, and a second conditional statement or series of statements usually preceded by the word ELSE. If the condition is true, then the first conditional statement or group of statements is executed; if the condition is false, then the second statement or set of statements is executed.

Impact printer A printer which forms characters by physically striking a ribbon and paper.

Implementation The act of finishing or installing a program or a system.

Independent software vendor A business concern, other than a hardware vendor, which offers computer programs for sale or lease.

Index (ANSI) (1) An ordered reference list of the contents of a file or document together with keys or reference notations for identification or location of those contents. (2) To prepare a list as in (1).

Indexed sequential A file organization technique in which data are placed on a file in sequence and an index is maintained, thus allowing both sequential and direct access. This technique is designed to be used on magnetic disk exclusively.

Information (ANSI) The meaning that a human assigns to data by means of the known conventions used in their representation.

Information processing (ANSI) See Data processing.

Information processing machine A computer.

Information processing utility A business concern which offers numerous computing facilities including programming, software, systems analysis, computer time, etc., for sale or lease.

Input (ANSI) Pertaining to a device, process, or channel involved in the insertion of data or states, or to the data or states involved.

Input device (ANSI) The device or collective set of devices used for conveying data into another device.

Input/output (ANSI) Pertaining to either input or output, or both.

Instruction (ANSI) A statement that specifies an operation and the values or locations of its operands.

Instruction control unit See Control unit portion of CPU.

Instruction counter (ANSI) A counter that indicates the location of the next computer instruction to be interpreted.

Instruction set (ANSI: instruction repertoire) The set of operations that can be represented in a given operation code.

Instruction time (I-time) The portion of a CPU cycle during which an instruction is fetched and decoded.

Integrated adapter A hardware device, built into the CPU, which performs the functions of a channel by stealing cycles.

Integrated circuit (IBM) A combination of interconnected circuit elements inseparably associated on or within a continuous substrate.

Integrated data base A data base whose parts are linked or otherwise integrated.

Integration In file processing, the degree of relationship between files.

Intelligent terminal A terminal with some logical capability.

Interblock gap (ANSI: block gap) An area on a data medium used to indicate the end of a block or record.

Interface (ANSI) A shared boundary.

Interrecord gap (ANSI: record gap) An area on a data medium used to indicate the end of a block or record.

Interpreter (ANSI) (1) A computer program that translates and executes each source language statement before translating and executing the next one. (2) A device that prints on a punched card the data already punched in the card.

Interrupt (ANSI) To stop a process in such a way that it can be resumed.

I/O (ANSI) An abbreviation for input/output.

I/O-bound A program or computer system which is restricted or limited in processing speed by its I/O devices.

I/O device An input or output device.

I/O device allocation Controlling the allocation of I/O devices among the several programs in a multiprogramming system.

Job (ANSI) A specified group of tasks prescribed as a unit of work for a computer. By extension, a job usually includes all necessary computer programs, linkages, files, and instructions to the operating system.

JOB card or **JOB statement** (IBM) The control statement in the input job stream that identifies the beginning of a series of job control statements for a single job.

Job control statement (ANSI) A statement in a job that is used in identifying the job or describing its requirements to the operating system.

K (ANSI) (1) An abbreviation for the prefix kilo; i.e., 1000 in decimal notation. (2) Loosely, when referring to storage capacity, two to the tenth power, 1024 in decimal notation.

Key (ANSI) One or more characters within an item of data that are used to identify it or control its use.

Key-to-disk Hardware designed to transfer data entered via a keyboard to magnetic disk or diskette. Also, the process of transferring data from a keyboard to magnetic disk.

Key-to-tape Hardware designed to transfer data entered via a keyboard to magnetic tape. Also, the process of transferring data from a keyboard to magnetic tape.

Keyboard terminal A terminal through which data can be entered to a data processing system by means of a typewriterlike keyboard.

Keypunch (ANSI) A keyboard-actuated device that punches holes in a card to represent data.

Label (ANSI) One or more characters used to identify a statement or an item of data in a computer program.

Label A header or leader on a volume of magnetic tape or on a direct access device containing information identifying the file, files, or records stored thereon.

Labor displacement The shifting of labor from one task to another in response to automation.

Library (ANSI) (1) A collection of organized information used for study and reference. (2) A collection of related files.

Line A communication medium connecting two or more points.

Line printer (ANSI) A device that prints all the characters of a line as a unit. Contrast with character printer.

Link (Webster) To join together....

Linkage (ANSI) In programming, coding that connects two separately coded routines.

Linkage editor (IBM) A program that produces a load module by transforming object modules into a format that is acceptable to fetch, combining separately produced object modules and previously processed load modules into a single load module, resolving symbolic cross references among them, replacing, deleting, and adding control sections automatically on request and providing overlay facilities for modules requesting them.

Load module (IBM) (1) The output of the linkage editor. (2) A program in a format suitable for loading into main storage for execution.

Local Connected to a computer by regular electric wires. In close proximity to the computer. Contrast with Remote.

Logging Maintaining records of computer use.

Logical record (ANSI) A collection of items independent of their physical environment. Portions of the same logical record may be located in different physical records.

Loop (ANSI) A sequence of instructions that is executed repeatedly until a terminal condition prevails.

Machine cycle The basic operating cycle of a CPU during which a single instruction is fetched, decoded, and executed.

Machine-level program A computer program in binary form capable of being executed on a computer.

Macro instruction (ANSI) An instruction in a source language that is equivalent to a specified sequence of machine instructions.

Magnetic core (ANSI) A configuration of magnetic material that is, or is intended to be, placed in a spatial relationship to current-carrying conductors and whose magnetic properties are essential to its use. It may be used to concentrate an induced magnetic field as in a transformer induction coil or armature, to retain a magnetic polarization for the purpose of storing data, or for its nonlinear properties as in a logic element. It may be made of such material as iron, iron oxide, or ferrite and in such shapes as wire, tapes, toroids, rods, or thin films.

Magnetic tape (ANSI) (1) A tape with a magnetic surface on which data can be stored by selective polarization of portions of the surface. (2) A tape of magnetic materials used as the constituent in some forms of magnetic cores.

Main frame (ANSI) Same as Central processing unit.

Main memory See Main storage.

Main storage (ANSI) The general-purpose storage of a computer. Usually, main storage can be accessed directly by the operating registers. Contrast with Auxiliary storage.

Mainline The primary route of logical flow through a program.

Maintenance (ANSI) Any activity intended to eliminate faults or to keep hardware or programs in satisfactory working condition, including tests, measurements, replacements, adjustments, and repairs.

Management information system (ANSI) (1) Management performed with the aid of automatic data processing. Abbreviated MIS. (2) An information system designed to aid in the performance of management functions.

Mark sense (ANSI: mark sensing) The electrical sensing of manually recorded conductive marks on a nonconductive surface.

Mass storage See Auxiliary storage and Bulk memory.

Mass storage device A hardware device on which amounts of data are stored on individually addressable data cartridges or cells.

Master file (ANSI) A file that is either relatively permanent, or that is treated as an authority in a particular job.

Master file update The process of maintaining a master file.

Master/slave system A multiprocessing configuration in which one computer controls another computer.

Matrix printer A printer which forms characters by printing a pattern of dots.

Megabyte One million bytes; more accurately, 1000K bytes.

Memory See Storage.

Memory management The allocation of main memory space on a multiprogramming system.

Memory protection (ANSI) An arrangement for proventing access to storage for either reading, or writing, or both.

Message characters Characters which precede and follow a message transmitted over a communication line.

Message switching The process of transferring messages between various communication media so as to ensure accurate transmission from the correct source to the correct destination.

MICR (ANSI) Magnetic Ink Character Recognition.

Microcomputer A very small computer; often a special-purpose or single-function computer on a single chip.

Microprocessor Synonymous with microcomputer.

Microprogramming (IBM) Programming with microinstructions.

Microsecond One millionth of one second.

Microwave (IBM) Any electromagnetic wave in the radio frequency spectrum above 890 megacycles.

Millisecond One thousandth of one second.

Minicomputer A small, digital computer.

MIS Management Information System.

Mnemonic code (ANSI: mnemonic symbol) A symbol chosen to assist the human memory, e.g., an abbreviation such as "MPY" for "multiply."

Modem (ANSI) (MOdulator-DE-Modulator) A device that modulates and demodulates signals transmitted over communication facilities.

Modular programming Writing a program as a series of separate but linked blocks of logic.

Modulation (IBM) The process by which some characteristic of one wave is varied in accordance with another wave or signal. This technique is used in data sets and modems to make business machine signals compatible with communications facilities.

Monitor (ANSI) Software or hardware that observes, supervises, controls, or verifies the operations of a system.

Multiplex (ANSI) To interleave or simultaneously transmit two or more messages on a single channel.

Multiplexer channel A data channel which multiplexes or overlaps the operation of two or more low-speed I/O devices.

Multiprocessing (ANSI) (1) Pertaining to the simultaneous execution of two or more computer programs or sequences of instructions by a computer network. (2) Loosely, parallel processing.

Multiprogramming (ANSI) Pertaining to the concurrent execution of two or more programs by a computer.

Nanosecond One billionth of one second.

National data bank A proposed data bank housing all federal government data.

Network (ANSI: computer network) A complex consisting of two or more interconnected computers.

Network (IBM) (1) A series of points interconnected by communications channels. (A private line network is a network confined to the use of one customer, while a switched telephone network is a network of telephone lines normally used for dialed telephone calls.) (2) The interconnection of electrical components.

Noise (ANSI) (1) Random variations of one or more characteristics of any entity such as voltage, current, or data. (2) A random signal of known statistical properties of amplitude, distribution, and spectral density. (3) Loosely, any disturbance tending to interfere with the normal operation of a device or system.

Nonimpact printer A printer which forms images through electrostatic or other nonimpact means.

NOT (ANSI) A logic operator having the property that if P is a statement, then the NOT of P is true if P is false, false if P is true.

Nucleus (IBM) That portion of the control program that must always be present in main storage. Also, the main storage area used by the nucleus and other transient control program routines.

Number system (ANSI) Loosely, a number representation system.

Numeric data Data consisting exclusively of digits; occasionally, in some languages, a decimal point is also permitted. Data whose individual digits are written in the positional notation of some number system.

Object code (ANSI) Output from a compiler or assembler which is itself executable machine code or is suitable for processing to produce executable machine code.

Object deck An object module in punched card form.

Object module (ANSI) A module that is the output of an assembler or compiler and is input to a linkage editor.

OCR (ANSI) Optical Character Recognition.

Octal number system (ANSI: octal) Pertaining to the number representation system with a radix of eight.

Off-line (ANSI) Pertaining to equipment or devices not under control of the central processing unit.

On-line (ANSI) (1) Pertaining to equipment or devices under control of the central processing unit. (2) Pertaining to a user's ability to interact with a computer.

OPEN An instruction or macroinstruction common to many languages whose function is to prepare a specific physical device and/or file for I/O.

Operand (ANSI) That which is operated upon. An operand is usually identified by an address part of an instruction.

Operating system (ANSI) Software which controls the execution of computer programs and which may provide scheduling, debugging, input/output control, accounting, compilation, storage assignment, data management, and related services.

Operation code (or op code) (ANSI) A code which represents specific operations.

Optical character recognition (ANSI) The machine identification of printed characters through the use of light-sensitive devices.

Optimization (Webster) (To achieve) the most favorable degree, condition, amount, etc.

OR (ANSI) A logic operator having the property that if P is a statement, Q is a statement, R is a statement, . . . then the OR of P,Q,R, . . . is true if at least one statement is true, false if all statements are false.

Organization (Webster) Any unified consolidated group of elements; systematized whole; especially a body of persons organized for some specific purpose, as a club, union, or society.

Output (ANSI) Pertaining to a device, process, or channel involved in an output process, or to the data or states involved.

Output device (ANSI) The device or collective set of devices used for conveying data out of another device.

Overflow (ANSI) That portion of the result of an operation that exceeds the capacity of the intended unit of storage.

Overhead Support, as opposed to direct, functions.

Packed decimal data Numeric data consisting of a series of decimal digits and a sign. Internally, each digit is represented by four bits. Some computers can perform arithmetic on such data.

Page A fixed-length portion of a program or data which can be transferred between main memory and a secondary storage device on a virtual memory system. Also, a fixed-length portion of a program that can be loaded into main memory and addressed independently of the rest of the program.

Paging Breaking a program into fixed-length increments. Also, the act of transferring pages between main memory and a secondary storage device.

Paper tape An input/output medium, similar to magnetic tape, on which data can be recorded as a pattern of punched holes.

Parity bit (ANSI) A check bit appended to an array of binary digits to make the sum of all the binary digits, including the check bit, always odd or always even.

Partition A portion of a computer's main memory set aside to hold a single program on a fixed-partition memory management system.

Partition management The act of controlling and implementing the subdivision of a partition for the use of independent subprograms; a function often performed by a data communication monitor on a time-sharing system.

Peripheral equipment (ANSI) In a data processing system, any unit of equipment, distinct from the central processing unit, which may provide the system with outside communication.

Personal computing A hobby concerned with the building and use of small, personal computers.

Physical record A single block of data as transferred between an I/O device and main memory; may contain several logical records.

Planning In the program development or systems analysis process, the act of determining the outline of a single, optimum solution to a problem.

Plug-to-plug compatible A peripheral device that can function with the main frame of another manufacturer without modification.

Pointer A link.

Polling (IBM) A technique by which each of the terminals sharing a communications line is periodically interrogated to determine whether it requires servicing. The multiplexer or control station sends a poll which, in effect, asks the terminal selected, "Do you have anything to transmit?"

Port A connection point for a communication line on a front-end device or a transmission control unit.

Port-o-punch A type of punched card in which the holes are prescored and are punched out manually with a stylus.

Positional notation (ANSI) A numeration system in which a number is represented by means of an ordered set of digits, such that the value contributed by each digit depends upon its position as well as upon its value.

Power, political The ability to control people and events.

Printer (IBM) A device which expresses coded characters as hard copy.

Priority (Webster) The quality or condition of being prior; precedence in time, order, importance, etc.

Privacy (Webster) (1) The quality or condition of being private; withdrawal from public view or company; seclusion. (2) Secrecy.

Private (leased) line A communication line intended for the use of a single customer.

Problem definition The first step in the program development or systems analysis process, concerned with determining, in general terms, what must be done.

Process (ANSI) A systematic sequence of operations to produce a specified result.

Process-bound See Compute-bound.

Processing (1) Executing instructions. (2) Converting data into information.

Program (ANSI) (1) A series of actions proposed in order to achieve a certain result. (2) Loosely, a routine. (3) To design, write, and test a program as in (1). (4) Loosely, to write a routine.

Program See Computer program

Program implementation See Implementation.

Program planning See Planning.

Program status word A doubleword on an IBM System/360 or System/370 computer containing such fields as the instruction counter and the comparison indicator.

Program testing See Testing.

Programmer (ANSI) A person mainly involved in designing, writing, and testing computer programs.

Programmer, application A person who writes or maintains application programs.

Programmer, system A person who writes or maintains system programs such as operating systems or data base managers.

Programmer/operator A person who both programs and operates a computer.

Protocol In data communications, a specific set of rules defining handshaking and message characters.

Punched card (ANSI) (1) A card punched with a pattern of holes to represent data. (2) A card as in (1) before being punched.

Purchased software Programs which are purchased or leased from outside rather than being written within an organization.

Query A request for specific data, usually made through a terminal and to a data comunication monitor.

Queue (IBM) A waiting line formed by items in a system waiting for services—for example, customers at a bank teller window or messages to be transmitted in a message switching system. To arrange in, or form, a queue.

Queueing The act of forming a queue.

Radix (ANSI) In positional representation, that integer, if it exists, by which the significance of the digit place must be multiplied to give the significance of the next higher digit place. For example, in decimal notation, the radix of each place is ten; in biquinary code, the radix of the fives place is two. Synonymous with base (3).

Random access See Direct access.

Randomize To compute relative record numbers from actual keys through any of a number of mathematical techniques.

Read/write head The mechanism which writes data to or reads data from a magnetic recording medium.

Real memory A computer's actual main memory which is directly ad-dressable by the CPU. Contrast with virtual memory.

Real time (ANSI) (1) Pertaining to the actual time during which a physical process transpires. (2) Pertaining to the performance of a computation during the actual time that the related physical process transpires, in order that the results of the computation can be used in guiding the physical process.

Record (ANSI) A collection of related items of data, treated as a unit; for example, one line of an invoice may form a record; a complete set of such records may form a file.

Redundancy The repetition of data in two or more places.

Redundant data Data which is repeated, in whole or in part, in two or more places.

Reel A single volume of magnetic tape.

Register (ANSI) A device capable of storing a specified amount of data such as one word.

Relative address (ANSI) The number that specifies the difference between the absolute address and the base address.

Relative record address The position of a record relative to the beginning of the file.

Relative record number See Relative record address.

Remote (1) At a distance. (2) Connected to a main frame via communication lines.

Remote access (ANSI) Pertaining to communication with a data processing facility by one or more stations that are distant from that facility.

Remote job entry Entering jobs into the regular batch processing job stream from a remote facility.

Response time (IBM) The elapsed time between the generation of a message at a terminal and the receipt of a reply in the case of an inquiry or receipt of message by addressee.

RJE See Remote job entry.

Roll-in (ANSI) To restore in main storage, data which had previously been transferred from main storage to auxiliary storage.

Roll-out (ANSI) To record the contents of main storage in auxiliary storage.

Rotational delay The time required for the desired record to rotate under the read/write heads once they have been positioned over the proper track on a disk or drum.

RPG (Report Program Generator) A business-oriented programming language designed to support the generation of reports.

Scheduling Determining the sequence in which programs will be loaded and/or executed.

Scientific notation A system for representing numbers as a decimal fraction multiplied by a power of ten.

Second generation (IBM) A computer utilizing solid-state components.

Secondary storage See Auxiliary storage.

Security (Webster) Something that gives or assures safety; safeguard.

Seek time The time required to move the read/write head mechanism of a direct access device to a desired position.

Segment (ANSI) (1) To divide a computer program into parts such that the program can be executed without the entire program being in internal storage at any one time. (2) A part of a computer program as in (1).

Segmentation See Segment (1).

Selector channel A data channel designed to connect high-speed I/O devices to a computer, and operating in a burst mode without multiplexing.

Semiconductor memory Memory composed of semiconductor components or integrated circuits.

Sequential file A file of records organized in a fixed sequence; for example, a file of punched cards or a file on tape.

Sequential file processing Processing the records in a file in fixed sequence.

Service bureau A firm offering data processing or data communication services for sale or lease. Usually applied to a firm not associated with one of the main frame manufacturers or one of the communication common carriers such as Bell Telephone, or to a separate subsidiary of one of these major firms.

Setup (ANSI) (1) In a computer which consists of an assembly of individual computing units, the arrangement of interconnections between the units and the adjustments needed for the computer to solve a particular problem. (2) An arrangement of data or devices to solve a particular problem.

Simplex Data transmission in one direction at a time. Synonymous with half-duplex.

Software (ANSI) A set of computer programs, procedures, and possibly associated documentation concerned with the operation of a data processing system, e.g., compilers, library routines, manuals, circuit diagrams. Contrast with hardware.

Sort (ANSI) To segregate items into groups according to some definite rules.

Sorting The act of putting items into order or segregating items into groups.

Source code Program statements written in a source language.

Source data Data in the form in which it is originally recorded.

Source data automation The use of special equipment to collect data at its source.

Source deck A source module in punched card form.

Source document A document containing source data.

Source module (ANSI: source program) A computer program written in a source language. Contrast with object program.

Special-purpose computer (ANSI) A computer that is designed to handle a restricted class of problems.

Spooling Moving data from a slow I/O device to a high-speed I/O device prior to moving it into main memory so as to help minimize the speed disparity between the computer and I/O. On output, the order of data movement is reversed.

Standard interface Converting data to (or from) a common code.

Statement (ANSI) In computer programming, a meaningful expression or generalized instruction in a source language.

Storage (ANSI) (1) Pertaining to a device into which data can be entered, in which they can be held, and from which they can be retrieved at a later time. (2) Loosely, any device that can store data. (3) Synonymous with memory.

Storage allocation (ANSI) The assignment of blocks of data to specified blocks of storage.

Storage protection See Memory protection.

Stored program A series of instructions placed in a computer's main memory to control that computer.

Structured programming Planning and implementing a program as a series of linked logical modules, paying special attention to documentation, testability, and program clarity so as to simplify program debug and maintenance.

Suboptimization The best, but from a subsystem point of view.

Subprogram See Subroutine.

Subroutine (ANSI) A routine that can be part of another routine.

Subsystem A portion of a system.

Supervisor (IBM) A routine or routines executed in response to a requirement for altering or interrupting the flow of operation through the central processing unit, or for performance of input/output operations, and, therefore, the medium through which the use of resources is coordinated and the flow of operations through the central processing unit is maintained. Hence, a control routine that is executed in the supervisor state.

Surveillance (Webster) Watch or observation kept over a person, especially one under suspicion or a prisoner.

Synchronous (IBM) Occurring concurrently, and with a regular or predictable time relationship.

Synonym A record whose computed or randomized relative record number is identical to that of a different record.

System (ANSI) (1) An assembly of methods, procedures, or techniques united by regulated interaction to form an organized whole. (2) An or-

ganized collection of men, machines, and methods required to accomplish a set of specific functions.

System software Programs or routines that belong to the entire system rather than to any single programmer and that (usually) perform a support function. Contrast with application program.

Systems analysis (IBM) The analysis of an activity to determine precisely what must be accomplished and how to accomplish it.

Systems analyst A person who practices systems analysis. A professional who analyzes systems from management's broad total-system point of view but who does not share in management's responsibility or authority.

Tape drive (ANSI) A device that moves tape past a head.

Telecommunications (ANSI) Pertaining to the transmission of signals over long distances, such as by telegraph, radio, or television.

Telephone network A network of telephone lines; the Bell system is a good example.

Terminal (ANSI) A point in a system or communication network at which data can enter or leave.

Terminal A piece of hardware designed to be placed at the terminal of a communication network for the purpose of entering or obtaining data.

Testing The process of assuring that an implemented program or system actually solves the problem that it is intended to solve.

Third generation (IBM) A computer utilizing SLT components.

Throughput (IBM) A measure of system efficiency; the rate at which work can be handled by a system.

Time-sharing (ANSI) Pertaining to the interleaved use of the time of a device.

Time-slicing Breaking the time of a CPU into a series of brief slices that are allocated to different programs in turn. Common on a time-shared computer.

Timer The computer's internal clock.

Top-down approach Solving problems by starting with a broad total-system point of view and gradually introducing details, layer by layer, until a solution is obtained.

Total-system point of view Considering the impact of a decision or course of action on the total system rather than on only a portion of the system.

Track (ANSI) The portion of a moving storage medium, such as a drum, tape, or disk, that is accessible to a given reading head position.

Transaction A single input record or a single query. Usually associated with a time-shared or real-time system rather than with a traditional batch processing system.

Transmission (ANSI) (1) The sending of data from one location and the receiving of data in another location, usually leaving the source data unchanged. (2) The sending of data. (3) In ASCII and communications, a series of characters including headings and texts.

Transmission control unit A control unit that interfaces data transmissions.

Turnaround (IBM) The elapsed time between submission of a job to a computing center and the return of the results.

Turnkey system A computer system that can be used by an untrained or unsophisticated operator.

Unemployment (Webster) The state of being unemployed.

Unit record (IBM) Historically, a card containing one complete record. Currently, the punched card.

Universal Product Code A bar-code, printed on a supermarket package, which uniquely identifies the product.

UPC Acronym for Universal Product Code.

Utility program (ANSI: service routine) A routine in general support of a computer, e.g., an input/output diagnostic, tracing, or monitoring routine.

Variable (ANSI) A quantity that can assume any of a given set of values.

Variable cost A cost that varies with activity. Contrast with fixed cost.

Variable-length region Space allocated to a program under dynamic memory management.

Verification The act of verifying. See Verify (2).

Verifier A machine similar to a keypunch used to verify.

Verify (ANSI) (1) To determine whether a transcription of data or other operation has been accomplished accurately. (2) To check the results of keypunching.

Virtual memory Memory space on a secondary storage device that is used to hold programs and data on a virtual memory system. Instructions and data must be transferred from this virtual memory into real memory prior to execution or processing.

Virtual storage See Virtual memory.

Virtual storage access method An access method or file organization in which data is stored on a secondary device in fixed-length segments or pages and transferred into real memory much as program pages or segments on a virtual memory system.

Voice-grade line (IBM: voice-grade channel) A channel suitable for transmission of speech, digital or analog data, or facsimile, generally with a frequency range of about 300 to 3000 cycles per second.

Voice print A technique for verifying an individual's identity by the pattern produced by his or her voice.

Volatility On data files, a measure of the frequency of additions to or deletions from the file.

Volume (IBM) That portion of a single unit of storage media which is accessible to a single read/write mechanism.

Volume table of contents A list of the contents of a volume, including the physical location of key fields or files.

Wait state (IBM: wait condition) As applied to tasks, the condition of a task such that it is dependent on an event or events in order to enter the ready condition.

Wait time The time during which a program or a computer waits for the completion of other activities.

Wide-band channel A communication channel capable of carrying data at a rate higher than a voice-grade channel.

Word (ANSI) A character string or bit string considered as an entity.

Index

Index